John Locke's labor theory of property is one of the seminal ideas of political philosophy, and helped to establish its author's reputation as one of the leading social and political thinkers of all time. Through it Locke addressed many of his most pressing concerns, and earned a reputation as an outstanding spokesman for political individualism – a reputation that lingers widely despite some partial challenges that have been raised in recent years. In this major new study Matthew Kramer offers an extensive critique of the labor theory and investigates the consequences of its downfall. With incisive analyses of the merits and failings of many aspects of Locke's political thought, Kramer advances a powerful challenge to Locke's image as an individualist. Employing a rigorously philosophical methodology, but remaining aware of the insights generated by historical approaches to Locke, Kramer concludes that Locke's political vision was in fact profoundly communitarian.

John Locke and the origins of private property

John Locke and the origins of private property

Philosophical explorations of individualism, community, and equality

Matthew H. Kramer
Churchill College, Cambridge

CAMBRIDGE
UNIVERSITY PRESS

PUBLISHED BY THE PRESS SYNDICATE OF THE UNIVERSITY OF CAMBRIDGE
The Pitt Building, Trumpington Street, Cambridge, United Kingdom

CAMBRIDGE UNIVERSITY PRESS
The Edinburgh Building, Cambridge CB2 2RU, UK
40 West 20th Street, New York NY 10011–4211, USA
477 Williamstown Road, Port Melbourne, VIC 3207, Australia
Ruiz de Alarcón 13, 28014 Madrid, Spain
Dock House, The Waterfront, Cape Town 8001, South Africa

http://www.cambridge.org

First published 1997
First paperback edition 2004

Typeset in 10/12pt Plantin

A catalogue record for this book is available from the British Library

Library of Congress Cataloguing in Publication data

Kramer, Matthew H., 1959–
John Locke and the origins of private property: philosophical explorations of individualism, community, and equality / Matthew H. Kramer.
p. cm.
Includes index.
ISBN 0 521 58412 4 hardback
1. Locke, John, 1632–1704. Communitarianism – History – 17th century. 3. Individualism – History – 17th century. 4. Equality – History – 17th century. 5. Labor – History – 17th century. 6. Right of property – History – 17th century. I. Title.
B1295. K73 1997
330.1′7–dc20 96–44671 CIP

ISBN 0 521 58412 4 hardback
ISBN 0 521 54890 X paperback

Transferred to digital printing 2004

Contents

Preface

John Locke and the Origins of Private Property began as a chapter in an unfinished book that was to be entitled *Encounters with Liberalism*. Like the other chapters of that book which I actually wrote, this study of the labor theory of ownership has swelled far beyond its originally foreseen dimensions. Not only does this volume subject the labor theory to minute examination, but it also tackles a number of variously connected issues; and, after sustainedly perusing Locke's theory and a host of surrounding problems, this book presents a large medley of citations that go some way toward revealing the enormousness of the literature on Locke and his labor theory.

Chapter 1 describes the basic approaches and objectives of the analyses in this book. Some further comments are appropriate here. An initial point should be obvious to any careful reader but should now be affirmed expressly: this book does not engage in either an acclamation or a denunciation of the substance of Locke's political views. Though a central aim of this study is to show that the apparent individualism of Locke's labor theory of property is rooted in a thoroughgoing communitarianism, my arguments that arrive at such a verdict will make no effort to applaud or condemn their findings. Censorious remarks that occur herein are strictly analytical – targeted against the invalidness of Locke's reasoning, and not against the putative balefulness of his outlook. The task of reviling or endorsing Locke's politics is left to anyone who feels strongly about such matters.

A second observation should help to clarify the ideal of "communitarianism" that has just been invoked. Though my second chapter and some portions of other chapters will seek to specify with precision the communitarian ideal which this book discerns in Locke's writings, an anticipatory remark is here advisable for the sake of warding off potential confusion straightaway. Collectivism or communitarianism, as understood in the present volume, can be defined roughly as the moral/political prioritization of collective needs over any individual's needs. In a fully communitarian world, the collectivity's superior status *vis-à-vis* individuals is a blanket precedence; individual rights can exist in such a world, but they exist only insofar as they can advance the collective good. That is, the entitlements attached to each person are assigned thereto solely on the basis of communal requirements and objectives. Now, in light of this rudimentary definition and in light also of chapter 2 (and the germane comments in other chapters), we ought to shy away from alternative notions of "communitarianism."

For example, readers should not surmise that this book perceives communitarian obligations as derivable only from the presence of collectivities that are smaller than the whole human race. Were specific communal structures indispensable for the sway of communitarian duties, the ideal of communitarianism would gain no purchase in the presocietal state of nature; but because communitarianism or collectivism as here defined can reach to all human agents simply by virtue of their membership in the human species, we should have no misgivings about the relevance of communitarianism to life in the state of nature. Throughout this book, my references to the full priority of communal welfare over individual welfare should be taken as references to the full priority of *humankind's* welfare. After all, Locke avouched that the sundry members of "*Mankind are one Community*, make up one Society distinct from . . . other Creatures," and he posited one "great and natural Community" before civilization (TTG, II, §128, emphasis in original).

Another misconception to be avoided, in regard to communitarianism, is the belief that this study tries to highlight a blend or junction of communitarian elements and individualistic elements in Locke's thought. As my first chapter has emphasized at its outset, this book reveals not a mixing of the two groups of elements but a total absorption of the one by the other. Far from simply *combining* with individualistic strands, Locke's communitarianism *envelops* and *pervades* them. As was mentioned above, the individual rights in a thoroughly communitarian world obtain if and only if they optimally promote collective ends; and since the general theme of this book is that a Lockean state of nature indeed would be communitarian through and through, we know that the individual rights therein would obtain precisely because they furthered collective goals. Instead of merely being coupled with individualism, the communitarianism in a Lockean state of nature would engulf individualism and would employ it for communitarian purposes. Individualism was never absent, but was starkly epiphenomenal.

A final main point to be noted here is the centrality of God and His edicts in many parts of this study. To some degree, the recurring appearances of God in this book have stemmed from my atheistic preoccupation with the Bible (on which I have been writing a commentary for the past thirteen years). But the chief reason for the salient presence of the Almighty throughout my critique of Locke is the overwhelming importance of religion for Locke himself. As will be remarked several times, some key principles and arguments which Locke put forward were striking evidence of his faith in a benign Ruler of the world – or, at least, they were striking evidence of his need to take the dominion of such a Ruler for granted. Without explicit or tacit affirmations of God's benevolent reign, the principles and arguments that have just been noted would crumble under the slightest challenge. And so, unless we presume that Locke deliberately ventured arguments which he almost surely would have assessed as gravely flimsy, we should recoil from the notion that the author of the *Two Treatises of Government* was a furtive atheist. Given the preposterousness of such a notion, it would not warrant any consideration or rebuttal if it had hardly ever surfaced among the exegeses of Locke's ideas; yet, because disciples of Leo Strauss have busily endeavored to prove that Locke indeed was a crafty nonbeliever, the present point must be highlighted. In defiance of the Straussians' efforts to "confirm" their dogmatic view that Locke was a secret atheist, we shall time and again discover that his stances and reasoning committed him to the postulation of God's actuality. Though such logical commitments would not *entail* any personal commitment, they would *suggest* a personal commitment quite strongly. (For additional comments on the wiles of Straussianism, see Matthew Kramer, "Book Review," 26 *Locke Newsletter* 196 [1995] [reviewing Michael Zuckert, *Natural Rights and the New Republicanism*].)

I began *John Locke and the Origins of Private Property* in November 1992, and completed it in February 1995. During most of that period I was living in Madison, Wisconsin, where I enjoyed a Visiting Fellowship at the Institute for Research in the Humanities. I extend my warm thanks to everyone at the Institute, most members of which are listed in the next paragraph. I am equally delighted to thank both Churchill College and the University of Cambridge's Faculty of Law, where I wrote the first chapter of this book at the outset of 1995. My return to Cambridge has been most pleasant.

In addition to my mother and father, many people have won my gratitude for their constant supportiveness. I thank Richard Fisher and the Cambridge University Press's readers for their extremely careful and astute attention to my book. I am equally indebted to Hilary Scannell for her invaluable copy-editing, which has greatly improved the book's style and substance. More generally, at the risk of leaving out someone who should be noted, I must convey my appreciation to the following friends:

Klaus Berghahn, Paul Boyer, James Crawford, Neil Duxbury, Loretta Freiling, Jerry Frug, Mark Goldie, Phil Harth, Doug Kelly, David Kennedy, Duncan Kennedy, Isaac Kramnick, Dave Lindberg, David Loewenstein, Martha Minow, Steve Nadler, Richard Parker, Jon Roberts, Nigel Simmonds, Carole Smith, Elisabeth Sponheim, John Tiley, Howard Weinbrot, Kay Zakarian, and Lindy Zakarian. I owe an especially profound debt of thanks to Nigel Simmonds, who perused most of this book in typescript.

A moment ago, I adverted to my parents. I owe far more to them than to everyone else. My father, happily, is alive and well to receive my thanks. My mother, alas, is not; she died in October 1993 while undergoing a course of treatment for the terrible illness of acute leukemia. To the memory of Eunice Kramer, with love, I have dedicated this volume.

Abbreviations

TTG John Locke, *Two Treatises of Government* (Cambridge: Cambridge University Press, 1967, 2nd edn.) (P. Laslett ed.), cited with treatise and section numbers.

EHU John Locke, *An Essay concerning Human Understanding* (Oxford: Oxford University Press, 1975) (P. Nidditch ed.), cited with book, chapter, and section numbers.

ELN John Locke, *Essays on the Law of Nature* (Oxford: Oxford University Press, 1954) (W. von Leyden ed.), cited with page numbers.

LT John Locke, *A Letter on Toleration* (Oxford: Oxford University Press, 1968) (R. Klibansky ed., J. Gough trans.), cited with page numbers.

STE John Locke, *Some Thoughts Concerning Education* (Oxford: Clarendon Press, 1989) (J. W. Yolton and J. S. Yolton eds.), cited with section numbers.

Part I

Introduction

1 A philosophical approach to philosophy

Sustained encounters with political theories involve protracted labor. In a study of John Locke's political thought, we thus do well to train our attention on the Lockean view of the just rewards for toil. Locke's labor theory of ownership has helped to win a place for its formulator among the great thinkers in Western civilization. That theory has correctly been viewed by sundry commentators as one key means by which Locke grappled with many of his most pressing concerns. It has also helped to give Locke a reputation as an eloquent spokesman for political individualism – a reputation that lingers widely in the face of some partial challenges during recent years. Therefore, by concentrating on the nexus that Locke postulated between work and ownership, I aim to probe the fundaments of his political thinking.

More exactly, this book tries to ferret out the reversals which Lockean individualism undergoes – reversals based on precisely the individualistic line of thought which they undo. In some respects, this study will countenance the conventional view of Locke as a supporter of economic and political atomism. In most salient respects, however, my critique will cast grave doubt on that conventional judgment; and the doubts posed here are more worrying and wide-ranging than those raised by several other recent interpreters of Locke. In the course of laying stress on the individualistic theses which Locke upheld, this book will demonstrate that those theses undermine the integrity of individualism. Whereas previous re-evaluations of Locke have classified his perspective as a *composite* or *blend* of individualism and communitarianism, the present study shows that Locke's individualism must *reduce* itself always to a thoroughgoing communitarianism (under which the rights of the individual in the state of nature were but facets or offshoots of humankind's collective ideals and purposes).[1] Though staunchly individualistic, Locke precluded himself from being individualistic. Or so this book argues.

[1] As should be clear from my preface's statement of the conception of communitarianism that is operative in this book, I am not attempting to associate Locke with the modern "communitarianism" of writers such as Charles Taylor, Jean Bethke Elshtain, Michael Sandel, and Alasdair MacIntyre. Although there is some considerable overlapping between present-day communitarianism and the communitarianism discussed in this

In other words, I focus on the complete interpenetration of communitarianism and individualism, and thus refrain from positing a mere mixture of those values. Far from discovering simply that Locke tempered his sociopolitical atomism with a weighty dose of collectivism, we shall see that his atomism was itself utterly collectivistic. We shall find that a blending of values was out of reach, for one value engulfed the other entirely. My conclusions will deal with theses to which Locke's arguments are logically committed, as well as with theses which his arguments directly proclaim. As will become evident, Locke overturned his positions through the very reasoning he employed to advance them.

Before scrutinizing the labor theory of property, however, this book presents three chapters with other foci. After chapter 1 articulates the methodological guidelines and concerns that inform the rest of the book, chapter 2 will clarify some of the central concepts on which my critique of Locke must draw. Next, chapter 3 explores Locke's reflections on the basic equality of people. His conception of equality has played a large and praiseworthy role in the development of the most enlightened political assumptions that obtain in the modern West; but his efforts to justify and expound his stance were bestrewn with blunders that still ensnare many theorists. By chastising Locke for arrant non sequiturs and other instances of confusion, I warn against some mistakes that have largely gone undetected. Finally, chapters 4–6 peruse the complexities of my main topic: the acquisitive rights and powers that were attained or exercised through human work in the state of nature.

A philosophical focus

As the title of this chapter indicates, my book will train its scrutiny on the philosophical merits and failings of the theories which Locke propounded. I do not venture to highlight the concrete circumstances that surrounded the drafting and the reception of the *Two Treatises of Government*. No one will find here any lengthy analysis of Locke's motives or of the rivalries and the altercations on which his renowned political texts would leave their enduring imprint. Not only will the tussles of religious and political jockeying remain unexplored, but so will the high-flown intellectual frays that pitted Locke against men such as Hugo

book, the two are not identical, and I am certainly not endeavoring here to expound or join the modern controversy. (For my own laconically expressed doubts about modern communitarianism, see Matthew Kramer, "Our longest lie: irreligious thoughts on the relation between metaphysics and politics," 37 *Philosophy Today* 89, 93–4 [1993]; Matthew Kramer, *Critical Legal Theory and the Challenge of Feminism* [Lanham: Rowman and Littlefield, 1995], 10–12.) As I observe in my preface, I have chosen "communitarianism" as a label because it accords with Locke's patterns of usage, rather than because of its connotations in substantive political debates among my contemporaries.

Grotius and Robert Filmer and Thomas Hobbes. Instead of focusing on the practical and intellectual contexts of Locke's writings, this book devotes its attention to the soundness of his arguments. Rather than judge his lines of reasoning on the basis of their serviceability in particular quarrels, I judge how well they fare when they have been lifted out of those quarrels and assessed for their lasting strength.

Of course, any interpretation of a text must depend upon a host of semantic and rhetorical assumptions; and assumptions built on copious knowledge of the relevant historical settings can forestall smug anachronisms and easy oversimplifications and sheer bemusement. An extensive familiarity with the uses of vital terms and broader patterns of discourse in a multitude of related texts should hone the sophistication of one's interpretive stance. Much the same can be said about an extensive familiarity with the institutional conflicts and controls that structured the site of a text's emergence. When coming to grips with Locke's *Two Treatises of Government*, for example, a critic stands to profit immensely from a learned awareness of the great natural-law tradition in Western thinking and also from a learned awareness of the acrimonious struggles in Britain during the seventeenth century. To be sure, a wide knowledge of intellectual currents and religious/political forces cannot guarantee that one's encounters with any specific text will be fertile and illuminating. Yet, while no assurances are available, a thorough acquaintance with the pertinent contexts will indeed supply leverage for fruitful readings.

All the same, to underscore the advisability of apprehending a text's location in a throng of ideas and social matrices is not to imply that every fitting analysis must dwell on those ideas and matrices. One can rely upon a knowledge of history without invoking the details of one's knowledge expressly, and in fact without highlighting the circumstances of history at all. Such an approach, indeed, will characterize this book.

While an awareness of the interaction between arguments and their contexts is extremely useful for understanding the arguments' specificities, a gauging of their soundness must proceed not by looking at their furtherance of some ends in their original times and places, but by checking how well their premises support their conclusions when detached from those original sites. What interests the philosophical reader is the lasting power or speciousness of an argument, in contrast with the time-bound endeavors which the argument was fashioned to serve. Hence, a philosopher will typically be inclined to discuss the worldly impacts of theories with great brevity, if at all.

Historical knowledge, handy though it may be for improving the adroitness and subtlety of one's readings, does not supplant the methods and skills required for the philosophical evaluation of texts. It merely helps to refine one's overall understanding of any argumentation on which one's philosophic techniques are then brought to bear. By itself, historical knowledge will serve the philosopher only as a preliminary footing for judgments about the soundness and the logical implications of theories. One's alertness to the contexts of history will not predecide the nature of one's approach to the paths of reasoning that emerged in those contexts. More specifically, it does not oblige one to call attention to the influence of those contexts upon those paths. One can omit to highlight that influence, and can appositely discuss instead the logical rigor of the influenced argumentation.

Intersections between philosophy and history

Until now, this chapter has emphasized the differences between history and philosophy; the time has arrived for me to underscore some interrelations and similarities between those two disciplines. The utility of the former discipline in the service of the latter has already become clear. On the one hand, when a philosophical theorist mulls over the virtues of sundry arguments by constructing and refining those arguments without engaging in sustained interpretations of other people's works, the historian's approach to texts is quite obviously beside the point. But, on the other hand, a philosophic dissection of argumentative routes can stem also from an effort to interpret some writings that develop those routes. Philosophic analyses in the form of critical expositions and jousting are as widespread as are independent musings that remain aloof from explicit confrontations with other texts. *John Locke and the Origins of Private Property*, for example, will assess a number of far-reaching arguments via an extensive interpretation of Locke. Thus, for the present study and for broadly similar studies, the value of pertinent historical information is great indeed – because an acquaintance with various historical currents will tend to improve the sensitivity of one's grasp of the theories that were shaped by those currents.

Among the ways in which historical information can redound to one's benefit is that it sharpens one's linguistic acuity. When we take cognizance of words' historically varied uses, we can better perceive that words which look familiar may carry strange meanings. Critics of the *Two Treatises of Government*, for instance, should recognize the diverse meanings that Locke and his contemporaries attached to the word "equality"; unless we are aware of the several meanings presupposed by Locke, we shall plunge into oversimplifications. At a level more far-reaching than that of individual terms, a knowledge of historical contexts will strengthen one's ability to divine the presence and roles of certain general patterns of discourse. Modes of argument and ways of construing problems gain a visible import when the interpreters who confront them are prepared to discern them. (Likewise, the *absence* of some specific argumentative modes and some specific ways of construing problems will gain a visible import when interpreters are prepared to notice that such features are missing.) More broadly still, a profound awareness of history can help an analyst sometimes to make sense of highly perplexing doctrines by seeing them as maneuvers in political and social debates. Such an awareness, furthermore, can help to avert any comically ahistorical censure or praise of a classic theory.

At many levels, then, from the uses of individual words to the deeper patterns of language to the general influence of society on theoretical outlooks, the importance of history for the texts of philosophy is prodigious; anybody engaged in an analysis of those texts should therefore become attuned to their historical circumstances. No philosopher should neglect the capacity of historians to illuminate the theories and arguments of which the philosopher then judges the merits. (To be sure, as I have contended, the important bearing of history on the views of philosophers does not mean that every worthwhile exegesis has to discuss overtly the interweaving of historical situations and particular texts. One's knowledge of intellectual and political currents can inform one's interpretations without being highlighted therein. One's knowledge can suitably remain helpful background knowledge. Moreover, an acquaintance with intellectual and political settings is per se clearly not enough for a philosophical verdict on the soundness of any line of reasoning. To arrive at such a verdict, an analyst has to employ techniques and consider problems that lie beyond the techniques and problems of historical studies.)

If someone taking a philosophical approach to philosophy can benefit from historical learning, somebody who takes a historical approach to philosophy can benefit likewise from some philosophical acumen. Although many of the questions facing the historians of philosophy are empirical and not metaphysical or deductive, some of the questions do belong to the realm of metaphysical speculation. Let us briefly look, for example, at the issues that will arise when a historian asks if such and such a theorist did genuinely espouse two views that may seem to be at odds. Very likely, the most important question that will have to be raised is whether the particular theorist deemed the patently clashing views to be reconcilable and conjoinable. Or perhaps the question that should be raised is whether the theorist simply overlooked the egregious conflict between the views (and thus held blithely to both of them). Or maybe the most pertinent question is whether the theorist showed a Whitmanian insouciance about contradictions between his tenets. If the answer to one of these inquiries is plainly "yes," the historian will harbor no reservations about detecting incompatible standpoints in the work of a single writer. Now, notice that each of the suggested inquiries is indeed a historical inquiry, which concentrates on the attitudes of a given theorist. We descry those possible attitudes – which, insofar as they can be known, are gleanable solely from the theorist's germane writings and from other people's accounts – by plumbing some appropriate texts, and not by abstract argumentation that can render its verdicts a priori. But notice as well the philosophic assumption which generates the foregoing three inquiries: the assumption that certain views do indeed conflict with each other.

Detecting the disharmoniousness or the harmoniousness of the relation between two viewpoints is a philosophical exploit. For such a task, an interpreter must make judgments about the logical implications and the logical boundaries of each viewpoint. Exactly such judgments underlie the three inquiries that were broached above. After all, if a historian has not concluded that certain standpoints jar with each other – if she has no grounds for presuming that the logical implications of one such standpoint conflict with those of another – she will scarcely need to determine why a theorist would not have shunned the inconsistencies between the two standpoints. Hence, only by having marked the logical bearings of particular doctrines can a historian feel a need to explain why somebody chose to support doctrines that collide with each other. And only by having knowingly or unknowingly marked the logical bearings of particular doctrines can a historian see *no* need to explain why somebody failed to regard the doctrines as uncombinable.

When an exegete asks why someone would embrace incompatible stances, he has concluded that the propositions entailed by either stance are logically incompatible with those of the other. When an exegete does not consider two stances to be at odds, and when he has therefore not been taken aback by somebody's joining of those stances, he has concluded that the propositions entailed by either stance are logically compatible with those of the other. So, whether a historian doubts the possibility or takes for granted the possibility of reconciling two theses, he commits himself to a philosophical verdict on the nature of each thesis. In that respect, a historian of philosophy cannot avoid being a philosopher. Thus, given that a reliance on philosophical judgments is inescapable, the historian is well advised to make such judgments reflectively and observantly – rather than precipitately or by default.

The philosophic perspective and the explanation/understanding dichotomy

The dyad of "explanation" and "understanding" is a potential source of confusion, both because its categories approximate the perspective of this book while significantly diverging therefrom, and because those categories often have been entangled with other foci. As here construed, a project of "understanding" seeks to describe a writer's arguments and positions from the writer's own vantage point. Instead of tracing a thinker's outlook to deep psychological or social determinants of which the thinker would have been unaware or only dimly aware, an exploit of "understanding" involves the faithful reconstruction of any viewpoint along lines that would be familiar and congenial to the person holding the viewpoint. Understanding, then, consists in trying to see an author and her opinions in the way that she saw herself. It proceeds by taking a writer's nonironical utterances at face value, and therefore disdains to treat her outlook principally as an epiphenomenon that instantiated some broader forces which the writer largely or wholly failed to discern.

Now, we should avoid two glaring misconceptions that might impede our grasp of what a project of understanding entails. First, we should not think that such a project must sympathize with the aims of the writer(s) whose beliefs it examines; we ought not to overlook countless motives that can spur one's attempts to reconstruct the doctrines of any theorist. To expound the convictions of an author in the author's own terms is not perforce to approve of those convictions; having elaborated an author's views in ways which the author would have recognized and endorsed, an analyst may then harshly denounce those views for moral reasons or political reasons. When one understands a writer as the writer would understand himself, one has an efficacious point of departure for an onslaught against his attitudes. Thus, for instance, when certain scholars have tried to understand Locke's theory of property in Indian-disparaging terms which Locke himself knew and favored, they have clearly done so in order to bewail the express chauvinism of the *Second Treatise of Government.*[2]

Second, we should not presume that a project of understanding must

[2] Among the analyses that I have in mind here are those of Wilcomb E. Washburn, "The moral and legal justifications for dispossessing the Indians," in James Morton Smith (ed.), *Seventeenth-Century America* (Chapel Hill: University of North Carolina Press, 1959), 15, 22–3; Wilcomb Washburn, *Red Man's Land/White Man's Law* (New York: Charles Scribner's Sons, 1971), 38, 143; William Cronon, *Changes in the Land* (New York: Hill and Wang, 1983), 78–9; Peter Hulme, "The spontaneous hand of nature: savagery, colonialism, and the Enlightenment," in Peter Hulme and Ludmilla Jordanova (eds.), *The Enlightenment and its Shadows* (London: Routledge, 1990), 16, 25–34; Robert Williams, Jr., *The American Indian in Western Legal Thought* (New York: Oxford University Press, 1990), 228–9, 246–9, 300; James Tully, *An Approach to Political Philosophy: Locke in Contexts* (Cambridge: Cambridge University Press, 1993), chapter 5; and Barbara Arneil, "The wild Indian's venison: Locke's theory of property and English colonialism in America," 44 *Political Studies* 60 (1996). See also Chester Eisinger, "The Puritans' justification for taking the land," 84 *Essex Institute Historical Collections* 131 (1948); James Axtell, "Through a glass darkly: colonial attitudes toward the native Americans," 1 *American Indian Culture and Research Journal* (1974), 17–18; Peter Thomas, "Contrastive subsistence strategies and land use as factors for understanding Indian-white relations in New England," 23 *Ethnohistory* 1, 4–5 (1976); Nicholas Griffin, "Aboriginal rights: Gauthier's arguments for despoliation," 20 *Dialogue* 690 (1981).

exclude attentiveness to historical backgrounds. Consistent with fierce rebukes, the objective of understanding is equally consistent with a focus on the occurrences and debates that structured the scene wherein a text evolved. On the one hand, admittedly, an emphasizing of historical contexts can be a route for attributing the main concerns of a theorist to forces that hardly entered his consciousness. On the other hand, such an emphasis can likewise be used for fleshing out the preoccupations that absorbed a theorist's mind. If the arguments in a text were fashioned chiefly as a response to well-defined positions in other texts or to well-defined happenings in the broader world, then a good acquaintance with those happenings or those other texts will clearly prove vital for an effort to understand the responsive argumentation. Though an explicit highlighting of the other texts or the affairs in the broader world is always forgoable – as this chapter has previously affirmed – it can bring a lot of rewards. And, again, whether invoked squarely or left implicit, a *knowledge* of the relevant other texts and the relevant worldly circumstances is crucial; we never can come to grips with anyone if we know very little about the problems to which he was reacting. Hence, not only will the training of one's attention on history be compatible with one's striving to understand the outlook of any theorist, but it also can very often aid such striving immeasurably.

Quite different from a project of understanding is a project of explanation. While a project of the former sort is an endeavor to rehearse views in the ways that their exponents themselves perceived them, a project of the latter sort is an endeavor to *account for* views by pointing to a variety of determinants, which shaped and governed the consciousness of theorists but lay beyond their ken. An explanatory approach does not accept anybody's verdicts and reasoning at face value; it pierces through them as the epiphenomena or signals of deeper causes. Those causes are to be found outside a theorist's writings, in the muddy roots of the theorist's psyche or in the vectors of social institutions and conditions. Those deep causes have gone unrecognized in the theories which they have engendered – or, at most, they have been only obliquely recognized. They have contributed hugely to the creation of texts despite the fact that their formativeness has not been apparent to the authors of the texts. In sum, whereas a project of understanding will treat an author's positions as *replies*, a project of explanation will treat them as *results*.

Some frequent mistakes about the posture of explanation are invertedly parallel to the frequent mistakes about the posture of understanding. An explanation does not necessarily set out to impugn the worthiness of the theories which it explains; nor does it invariably proceed via a focus on historical contexts. To be sure, a proposed explanation of someone's views can seek to discredit her lines of thought by showing that they were spawned by unattractive determinants. A Marxist critique that highlights the class-based origins of political values, and a Nietzschean attempt to trace religious piety to shame and fear, are obvious examples. Nonetheless, such hostile explanatory accounts are not the lone options. Hosts of neutral or supportive accounts will coexist with any jaundiced appraisals. A charting of the connections between a theory and the theory's surroundings can enable admirers to applaud the ingenuity or the well-adjustedness of the theory; and the drawing of such connections likewise can allow an impartial analyst to enjoy a richer sense of the theory's station. To explain is not ineluctably to deride.

Perhaps not so evident is the sunderability of explanatory theses from historical foci. If an explanation consists in marking the ties between a theoretical viewpoint and some factors beyond the viewpoint, does it thus have to plight its troth to the concerns and methods of historians? Our response to this question should be negative, as the stimuli that are deemed germane for explanatory purposes can transcend all specific contexts. Think, for example, of a Freudian who wants to explain a creed with a reference to the profound yearnings in the psyche of the creed's major spokesman. As portrayed by unabashed Freudians, such yearnings are timeless elements of the human condition rather than distinctive outgrowths of specified periods and places. An equal slighting of historical currents will attend a geographic determinism that ascribes the outlook of a philosopher to the nearly unchanging facets of his or her environment. In short, one's choice between explanation and understanding does not predecide one's position in the debates over the relative merits of contextualizing and noncontextualizing approaches.

Such, then, are the categories of explanation and understanding. How does the present volume's analysis relate to each of those two endeavors? First, it aligns itself with projects of understanding in its acceptance of Locke's key principles and terms at face value. This book eschews the explanatory aim of accounting for the tenor of Locke's positions by reference to some forces or promptings that inspired those positions from without. Neither a historical explanation nor any other species of explanation will emerge in this book to highlight the extrinsic causes that shaped the *Two Treatises of Government*. Moreover, I address some of the specific problems which Locke addressed, and I make no effort to ignore the basic postulates that structured his theory. Instead of wishing that Locke had tackled some other questions, this book will concentrate on the questions that did absorb him. And instead of disregarding his prime axioms, we shall grant those axioms arguendo. In these respects, and furthermore in my abstention from any searching for some unacknowledged wellhead of Locke's ideas, the present book will cast its lot with exegeses that are oriented toward understanding. It seeks to engage with Locke on the turf that he himself chose.

Though concordant in these notable ways with the objective of understanding, the analysis offered by this book will also significantly *depart* from that objective. This book attempts to unearth grave difficulties in Locke's arguments – difficulties not glimpsed by Locke himself. Having taken his axioms as givens, we proceed to observe that he committed some downright blunders in the argumentative uses to which he put those axioms. Instead of opting to recapitulate his arguments in a manner that he himself would elect, this study will plumb his arguments very closely in order to reveal that their premises cannot sustain their conclusions. By faithfully cleaving to the tenets with which Locke started, this book will show that he bound himself to verdicts that run athwart the verdicts which he himself advanced. Having found that his central postulates carry implications which he never divined, we then explore the reach of those implications at length. With this ferreting out of unseen aspects of Locke's credo, the current volume's analysis bears a resemblance to explanatory approaches.

Note that the critiques herein will diverge from projects of understanding that display moral/political indignation. As was remarked above, an effort to understand does not entail a ringing endorsement of the position(s) under investigation. Someone can choose to understand a doctrine precisely in order to decry it. Here the goal is quite different. The current book does not judge the labor theory of property on ethical or political grounds, but only on analytical grounds. Moreover, unlike a politically disaffected project of understanding – which, like every other project of understanding, seeks to recount a person's views as the person would define them herself – this book does not attempt to reconstruct Locke's positions in ways that would tally with his own idea of what the *Two Treatises of Government* had accomplished. Far from trying to map the course of his reasoning as the solid trail that Locke presumed it to be, we map it as a treacherous route that necessitated some conclusions starkly incompatible with those which he drew. To be strictly faithful to Locke, we have to spurn his own account of what he managed to prove.

In short, the categories of understanding and explanation do not fit smoothly with the critiques that form the rest of this book. Those critiques will strive for the loyalty or closeness of understanding and for the distance or unsettlingness of an explanation. Neither an attempt to rehearse Locke's stances by his own lights, nor an endeavor to account for his stances by imputing causal responsibility to something outside his texts, my reappraisal of Locke unfolds as an immanent transvaluation.

A postscript: some concluding caveats

On several occasions in the subsequent chapters of this book – in the notes and also in the main text – I offer caveats about some specific terms that have been employed therein. This postscript presents a few additional cautionary remarks that are somewhat more wide-ranging.

First, this book expounds the germane portions of Locke's theories as if those theories take lone individuals to be the primary elements or stuff of human existence. Yet, as any careful readers will hardly fail to have noticed, Locke presumed generally that the basic moral units of human life were families – rather than solitary agents who had somehow remained aloof from every bond of intimateness before the growth of society. Nevertheless, my presentation of Locke's ideas is not distortive. Even if one has put aside the medley of arguments where Locke wrote of individual human beings as though they were completely detached atoms in the state of nature, and even if one has duly underlined the significance of the family in a Lockean world, one should not bridle at my de-emphasizing of the family throughout the chapters below. References in those chapters to individuals can almost always be viewed likewise as references to individual *families*.

In the state of nature and in every successive period, each breadwinner was responsible for meeting the needs of the dependents within his or her family; thus, any claim (or just about any claim) by a breadwinner to receive certain goods was also in effect a claim by his or her dependents. That is, because each family was an ethical unit sharing most claims and burdens, virtually nothing of substance will be lost if my statements about individuals are construed as statements about individual families. Such a construction is inappropriate at only one juncture – a juncture (in chapter 6) at which this book maintains that some dependents in the state of nature would have no rights to get their needs fulfilled by breadwinners. Everywhere else, the shift from "the individual person" to "the individual person plus his or her family" can go ahead without bumps. The very smoothness of that transition, however, has meant that I can leave it unbroached without distorting Locke's theory. And because persistent references to the place of the family would have been exasperatingly awkward for my prose, I have seized the chance to avoid such references while not being unfair. Constant reminders of the key familial duties that prevailed in Locke's state of nature are entirely unnecessary and would have been most irksome in their clumsiness.

For a second caveat, let us note that statements about "rights" occur throughout this book. Save when the immediate contexts or express statements have signaled otherwise, my various references to the rights and powers of ownership apply to *originary* rights and powers attained through the originary appropriation of assets from the unowned bounty of nature. The majority of those references do not apply to the derivative rights and powers gained via transfers of primal holdings.

Third, when drawing the consequences that flow from the collapse of Locke's theory of property, this book has not troubled to distinguish between wealth-maximization and welfare-maximization. In part, my overlooking of that dichotomy has ensued from the fact that Locke never really acknowledged it himself when stressing the great importance of human flourishing. In part, also, my obscuring of the divide between wealth-maximization and welfare-maximization is due to the fact that those distinguishable objectives converge in multitudinous ways (even if we construe the objectives in a manner that accentuates their discordancies); though wealth-maximization and welfare-maximization are not identical, they do overlap considerably. And in part, finally, my scanting of the discrepancies between those objectives has resulted from the fact that such discrepancies are completely immaterial for the purposes of this book. My critique will apply in full to a Lockean world pursuing wealth-maximization *and* to a Lockean world pursuing welfare-maximization. Hence, we are not compelled to discriminate between these two sorts of maximizing ideals.

Finally, this book often describes originary entitlements as having been "granted" or "conferred" or "allotted" or "apportioned" or "bestowed" or "awarded" or "assigned." Such verbs and their cognate nouns do not proleptically denote the workings of a governmental body with distributive powers; rather, they denote the workings of natural law. What conferred or apportioned or allotted or bestowed or granted or assigned or awarded the originary entitlements was the natural law (or God, whose will the natural law set forth). Because the natural law ordained the appropriate distributions of assets in the state of nature, it defined people's legitimate holdings – notwithstanding the absence of governmental institutions. Thus, with my numerous references to the assigning or conferring or granting of people's holdings, I do not commit the blunder of presupposing the existence of governmental agencies in the presocietal era. Instead, such references pertain to the natural law's prescribing of all originary distributions.

2 Preliminary matters

Before we study Locke's reflections on equality and his labor theory of ownership, two discussions will help to avert confusion by sharpening this book's principal terminology. The first discussion presents an analytical framework of entitlements, a framework that supports the drawing of key distinctions within the subsequent critiques of Locke's theories. The second and shorter discussion clarifies the words "individualism" and "communitarianism" by staking off their political meanings from their nonpolitical or nonnormative meanings.

Hohfeldian preparation

All legal and moral philosophers should be grateful to Wesley Hohfeld, an American jurist, for his attempts to bestow precision on the language and concepts that suffuse normative inquiries.[1] Hohfeld managed to sift four senses that had become attached to the word "right." In regard to each of the four entitlements that he traced, he defined as well a correlative position; he grasped that each entitlement must always entail a posture in

[1] The two most important essays by Hohfeld are "Some fundamental legal conceptions as applied in judicial reasoning," 23 *Yale Law Journal* 16 (1913); and "Fundamental legal conceptions as applied in judicial reasoning," 26 *Yale Law Journal* 710 (1917). Both of those essays are reprinted in Hohfeld's *Fundamental Legal Conceptions* (New Haven: Yale University Press, 1923) (Walter Cook ed.), which was published posthumously. I discuss Hohfeld extensively in my long essay "Rights without trimmings," which will appear in a book (*Getting Rights Right*) co-written by Nigel Simmonds, Hillel Steiner, and myself. For some very good analyses of Hohfeld, see Karl Llewellyn, *The Bramble Bush* (New York: Oceana Publications, 1951), 95–101; John Finnis, "Some professorial fallacies about rights," 4 *Adelaide Law Review* 377 (1972); Duncan Kennedy and Frank Michelman, "Are property and contract efficient?" 8 *Hofstra Law Review* 711, 751–3 (1980); L. W. Sumner, *The Moral Foundations of Rights* (Oxford: Clarendon Press, 1987), 18–31; Nigel Simmonds, "The analytical foundations of justice," 54 *Cambridge Law Journal* 306 (1995). (The essay co-authored by Duncan Kennedy, along with Kennedy's other critiques of the law-and-economics movement, has helped to shape my approach to the efficiency-oriented justifications of proprietary rights, which I discuss later.) Confused and uncomprehending attacks on Hohfeld still appear now and then, alas. For an egregious example, see Arthur Jacobson, "Hegel's legal plenum," 10 *Cardozo Law Review* 877 (1989).

relation to which it has its effect. Thus, Hohfeld's work is of the greatest importance for our aims, both because it marks essential divergences among concepts and because it underscores the reciprocality of secureness and prohibitions.

Hohfeld devised his theory of entitlements with a largely jurisprudential hue for application to contexts where institutions of governance have emerged as the means of bringing disciplinary force to bear against anyone who flouts a right. But his approach can easily be extended to cover moral problems and discourses in which the punitive workings of the law do not figure saliently or directly. That is, although Hohfeld presupposed a system of governmental compulsion behind the asserting of people's claims, his insights apply as tellingly to the varied circumstances in which the only backing for claims will lie in reprehension, moral authoritativeness, and individuals' acts of outrage. For his overarching scheme as generalized here, sanctions can consist in upbraiding or in personal retribution as well as in legal punishments by a full-blown state.

Hohfeld first explained the entitlement for which he reserved the appellation of "right." Being endowed with a right (which Hohfeld also labeled as a "claim") consists in being normatively protected against someone else's interference or in being entitled to someone else's assistance or remuneration, with regard to a certain action or a certain state of affairs. The person who is required to abstain from interference or to render assistance or remuneration is under a duty to behave so. A right or claim, then, is the legal position created through the imposing of a duty on someone else. If a person *X* has a claim against a person *Y* to be free from interference with *X*'s project *P*, then *Y* has a duty to abstain from interfering with *P*; conversely, if *Y* has a duty to abstain from interfering with *P*, then *X* has a right to be free from any such interference by *Y*. Anyone who violates a right has thereby failed to live up to the imperatives of a duty. When a person's neglecting of a duty becomes known, it ordinarily triggers sanctions – whether the sanctions unfold as mere disapproval or as something more violently coercive.

Hohfeld next described the entitlement that he dubbed a "privilege." To have a privilege to engage in a certain action is to be free from a duty to eschew the action; likewise, to have a privilege to abstain from a certain action is to be free from a duty to undertake the action. Like a right, each privilege is held by a specific person or group of persons against another specific person or group of persons. The person against whom the privilege is held has a no-right concerning the activity or state of affairs to which the privilege pertains. Nonetheless, although that person has no *right* to the cessation of the activity or state of affairs, he himself may well have a *privilege* to interfere. He cannot successfully have recourse to the mechanisms of public governance, but he can have recourse to his own devices (within the confines imposed by the privilege-holder's rights).

Consider an example. Suppose that *Z* enjoys a privilege, against *Y*, to express opinions about various public matters. *Y* therefore cannot correctly maintain that his rights are violated by *Z*'s pronouncements on the matters in question. As a consequence, there will not occur any warranted governmental intervention in order to uphold *Y*'s rights. Yet, although *Y* cannot rely on the coercive mechanisms of government to stop *Z* from speaking, he can do his utmost himself to interfere with *Z*'s voicing of opinions – so long as he does not violate any of *Z*'s rights (such as the right to be free from physical assaults). Perhaps *Y* will contort his face in ways that cause *Z* to laugh helplessly and thus to stop speaking. Or perhaps *Y* will make so much noise that he drowns out *Z*'s words and thereby causes the frustrated *Z* to desist from further pronouncements. Whatever be the exact methods of interference, *Y* himself enjoys a privilege to impede the exercise of *Z*'s privilege, within the constraints imposed on *Y* by *Z*'s rights. (Of course, if *Z* has a right to be free from any such obstructive behavior by *Y*, then *Y* will owe a duty to *Z* to refrain from such behavior and will accordingly not enjoy a privilege to engage in it.)

One of the most important features of the relationship between rights and privileges is the absence of any entailment between them. A right to do ϕ – that is, a right to be free from interference with the doing of ϕ, or a right to be assisted in the doing of ϕ – will not entail a privilege to do ϕ and is not entailed by such a privilege. Someone can have a right to be free from interference with the carrying out of some act which she has no privilege to perform, and someone can have a privilege to carry out some act even though she is not entitled to be free from manifold obstacles that prevent her from performing the act successfully.

The latter of the two points just mentioned, the point that a privilege to do ϕ will not entail a right to be free from interference with the doing of ϕ, is quite straightforward and has already been touched upon. In the Hobbesian state of nature (including parts of New York City), no one has any Hohfeldian rights to noninterference even though everyone has a privilege to do all that is necessary for survival. In less bizarre situations as well, we find that a privilege to do ϕ cannot per se entail a right against any interference with the doing of ϕ. Think, for example, of a merchant who is free – within the confines of antitrust laws, antifraud laws, and the like – to outperform his competitors and thus to take business away from them. Although the competitors are not entitled to be shielded from the merchant's permissible striving, they likewise almost certainly do not have any duties to refrain from selling their own wares expeditiously (within the confines of the aforementioned laws). If each merchant has a privilege to peddle his goods with rapidity, then each has no entitlement to be insulated from the other merchants' similar practices which sap the efficacy of his own endeavors. Each has a privilege without having a cognate right.

Less easily grasped than the absence of entailment between privileges and rights is the absence of entailment between rights and privileges. Quite plainly, a legal or moral privilege to do ϕ does not entail a legal or moral right to be unimpeded in the doing of ϕ; equally surely, but less plainly, a legal or moral right to be unimpeded in the doing of ϕ does not entail a legal or moral privilege to do ϕ. Someone can have a right to be unobstructed in the performance of an activity which she is not allowed to perform. In order to see this point clearly, we should look at an example that is more elaborate than those offered so far.

Suppose that a huge factory begins to operate along the shore of a lake. Noxious discharges from the factory contaminate the lake's waters so badly that the fishermen who once earned their livelihood on the lake are forced out of business. As effluents continue to spew into the once vibrant body of water, the fishermen sue the factory's owner for his violation of their right to noninterference with the plying of their trade. The court holds that the fishermen should indeed be awarded damages for the fouling of the lake and for the consequent loss of their livelihood. (Most likely the damages are in the form of a lump-sum payment, but they can also be in the form of year-to-year payments. Note that the granting of an injunction against the factory would introduce certain complications into this example but would not alter its basic point at all.) Nonetheless, despite the compensation for the factory owner's breach of his duty to abstain from spoiling the waters, the fishermen remain disgruntled. They make their way to the factory's outlet pipes, where they manage to occlude the pipes and thus force a temporary shut-down of the factory's operations. Once again the parties to the dispute appear in court, but now the factory owner sues the fishermen for their obstruction of his outlets which has caused quite extensive interference with the running of his business. The court now holds that the factory owner should be awarded damages for the fishermen's breach of their duty to abstain from interfering with the normal operations of his factory. Albeit the factory owner does not have a privilege to emit large quantities of toxic substances into the lake, he has a right to be unimpeded in the discharge of these emissions.

In the scenario just sketched, the factory owner has an obligation to abstain from polluting the lake but also has a right to be unhindered in his pollution. If we were to adopt a somewhat loose "right to do" phrasing,[2] we could say that the factory owner has a right to commit a wrong – or a right to undertake what he is not permitted to undertake. If we opt instead for more accurate but less exciting terminology, we should say that the factory owner has a right to be free from interference with his perpetration of a wrong. His enjoyment of a right to be unobstructed in his processes of manufacturing does not entail his enjoyment of a privilege to carry out the processes that should be unobstructed.

Third among the entitlements that Hohfeld delineated were "powers." Someone who holds a power can expand or reduce or otherwise modify, in particular ways, his own entitlements and the entitlements held by some other person(s). Someone who bears a liability, on the other hand, is exposed to the exercise of a power; the entitlements of the liability-bearer are open to being amplified or diminished or shifted in certain ways. In short, a power consists in one's ability to change legal or moral relations, while a liability consists in one's susceptibleness to undergoing a change brought about by the exertion of a power.

One's exposure to changes in one's entitlements is by no means always unpleasant. A promisee can benefit greatly from the entitlements vested in her by a promisor, and an heir can benefit greatly from the entitlements vested in him by a will. Of course, not all changes imposed on one's legal or moral standing by someone else are desirable from one's own perspective; but many such changes are indeed desirable, and thus a liability to the imposition of such changes is not necessarily onerous at all.

"Immunities" and "disabilities" are the other main terms in the Hohfeldian lexicon. The holder of an immunity is not exposed to the exercise of a power by someone, with respect to any entitlements covered by the immunity. If *X* has an immunity from an effort by *Y* to alter *X*'s proprietary rights in a piece of land, for instance, then *Y*'s efforts will come to nought. With regard to those proprietary rights, *Y* will have run afoul of a disability. Perhaps various other people can change *X*'s proprietary rights – or perhaps not – but, in any event, *Y* will be unable to change them so long as *X* has an immunity that shields her from his attempts.

The connections between the two second-order dyads of legal posi-

[2] As Glanville Williams has remarked: "No one ever has a right to do something; he only has a right that some one else shall do (or refrain from doing) something. In other words, every right in the strict sense relates to the conduct of another." Glanville Williams, "The concept of legal liberty," 56 *Columbia Law Review* 1129, 1145 (1956). Though the urge to talk about someone's right to do something is probably irrepressible even among analysts of Hohfeld, we should recognize that such talk is in fact referring to an entitlement which requires that a *duty-bearer* forgo interference or afford assistance or provide remuneration.

tions (the immunity/disability axis and the power/liability axis) are precisely similar to the connections between the two first-order dyads (the right/duty axis and the privilege/no-right axis). Just as a liability is the absence of an immunity, so a no-right is the absence of a right; and just as a disability is the absence of a power, so a duty to abstain or to do is the absence of a privilege to do or to abstain. Note that immunities are the second-order counterparts of rights, while powers are the second-order counterparts of privileges. Just as a privilege must be specified by reference to the privilege-holder's latitude, so a power must be specified by reference to the power-holder's legal or moral ability. Likewise, just as a right has to be specified by reference to what the duty-bearer must do or not do, so an immunity has to be specified by reference to what the person disabled by the immunity cannot do.

Having reviewed the analytical scheme which Hohfeld devised, this section will end with observations which clarify that scheme and which adumbrate its bearing on Locke's account of property. First, Hohfeld's approach indeed was purificatory and definitional, not substantive or empirical. With his theoretical structure, centered on negations and correlations, Hohfeld charted the principles of deontic logic with verve. To be sure, any such exploration has numberless points of contact with the structures of legal and moral arguments, for quite the same reasons that analyses of truth-functional logic can apply in countless ways to the structures of nonnormative arguments; in either case, a study of logic will help us to verify the strength of a line of reasoning or to apprehend the stumbles therein. Hohfeld's discussions have particular merit in revealing and averting the glib conflation of distinct categories. But the provision of formal standards for the evaluating and refining of argumentative soundness is quite different from the pressing of normative or empirical claims. Hohfeld's framework does not prescribe the substance or distribution of our entitlements, nor does it endeavor to track the distribution or the substance empirically, nor does it attempt to follow the settled patterns of usage that have shaped juridical writing. Its purpose is the formal assessment and correction of the prevailing patterns of usage.

Now, in view of the starkly analytical nature of Hohfeld's theory, an attempt to confute his theory by reference to empirical data is at best ill-conceived. A seeming refutation of Hohfeld through empirical counter-evidence will either have made some outright blunders or have started with definitions at odds with those laid down by Hohfeld. That is, all such "refutations" are either wrong or beside the point. For people who adhere to the definitions that Hohfeld set, his lines of analysis are rules of logic that cope with all empirical data of any kind.

To be sure, we can point to any number of precepts that will obviously tangle the Hohfeldian categories in double binds. Think, for instance, of an authoritative leader who commands her subordinates to disobey all authority; her instruction is the exercise of a power if and only if it does not succeed in being the exercise of a power. But such examples fall far short of rebutting Hohfeld's picture of the inherent correlations between entitlements. Instead, they show that his picture of correlations must abound with antinomies to which every other mode of analysis must likewise be subject. We can hardly escape the paradoxes of the self-subverting command by choosing non-Hohfeldian definitions of legal/moral entitlements. Further, the paradoxes do not simply negate the bonds between liabilities and powers or between rights and duties. *Au contraire*. When understood within Hohfeld's scheme, the paradoxes must presuppose and confirm such bonds while deranging them. The person who demands the flouting of her demands will have exercised a power and thereby traded upon a liability if and only if she has failed to do so. In other words, the logic of her decree does not eradicate the connections between legal positions, but keeps those positions *and their unremitting connections* always ensnared in double binds. Liability–power correlations engulfed in whirlpools of incoherence are liability–power correlations nevertheless.

For a second point of clarification, we should briefly probe the debate between the "interest theory" and the "choice theory" of rights. Analysts who uphold the former theory maintain that rights exist through the imposing of obligations designed to advance the interests of persons. Analysts who plump for the latter theory contend that rights do not exist unless the right-holders can seek or waive the enforcement of the duties that attach to various other people; when a person lacks competent discretion to choose enforcement or nonenforcement, she cannot hold any rights. (A more exact statement of the interest theory can run as follows: [1] Necessary but insufficient for *X*'s actual holding of a right is that the right, when actual, preserves an interest of *X*'s. [2] *X*'s being competent and authorized to demand the enforcing of a right is not sufficient or necessary for *X* to be endowed with that right. A more exact statement of the choice theory is the following: [1] Sufficient and necessary for *X*'s holding of any right is *X*'s being competent and authorized to demand or waive the enforcing of the right. [2] *X*'s holding of any right does not necessarily involve the guarding of any interest of *X*'s. [3] The potential of any right to guard some interest of *X*'s is not enough per se for *X*'s actually possessing that right.)

In short, the advocates of the choice theory contend that rights and claims are not equivalent. Unlike Hohfeld, they apply the label of "rights" only to claims that are coupled with powers of enforcement/waiver in the hands of the claim-holders; they do not attach the label of "rights" to claims that are unaccompanied by such powers in the hands of the claim-holders. Not only do the adherents of the choice theory submit that each claim must be enforceable if it is to qualify as a genuine claim – a proposition with which any adherent of the interest theory would firmly agree – but they also insist that each claim must be enforceable and waivable *by the claim-holder* if it is to qualify as a right. A champion of the interest theory, by contrast, is happy to join Hohfeld in using "claim" and "right" interchangeably.

We are now in a position to see why Hohfeld's account of jural relations is strictly neutral between the interest theory and the choice theory, notwithstanding that the interest theory's application of the term "right" is more in keeping with Hohfeld's own patterns of usage. The key point here is that a Hohfeldian claim *can* be combined in a single person with a Hohfeldian power of enforcement/waiver but does not *have* to be so combined. Nothing prevents such a conjunction, and nothing necessitates it. As far as Hohfeld's analytical scheme is concerned, then, the difference between the interest theory and the choice theory is simply a matter of labeling. If the exponents of the choice theory want to use only the label "claim" for the entitlement which Hohfeld styled as either a "claim" or a "right," and if they want to reserve the word "right" for a claim accompanied by a power of enforcement/waiver in the hands of the claim-holder, then their departure from Hohfeld's scheme is merely terminological. They are not proposing any combinations or correlations which Hohfeld revealed to be untenable. So long as the choice theorists recognize that rights as they define them are correlative with duties-plus-liabilities rather than simply with duties, they will have adhered faithfully to the matrix of correlations and negations which Hohfeld set forth.

Finally, let us explore the bearing of Hohfeld's usages and analyses on my investigations of Locke's *Two Treatises of Government*. Hitherto, I have occasionally employed Hohfeldian terms in just the way that Hohfeld employed them; but I have also sometimes used those words with quite different meanings. Henceforward, this book will cleave much more consistently to the usages specified by Hohfeld. Now and then, however, some or another word from his lexicon may carry its broad quotidian sense (or senses) in lieu of its precise Hohfeldian sense. At any point where one of these terms appears, the context should plainly indicate whether a Hohfeldian or non-Hohfeldian meaning is being conveyed. (Likewise, the proper choice between a Hohfeldian meaning and a non-Hohfeldian meaning for any of these words as used heretofore can easily be divined from the context.)

Naturally, the correspondence between the language of Hohfeld and the language of Locke is pretty meager. In the first place, although Locke rarely if ever was as loose with his argot as he often is derided for having been, he clearly never exhibited a Hohfeldian penchant for precision. Furthermore, he could hardly seek to follow guidelines for usage that were developed more than two hundred years after he had died. Unsurprisingly, then, the value of Hohfeld's work for the present book does not lie in a substantial coincidence between Hohfeld's and Locke's patterns of language. A certain amount of overlapping exists, of course, but not in abundance. Instead, Hohfeld's work is valuable because it enables the clarifying and tightening of Locke's theory – and because it therefore enables us to discern with exactitude the theory's strength *and* shakiness. As a result, moreover, we can detect some facets of the Lockean theory that have eluded the attention of all or most other critics, and we can shun interpretations of Locke which Hohfeld's insights will expose as philosophically unacceptable. In short, the application of Hohfeld's lexicon here accords with the central tenor or focus of the critique delivered in part III, which investigates the profound dynamic of the labor theory of property while tracing how that dynamic often works against Locke's own descriptions of it.

Collectivism contra collectivism

Part III of this book will attempt to show that Locke's individualistic prescriptions concerning property turn out to be communitarian through and through. As a preliminary matter, this thesis needs some definitional clarification; words such as "individualism" and "atomism" and "communitarianism" and "collectivism" have borne a welter of meanings. In particular, we should take account of a contrast between the ethical and nonethical senses of these terms.

A full-scale treatment of the divide between the nonethical and the ethical would have to consider many queries and difficulties that need not trouble us here. For our present purpose, we can view that divide as an essential gulf between inquiries which concern "how things hang together" and inquiries which concern "how people should interact." The former group of topics is focused on the conditions of human agents and other things as they *are* or *were* or *could* be or *must* be. The latter group of topics is focused on the conditions of human beings and their interrelationships as they *ought* to be. Here the word "ought" carries a moral charge. Nonethical positions unfold by describing and explaining, and do not seek to commend value-laden stances; ethical positions, by contrast, with their emphasis on how people ought to live, do prescribe moral choices.

Worthy of special mention is the capacious breadth of the class of nonethical affairs. Such affairs include all the diverse topics explored in any academic fields and in other discourses, insofar as analyses of the topics do not aim solely at moral prescriptions. Hence, nonethical debates form a set extending not merely to the concerns of disciplines such as sociology and psychology and chemical engineering, but also to abstract questions of ontology and epistemology. Metaphysical questions fall within the nonethical category of the nonethical/ethical disjuncture, along with countless questions relating to mundane realms of existence. Here what matters is not whether positions have to justify their theses a priori through conceptual arguments or whether they have to justify their conclusions a posteriori by using interpretive procedures and observational tests; rather, the lone thing relevant is whether an outlook consists in moral judgments and pronouncements or not.

Nonethical atomism and nonethical communitarianism

As applied to the basic headings of "individualism" (or "atomism") and "communitarianism" (or "collectivism"), the split between nonethical and ethical theses will cut along foreseeable lines. Nonethical individualism, which has a place in nearly all social sciences and biological sciences and in almost all spheres of the humanities, is a doctrine holding that the individual human agent evolves as a completely or largely self-sufficient actor who shapes his course as the individual that he becomes. Instead of having been fundamentally shaped by other people's molding of his desires and perceptions, each agent will have sparked and fostered his own development from sources within himself. Human beings may well establish warm ties of social intercourse, but the intercourse scarcely plays an *essential* role in constituting the selves of those who establish it. Self-development is precisely *self*-development, taking place within individuals who each enjoy fundamental autonomy *vis-à-vis* one another. That autonomy endures, regardless of how extensive is the interaction among the autonomous agents.

This kind of individualism can emerge in a multitude of specific forms, which vary in their degrees of subtleness and insightfulness. They figure prominently in many of the empirical disciplines such as anthropology, psychology, and biology, where the fashioning by the self of itself is pictured as ensuing from genes or instincts or cognate mechanisms. Nonnormative individualism has appeared in philosophy as well, again and again. When advanced as a philosophical outlook, it does not ground itself on any factors like genes or instincts that are only to be discovered empirically; it grounds itself a priori, rather, by pointing out the conceptual necessity of ascribing all impulses and conscious states to the irreducibly exhaustive self-presence of each agent who experiences those states and those impulses. Nevertheless, the philosophical version of nonethical individualism shares the central theme of the mundane versions – the theme of the primacy of individual human subjects over collective practices and arrangements. And the philosophical version also joins with the mundane versions by arguing for the thesis of individual primacy in nonnormative terms which carry no moral messages or entreaties (though these starkly nonethical positions can readily combine with moral stances of any stripe).

Nonnormative communitarianism or collectivism, which enjoys as much salience as individualism in a host of fields, is a credo that affirms the priority of collective structures and understandings over the thoughts and wills of individual agents. According to this position, the general outlooks that individuals hold are functions of the interpretive, analytical, and practical frameworks which have been produced through the myriad exchanges of individuals with one another. Collectively crafted schemes of thought and behavior overarch the perceptions of anybody within the sway of those schemes; their sway determines the standards of acceptability and conceivability to which sane perceptions have to conform.

Communal fashioning of the codes that govern ideas and conduct can take a boundless number of routes. Nothing whatever in nonnormative communitarianism implies that the collective molding of individuals' attitudes will require supportive and warm relationships of esteem among the people involved. Further, this doctrine of communitarianism does not imply that the multifaceted processes in which people are formed by one another must operate through well-planned and well-organized institutions for collective deliberating. The overarching frameworks which set the options for individual viewpoints can encourage and perpetuate selfish viewpoints; likewise, those frameworks can produce their effects in ways not consciously organized and perhaps not even desired. Communally forged determinants of individuals' acts and thoughts *can* promote hearty fellowship and extensive consultations, but certainly never *have* to do so. A collective process of subjectivity-formation remains collective even when it teaches each person – through the egoistic behavior and egoistic values of other people – to regard others principally as impediments, rather than as contributors, to his or her well-being. In a society filled with selfish boors, people shape one another as boors by acting piggishly in their manifold contacts with one another and by expecting like behavior to be returned. In this case, just as much as in all the processes that give rise to unselfish mind-sets, the constitution of subjectivity has indeed been attained through patterns of collective exchanges, notwithstanding that the collective achievement has consisted here in the tendency of people to act brusquely toward one another. Thus, people can acknowledge the source of their identities in communal practices while declining to show much gratefulness or solicitude therefor; they will fail to evince gratitude unless they cling to the normative assumption that the relevant processes should win their support and unselfish concern.

Nonethical credos of communalism, like nonethical credos of individualism, have taken both empirical and philosophical forms. In disciplines such as sociology, psychology, and linguistics, the focus on collective arrangements has come about as environmental determinism. Analysts concentrate on the major institutions and forces of the social environment which people have wittingly or unwittingly created together; these myriad institutions and forces – such as language and economic structures and kinship systems and mass-media advertising – are jointly or severally portrayed as exerting a profound and decisive impact on the ways people think.

As a philosophical theory, nonnormative communitarianism has advanced the view that reality is a "social construct." Far from being an empirical doctrine based on observations of the roles of certain environmental features in shaping our thoughts and sentiments, this philosophical theory delineates the underlying conditions of any knowledge or consciousness whatsoever. It affirms that truths attain their posture as such through categorizing schemes which are always variable but which transcend and mold the perceptions of discrete agents. (In a theological vein, nonmoral communitarianism attributes primacy not to varying frameworks of assumptions and concepts, but to the enduring governance of a comprehensive Creator. Although such an attribution nearly always consorts with fervid stances on the problems of ethics, it is strictly nonnormative in itself.)

Now, just as the countless metaphysical species and the countless mundane species of nonnormative atomism converge in underlining the precedence of individual agency, so the multitudinous species of nonnormative collectivism converge in underlining the precedence of supraindividual structures. And, of course, the varieties of nonnormative collectivism likewise converge in being starkly analytical or descriptive. Nonmoral communitarianism can attach itself to untold sets of prescriptions, but the reason for its great flexibility in securing such attachments is that it does not lay down any prescriptions on its own.

Normative atomism and normative communitarianism

Were my book to engage sustainedly with Locke's epistemological and psychological theses, it would do well indeed to take the nonethical approaches to individualism and communitarianism as its guiding threads.[3] Here, however, my focus will lie on some crucial strands of Locke's political theory. Hence, the *normative* conceptions of communitarianism and individualism will function as the analytical mainstays in my encounters with Locke's ideas about equality and the acquisition of property. Because the nonmoral versions of communitarianism and individualism contrast quite sharply with the moral versions in their sweep and tenor, my conspectus of the former versions has helped to define the latter versions by making clear what they are not.

Ethical individualism, as here construed, does not amount straightforwardly to a thoroughgoing translation of its nonethical counterpart into a prescriptive vocabulary. It does diverge from its counterpart by taking prescriptive stands on some moral and political questions, but it also distinguishes itself by confining its scrutiny to certain modes of behavior. Individualism here refers to an outlook that countenances selfish actions which bespeak little sense of responsibility or concern for anyone who might be harmed by them. Somebody who espouses normative individualism thus declares that people *should* behave selfishly and heartlessly. Not only should people never take account of the general interests of society when they plan their various projects, but they likewise should keep themselves from taking account of *any* interests beyond their own greedy and self-indulgent desires. According to devotees of normative individualism, feelings of compassion are both gratuitous and extremely ill-advised; no one is obligated to have such feelings or to act upon them in any way, and no one who is intelligent will permit such feelings to intrude on his self-devotion.

Of course, many advocates of normative individualism have argued that the unabating pursuit of selfish interests by people will redound to the benefit of society as a whole. An invisible hand or a cognate mechanism supposedly ensures that the private vice of egoistic grasping will operate as a public virtue. This hopeful stance is obviously consistent

[3] I do not mean to suggest, of course, that Locke viewed his epistemological/psychological doctrines as purely nonethical. Quite the contrary; he clearly saw those doctrines as facilitative of human beings' compliance with God's will. Nonetheless, the links between the epistemological and the ethical which Locke perceived as inherent can and should be perceived by modern philosophers as contingent. Although someone putting forward a philosophic critique of the *Essay concerning Human Understanding* would have to take account of the ethical aspirations which suffuse that text, he or she could gauge the merits of its doctrines by reference to strictly analytical criteria.

with diehard atomism, for the modes of behavior that it prescribes are the exact modes prescribed by theorists who acclaim selfishness as just and warranted irrespective of its ability to promote the public weal. Normative individualism retains its character as normative individualism so long as it commends egoism or self-reliance and discourages altruism. Any number of motivating factors – such as a desire for efficiency or an earnest respect for natural rights or a fear of the tyranny that lurks in all centralized direction and planning – can undergird the patterns of approval and disapproval that are the hallmark of individualist ethics.[4] Relevant here, in other words, is the favoring of self-centeredness; the perceived justification for prescribing the self-centeredness is of ancillary importance.

Regardless of the factors behind the lauding of moral individualism, its champions can propound their doctrine with varying degrees of tenaciousness. On the spectrum of fervor, the extreme position of zeal is occupied by the fanatical Social Darwinists whose outlook will be discussed in chapter 3. From the vantage point of those zealots – who are much more pugnacious than most true Social Darwinists – the ideal of individualism calls for a violent struggle in which nary an obligation is owed by anyone to anyone else. Like the Hobbesian state of nature, the world envisioned by the crude Social Darwinists is a world where might equals right and where allowable self-devotion confronts no limits at all. But this hell of unrestrained bloodshed looms as only the most horrific variant of normative individualism. Sundry other interpretations of the individualistic ideal will set trammels on overweening hoggishness by proposing duties that require certain levels of moderation and decency and forbearance. Such duties can reach as far as the duties of nonaggression that Locke proclaimed in his *Second Treatise*, whereby no one was allowed to "take away, or impair the life, or what tends to the Preservation of the Life, the Liberty, Health, Limb or Goods of another" (TTG, II, §6). Though the basic Lockean duties are described as a mild form of communitarianism in most of my next chapter, they also can aptly be classified as a mild form of individualism. After all, people who are morally bound to shrink from any unprovoked violence can remain quite free to display frosty indifference toward one another; a stark obligation to forgo murder and pillaging does not in itself encompass an obligation to show care for the needs of others with bountiful assistance (or even with the most niggardly assistance). If a network of entitlements has authorized no demands for active succor, it arguably merits being labeled as "individualistic" even if it largely or wholly outlaws aggressive conduct.

[4] Plainly, none of these factors leads perforce to a strong individualism.

Hitherto, this discussion of moral individualism has perhaps furnished an unduly banausic picture. Readers may have inferred that self-absorption or egoism inevitably amounts to a crass preoccupation with the garnering and enjoyment of material goods. To be sure, an inference along those lines will not really go astray in regard to my critiques of Locke, because most of the major arguments and analyses that are ventured herein indeed will depict self-devotion as acquisitive grasping. Nonetheless, individualistic self-assertion can eschew a greedy attachment to material wealth, and can instead favor moral and intellectual autonomy as its highest good. When Nietzsche reviled communitarian politics, he was hardly championing bourgeois possessiveness and consumerism; rather, he was striving for freedom from traditional and current criteria of morality. For him, the praiseworthy man was not the avaricious accumulator of goods, but the "sovereign individual, like only to himself, liberated again from morality of custom, autonomous and supramoral."[5] Hence, although my critiques of Locke will understand moral individualism as a doctrine of self-indulgent rapacity, the quest for self-determining liberation from ties of kith and kin has sometimes evolved with nobler bearings.

Whereas moral individualism prescribes self-reliance, the creed of moral collectivism sings the praises of comradeship and mutual sacrifice. Solidarity here replaces autonomy as the cardinal virtue. Proponents of normative communitarianism admire patterns of social intercourse in which people harbor sentiments of responsibility and affection for one another. Not any more is selfish gratification viewed with overriding respect; now such gratification is distrusted as interfering with the solid emergence of the bonds that make up a tightly woven society. In a communitarian social order, the regime of entitlements will provide for extensive claims by each person on everybody else. The satisfying of individual needs has now become a mere offshoot of the satisfying of social needs and ideals. In other words, the entitlement or moral ability of everyone to supply himself with goods is filtered through the collective entitlement of people *en masse* to gain and distribute goods among themselves. Communal requirements will subordinate the requirements of individuals, who get what the overarching interest of the community allows them to get. Each person must stand ready to sacrifice the indulgence of his own wishes, in order to effectuate the wishes of others. But each person justly can demand that people who benefit from the sacrifices should undertake corresponding sacrifices in turn.

[5] Friedrich Nietzsche, *On the Genealogy of Morals*, in *On the Genealogy of Morals and Ecce Homo* (New York: Vintage, 1967) (W. Kaufmann and R. Hollingdale trans.), 59 (essay II, §2).

As will be thoroughly explored from a different angle in the next chapter, one should staunchly avoid confusing egalitarianism and collectivism. In societies oriented to the latter ideal, people can lay claim to the wealth and skills of others with frequency because the wide-ranging good of the social unit will have trumped the narrower good of any person or set of persons. Yet this structure of sweeping and reciprocal obligations does not perforce amount to a structure of equality. People owe an array of duties whereby they always have to contribute to the public well-being as far as possible – but the definition of the "public well-being" can include pronounced hierarchies. So long as people are obligated to put the interests of their community above their own particular interests, they reside in a communitarian setting; thus, a welter of gaping inequalities will not detract from the communitarianism of a social arrangement, if the inequalities are construed as serving the general welfare of the people who live under such conditions.

An example here may help to accentuate the disjunction between equality and community. Let us recall the early Christians as portrayed in the Acts of the Apostles. On the one hand, the followers of the Christian creed subjected themselves to a communitarian style of life that can seem dreadfully cloying to a modern observer. We are told that "all who believed were together and had all things in common; and they sold their possessions and goods and distributed them to all, as any had need" (Acts 2:44–5). Slightly later in Acts, we find an even stronger account of the firm unity of the Christians:

> Now the company of those who believed were of one heart and soul, and no one said that any of the things which he possessed was his own, but they had everything in common . . . There was not a needy person among them, for as many as were possessors of lands or houses sold them, and brought the proceeds of what was sold and laid it at the apostles' feet; and distribution was made to each as any had need. (Acts 4:32, 4:34–5)

Yet, as this quotation reveals, the suffocating collectivism of the devout was hardly any guarantor of equality. When giddy believers sold their assets in order to contribute the proceeds to a common fund, they laid their takings at the apostles' feet. This gesture both ratified and reinforced the superior positions held by the divinely entrusted leaders of the community, at whose hands "many wonders and signs were done" (Acts 2:43).

Indeed, the Christian apostles reigned in a fashion that may strike modern analysts as curiously familiar. Like much more recent experiments in communism, the early church enforced the collectivist ideal with despotic ardency. Having caught Ananias and Sapphira when they pretended to have given the church the total proceeds from the sale of their land, the gracious Peter unceremoniously consigned them to death in a manner reminiscent of Stalin (Acts 5:1–11). Peter's heartless judgments not only served to uphold the strong communitarianism of the faithful – as "more than ever believers were added to the Lord" (Acts 5:14) – but also vividly manifested the domineering ascendancy enjoyed by the inner circle of the devout. As the wide-eyed author of Acts proudly informed his readers, the apostles soon elicited reverence from the humble underlings of their flock: "Now many signs and wonders were done among the people by the hands of the apostles. And they [the apostles] were all together in Solomon's Portico. None of the rest dared join them, but the people held them in high honor" (Acts, 5:12–13).

In sum, the early church grew with a combination of hierarchy and fellowship that has also characterized (in varied blends) a host of other communities, both religious and nonreligious. Solidarity *can* conjoin with equality but can likewise fail to do so. Although hierarchies can drive people asunder, they can also nourish potent and lasting nexuses of allegiance. Supplied with a focus through the rituals, symbols, assurances, and appeals of leadership, the communal nexuses may often become firmer than they usually do within less stratified schemes of human association. Such effects are not preordained but are always possible. Thus, far from necessitating a regime of equality, the abundant claims that people exert on one another in communitarian social orders can blossom and persist while inegalitarianism thrives.

We should note one further clarificatory point about ethical communitarianism. Until now, my references to communitarian bonds have run together the aspects of subjectivity and objectivity. This discussion has tended to imply that people who live within the sway of communitarian mandates will possess sweet-tempered outlooks that nicely harmonize with the obligations which those people must shoulder. When subjective impulses and objective duties square with each other, human agents are pleased to carry out the responsibilities which they are called upon to fulfill. In such circumstances, obligation generally coincides with affection; obligation coexists with a *sense* of justified obligation.

Yet, as should have been unmistakably clear to anybody who visited the former Soviet Union during its heyday, the coincidence between feelings and imperatives can often break down. People may harbor very little concern and friendship for one another even though they belong to a society that imposes wide-ranging dictates of collective responsibility and care. Obligation does not *exclude* affection, but certainly it does not *entail* affection, either.

When human beings are governed by communitarian norms while

cherishing almost no communitarian inclinations, they can opt to comply grudgingly with their duties, or else they can somehow shirk their duties. Whether self-absorbed people flout the altruistic requirements with which they have annoyingly been encumbered, or whether they elect to grin and bear such requirements, the requirements compose a matrix that can aptly be deemed "collectivist" or "communitarian." If people owe many obligations to one another for sustenance and general support, their overall regime of entitlements is a regime of mutual responsibility no matter how dismissively it comes to be fleered (or overlooked) by those to whom it applies; matched or not by communitarian sentiments within people's breasts, an existing structure of communitarian rights and duties and powers will abide as a structure of *communitarian* prescripts.

Justified omissions These preliminary remarks have sought to stress the divide between the normative and nonnormative versions of collectivism and atomism in order to convey more clearly the tenor of the normative versions. However, just as significant has been a closely related purpose. By emphasizing the differences between the normative and nonnormative credos, these remarks have helped to explain the scantiness of attention devoted to the nonnormative credos by the rest of this book.

As should be quite apparent, no necessary connections join ethical individualism or ethical communitarianism to either of their nonethical counterparts. After all, not only do the ethical outlooks train their scrutiny on what *should* be rather than on what *is* or *was* or *might* be, but they also limit their focus by considering and prescribing only certain species of conduct (selfish or solicitous). Given this reorientation and this constricted breadth of inquiry, the questions tackled by the normative doctrines will differ pronouncedly from the questions tackled by the nonnormative doctrines. Stances on the ethical questions cannot entail, or be entailed by, specific stances on the nonethical questions – though of course a multitude of *contingent* links can form between these two kinds of stances. (Among the horde of contingent ties that can emerge is the frequent junction of normative collectivism and a psychological proposition advanced by some of the advocates of nonnormative collectivism who work in the social sciences. What I have in mind specifically is the junction of normative collectivism and the psychological proposition that ample duties-to-furnish-succor will promote traits like sympathy and forbearance in people's characters. The prediction about the development of people's characters scarcely has to join with any ethical credo that regards traits like sympathy and complaisance as desirable, nor does any such credo have to join with the aforesaid prediction; but the credo and the prediction have in fact commonly interlocked.)

Thus, since the associations between our normative viewpoints and our nonnormative viewpoints are always variable rather than ineluctable, and since any specific standpoints of either type can therefore be probed quite separately from any specific stands of the other type, our focus on the doctrines of moral atomism and moral collectivism will enable us to shelve all disputes that center on the nonmoral counterparts of those doctrines. While engaging in a critique of the atomism and communitarianism that informed Locke's jurisprudential and political notions, we can warrantedly refrain from exploring the atomism and communitarianism that informed his psychological and metaphysical theses.[6]

[6] I should emphasize again my recognition that Locke himself saw intrinsic connections between some normative aspects and some nonnormative aspects of his various positions. Were I an intellectual historian rather than a philosopher, I would expound those postulated connections at length.

Part II

On equality

3 Equality unlocked

This chapter will try to disentangle some key issues which Locke persistently ran together. By contrast with the investigation of the labor theory of property in my subsequent chapters, this chapter does not seek to highlight a profound overturning of Locke's ideals. Rather, the chief aim here is to show that answers to certain questions do not entail specific answers to various other questions. We shall find that Locke went astray in presupposing that an insistence on equality is necessarily bound up with an insistence on other specified values.

One main caveat deserves to be registered at the outset. The complaints here about Locke's vision of equality do not aspire to prevent all linking of disjoinable questions; instead, my target consists in the belief that such questions are *ineluctably* yoked together in certain ways. Purportedly automatic associations, not explicitly contingent associations, come under fire. Nothing stated here will deny the obvious fact that sundry values which can be separated are often found together (perhaps in modern discourses or perhaps in the discourses from some bygone age). To rebut the notion of unavoidable ties between particular values is decidedly not to overlook the welter of avoidable ties that have emerged during any number of periods throughout history. We indeed should acknowledge that avoidable ties can well prove strong and lasting and broadly influential, even while we insist that they are in fact avoidable.

Applied more specifically to Locke, this caveat emphasizes that the orientation of this chapter is philosophical rather than historical. Nowhere in the analyses below does Locke receive criticism solely for having tried to build connections between the norm of human equality and other important topics. Had Locke made clear the contingency of the links he forged, he would have rendered superfluous the clarificatory goal of this chapter. Alas, however, he exhibited and encouraged confusion by implying that his stance on equality had to join *perforce* with his stances on certain other issues. Rather than merely urging that his combinations of views were plausible or desirable, he portrayed the views as inextricably yoked together. He gave the strong impression that anyone who concurred with him about the principle of equality would also have to concur with him about the values which he connected to it. That impression is what the criticisms here will seek to dispel.

The denaturing of social equality

Let us look first, then, at a breach of the "is"/"ought" barrier. From this angle, one blunder by Locke was to derive the norm of political equality from a thesis about physical and mental equality. Near the beginning of the *Second Treatise of Government*, he announced that the alikeness of people's faculties would disallow any natural dominance of specific human agents *vis-à-vis* others. Locke believed that any fair-minded analyst would have to avouch that persons largely equal in wits and brawn should also be equal in their everyday intercourse (until they had left the state of nature):

> [A]ll the Power and Jurisdiction [in the state of nature] is reciprocal, no one having more than another: there being nothing more evident, than that Creatures of the same species and rank promiscuously born to all the same advantages of Nature, and the use of the same faculties, should also be equal one amongst another without Subordination or Subjection, unless the Lord and Master of them all, should by any manifest Declaration of his Will set one above another, and confer on him by an evident and clear appointment an undoubted Right to Dominion and Sovereignty. (TTG, II, §4)

Here we properly may chastise Locke for seeking to jump from the descriptive to the prescriptive. From the fact that people were generally alike in strength and capabilities, he concluded that people were morally alike in that no one could properly enjoy nonconsensual control over fellow human agents (apart from those agents who had monstrously violated the law of nature). Human beings patently all belonged to the same species, with roughly similar natural endowments; hence, Locke insisted, they were bound to refrain from wielding any dominion over one another in their presocietal state.

Readers of Locke have often argued that his egalitarianism bespoke his deep absorption in the New Testament. For instance, John Dunn declares that "Jesus Christ (and Saint Paul) may not appear in person in the text of the *Two Treatises* but their presence can hardly be missed when we come upon the normative creaturely equality of all men in virtue of their shared species-membership."[1] Now, in one obvious and important way, Dunn and other exegetes are on solid ground: Locke matched Christ and Saint

[1] John Dunn, *The Political Thought of John Locke* (Cambridge: Cambridge University Press, 1969), 99.

Paul in his insistence that people's homogeneity as human beings would override all heterogeneity and disparities. Yet, in other crucial ways, Locke's egalitarianism tended more to *overthrow* the priorities and the foci of the New Testament than to *recapitulate* them. When Jesus and especially Paul underscored the profound commonalities among human beings as creations of the Almighty, they did so in order to discount the significance of values such as equality or hierarchy within this vale of tears. Exactly because they portrayed the Christians in earthly bondage as freedmen of the Lord, and portrayed the Christians possessing earthly freedom as the Lord's slaves, they felt no qualms about instructing their faithful comrades that "[e]very one should remain in the state [such as slavery] in which he was called" (1 Corinthians 7:20). To be sure, this bland acceptance of hierarchy by Paul and Jesus was not a preordained consequence of their metaphysical holism; furthermore, these two men were sometimes less than unalloyedly quietistic in their remarks about the inegalitarian practices of sublunary life. But the center of their concern lay in an otherworldly level of human similitude, a level that generally overcame their interest in pushing for equality at the level of mundane institutions.

Locke proceeded quite differently. While harboring few if any doubts about the supramundane equality to which the New Testament had ascribed the utmost importance, Locke concerned himself with a mundane type of equality in most parts of the *Two Treatises of Government* where he wrote about human likenesses. He focused on similarities among human agents in regard to key observable traits. And he drew from his observations a general norm for human life in this world: a norm that debarred political inequalities among people within the state of nature (and thus a norm that established the abiding need for consent by people to the submergence of their natural equality in favor of political rulership). For Locke, the central fact of equality was the sharing of basic aptitudes by all people during their time on earth – a fact which implied that all human beings deserved equal liberty.

A circumscribed objection to Locke's analysis could advert to the many differences among human agents, differences to which Locke was far from blind. He himself contended that basic similarities among persons left a lot of room for specific variations and inequalities:

Though I have said above . . . *That all Men by Nature are equal,* I cannot be supposed to understand all sorts of *Equality*: *Age* or *Virtue* may give Men a just Precedency: *Excellency of Parts and Merit* may place others above the Common Level: *Birth* may subject some, and *Alliance* or *Benefits* others, to pay an Observance to those to whom Nature, Gratitude, or other Respects may have made it due; and yet all this consists with the *Equality*, which all Men are in, in respect of Jurisdiction or Dominion one over another, which was the *Equality* I there spoke of, as proper to the Business in hand, being that *equal Right* that every Man hath, *to his Natural Freedom*, without being subjected to the Will or Authority of any other Man. (TTG, II, §54, emphasis in original)

A limited objection here could proceed by pointing out that Locke failed to justify his stand on the unallowableness of interpersonal dominion in the state of nature. Any such stand attaches greater importance to the general likenesses among people than to their specific divergences. Given that Locke was well aware of both the divergences and the likenesses, he endowed the latter with an inexplicably special bearing on social intercourse when he wrote that such intercourse in the state of nature should not be marked by interpersonal dominion among adults (until people chose to exit the state of nature by forming civil society). In relations of natural liberty, according to Locke, the general traits which all people had in common would override the traits that served to distinguish people from one another. Yet, a critic can justly ask, why should anybody concur with Locke's favoring of samenesses over inequalities? Locke was not flatly incorrect to highlight the common features and to accord less weight to distinctive features, but he was flatly incorrect to regard his position as *uniquely* cogent and proper.

Anybody is entitled to feel that natural differences among human beings should have resulted in the subordination of many people by others long before the emergence of political institutions. From this perspective, Locke's decision to focus on the attributes which all human agents shared as a species was unfortunate and misguided. Why should qualities setting people apart from other animals be one's touchstone for prescribing the sorts of interaction that were legitimate *within* the species of human agents? Should we not instead find our touchstone in qualities setting people apart *from one another*? If the distinctive traits of individual human beings were not substantial, then a focus upon such traits would perhaps lead to the same overall prescription that Locke commended: an egalitarian absence of dominion. But, given that Locke himself showed scant reluctance to acknowledge how striking the disparities among people were, a shift of focus (to a focus on the disparities) would lead to a corresponding mutation in one's substantive verdict. Dominion and hierarchy, not strict equality, would then be most suitable for the state of nature.

To be sure, the critic of Locke might add, all people who were not imbeciles could attain the knowledge required for the possession and exercise of moral judgment. But, the critic would urge, the fact that all or most people were alike in their general capacity for moral reflection did not commit the earliest human creatures to the norm of egalitarianism.

Although the common ability of people to act as moral agents did separate the human species from brutes, it never could per se warrant inferences about the appropriate relations among the members of that species itself in any period. If we are laying stress on the attributes that marked people off from one another – attributes such as age or wisdom or "excellency of parts" – we can submit that people's sharing of the capacity for moral judgment would not outweigh their many divergent traits. And we thence can hold that subordination and hierarchy were felicitous social patterns for the primeval stage of human development (and also for every subsequent stage, of course). Our knowing of the human ability to comply with ethical demands, like our knowing of other qualities which people had in common, will never oblige us to attach more importance to those common qualities than to qualities that were not as widely shared.

Of course, the argument just sketched here in opposition to Locke has failed to build a conclusive case for emphasizing the inequalities among people and for playing down their affinities. The anti-Lockean stance on this matter is as plausible as Locke's, but is not irrefragable or decisive. Supporters of Locke will clearly not accept that the general traits shared by almost all members of the human species had little relevance for determining the best social arrangements within the species. No one should hope or fear that any critic of Locke can furnish proofs which will settle once and for all the relative importance of human differences and human likenesses. But we hardly need definitive proofs in favor of inegalitarianism, to perceive that Locke's equality-centered picture of humankind's natural state is itself very far from incontestable or definitive. Locke stoutly acknowledged people's similarities *and* their differences, but chose to accentuate the former when he wrote about natural freedom. When substantive verdicts hinge so baldly on unsupported choices of emphasis, they are bound to be inconclusive. Who sets the tone calls the tune.

In addition to criticizing Locke's one-sided focus on the general endowments that earmarked people as members of the same species, we can raise a still bolder challenge. Locke stumbled not merely by presuming that there was "nothing more evident" than his stance on natural equality, but further (and even more profoundly) by seeking to educe his normative tenets from nonnormative starting points. In other words, Locke's failure to vindicate his normative stance arose not only from his failure to vindicate his skewed focus on the traits people had in common, but additionally and chiefly from his assuming that a normative standpoint could be justified on the basis of nothing more than some premises about human nature. Here Locke tied his hopes to a conflation of "is" and "ought," as he ventured to sustain his ethical views by looking merely at certain natural characteristics of humankind.

In a number of contexts, to be sure, Locke exhibited an awareness of the "is"/"ought" distinction. He observed that "an Argument from what has been, to what should of right be, has no great force" (TTG, II, §103), and he ridiculed his opponents' thesis that "the Example of what hath been done, be the Rule of what ought to be" (TTG, I, §57). Likewise, he scorned the anodyne belief that "what happens . . . to be preserved, God is careful to preserve as a thing therefore to be esteemed by Men as necessary or useful" (TTG, I, §147). Yet, although Locke repeatedly declared that we can draw no safe inferences about the ways people *should* act from the ways people *do* act, he forsook his notably careful attitude toward the "is"/"ought" cleft when his explanans was the underlying features of human bodies and human psyches (rather than shameful conduct in which those bodies and psyches engaged). On the observed fact of an equal distribution of many general capacities among the creatures belonging to the human race, Locke based his normative view that human individuals naturally possessed equal rights.

For the sake of discussion, let us grant that Locke indeed was correct to highlight people's sharing of general attributes and thus that he correctly de-emphasized the ways in which people were not alike. Nonetheless, even if we side arguendo with Locke (to some extent) by giving primary attention to the qualities people shared, we can still reject his assumption that a parity of endowments – mental and physical endowments – would entail a parity of rights or a parity of freedoms. Locke erred in supposing that the fact of nonnormative equality would itself count in favor of the ideal of normative equality. Locke's nonnormative starting point could never per se advance his normative goal, since anyone can counter by affirming that human agents who were broadly alike in their abilities could justly treat one another as prey for the imposing of servitude. This reply, of course, would not be decisive; but it squares with Locke's nonnormative starting point as smoothly as his own normative verdict.

From the inegalitarian viewpoint, a pronounced focus on the nonnormative similarities among human creatures may be important, but exclusively because it can underline the turmoil involved in the establishing of dominion. With such a focus, an analyst will conjecture that the natural state of humanity abounded in discord if a number of people there accepted the moral thesis that human beings were entitled to dominate their fellows; creatures with the same basic capacities must have struggled intensely if they lived by the rule of dominance and subordination. However one may choose to regard their strife – whether one portrays it as a keen spur to progress or as an unavoidable source of woe – one should suspect that it was rampant indeed during the state of nature (if quests for dominance were viewed generally as permissible). In short, one's descriptive focus on the traits that characterized the overwhelming majority of people will here result in a descriptive conclusion. That conclusion can be evaluated in many ways, even by observers who agree that people within the state of nature were fully warranted in doing their best to subjugate one another.

Locke could aptly have used his stress on people's common abilities in order to highlight the regrettable mayhem that very probably would have flowed from the legitimizing of servitude in the natural state of the human species. Had Locke put forth an argument similar to the one recounted in my last paragraph, and had he deplored the conflicts that very likely would be associated with inegalitarian ambitions among people residing in the state of nature, he would thereby have stayed away from an illicit "is"/"ought" crossover. Neither his descriptive conclusion pointing to the probability of extensive strife, nor his value-loaded conclusion branding as unacceptable the envisioned strife, would have placed itself beyond all dispute; but neither of those conclusions would have been a glaring non sequitur.

Unfortunately for Locke, however, he was not satisfied with simply basing a prescriptive egalitarianism on the need to avert the dangers of inegalitarianism. He instead made bold to educe his normative principle, his principle against servitude in the state of nature, from his non-normative perception that human subjects were roughly equal in their endowments. "[B]eing furnished with like Faculties, sharing all in one Community of Nature, there cannot be supposed any such *Subordination* among us, that may authorize us to destroy one another, as if we were made for one anothers uses, as the inferior ranks of Creatures are for ours" (TTG, II, §6, emphasis in original). Even if one adopts the view that people's overall capabilities were uniform by and large, one can certainly refuse to credit the deduction by which Locke held that people's rights and privileges of autonomy in their interactions with one another should have been uniform.

The equality of unfreedom

In this brief discussion, we shall probe a further argument in which Locke depended on a specious transition from fact to mandate. But, instead of continuing to chide Locke for having run together normative and non-normative matters, this chapter shifts direction by seeing that he likewise conflated the ideals of liberty and equality. Although we here shall continue to scrutinize the basic line of analysis by Locke that we studied above, we now shall reconceive the analysis and the blunder therein. Even if we consider Locke's analysis to be normative in its premise as well as in its outcome, and therefore even if we decline to hold Locke guilty of violating the "is"/"ought" gap, we can censure him for conflating some distinct questions.

In the course of the *First Treatise of Government*'s attack on Robert Filmer, Locke summarized his own perception of the natural prerogatives of human beings:

> Man has a *Natural Freedom*, notwithstanding all [Filmer] confidently says to the contrary, since all that share in the same common Nature, Faculties and Powers, are in Nature equal, and ought to partake in the same common Rights and Priviledges, till the manifest appointment of God, who is *Lord over all, Blessed for ever*, can be produced to shew any particular Persons Supremacy, or a Mans own consent subjects him to a Superior. (TTG, I, §67, emphasis in original)

Let us now overlook the fallacy of moving from equal abilities to equal rights; in the present discussion, we shall arguendo accept Locke's view that the sameness of people's general endowments had a clear-cut normative bearing. Even so, we now can detect another fallacy in his statements. Having temporarily granted that the likenesses among human agents were both factual and prescriptive, one is not thus obliged to think that "Man ha[d] a Natural Freedom." In other words, Locke stumbled not just by having shown dogmatism when he combined his anthropology and his ethics, but also by having merged his various ethical positions too confidently. From his premise concerning human agents' naturally equal ranks and equal entitlements, he here derived his contention that the natural posture of human agents was a posture of freedom. Although Locke shortly became more circumspect about proposing this derivation – near the start of the *Second Treatise* he posited his affirmation of equal rights and his affirmation of liberty as distinct though closely related tenets (TTG, II, §4) – his misstep in the *First Treatise* calls for a quick reproof.

Someone believing in a natural equality of rights and of privileges has not ipso facto bound herself to uphold the value of human freedom, since everything must depend on the specifying of the rights and the privileges. Patterns of human life that fulfill the aim of strict equalitarianism can be patterns marked by a dearth of liberty; after all, human agents can be equal to one another in their confinedness. In two chief ways, with countless specific variations, the natural state of humanity could smother freedom through the development of an equal distribution of rights – inasmuch as the rights themselves would tend grossly to restrain freedom.

Of course, any structure of liberty-protecting rights must cabin freedom as well as secure it, since the holding of a right by any person will have imposed a duty on other people to respect that right. But rights and structures of rights can differ in the degree to which they authorize interference with modes of behavior that will cause no clear harm to anyone (apart from the possible harm to the people who carry out the behavior, and the possible harm to moralizers and quidnuncs who experience distress by fretting). Matrices of rights and privileges that permit little interference with most such modes of behavior were what Locke had in mind when he invoked the concept of "freedom" or "liberty."[2] As he explained in the *Second Treatise*: "[W]e must consider what State all Men are naturally in, and that is, a *State of perfect Freedom* to order their Actions, and dispose of their Possessions, and Persons as they think fit, within the bounds of the Law of Nature, without asking leave, or depending upon the Will of any other Man" (TTG, II, §4, emphasis in original). Keeping in view this general notion of "freedom," we shall ponder the two chief varieties of repressive egalitarianism – the two chief ways in which equality could prevail without ensuring that all or most people would enjoy very much liberty. These two chief ways are also, of course, the two main reasons that an attempt to derive liberty from equality is a blunder.

Freedom to abridge freedom

First, a situation of formal or initial equality could give rise to substantive inequalities that sharply abridged the freedom of many people. A state of nature that involved equal rights and equal privileges could indeed be quite an unpleasant setting where everyone was armed with a power and a privilege to subjugate as many other human beings by force as possible. (Throughout this argument, the term "power" bears its technical Hohfeldian meaning rather than its everyday meaning; it denotes an entitlement to change or expand or cancel entitlements.) If everyone held a right-engendering power to reduce as many other people to servitude as he or she could, then everybody would begin with rights and powers exactly similar to the rights and powers with which everybody else had started, and everyone would also begin with Hohfeldian liabilities equal to the Hohfeldian liabilities borne by everyone else. Each person would hold a power to win full rights of mastery by enthralling any of his or her counterparts, and each in turn would remain liable to be enthralled by those counterparts. As time went on, some people would enslave others and hence acquire rights of lordship, but everybody would have a power to subdue any person who was neither enslaved already nor endowed already with lordship over the aspiring subduer. Within this network of

[2] I am perhaps assimilating Locke too closely to John Stuart Mill (or to Mill's modern followers). Nonetheless, my basic point here is not at all weakened by the fact that Locke's conception of liberty was somewhat more restrictive than Mill's.

rights and powers, each person would have a duty to avoid interference with the rights of dominion exercised by each captor *M*, but everyone aside from *M*'s slaves would have a power to subject *M* to bondage. At least in a formal way, then, every person always would keep the basic power that was described in my penultimate sentence, and every person always would stay exposed to the wielding of that power by his or her contemporaries throughout the natural stage of human association.

A somewhat less complicated variety of this first main type of repressive egalitarianism, with a close resemblance to the Hobbesian state of nature, would occur through an equal distribution of privileges rather than an equal distribution of powers-to-create-rights. That is, everyone would always hold an entitlement to subdue the people around him or her, but the acts of subjugation would not result in the conferral of any rights. Dominance established by someone over somebody else would have a morally neutral posture, being neither transgressive of a duty nor confirmable by a right. Every person would be entitled to interfere with the lordship exercised over anyone else by anyone else, and slaves would be entitled to free themselves whenever an opportunity for revolt might arise. Of course, any slave would also be privileged to consign his master to servitude in the wake of a fruitful insurrection. Within this state of nature, everyone would possess an entitlement to clamp the yoke of bondage *on* others and to obstruct the imposition or retention of bondage *by* others. Conversely, each human agent would always live with the risk of being forced into servitude, and would also live with the risk of being toppled from any situation of mastery that had been achieved over someone else. Everyone would hold privileges that corresponded to all the privileges of everyone else; and everyone's rights and duties would likewise correspond in full to the rights and duties of everybody else, for no one would incur any duties or enjoy any rights.

Egalitarian officiousness

Even more damaging to Locke is a second way in which the norm of equality could fail to procure freedom and in fact could encourage the severest choking of freedom. This second major type of illiberal egalitarianism is perhaps more telling for our present discussion than the first type, because we here discover no rift between the form and the substance of equality (or between equal opportunities and equal results). Hence, even if we maintain that Locke's approach to equality was much less anemic than a drably formal approach, we still can recognize here that Locke committed an error when he referred to the principle of freedom as an essential aspect of the principle of equality.

A state of nature with conditions of substantive as well as formal equality could fetter individuals' latitude if the rights that people held in common were rights to overrule individuals' choices on a very wide range of matters. A state of nature did not include a full-fledged system of government, *bien sûr*, but it could include a widespread sense among people that many paths of conduct which might be chosen by individuals would run afoul of a shared right against anyone's adoption of those modes of conduct. Locke himself mentioned that the people residing in the state of nature could join with one another to redress infringements of natural law: "[H]e who hath received any damage [from a violation of natural law], has besides the right of punishment common to him with other Men, a particular Right to seek *Reparation* from him that has done it. And any other Person who finds it just, may also joyn with him that is injur'd, and assist him in recovering from the Offender, so much as may make satisfaction for the harm he has suffer'd" (TTG, II, §10, emphasis in original). Now, suppose that people within the state of nature believed that dictates of natural law commanded the following of certain dietary regimes, regimes of sexual conduct, patterns of sleep and exercise, and so forth. Everyone failing to abide by those codes of conduct would thus have brought upon his own head the punitive indignation of his contemporaries. Each human being had a privilege, and perhaps a duty as well, to punish anybody else's behavior that departed from the intrusive requirements set by natural law. Moreover, any person could act in concert with other people, if necessary, to enforce the mandates of natural law against the unruly and the deviant. People would collaborate intermittently to secure compliance by everyone with rigid norms that defined personal lifestyles, religious observances, and occupational choices. People would also intervene whenever necessary to block one of their fellows from pursuing attainments that would lie beyond the abilities of most persons. Within this primeval state, the human beings who were themselves incapable of excellence would sincerely resort to natural law as the basis for preventing the achievement of excellence by those who indeed were capable of it. No one could be allowed to disturb his counterparts by rising too high.

In such a state of nature, despite the absence of full-blown institutions of government, narrow-minded people would cooperate sufficiently to effect the ruthless regulation of sundry facets of life that are left by a liberal society to the discretion of individuals. Yet everybody would occupy a formal status and a substantive status equal to the formal status and substantive status of everyone else. Formally, all people would be alike because everyone would be entitled to enforce natural laws and to participate in collective measures for enforcing such laws. Substantively, all people would be alike because their collective interpretation and enforcement of the natural law would produce conditions of intellectual, social, and economic equality. Notwithstanding this strict equality, however, no one would enjoy much liberty.

Values joinable and disjoinable

These two principal ways in which the norm of egalitarianism for the state of nature could fail to guarantee or promote freedom within the state of nature – the way of formal equality as a uniform distribution of entitlements-to-exert-dominion, and the way of thorough equality as a suffocating conformity imbued with the lowliness and resentfulness that Nietzsche derided – would allow of multitudinous forms that could diverge quite markedly from one another in their specifics. Countless details and many broader features that are pictured in the foregoing accounts of repressive egalitarianism could indeed be modified or abandoned, without obscuring the basic point that equality and freedom are values which can impair as well as buttress each other. However numerous the modes of repressive egalitarianism were, they all would serve to refute the thesis that liberty must follow perforce from equal rights.

Conveyed with a slightly different emphasis, then, my current point is that a premise of equal rights can never enable us to draw conclusions about freedom, until we know the specific stuff of the rights. Unless the rights in the state of nature were rights that bolstered liberty (i.e. liberty as Locke understood it), any equal sharing of rights would in turn not bolster the cause of liberty. One has to specify people's rights and privileges in order to ascertain whether the equal distribution of them would tend to endow people with Lockean freedom. (We should observe that, in the *Two Treatises of Government*, Locke refrained quite deliberately from specifying much of the natural law. As he remarked: "[I]t would be besides my present purpose, to enter here into the particulars of the Law of Nature" [TTG, II, §12]. But in fairness we should also observe that, insofar as Locke did describe the natural law, he revealed that his preferred structure of equal rights would not resemble the structures of oppressive egalitarianism outlined above.)

In other words, we never can illuminatingly deal with the question of the actual ties between freedom and equality, so long as we discuss either of those ideals in abstracto. We need to confer substance on both ideals (though perhaps only a modicum of substance), before we can usefully discern the potential for a conflict or a supportive relationship between them. Having embraced the Lockean conception of liberty, one further has to state one's conception of equality in order to say whether liberty and equality would clash. Until one has started to flesh out one's vision of equality, one has neither affirmed nor denied the view that equal statuses would involve repressive social controls. Accordingly, one has neither posited nor excluded an incompatibility between the realization of liberty and the realization of equality – an incompatibility that would oblige one to choose between those values.

Of course, we can tailor our notion of equality to fit our notion of liberty; we can maintain that the state of nature involved a structure of equal rights that was built of rights which promoted liberty in whatever sense we have understood the ideal of "liberty." To achieve such custom-made harmony, however, what we have done is not to pluck our abstract concept or our specific version of equal rights from an abstract concept of liberty. Nor have we plucked our abstract concept or our specific version of liberty from a general theme of equality. Rather, we have opted for a specific version of one ideal with reference to the specific version of the other ideal that we support. We always can derive a fairly specific norm of liberty from a fairly specific norm of equality and vice versa, in that we can give an elaboration of either norm which is responsive to our detailed specification of the other norm. If one wants to make a case for both liberty and equality, one should indeed attempt to furnish an exposition of each ideal that takes account of one's exposition of the other ideal. Any different way of proceeding would be foolish. But what we cannot do is to draw a general or specific notion of one ideal from a pronouncedly abstract notion of the other. So long as either of those two ideals is pondered at a level of high abstraction, we cannot say much that is very illuminating about the tension or harmoniousness between them.

Egalitarian gruffness

Not only did Locke presume to derive his norm of liberty from his norm of egalitarianism in abstracto, but he further stumbled by tending to conflate the theme of equality and the theme of community. Having moved from the fact of human beings' shared capabilities to the norm of equal rights, Locke appealed to both that fact and that norm as grounds for another inference, an inference to the norm of community. From the premise that human agents were endowed with similar general faculties and that human agents thus deserved to be treated similarly, Locke drew the consoling message that human agents had to care for the needs of one another with fellowship and solicitude. Given that people were alike, they were bound to interact justly with one another in connections of mutual support and concern. Or so Locke reasoned.

Equality as balm?

We shall train our attention first on a minor instance of this faux pas. When recounting the early stages in the development of primeval society toward a full-fledged scheme of governance, Locke declared that the equality of possessions among the men in primitive social structures had warded off the antagonisms that would ensue from inequalities and emulous striving: "The equality of a simple poor way of liveing confineing their desires within the narrow bounds of each mans smal propertie made few controversies and so no need of many laws to decide them" (TTG, II, §107). To be sure, Locke vested the term "equality" in this passage with several meanings. He not only employed the term in reference to people's samenesses, but also invoked meanings of the term that are no longer assigned to it in the present day – meanings such as "due proportion" and "moderation" and "equability." Nonetheless, as will briefly be explained here, Locke saw the due proportion and equability of the earliest schemes of social concourse as vitally bound up with the level statuses of the human beings therein. Ergo, we can correctly treat the passage just quoted as a pronouncement tracing the realization of community to the realization of equal statures.

Locke's pronouncement stemmed in part from his view that people "who liked one another so well as to joyn into Society, cannot but be supposed to have some Acquaintance and Friendship together, and some Trust one in another; they could not but have greater Apprehensions of others, than of one another" (TTG, II, §107). But Locke was also putting forward a thesis about the inherent tendency of an equal distribution of rights and an equal parceling out of goods to minimize the sources of conflict and distrust among people. When the goods allotted in equal shares had been pathetically few and poor, at any rate, they had yielded "little matter for Covetousness or Ambition" (TTG, II, §107). After all, not only had everyone possessed no more than a scant collection of goods, but everyone had had virtually the same amount as everyone else. The exiguity and equality of people's holdings had dampened the competitiveness and resentfulness that prevail when lavish goods are apportioned unequally. And these pacific effects of general economic egalitarianism had acquired reinforcement from the sway of egalitarianism in the sphere of personal and political rights. As Locke never tired of stressing, primitive human agents recognized that they "were all *equal*, till by the same consent they set Rulers over themselves" (TTG, II, §102, emphasis in original). Equally invested with basic rights, and aware of that strict equality, the members of the earliest social structures had had no reason to begrudge anybody his or her rights. In this way, too, equality had promoted harmony. Locke could thus wax eloquent in extolling "the great confidence the Innocence and Sincerity of that poor but vertuous Age . . . gave Men one of another" (TTG, II, §110). He admired that age as "the *Golden Age* (before vain Ambition, and *amor sceleratus habendi*, evil Concupiscence, had corrupted Mens minds into a Mistake of true Power and Honour)" (TTG, II, §111, emphasis in original).

Although the story of Cain and Abel should provoke some serious doubts about this picture of an originary harmony, the picture is overwhelmingly wishful rather than unalloyedly wrong. With ample justification Locke could suggest that envy often flourishes when some people are much more wealthy than other people, and he also could sensibly declare that social frameworks with largely egalitarian allotments of basic goods would tend to produce less jealousy than would inegalitarian frameworks. Moreover, he could even hold that the paucity of covetousness in certain egalitarian arrangements might not be counteracted too significantly by any number of forces; in other words, he could even hold that the paucity of covetousness might bring about a state of communal warmth and support. Though Locke's recountal of a primitive Golden Age is exceedingly sugary, we should forbear from slighting it as void of all credibility.

Locke's error lay not in his having submitted theses wholly without merit, but in his taking for granted the inherent tilt of equality toward communitarian harmony. Pace Locke, the norm of egalitarianism could kindle and perpetuate strife at least as frequently as it could form and sustain solidarity. Thus, any peaceful ties of fellowship in the Golden Age which Locke pictured would be due to the general impulses of the human creatures involved, rather than to any decisive or ineluctable bearing of equality in support of community. In other words, given that the norm of equality per se could retard community in many circumstances, it procured its role as an unequivocal mainstay of solidarity within the *Two Treatises of Government* only because Locke coupled his belief in egalitarianism with a strikingly generous model of human nature. His portrait of the Golden Age relied utterly on that generous model; the value of equality had no independent weight.

Let us examine, then, the ways in which the norm of egalitarianism at the origins of human society could impede the development of tight-knitted relations marked by good will. (Once again, the texts of Hobbes lurk redoubtably in the background.) Though Locke played his strongest card when he indicated that greed and jealousy would thrive less if people's ranks were similar on the whole, he overstretched himself even here. After all, the meagerness of the disparities among human beings could heighten the potential explosiveness of any changes in the disparities. Fairly slight advances and setbacks would loom much larger when current differences among people were very small than when current differences were enormous. If the gaps that separated people were yawning chasms, then a marginal widening or a marginal narrowing of the gaps might almost be imperceptible; if, however, the gaps themselves were barely visible, then a widening or a narrowing of them could spark consternation in the people who had regressed *vis-à-vis* their fellows. Through such reactions, at least, the reign of egalitarianism in the early years of society might foster an acute susceptibility to envious strife.

Of course, an egalitarian social structure would not inevitably breed in people a fretful and keen alertness to shifts among their rankings. Moreover, such keen alertness could exist in a sharply inegalitarian social structure. When the apportionment of goods and other desiderata came to be highly skewed, people might resent even the slightest broadening of the gross disparities, and their pique could stem from the very hugeness of the disparities. Abject human agents, with far fewer comforts than other human agents enjoyed, might feel that their lowliness entitled them to be sheltered from any worsening of their stature. An augmentation of the gaps among people might seem intolerably unfair when the gaps already were large, whereas a similar augmentation might go unnoticed when the gaps were quite slender.

Nevertheless, there was an ineliminable possibility that the reign of egalitarianism at the dawn of society would exacerbate the competitiveness and insecure peevishness of human agents. Furthermore, this potential for the magnification of the impulse of jealousy would coexist with other possible ways in which the norm of equality could hamper the development of communal bonds. In accord with Gilbert's remark that "[w]hen every one is somebodee,/ Then no one's anybody" (*The Gondoliers*, Act II, lines 371–2), and in accord also with a distressed king's bitter plaint that "[t]hrough tattered clothes small vices do appear;/ Robes and furred gowns hide all" (*King Lear*, IV.vi.166–7), the reign of egalitarianism could encourage a general lack of respect among human beings for one another. When marked inequalities obtained, the people in the topmost positions could evoke reverence from the people in lowlier positions; the latter group might not just display esteem for their betters and might not just refrain from any attacks on them, but might likewise heed the counsel given by their superiors in favor of close ties of community and responsibility among people at every rank of the social system. Elite classes of people well could serve, through the very prestige of their positions, as mediating foci that would arouse and sustain the impulses of loyalty and affection in the people of lower classes. Nourished through the devotion which elite groups of people could attract, communal tight-knittedness might form more robustly than in a social framework guided by the norm of egalitarianism. After all, an egalitarian regime would offer no outstanding focus that could mediate and strengthen the impulses of communal solidarity. Such a regime, in which no person or class of people elicited popular reverence, would deprive itself of a source of strong cohesion.

Even more important, the human agents living in an egalitarian society could tend to feel confident about their chances of benefiting from the attacks they might mount against others. When everyone's overall position was just about the same as everybody else's, a lot of people could feel a brazen willingness to commit assaults for the sake of plunder. Impunity might attach to various deeds of violence that would incur harsh retribution in most other societies, where elite groups could wield enough strength to back up the norms which outlawed such deeds. Though some collective arrangements for enforcing laws would always exist even in a social structure that had no elite classes, such a diffuse scheme of enforcement would tend to operate with far less efficiency and smoothness than a hierarchical system where the lines of responsibility and command were much more definite (and where the deterrent factor of punitive coercion was thus more credible). Hence, a society of equals could prove to be a turbulent throng of individuals who showed equal readiness and confidence in the pursuit of rapine. Such a society would differ from the Hobbesian state of nature only because people in the society cooperated just enough to preserve the formal structure of their regime. Levels of frenzy would fall short of the chaos in the war of *omnium contra omnes*, but wide distrust and frequent pillaging would be the earmarks of a grimly atomized social matrix. By contrast, a highly inegalitarian social system might involve little turmoil; fear and reverence might discourage the humble classes from rebelling against the elite ranks, while scruples of honor or an absence of any need for further wealth might dispose the upper classes to treat the lower classes with benign condescension.

Not only could the members of a society of equals be more inclined to carry out depredations than would their counterparts in some inegalitarian schemes of life, but they also could be far more inclined to think that others would carry out depredations. Most human beings who lived in egalitarian societies at the dawn of civilization could not help knowing how inefficient the methods of law-enforcement were, and thus they rightly could anticipate that their fellows would be lured by the heady prospect of breaking laws with impunity. People who would themselves not be tempted to engage in plunder at all, and who might even show a healthy concern for ordinary people in need, would nonetheless guard vigilantly against onslaughts. Expecting attacks from any quarter at any time, people naturally disposed to be quite unthreatening might frequently have to go as far as to launch pre-emptive raids against others.

And, given that an egalitarian regime might force human agents of a placid bent to adopt belligerent modes of conduct, a regime of that sort might give a shuddersome stimulus to the tendencies of human agents who were disposed to be pugnacious and greedy. In a social system that created many opportunities for people to act as threats to the well-being of one another without much fear of incurring retribution, the danger of large-scale strife would become self-fulfilling; when each person looked upon everyone else as a probable assailant, each person would tend to conduct himself in ways that would vindicate everyone else's suspicious outlook.

Furthermore, even if one does not surmise that the anticommunitarian effects of egalitarianism would erupt very frequently into bloodshed, one can still insist on the separability of the norm of egalitarianism from the norm of communitarianism. Between a society of profound distrust and extensive rapine at one extreme and a society of warm loving-kindness at the other, there would fall sundry intermediate possibilities; and many of those intermediate social systems (based on the principle of equality) could quite justly be classified as devoid of mutual supportiveness. A society of equals might suffer very little from outbursts of pillaging while nonetheless failing to produce more than the slightest level of fellowship. People could behave selfishly and brusquely toward one another even if most of them eschewed the perpetration of outright violence.[3]

Let us recall that a society of equals might foster little if any reverence among its citizens for one another; such a dearth of reverence would ensue from the very uniformity of the statuses in egalitarian regimes. Yet the general disrespect that could reign among equal persons would not inevitably result in looting and fierce attacks. Instead, it might eventuate in a largely peaceful setting of frosty curtness where everyone interacted with his fellows gruffly but not too violently. Human agents could of course perceive other human agents as nothing more than means to be used for selfish ends, while recognizing that others were most serviceable as means when they were not subjected to brigandage. Cooperation among people who harbored little or no respect for one another could be a very chilly kind of cooperation indeed, with almost no displays of unselfish concern by anyone. Yet such a pattern of interaction, teeming with selfishness, would deserve the tag of "cooperation" to the extent that selfishness and callousness did not give rise to predatory assaults.

When we look anew at the tendency of egalitarian arrangements to

[3] Indeed, a society which resembles the one that I delineate in this paragraph (and in the next two paragraphs) may actually exist among the nomadic Hadza. See James Woodburn, "Minimal politics: the political organization of the Hadza of North Tanzania," in William Shack and Percy Cohen (eds.), *Politics in Leadership* (Oxford: Clarendon Press, 1979), 244–64.

promote license by impairing the effectiveness of disciplinary institutions, we find once more the potential for countless types of disagreeable atomism that would not give rise to many bloodsoaked scuffles. Instead of clearing the way for banditry, the lack of efficient mechanisms for punishing the violations of laws or rules might embolden people to exhibit impertinence and gross selfishness but not to engage in arrant plunder. In a society devoid of any efficient punitive scheme and also bereft of any strata of affluent people who could win and retain the loyalty of others by doling out a variety of perquisites, no one had very strong incentives to curry favor with anyone else by means of ingratiating conduct; yet the resultant piggishness might take merely the form of crass self-seeking, without numerous bursts of depredation. Although people in a primitive regime of egalitarianism would have little to lose by opting to commit deeds of plunder, all or most people might decide that the possible gains from plunder did not warrant the hazarding of the small risks involved. Since people might limit their rapacity and their brazenness to nonviolent routes of conduct (with a stony indifference toward the needs and desires of others), the dearth of effective sanctions against belligerence in egalitarian societies could breed many forms of chilly atomism unsoiled by frequent pillaging. Extremely self-centered people who could advance their interests with near-impunity might elect to further their interests by means other than despoliation and violence (and the attendant risks, which were fairly slim but greater than nothing).

Now, of course, the general arguments here advanced – the arguments about the cohesiveness derived from reverence and fear in hierarchical social structures, versus the atomism stemming from brazenness and irreverence in social schemes devoid of hierarchy – do not lay claim to incontestable soundness. Within any social order marked by extensive stratification, people in the bottom tiers of the order might resent and loathe the people occupying the positions at the top. Similarly, the people at the top might despise the people in lower ranks and might evince their contempt quite plainly through heavy-handed oppression. Further, the people on the topmost rungs of the social ladder might struggle fiercely among themselves to retain or enhance their powerful positions. Perhaps as a consequence of such struggles, or perhaps because of some other turmoil, the regime of law-enforcement in an inegalitarian social system could badly falter. An impaired mechanism for law-enforcement would in turn give free rein to miscreants at every tier of the social structure, who could prey upon their fellows and thus could push even the most stolid into a life of anxiousness and distrustfulness. Moreover, even if marauding and brouhahas might not proliferate, frostiness and hardheartedness could thrive.

By contrast, a social framework imbued with the ideal of equality might skirt or overcome the perils of atomism and achieve harmonious ties of trustfulness and solicitude. By and large, as Locke recognized, a primitive social unit that brought about conditions of nearly equal statuses would supply less fuel for the divisive passion of jealousy than a social unit that brought about conditions of hierarchic ascendance. Furthermore, the number of people who were disposed to rob their contemporaries for the sake of avoiding honest labor might be quite small. And, given this climate of extensive trust and cooperation, a diffusely organized scheme for the apprehension and punishment of wrongdoers could work very nicely.

In sum, a theory associating communal warmth with hierarchical institutions will be no more compelling and definitive than a theory associating communal warmth with egalitarian arrangements. Neither line of association is flatly wrong, but neither line is conclusive. Yet such inconclusiveness is exactly the point here. Equality is neither requisite nor sufficient for the growth of tight solidarity; and hierarchies are not requisite or sufficient for solidarity, either. Hence, the factors of inequality and equality are never decisive in allowing or checking the emergence of communitarian sentiments. At most, those factors perform the variable and secondary function of helping to define the exact forms that communal harmony or communal disharmony takes. They cannot determine whether harmony and responsibility will triumph or fail to triumph over disharmony and atomism. Equality and inequality each can associate with warm community *and* with heartless individualism. Accordingly, the decisive resolution of the battle between communitarianism and individualism has to flow from another source.

For Locke, the essential fount of solidarity (and the reason for the triumph of solidarity over indurate selfishness) lay in human nature. His unduly generous beliefs about human nature, and his generous beliefs concerning what human intercourse ought to be, enabled him to assume that originary networks of social and political life must have involved high levels of communitarian sentiment. Unlike the principle of equality per se, the promptings of human nature could guarantee or nearly guarantee the flourishing of communitarianism – if those promptings were as inclined toward communitarian fellowship as Locke judged them to be. If human creatures did indeed have a natural bent to display forbearance and solicitude, then they very likely would fashion structures of intercourse that gave free expression to their benevolent impulses. Those arrangements for compassionate intercourse would flourish until the cloying sweetness of humanity in the Golden Age had come to an end through the corruption of basic instincts.

Utterly crucial, then, to Locke's portrayal of Golden Age societies is his proposition, quoted earlier, that "those who liked one another so well as to joyn into Society, cannot but be supposed to have some Acquaintance and Friendship together, and some Trust one in another" (TTG, II, §107). Likewise indispensable is another statement already quoted, dealing with "the great confidence the Innocence and Sincerity of that poor but vertuous Age . . . gave Men one of another" (TTG, II, §110). Locke also made more general pronouncements on the inclination of people toward society. For instance, he began one of his chapters in the *Second Treatise* with the following statement: "God having made Man such a Creature, that, in his own Judgment, it was not good for him to be alone, put him under strong Obligations of Necessity, Convenience, and Inclination to drive him into Society, as well as fitted him with Understanding and Language to continue and enjoy it" (TTG, II, §77). A closely similar view appears in the *Essays on the Law of Nature*: "[Man] feels himself not only to be impelled by life's experience and pressing needs to procure and preserve a life in society with other men, but also to be urged to enter into society by a certain propensity of nature" (ELN, 157). These and comparable assertions, as we have realized now, demand to be viewed as independent theses that bear no necessary or intrinsic connection with the Lockean belief in egalitarianism. They stand on their own as postulates regarding the human race in general and early human beings specifically. By relying on such postulates, Locke could sketch his picture of supportiveness and obligingness in the earliest social and political frameworks. His general postulates were the sine qua non of his account; the theme of equality – the "equality of a simple poor way of liveing" – performed no self-sufficient or ineluctable role in strengthening the theme of community.

Kindly imperatives

For an even more conspicuous and important example of Locke's frequent confounding of the norm of equality with the norm of community, we may turn to his recountal of the fundamental conditions in the state of nature. After arriving at his verdict about the equal normative ranks of human beings from his descriptive premise about the equal faculties of human beings, Locke employed his normative verdict as a premise for another conclusion – a conclusion about the basic respect and self-control that moral agents were bound to exercise in their dealings with one another. He proclaimed: "The *State of Nature* has a Law of Nature to govern it, which obliges every one: And Reason, which is that Law, teaches all Mankind, who will but consult it, that being all equal and independent, no one ought to harm another in his Life, Health, Liberty, or

Possessions" (TTG, II, §6, emphasis in original). Locke explained that the duty to avoid harming other people was a key aspect of a broader duty to conserve other people's lives and welfare as much as possible: "Every one as he is *bound to preserve himself*, and not to quit his Station wilfully; so by the like reason when his own Preservation comes not in competition, ought he, as much as he can, *to preserve the rest of Mankind*, and may not unless it be to do Justice on an Offender, take away, or impair the life, or what tends to the Preservation of the Life, the Liberty, Health, Limb or Goods of another" (TTG, II, §6, emphasis in original).

Locke's stance here, his positing of a duty that obliged everyone to preserve other human agents, will receive close attention in part III of this book. What needs to be challenged now is the ostensible derivation of such a duty from the fact and the norm of human creatures' equality. Locke asserted that the "equal and independent" statures of human beings were the grounds for the obligation that lay on every human creature to forbear from harming her fellows (and for the obligation that lay on every human creature to provide sustenance to her fellows when necessary). Locke did not here avail himself of the consequentialist modes of argument which some of his predecessors – notably Hobbes and Hooker – had used. He declined to focus directly here on each person's self-interest as the fundament or provenance of everybody's duty to abstain from inflicting harm upon others. For him, the central justification of that duty did not rest on the proposition that everyone would enhance his or her material well-being if everyone complied with the duty. Rather, Locke pointed solely to the normative and nonnormative equality that characterized all human beings, whom God created "to last during his, not one anothers Pleasure" (TTG, II, §6). Because all people possessed "like Faculties," and because all people occupied the same basic moral footing "in one Community of Nature," we must conclude that "there cannot be . . . any such *Subordination* among us, that may Authorize us to destroy one another" (TTG, II, §6, emphasis in original). Given that people were alike in crucial respects, each person had to value the needs and aspirations of others. Or so Locke plainly wished his readers to think.

One can start to realize how extensively Locke confused the ideal of egalitarianism and the ideal of communitarianism, when one notices that his tenet relating to the moral equality of people is expressed here as a tenet regarding the "Community of Nature,"[4] and when one notices that

[4] On the basis of TTG, II, §128 ("*Mankind are one Community*, make up one Society distinct from all other Creatures" [emphasis in original]), I here am glossing the phrase "Community of Nature" as a way of referring to the natural equality of human beings with one another – their equality as the members of the highest species in God's creation. If the phrase denotes instead people's common access to the earth's material riches, my general point will remain completely intact.

his argument's conclusion about mutual restraint is expressed here as a dictum about the need to eschew "Subordination among us." From the postulate of the essential sameness of human beings, Locke tried to educe an obligation that required every human being to show respect for the fundamental welfare of others. He went astray in drawing this clear-cut verdict, because the sameness of human beings could just as rightly issue in a lack of concern by everyone for the needs and the well-being of everybody else. Moreover, the normative and nonnormative alikeness of human beings could aptly issue in any number of intermediate levels of concern and forbearance. Equality in itself could never serve as the touchstone for prescribing the amount of care and respect that human beings owed to one another.

To affirm that human agents in the state of nature had equal rights and privileges is not yet to specify what those rights and privileges were. An affirmation of equal rights and liberties, on its own, will inform us merely that the rights and the liberties enjoyed by each person were the same as the liberties and the rights enjoyed by anyone else. Alone, such an affirmation does not fill in the substance of the entitlements that were held by all. But until we know that substance, we shall have no grounds for saying whether a given act would transgress someone's entitlements, and thus we shall have no grounds for saying whether a given act would transgress the principle of equality by which the entitlements were apportioned. In turn, unless we have grounds for knowing whether a given act would flout the principle of equality, we shall have no grounds for saying whether anticommunitarian behavior was in agreement with the principle of equality or in tension with it. Hence, we shall have no grounds for saying whether the principle of equality would mesh with the principle of community, or not. Such a determination becomes possible only when we are apprised of the substance of the entitlements which everyone held. And since the general norm of equality could never per se define the substantive bearings of the rights and the privileges which were patterned with reference to that norm, it would play no role in establishing its own congruence or lack of congruence with the norm of community.

To illustrate this point, let us suppose that everybody alike retained a privilege to thrash and murder everyone else. Or perhaps everyone had a privilege to assault and murder everyone else in some prescribed ways only, and therefore everyone also had a right to security – a right to be free from any sort of attack or slaying that was not permitted. Given this pattern of entitlements, someone who made use of his privilege to commit murder (or to commit some specific types of murder) would clearly have conducted himself in line with the dictate of equality. After all, he availed himself of a privilege that was held not only by him but likewise by every one of his fellows. His victims were as entitled to murder him as he was to murder them. Hence, his slayings did not proceed from the assertion of an entitlement that was unavailable to anyone else. Because everyone held exactly the same privilege to commit homicide, the perpetration of any deed which gave effect to that privilege was the perpetration of a deed very strictly in keeping with the norm of equality. A murderous exploit would not encroach on anyone's rights, since no one had any right to be safe from murder (or from various kinds of murder); and the only privilege that would have to be exercised for the undertaking of the deed was a privilege shared by all human creatures. If the entitlements possessed by each person did include an entitlement to carry out the slaughter of other people, then acts of slaughter would not induce an illegitimate "Subordination among us." Indeed, if such an entitlement figured as an aspect of every human being's moral endowment, people would avoid the subordination of one another only when *everyone* was allowed to try to spill the blood of his fellows – at least until he had alienated the privilege to do so. Although any person could rebuff someone else's homicidal endeavors, no one adhering to the norm of equality could insist that somebody else was obligated to shrink from such endeavors.

A supporter of Locke may reply that any structure of rights and privileges in which people were entitled unprovokedly to destroy one another would indeed result in the subordination of many people by others. Not only would the perpetrator of homicide impose his aims on his victim, but, as a general pattern, people who were strong and fast and shrewd would fare better than people who were weak and slow and dull-witted. Everyone held the same entitlements, yet the substantive outcomes yielded by those entitlements would tend to congeal into sharp inequalities. In sum, the defenders of Locke may argue, the endowing of everyone with a privilege to commit murder would bring about an astonishing degree of "Subordination among us" at the level of particular acts and at the level of the broader relationships that were formed or intensified by those acts.

A second defense which the followers of Locke might advance is that his pronouncements on the "equal and independent" statures of human beings and on the need to avoid "Subordination among us" were only ways of imparting his belief that members of the human species should all die only of natural causes (and thus not at the hands of one another, except in cases of urgent self-defense or legitimate retribution). Locke suggested merely that human agents were equal in their common right to secureness from assaults. In other words, instead of trying to derive that shared entitlement from the fact and norm of equality, he understood that entitlement itself as the basic mode or source of equality among people – whose possession of that entitlement distinguished them from all other animals. Although the abstract theme of equality did not pre-ordain a right to be free from murder and unprovoked attacks, the sharing of such a right itself would be a crucial version or instance of the abstract theme. A common right to security could never *flow* perforce from the general rule of egalitarianism; but, the champions of Locke might contend, it well could *instantiate* that rule.

Equality according to whom? Let us deal in turn with these two postulated objections. To the charge that an unacceptable state of "Subordination among us" would arise from individual acts of homicide and from the general advantages that would accrue to sturdy and intelligent people when homicide was allowed, we have to respond by making a distinction between legitimate and illegitimate hierarchies. As was described earlier, Locke readily acknowledged a host of ways in which people differed markedly – and in which they thus might deserve unequal allotments of the benefits arising from any number of distributional choices. While tenaciously pointing up the fundamental equality of people, Locke stressed as well that people's basic alikeness scarcely led to the imposition of *all* "sorts of *Equality*: *Age* or *Virtue* may give Men a just Precedency: *Excellency of Parts and Merit* may place others above the Common Level: *Birth* may subject some, and *Alliance* or *Benefits* others, to pay an Observance to those to whom Nature, Gratitude, or other Respects may have made it due" (TTG, II, §54, emphasis in original). Locke affirmed that any system which took account of the underlying equality of people, in some respect or another, would have to leave room for inequalities in a myriad of different respects. But, as long as the fundamental sameness of people had been sedulously respected, the disparities among people were unobnoxious and legitimate when appraised by the standards of the relevant system. As Locke declared after noting some of the many types of inequality that he viewed as both desirable and inevitable: "[A]ll this consists with the *Equality*, which all Men are in" (TTG, II, §54, emphasis in original). Although applied by Locke to his own conception of equality, this basic point – his point about the warrantedness of sundry hierarchies within a matrix of rights that gave effect to the deep equality of human beings – extends with full force to *any* structure of equal rights and privileges, since any such structure must create some inequalities in order to secure a desired pattern of equality.

Insofar as any matrix of entitlements did not function in a way that diverged from the central principle of equality on which the matrix had been founded, any uneven set of advantages that evolved would not amount to noxious "Subordination among us" (when judged with reference to the criteria laid down by the scheme of entitlements itself).

Accordingly, a regime of entitlements that conferred on everyone a privilege to slaughter everybody else would sow no *illegitimate* hierarchies, even if it unrelentingly favored people who were cunning and tough. Or, at least, we can say that it would breed no illegitimate hierarchies, if its own standards of "legitimacy" are the criteria on which we draw to assess it; after all, any such regime of entitlements that operated in accordance with its design would serve to realize its vision of equality – its peculiar vision of equality as the sharing of an entitlement to engage in murder. Substantive inequalities produced by compliance with that strange vision would be no more nettlesome for proponents of such a vision than duly meritocratic hierarchies and other hierarchies were troublesome for Locke.

Now, of course, Locke would clearly have rejected the view of human equality as the holding by every person of an entitlement to carry out slayings. Such a conception of equality, when gauged by the moral standards to which Locke cleaved, would obviously engender unacceptable patterns of "Subordination among us." It would "Authorize us to destroy one another, as if we were made for one anothers uses, as the inferior ranks of Creatures are for ours," and thus it would run afoul of Locke's insistence that human beings were made by God "to last during his, not one anothers pleasure" (TTG, II, §6). Yet, far from clashing with anything maintained here, the fact that Locke would have scorned a homicide-promoting conception of the theme of equality is a fact which bolsters the view advanced throughout this discussion. Nothing in the abstract norm of equality for the state of nature could predetermine the outlawing of homicidal behavior. Locke thus made an unsupportable leap when he inferred basic duties of nonaggression from the existence of strictly "equal and independent" postures. What bore decisively on the presence of such duties was not the *equal allocation* of rights and privileges, but the *substance* or the *tenor* thereof. Someone who points merely to the equal apportioning of entitlements in the state of nature has left open the chance that the major entitlements in question were strongly anticommunitarian. (And, as will presently be explained, someone who points merely to people's endowment with communitarian rights in the state of nature has thus left open the chance that any number of their entitlements were not apportioned equally.)

In itself, the fact of an equal distribution of all entitlements will not indicate the level of communitarian closeness which the entitlements prescribe or should have prescribed. As is illustrated by the hypothetical social scheme which vested in everyone the privilege to commit murder, the equal allocation of rights and privileges would be wholly compatible with an absence of any communitarian content in the rights and the privileges. To know the communitarian or anticommunitarian leaning of our entitlements, we have to know what they are; yet, to know what the entitlements are, we never can resort merely to the fact that they are held by everybody alike. Thus, Locke's apparent derivation of peace-encouraging duties from the theme of human equality was in fact his specification of the rights and privileges which the "equal and independent" human beings held. For Locke, equality meshed with community and forbearance *just because* the entitlements which he viewed as falling within the sway of equality were entitlements that established the obligation to show forbearance. In other words, Locke's emphasis on equality could engender its reassuring verdict only because that emphasis conjoined with the reassuring doctrines of his religion. In the absence of his belief that God barred people from undertaking aggression, and in the absence of some equivalent belief focused on secular considerations, his insistence on equality would not have been matched by an insistence on harmonious interaction. In sum, far from being able to ground the duties of nonaggression in the bare ideal of equality, Locke had to ground them in religious precepts which shaped the substance of the entitlements to which the ideal of equal distribution applied. Because he had placed the rabbit of peacefulness in the hat of fundamental equality, we should hardly be surprised by his success at pulling that rabbit out of that austere hat.

Before we tackle the second way in which supporters of Locke might try to vindicate his remarks on normative equality and forbearance, we should briefly take notice of one more argument that can be used to parry the first defense which those supporters might raise. Thus far, while examining the view that the retention by everyone of a privilege to commit homicide would lead to invidious "Subordination" among people, we have arguendo taken for granted that the universal holding of such a privilege would indeed result in subordination. To distinguish between legitimate and illegitimate domination is to presume that domination occurred. Here we shall continue to presume that the effects of a universal entitlement to carry out murders would approximate the effects against which Locke's supporters might warn. But we shall now resist the branding of those effects as subordination or domination.

To be sure, the systematic favoring of intelligent and powerful human agents would be regarded as manifest domination under most codes of ethics, particularly when the stakes of life and death were involved. But under a code of morals that vested everyone with a privilege to commit homicide, the inequalities nurtured by the sharing of that privilege might fail to count as domination at all (even as legitimate domination). A structure of entitlements that engendered grossly disparate outcomes could be seen as the only pattern of entitlements that would duly treat people equally, in the sense that it would handle like people alike by giving everybody exactly what he deserved on the basis of an overarching criterion. That is, one's prime concern when one supports the murder-permitting scheme of entitlements may be the results that followed from the scheme, rather than its groundwork of universal privileges. Someone enamored of the scheme may regard the victimizing of certain people and certain classes of people not as a subordinate feature that we grudgingly ought to sanction, but as the foremost reason for approving the scheme. If one feels utter disdain for the people or groups of people who were the likely victims, and if one furthermore maintains that they could be singled out only retrodictively, one will hold that the best structure of entitlements was a structure which allowed everyone to slay everyone else.

Apologists for that structure can portray it and its results as aptly egalitarian in two principal ways. First, of course, it would provide the same entitlements and thus the same general opportunities to all people. In addition, even the bloody outcomes of such a matrix of entitlements can be classed as egalitarian, by gruff Social Darwinists who believe that those outcomes would render to each person whatever he had deserved. Against the background of such a scheme of entitlements, each person would stand a chance of flourishing and surviving in proportion to his or her adroitness at outwitting and overmastering other people. Therefore, if one genuinely assumes that the proper touchstone for granting or denying various claims to sundry desiderata was everybody's relative fitness in a bruising struggle for life, one can submit that the outcomes of such a struggle would confer on no one either more or less than was merited. Winners and losers would reveal their respective skills by keeping or forfeiting their lives, and thus would earn their rewards or hardships by being measured against the same criterion. From the quaint perspective of someone who avouches that truly equal treatment for all the members of the human race must entail their being measured against the single standard of their ability to survive, the use of a more humane criterion would amount to grossly unequal treatment. After all, greater humaneness would curtail the well-deserved flourishing of the strong and the crafty in the interest of the weak and the oafish.

For the radical Social Darwinist, the introduction of a more humane criterion would occasion wrongs akin to the wrong that most of us perceive in a blunt refusal to pay workers more money when they have toiled more lengthily than their fellows. Think of Christ's Parable of the Laborers, where the vineyard owner compensated each of his hirelings with a single denarius although some hirelings had worked much longer than others. Certain theorists might classify the uniform level of the laborers' wages as an instance of equal treatment for all. But such a view is hardly compelling, and is indeed less plausible than the view that the workers suffered unequal treatment when their boss failed to remunerate their efforts in accordance with the extent of their services. If we look for a direct correlation between the level of wages and the length of work when we judge the equality or inequality of various people's incomes, we clearly then must call for pronounced disparities among the incomes qua flows of money. We must do so, at any rate, if we hope to equalize the incomes qua reimbursements for periods of labor performed. Given our touchstone for determining the equality or inequality of people's conditions, we shall be upholding an inequality of conditions if we plump for the equalizing of wages qua flows of money. Gaps among the monetary levels of wages will have won our support as instances or manifestations of equal treatment.

Our extreme Social Darwinists will feel very much the same way about the yawning gaps among people's situations that would emerge during the all-out struggle for life in the state of nature. For these extremists, the only outcomes that harmonized with the norm of equality among persons were outcomes that matched each person's welfare with his ability to survive and to flourish in the aforementioned struggle. Given this unusual touchstone for assessing the inequality or equality of human agents, an effort to equalize the standing of human agents in any other respects would be a withholding of equal treatment. In parallel with the notion that any treatment of human agents as equals would involve the adjusting of their levels of reimbursement to take into account the duration of their work, the zanier Social Darwinists will contend that the treatment of human agents as equals must involve the bestowing of rewards (especially the reward of continued life) in allotments that would reflect the skill and tenacity of people as they pursued a war of *omnium contra omnes*. A less stratified distribution of goods would infringe the equality of human beings by handing out far more benefits to the doltish and the puny than they deserved.

This new reply to the first of the objections which Locke's defenders might raise is different from my earlier retort, but the divergences between them are rather tenuous while the similarities are crucial. We once again should look at the Parable of the Laborers. Here, however, we need to modify the story in two closely connected ways. Let us first assume that the owner of the vineyard opted to pay his workers different amounts of money that would reflect the different amounts of time which the workers had spent toiling for him. And let us assume further that the laborers in the vineyard were satisfied with the owner's method of compensation. Now, the contented state of the laborers might derive from their perception that they had clearly not received equal treatment and that the inequality of the treatment was fully justified (because their periods of toil were themselves unequal). Such an attitude would align with my initial riposte to Locke's followers, by distinguishing unacceptable from acceptable hierarchies. Yet the laborers' satisfaction might spring not from a sense of justifiable inequalities, but from a disarming sense of equality. If the workers gauged equality on the basis of a correspondence between income and the length of toil, rather than on the somewhat cruder basis of the varying sums of money that they had pocketed, they would view the disparities among their levels of earnings as the means by which true equality had been realized. Such an attitude would of course align with my second way of countering Locke's defenders, where we noted that disparate rewards could amount to manifestations of a strict egalitarianism. By that standard, a strict uniformity of rewards would amount to the slighting of intelligent and vigorous people for the sake of the stupid and the feckless.

Differences between these two types of satisfaction on the part of the workers are primarily differences between labels, rather than differences of substance. In the first account of the workers' contentedness, disparities were perceived as legitimate inequalities; in the second account, the workers saw disparities as marks or modes of equality. At least in the present case, however, the different characterizations – "justified inequality" versus "true equality" – would make no practical difference. Although the laborers in the first depiction would employ standards for "what should count as equality" that diverged from the standards of equality used by laborers in the second depiction, the criteria for "what should count as desirable and just" diverged not at all between these two renderings of the parable.

Likewise, the differences between our two accounts of the Social Darwinist perspective are chiefly differences between labels. Whether the extreme Social Darwinists view the upshot of the war of each against all as a condonable state of inequality or as the effectuation of pure equality, they regard that war as highly commendable because they esteem it as the guarantor of human equality. In our first version of extreme Social Darwinism, the all-out fray would serve to realize equality by sustaining a formal network or baseline of entitlements which were equally apportioned and which included the privilege to commit murder; in our second version of extreme Social Darwinism, the all-out fray would serve to realize equality by producing for each person the substantive results that he or she had merited.

Of course, any decent person will scorn the Social Darwinists' vision of equality. Just as nothing can ensure that workmen will have a sense of being treated equally when they get exactly the same amounts of money for their varied amounts of labor, and just as nothing can ensure that they will have a sense of being treated equally when they get *varying* amounts of money for their varying amounts of labor, so nothing can oblige us to agree with vehement Social Darwinists in their understanding of equality. By essentially the same token, however, nothing in the abstract theme of equality can demand the repudiation of the Social Darwinists' views. Their views, as expounded here, are very much a conception of equality – albeit a conception that will strike most people as daft and hateful. Thus, however rebarbative the murder-permitting doctrine is, we do not rule it out when we affirm that all adequate moral stands must respect the norm of human equality. Extreme Social Darwinism's general condonation of murder can pass the equality-respecting test with flying colors; after all, the universal allowability of murder involves a thorough equality among human beings in the possession of all entitlements.

Hence, given that the abstract theme of equality is consistent with even the most hellishly strife-ridden human intercourse, we should scarcely perceive it as requiring a harmonious and solicitous way of life. Only when our concrete entitlements are themselves promotive of solicitous ways of life, will the equal allocation of the entitlements be likewise. In other words, before the ideal of equality can point toward community, it must join with some benignly communitarian principles which set the bearings of our entitlements.

As was explained earlier, Locke's own soothing conception of entitlements came from his religious beliefs:

> The *Idea* of a supreme Being, infinite in Power, Goodness, and Wisdom, whose Workmanship we are, and on whom we depend; and the *Idea* of our selves, as understanding, rational Beings, being such as are clear in us, would, I suppose, if duly considered, and pursued, afford such Foundations of our Duty and Rules of Action, as might place *Morality amongst the Sciences capable of Demonstration.* (EHU, IV, iii, §18, emphasis in original)

Readers who decline to share Locke's faith in a noble Being should adopt quite a jaundiced view of his effort to extract harmony-requiring duties from the "equal and independent" statuses of all persons. The equality of statuses in itself was simply not sufficient to yield his sanguine conclusions. We need to inquire about the *substance* of the privileges and the rights that composed each natural status; and, in the absence of a benevolent Being, the substance of those entitlements was not as reassuringly predetermined as Locke supposed.

From deduction to dogma We shall conclude this discussion by returning to the second major defense of Locke that his supporters might raise – i.e. the suggestion that Locke adverted to peace-promoting duties not as imperatives which he hoped to *derive* somehow from the abstract theme of human equality, but as basic imperatives that *molded* his vision of equality. According to this defense, Locke invoked crucial obligations as his chief means of specifying and circumscribing the general norm of equality, rather than as precepts deducible from that norm. Instead of perpetrating a gross non sequitur by trying to draw community from equality, he proceeded in a much more incisive fashion by laying out a communitarian picture of equality.

To this line of defense my discussion will respond in four ways, of which the first two will be exceedingly brief. My third reply will counter the new defense of Locke with an argument that (to some degree) resembles the arguments which have parried the initial line of defense. In other words, that reply will submit that countless forms or principles of equality would not favor community. My fourth response will opt for a different tack. Rather than argue once again that equality was never *sufficient* to establish communitarian bonds in the state of nature, the fourth riposte will emphasize that the equal allocation of rights and privileges was not *necessary* to establish such bonds. Neither essential nor sufficient for the reign of fellowship and mutual responsibility, the reign of equality in abstracto could never play a decisive part in the furthering or the hindering of communitarian aspirations.

Interpretative extravagance As a reconstruction of Locke's own argument in the *Second Treatise*, the postulated defense has left much to be desired. Perhaps Locke should have proceeded in the manner which the defense suggests, but any contention that he did thus proceed is (at best) one-sided and overgenerous. Taking for granted that equality was equality conjoined with religious precepts defining the substance of our entitlements, Locke believed that the notion of equality would suffice as a ground from which a rational human being should infer obligations. Or, at least, we can readily conclude that Locke felt this way, when we focus on a key passage in the *Second Treatise*. In that passage, which does not jar at all with other relevant passages, Locke declared that "Reason, which is [the Law of Nature], teaches all Mankind, who will but consult it, that being all equal and independent, no one ought to harm another in his Life, Health, Liberty, or Possessions" (TTG, II, §6). Here the violence-retarding duties figured not as the means of fleshing out the abstract principle of equality, but as consequences derived therefrom. We presently come upon another such flow of derivation: "[B]eing furnished with like Faculties, sharing all in one Community of Nature, there cannot be supposed any such *Subordination* among us, that may Authorize us to destroy one another, as if we were made for one anothers uses, as the inferior ranks of Creatures are for ours" (TTG, II, §6, emphasis in original). Here the violence-retarding duties stemmed from both the fact and the norm of equal ranks – that is, from the state of "being furnished with like Faculties," and also from the norm of the "one Community of Nature." Indeed, as we previously observed, Locke described the duties of nonaggression as duties aimed at scotching the growth of inadmissible hierarchies ("Subordination among us"); those hierarchies, if permitted to bloom, would clash with the equality of the general aptitudes and entitlements.

Locke, to be sure, did supplement these appeals to equality with appeals to the pious tenet that human beings were "made to last during [God's], not one anothers Pleasure" (TTG, II, §6). This pious tenet did contribute to spelling out the entitlements and the sort of equality that Locke perceived as appropriate for the members of humankind. If embraced, it could indeed help to buttress certain strands of the reassuring conclusions that Locke proposed, for it itself would amount to the cardinal norm in those conclusions. But, although the invocations of God could fulfill their purpose – if we credit religious dogmatism as an apposite ground for the achievement of such a purpose – they could hardly excuse or salvage or erase Locke's appeals to equality; in fact, they now serve to underscore the foolishness and irrelevance of those appeals. Locke, despite his overt reliance on a religious doctrine of nonaggression, felt a need to enhance his case by pointing to our "equal and independent" positions and our "being furnished with like Faculties" and our subsumption in "one Community of Nature." Not only were these references to equality futile, but they were utterly superfluous. When Locke proclaimed that the Deity had forbidden any unprovoked bloodshed, he thus supplied himself with everything he needed in order to underpin and authorize his pronouncements against the bloodshed.

For a devout person who thinks that God has condemned our harming of one another (in the absence of provocation), no further grounds will have to be cited for the establishment of duties that give effect to God's will. Whether the pious person has come to know God's will through reflection or through the Scriptures, she must be very "careful to do therefore as the Lord your God has commanded you; you shall not turn aside to the right hand or to the left" (Deuteronomy 5:32). If God has imposed duties of nonaggression on all people, then such duties enjoy the firmest possible grounding. Attempts to fortify the justification of those duties with references to our common aptitudes and our "equal and independent" postures are entirely gratuitous. Thus, although Locke's religious axioms did indeed flesh out his notion of equality, they did not strengthen or warrant his appeals to equality in abstracto. Far from salvaging those appeals, the religious dogmas showed them to be redundant and pointless.

Hence, if supporters of Locke insist that pronouncements on duties of nonaggression served as his vehicles for defining the concept of equality rather than as derivations from it, they will give Locke the benefit of too many doubts. They will have glossed over his deducing of obligations from the principle of equality in abstracto. Or, if they seek to vindicate those abstract deductions by highlighting the sacred mandates with which Locke blended them, the pointlessness and superfluousness of the deductions will have become apparent. Given the repeated attempts by Locke to invoke the nebulous ideal of equality as a ground for his exhortations against violence, his defenders can hardly rescue him by adverting to the specific dogmas that supplemented his vacuous ideal; because his dogmas were in themselves sufficient to yield his humane exhortations, and because his reliance on his vacuous ideal of equality contributed nothing to the force or role of the dogmas, his emphasis upon those specific dogmas made glaringly redundant the invocations of his vapid ideal. References to specific prerogatives of the Maker were not mere supplements to the abstract theme of egalitarianism. Instead, they alone bore the justificatory burden which the abstract theme was supposed to bear.

On the all-encompassing might of all-encompassing might When directing attention to the prerogatives of our Fashioner,[5] Locke announced that human beings were "made to last during [H]is, not one anothers pleasure" (TTG, II, §6). As has just been observed, this tenet enabled Locke to posit duties of nonaggression that applied to all people. Moreover, this basic precept – whereby only the Creator could rightfully "destroy his own Workmanship" (TTG, I, §53) – also underlay Locke's insistence that human beings were not entitled to commit suicide or even to sell themselves into bondage (TTG, II, §§6, 23–4, 135). We ought not to be surprised, then, if Locke's supporters focused upon this dogma as the essential fountainhead of his views concerning our equal statuses.

Now, let us grant Locke's assumptions that human lives and capacities were the products of "one Omnipotent and infinitely wise Maker" (TTG, II, §6), and that the Maker had exclusive and full authority to determine how long His sundry creatures ought to abide. Arguendo we can agree with Locke (in ELN, 157), and with Saint Paul and with Isaiah, that lumps of clay can never have grounds for questioning the will and the governance of the potter who molds them. Nevertheless, despite our

[5] Here and elsewhere throughout this book, I employ "prerogatives" (or "prerogative") as a synonym for "entitlements" (or "entitlement"). I decline to follow the *Second Treatise* in its use of the term "prerogative" to denote the latitude of governmental officials who are charged with giving effect to legislation.

having granted so much, we clearly can reject Locke's presumption that human beings were obligated to avoid harming themselves and to avoid harming their fellows unprovokedly. In other words, we still can eschew his sense of a necessary conflict between the proposition that "God made persons to last as long as He pleased" and the proposition that "God made persons to last as long as they pleased."

Here we have to turn upon Locke an argument of the sort that Shakespeare had Polixenes wield against Perdita in *The Winter's Tale* (IV.iv.89–97). There Polixenes challenges the distinction that his future daughter-in-law has made between natural growth and human efforts to change such growth. Because human beings who affect Nature's course can do so only by employing the means which Nature has put at their disposal, "[t]he art itself is Nature." And because the human beings who trade upon natural forces are themselves the products of natural forces, "Nature is made better by no mean/ But Nature makes that mean."

Likewise, given the premise that the world and all its inhabitants attained their being and their roles through the might of an omnipotent God, the slaying of one inhabitant by another would occur within the whole scheme of things that God had devised. Given that human beings were all "the Servants of one Sovereign Master, sent into the World by his order and about his business" (TTG, II, §6), someone who unprovokedly put a violent end to the life of somebody else had thereby gone about the business of God. As servants of the one all-ordaining Master, people who shed the blood of other people had caused their victims to last as long as God had prescribed. Because homicidal people and homicidal weapons owed their existence and their roles to the all-embracing control of God, a brutal murder would give effect to God's will as much as would a conciliatory act. When people let one another live no more than to the extent of "one anothers Pleasure," they ipso facto let one another live to the full extent of God's pleasure.

Now, the champions of Locke would doubtless reply by submitting that the Lockean God was a benevolent God, and that the roguish acts committed by human beings were violations rather than realizations of God's will. God bestowed His love on each human being as a "wonderful . . . piece of Workmanship" (TTG, I, §86), and intended the preservation of each as far as possible. But He created and loved these splendid pieces of workmanship as fallible beings, since He Himself was the lone infallible Being. Though the might of God extended everywhere, and though His constant solicitude for His creatures extended to human creatures above all, He had made human beings merely *capable* of the harmony and virtue that He demanded from them. God forbore from endowing human agents with the infallibility that belonged to no one but Him. He "made man such that these [natural-law] duties . . . necessarily follow from [man's] very nature" (ELN, 201), but He scarcely had guaranteed that the various members of the human race would conduct themselves in accordance with the fine nature they possessed. Because men and women were indeed men and women rather than veritable peers of God, they could sin at any time and could thereby lapse from performing their essential roles as God's servants. God did not merit any share of responsibility for the wrongs to which human beings stooped when they deviated from the hard way of righteousness that He had laid down for them. As Locke explained in the *Essay concerning Human Understanding*:

> But yet there is a case wherein a Man is at Liberty in respect of *willing*, and that is the chusing of a remote Good as an end to be pursued. Here a Man may suspend the act of his choice from being determined for or against the thing proposed, till he has examined, whether it be really of a nature in it self and consequences to make him happy, or no . . . And here we may see how it comes to pass, that a Man may justly incur punishment, though it be certain that in all the particular actions that he *wills*, he does, and necessarily does will that, which he then judges to be good. For though his *will* be always determined by that, which is judg'd good by his Understanding, yet it excuses him not: Because, by a too hasty choice of his own making, he has imposed on himself wrong measures of good and evil; which however false and fallacious, have the same influence on all his future conduct, as if they were true and right . . . The eternal Law and Nature of things must not be alter'd to comply with his ill-order'd choice. If the neglect or abuse of the Liberty he had, to examine what would really and truly make for his Happiness, misleads him, the miscarriages that follow on it, must be imputed to his own election. (EHU, II, xxi, §56, emphasis in original)

Because people strayed from the imperatives of God's will through "too hasty choice[s] of [their] own making," their homicides and their numerous other sins diverged from the paths that the Creator set for the world to follow. Knavish acts, in short, did not serve God's pleasure.

This earnest defense will pose two difficulties for Locke. First, of course, it will raise the hoary problem of accounting for evil in a universe governed by a perfectly righteous and omnipotent God. Locke's basing of his theodicy on the freedom that attached to all human agents, who had "Liberty in respect of willing" – i.e. Locke's sense that their freedom brought upon them the *ultimate* responsibility for their turpitude, as well as responsibility for it at a mundane level – was no more satisfying or cogent than the myriad other doctrines that have surfaced throughout the centuries in vindication of God. A question from the Book of Isaiah rings loudly still: "O Lord, why dost thou make us err from thy ways and harden our heart, so that we fear thee not?" (Isaiah 63:17).

Second, and even more important for our present strand of analysis, the attempt to buttress Locke's distinction between God's pleasure and people's pleasure must advert to the great benevolence of the Deity. It must thereby introduce a consideration which goes beyond the pronouncement that the members of the human species were all the "Workmanship of one Omnipotent, and infinitely wise Maker" and were "his Property, whose Workmanship they are" (TTG, II, §6). That is, to mount a defense of Locke's distinction, his apologists will have to press a substantive thesis about the Maker's benignity, and thus they will have obliged themselves to do much more than contend flatly that people were servants of the all-powerful and all-knowing Maker who had invested everybody with life. God qua omnipotent and omniscient Creator is not enough for the purpose; Locke's champions will have to rely on God qua benevolent Creator.

In other words, we once again have discovered that the abstract theme of equality would never suffice to ground the imposition of the duties that Locke commended. From the fact or suggested fact that every person was produced by God, and from the norm that God's absolute dominion extended to every part of His workmanship, no comforting conclusions follow. Not until we know that the all-encompassing Craftsman frowned upon the violent destruction of His human creatures by one another, can we justify a belief that His dominion laid a duty on every one of His servants to refrain from unprovoked onslaughts. Such a duty could never come just from human agents' equal positions as the products of divine craftsmanship or just from their equal standing as the Lord's servants; a belief in the all-comprehending sway of God's creative dominion can support very well the charge that murders and countless other misdeeds by human agents must draw their impetus from the guiding hand of the Lord. As Job proclaimed bitterly: "Who . . . does not know that the hand of the Lord has done this?/ In his hand is the life of every living thing and the breath of all mankind" (Job 12:9–10).

Thus, by lending emphasis to the equal postures of human beings as God's creations and servants who were governed constantly by His will, we can quickly move toward the inference that the Deity prompted vile and murderous actions with the same ineludible force which He exerted in prompting all other actions. Such an inference occurred, naturally, to the freethinker from Uz: "[God] destroys both the blameless and the wicked" (Job 9:22). To prevent our concluding that God indeed must drive and countenance every ghastly act of destruction – a conclusion which leaves no room for acts of destruction that would not be carried out at God's behest, and which therefore leaves no room for God's laying down of duties of nonaggression – the supporters of Locke must echo Locke himself by insisting on the Deity's goodness and His consequent disapproval of wicked modes of behavior. This insistence will underscore the abiding potential for a gap between "what occurred" and "what occurred in line with God's pleasure." It will indicate that actions which occurred in line with God's pleasure would invariably be good. Such an insistence will accordingly clear the space (between the actuality of "is" and the commendability of "ought") that is needed for the positing of duties of nonaggression which stemmed from God. But the insistence will accomplish this task only by fleshing out the bare theological notion that equality lay in people's wholesale subjection to the will of their common Maker. Instead of clinging to that bare premise of equality, the supporters of Locke will have to amplify it by deeming the Maker to be perfectly good; such an amplification will allow us then to infer that God imposed duties upon His creatures which befit His own loving-kindness. In effect, the amplification will emerge as an unforgoable thesis stating the salutary entitlements with which the Fashioner had endowed every one of His human products. Without that vital thesis, the comments on people's "being all the Workmanship of one . . . Maker" and on their being "his Property, whose Workmanship they are" do not tell us anything about the rights and the privileges that people enjoyed.

We discover afresh what we discovered before. Any abstract norm of equality – here, equality as people's common subjection to their common Creator – would leave undefined and therefore leave unresolved the nature of the entitlements to which the rule of equality would pertain. A pronouncement dealing with the substance of people's God-given entitlements must base its specific tenor on specific beliefs about God (and hence on specific beliefs about the entitlements that God would deem to be most appropriate for His human pieces of handicraft). Rosily benign conclusions have to draw their support from rosily benign starting points, not from starting points that are purely abstract and formal.

From the invalidity of deductions to the silliness of postulations

When we focused on the aspiration of Locke to ground human beings' peace-encouraging duties on the human beings' "equal and independent" ranks, we saw that those duties can be readily classified as promotive of inequality. If we think that the general value of equality is realized when people flourish or founder in accordance with their ability to look after themselves and to discomfit their fellows in an uncompromising state of belligerence, then we shall condemn any other modes of life for failing to treat all persons as equals. In a social order which limits the aggression of the sly and the brawny and which therefore protects the clumsy and the weak, the people who are curbed may fare worse than in an anarchic rivalry, and those who are shielded will almost certainly fare much better than they otherwise would; and so, for anyone who thinks that people deserve no less and no more than they can seize in a state of unchecked combat, the curbing of that combat through some duties of nonaggression is an inegalitarian project that impedes the goal of distributing to each human agent his or her due.

We are here supposing that the defenders of Locke have reconstrued his efforts to derive duties of nonaggression from the general equality of human beings, and thus that his supporters now understand those duties not as derivatives from the theme of equality but as ways of instantiating and specifying that theme. What would strike most readers as a deductive argument is now redefined as a prescription with which Locke fleshed out the norm of egalitarianism. Unfortunately for his supporters, their reconception of his peace-encouraging duties does not eliminate the potential for an assessment of those duties as inegalitarian and thus as undesirable. Indeed, the new understanding of Locke's position will have left this whole problem just as glaring as ever, for the new approach continues the attempt to collapse the value of equality and the value of community into each other. In the eyes of someone who rejects the Lockean standard for determining the equality of people's positions, Locke's conflating of equality and community is as ill-advised in the form of a stipulation as in the form of a derivation.

Let us return to the example of the laborers in the vineyard. For a vineyard proprietor whose touchstone of equal treatment is focused on the amounts of money that laborers (and other people as well) have pocketed – irrespective of the length or the skillfulness of anybody's exertions – the only way to treat persons equally is to give every person exactly the same income. Regardless of how long someone has labored, and regardless of whether someone has truly labored at all, each person is entitled to receive no more and no less remuneration than anyone else. Such an entitlement prevails, at least, if equality is the norm of distribution and if equality is defined as level incomes that do not vary to take account of differing lengths of toil. Under such a criterion of equality, the uniform streams of income accrue to people qua people; the streams of income do not accrue, in varying amounts, to people qua diligent or idle workers. According to this level-incomes standard of equal treatment, a mode of payment that adjusts people's earnings to reflect their disparate hours of toil can appropriately be censured as inegalitarian.

Now, for anybody who takes this rather unsophisticated view of equality, the concept of equal treatment can never rightfully be invoked as a basis from which we can deduce the need to graduate the amounts of people's earnings (in order to bestow on industriousness and talent their due rewards). Any such deduction will strike proponents of the level-incomes criterion as a daft non sequitur. But the supporters of that criterion will also bristle if they are asked to sanction a graduated-incomes plan as a means of lending substance to the norm of equality. Given that the proponents of the level-wages conception of equality have frowned on disparate earnings as the marks and causes of inegalitarianism, they will hardly be receptive to labeling disparities as "equality" – any more than they are receptive to seeing disparities as arrangements that are *deducible* from the norm of equality. If the deducing of certain inequalities from the theme of equality is defined as a crass non sequitur and indeed a contradiction, the styling of those same inequalities as a pattern of equality is a flagrant mistake. One should avoid applying the designation of "*X*" to things that are not *X*, just as much as one should avoid deducing from the existence or desirability of *X* the existence or desirability of a thing that clashes with *X*.

We find a parallel situation, of course, when we turn to the view that laborers have not secured really equal treatment unless their incomes have corresponded to the proficiency and extent of their work. Someone who espouses that view will patently not accede to the deriving of a uniform-wages principle from the goal of equality. By allowing everyone to pocket the same amount of money despite the very different amounts of work that individuals have carried out, the uniform-incomes policy renders unequal treatment. It therefore is not a program that can validly be derived from the general norm of equality. And, if deductive reasoning can never correctly place the uniform-wages policy within the scope of egalitarianism, then one's specifying or stipulating of terms ought likewise to stay away from classing such a policy as a mode of equal treatment. After all, from the viewpoint of anyone who regards equality as the tailoring of remuneration to achieve a match between people's earnings and the lengthiness of their work, an effort to deduce the uniform-earnings program from the theme of equality must fail not just because other inferences are possible, but because the uniform-earnings program is at odds with the very theme from which it supposedly is to be deduced. From this viewpoint, to designate the uniform-incomes measure as equal treatment is to fix the label of "*X*" on something that is clearly not *X*. Such a tag will carry no more persuasive force when engendered through stipulation than when engendered through deduction. From this perspective, anybody who calls for uniform wages in the name of equality will seem, à la Humpty Dumpty, to be defining his terms as he chooses but in defiance of guidelines that would keep him from putting forward obvious nonsense.

Let us come back to the attempt by Locke to establish duties of nonaggression that were incumbent on human agents. Given that countless tenable understandings of equality can joust with Locke's own understanding, his insistence on peace-promoting duties will hardly fare much better when interpreted as the specifying of equal statuses than when seen as the deducing of specificities from those statuses before the statuses have been specified. (For the sake of vividness, this discussion will advert to the Social-Darwinist credo; but one clearly should not forget that a multitude of less savage creeds are similarly available to contend with Locke's vision of the equal postures that were enjoyed by members of the human race.) Social Darwinists, faced with Locke's assertion that peace-promoting duties were the apposite means of fleshing out the norm of equality, will feel like resolute atheists who have been confronted with Paul's entreaty that "[i]f any one among you thinks that he is wise in this age, let him become a fool that he may become wise. For the wisdom of this world is folly with God" (1 Corinthians 3:18–19). That is, the perfervid Social Darwinists will have branded Locke guilty of an idiosyncratic use or abuse of language by which he designated as "*X*" a milk-toast scheme of entitlements that was glaringly not *X*. The Lockean vision will provoke the scorn of these extremists as a negation of true equality. From their perspective, the attempt to classify peace-encouraging obligations as the vehicles or the guarantors of human equality will appear to do with the terms "equality" and "equal" what Locke derided Filmer for doing with the words of the Holy Writ:

> [T]he goodness of his Cause . . . required in its Defender Zeal to a degree of warmth, able to warp the Sacred Rule of the Word of God, to make it comply with his present occasion; a way of proceeding, not unusual to those, who imbrace not Truths, because Reason and Revelation offer them; but espouse Tenets and Parties, for ends different from Truth, and then resolve at any rate to defend them; and so do with the Words and Sense of Authors, they would fit to their purpose, just as *Procrustes* did with his guests, lop or stretch them, as may best fit them to the size of their Notions: And they always prove like those, so served, Deformed, Lame, and useless. (TTG, I, §60, emphasis in original)

The fact that we can interpret Locke's egalitarian pronouncements as specifications of the concept of equality, rather than as deductions from it, will make little or no difference for the Social Darwinists. In either case, Locke presented inegalitarianism as equality; and therefore in either case he badly misused his terms.

Champions of Locke might now submit that a crucial difference remains between his fleshing out of the principle of equality and a derivation of consequences therefrom. Had Locke made bold to derive his peace-encouraging obligations from the abstract norm of equality, he would have indeed produced a grossly invalid argument. But, the supporters of Locke might argue, an account that proceeds by stipulation rather than by deduction will have skirted the problem of invalidity.

Unlike arguments, stipulations partake of neither invalidity nor validity. Instead, they partake of more substantial or less substantial degrees of boldness and acuity and persuasiveness and flexibleness and open-mindedness. At most, then, Locke perhaps can be charged with dogmatism; he cannot properly be charged with blunders in reasoning. In fact, given the attractions of Locke's construal of equality, a complaint about his dogmatic style will bespeak the churlish spirit of the complainer more than it will tell against Locke – at least in the eyes of Locke's devotees.

For the sake of argument, this discussion henceforth will acquiesce in the posited distinction between the outright error of invalidity and the more excusable fault of dogmatism, aside from noting that any such distinction is far more problematic than it might at first seem. (It is problematic because the drawing of unsupported conclusions from a set of premises can be viewed as arising from a blinkered and oversure interpretation of the scope of those premises.) Having conceded for the moment the divide between dogmatism and invalidity, we can still object to Locke's presenting of his dogmatic theses as theses focused on the norm of egalitarianism. To expound duties of nonaggression as the principal vehicles for the Maker's conferring of substance on human agents' "equal and independent" statures was to add nothing to an exposition that approached the duties much more directly as the Maker's demands on people for general cooperation and harmony. When one has collapsed the principle of equality and the principle of community by understanding the former as a variant of the latter, one has taken away the independent role of the former.

Leaving the value of equality without any independent substance, the appeals to that value in a pronouncement on communitarian obligations will have thus sown the ground for two main types of confusion: a sense that upholding the communitarian obligations must entail the upholding of the norm of equality *tout court*, and a sense that championing the norm of equality must entail the championing of the communitarian obligations. To see why each of these perceptions is ill-advised, we should picture two general groups of people. On the one hand, certain people may well applaud the duties of nonaggression while disavowing any support for the ideal of equality. Such people explicitly or implicitly define the notion of equal statuses in terms very different from Locke's. These people decline to join with Locke in making the value of equality a mere function of the value of community, and hence their support for basic duties which give effect to the latter value does not oblige them to seek the realization of the former value. Indeed, their favoring of the duties of nonaggression commits them to opposing the realization of equality as they understand it.

On the other hand, certain people may espouse the theme of equality while looking aghast at some or all of Locke's communitarian impositions. Whether these people have defined our equal postures by reference to material wealth or social standing or any other suitable index, they agree in scouting Locke's definition of those postures as shared entitlements to freedom from unprovoked harm. Thus, given that these people are against such entitlements, their firm attachment to the cause of egalitarianism indicates that they look askance at Locke's conflation of equal ranks with bans on aggression. Should these people ever come to adopt the Lockean conception of equality while retaining their current political preferences, they will cease to plump for the realization of equal postures. In other words, they will act in much the same way as people who insist on rewarding diligent toil through graduated incomes and who construe the norm of equality as a suffocating prescript which bars remunerational disparities.

Now, Locke's dogmatic specifications of equality implied that the two positions just sketched – the combination of peace-promoting duties and inegalitarianism, and the combination of scorn for peace-encouraging duties and acclaim for the ideal of equality – would jar or accord with his own position exactly insofar as they jarred or accorded with his view of equality. That is, by opting to express the pursuit of harmony as the pursuit of equality, Locke suggested that no one could disagree with either type of pursuit while countenancing the other. Yet, when we re-examine the two positions outlined above, we find the following points: both positions depart from Locke in the meanings they ascribe to "equality"; the first position has departed from the second position and from Locke by failing to advocate the norm of equality; the second position has departed from the first and from Locke by disapproving of Lockean peace-encouraging duties. Instead of any straightforward match between the commending of such duties and the commending of equality, we discover a pattern that betrays the sunderableness of these two foci of commendation.

We do indeed come upon straightforward paths of linkage, however, when our comparison of each of the positions above with Locke's position is focused on attitudes toward community. Because the first of the viewpoints above has agreed with Locke in regard to the extent of people's responsibility for the general well-being of one another, it concurs entirely with him about our duties of nonaggression. Because the latter of the viewpoints above has *not* agreed with Locke in regard to the extent of people's responsibility for the general well-being of one another, it has disagreed partially or fully with him about the duties of nonaggression. Here the patterns of consonance and conflict are quite perspicuous: if a standpoint places at least as much importance on communitarian values as Locke did, then it sides with him in affirming basic duties of nonaggression; if a standpoint has attached less importance to communitarian values than Locke did, it has frowned on some or all of his peace-encouraging duties. Views about equality are here beside the point, since these appraisals of the duties of nonaggression have been wholly shaped by views about community.

Of course, some people in the first group above may place even more importance than Locke upon communitarianism. Not only will the duties of nonaggression meet with their heartiest approval, but much more sweeping ties of responsibility will also win their endorsement. Such people may therefore go well beyond Locke's champions in postulating duties more far-reaching than the duties of nonaggression. Disputes of this kind, however, are perfectly consistent with what has here been argued. In the first place, all the parties to the dispute still agree about the inclusion of an aggression-prohibiting mandate within the packet of the vital responsibilities that every man and woman must shoulder. More important, the tiffs between the Lockeans and their zealously humane counterparts are disputes about the level of communitarian prospects and aspirations which a society should attempt to realize. Such wrangles arise from the sundry attitudes people take toward the fellowship and the mutual concern on which the proponents of communitarianism set their sights. Attitudes toward equality are beside the point.

Now, given that the theme of equality in abstracto is void of content and is thus protean, it lends itself to being invoked as Locke invoked it, just as it lends itself to being invoked in every other fashion conceivable. We have observed already, at least for the sake of argument, that Locke's conflation of equality and community sheds its character as an outright bungle when it is deemed to be an unsupported assertion rather than a faulty deduction. Anybody can side with Locke by supporting both the peace-encouraging obligations and the general principle of equality; nor is it an outright error to join with Locke by specifying that principle in terms of those exact obligations. Yet, although nothing really prevents the reduction of the norm of equality to a function of the norm of community, we still can ask whether such a conflation helps to promote analytical sharpness.

On the basis of what has been said already, we should notice two reasons for shrinking from this conflation. First, the invocations of equality in discussions of peace-engendering duties are superfluous. Through such invocations, the ideal of "equality" refers only to the aspects of human life to which the principle of "community" refers – the aspects that make up the extent of people's solicitude for the welfare of one another. That is, such references strip the egalitarian ideal of its independent bearing. When "equality" has come to denote the presence or absence of specific rights and responsibilities by which people concern themselves with the needs of one another, then the terms "equal" and "equality" have become dispensable verbiage; those terms have then redundantly come to stand for entitlements which the language of "community" can signal very well on its own.

We have to take pains here to distinguish certain facets of Locke's approach. By insisting on the duties of nonaggression as the basic responsibilities incumbent on human beings, Locke advanced theses about the substance of human beings' entitlements and also about the distribution of those entitlements. He asserted that people had rights to be free from any unprovoked harm, and that every person had such a right. The latter part of his assertion did indeed pertain to equality. It offered the view that, in regard to the holding of fundamental rights and privileges, human beings would stand as equals. Locke was here taking aim at men such as Robert Filmer, who had declared that only kings were possessed of any God-given rights. Yet, as I have argued, the principle of equality in the distribution of entitlements would per se not do anything to define the substance of the entitlements. Such a principle would establish merely that the same rights and privileges accrued to all people, and it could therefore extend just as fittingly to harsh entitlements as to humane entitlements.

Locke went astray by treating as indivisible the question of substance and the question of due apportionment. Even when we classify his remarks on peace-encouraging duties as remarks that were strictly designative rather than inferential, we can frown on his designating as "equality" both the universal apportionment *and* the humane cast of people's duties. To insist that everyone enjoyed the same basic privileges and rights was to espouse a view about the equality of human beings; however, to contend that those entitlements effectively banned aggressive deeds was to espouse a view about the concern which people were duty-bound to exhibit for the well-being of one another. Instead of functioning as a thesis about equality, the latter view was a communitarian thesis – a thesis which might well combine with pronouncements in favor of equality but which never itself formed an integral part of such pronouncements. It addressed the substance rather than the distribution of people's rights and privileges. Thus, since abstention from aggressive behavior was a communitarian posture describable in communitarian language, and since that language was quite disjoinable from the language of "equality," a reliance upon the discourse of egalitarianism for the task of commending the substance of the peace-securing duties was pointless and gratuitous.

A second major reason to avoid the argot of "equality" when one seeks to describe the general cast of communitarian rights and obligations is that the confounding of solidarity with equality will muddle the chief issues at stake in any evaluation of Lockean peace-promoting duties. When we pass judgment upon those duties, we must consider *both* the level of responsibility required of people for one another *and* the degree of uniformity among the responsibilities that are imposed on various people occupying various stations. Although in ordinary debates these two decisions will often go ahead pari passu, they lend themselves to being divided conceptually. No way of dealing with the first of these two assessments requires any particular way of dealing with the other assessment, or vice versa. Hence, to employ the language of "equality" in one's answers to *both* problems is to obscure their separateness; not only does that out-of-place language fail to add anything of value when we invoke it to address topics that should be analyzed with the argot of "community," but it adds an extra layer of murkiness to discussions that are murky enough without it.

When evaluating the peace-securing duties announced by Locke, all or most observers will very likely accept that the announced duties would impose on people at least a modicum of answerability or accountableness for the essential well-being of others. Of course, disputes will forever rage about the meagerness or the amplitude of the Lockean obligations. Some theorists may see those obligations as having struck a fair balance that assigned due weight to individual freedom and collective responsibility in the state of nature. A more individualistic observer may perceive the Lockean duties as heavy-handed controls that went too far in checking the strenuous competition of human agents for raw survival (and their competition for ancillary desiderata, of course). Someone of a communitarian bent may view the peace-encouraging interdictions as paltry shields which curbed the ghastliest tendencies of human creatures but which did very little to bring about a full-blown sense of community. (In fact, someone enamored of communitarianism may even worry that the Lockean obligations could induce people to think that nothing more was owed to their fellows than what the obligations prescribed.) Countless other positions, falling somewhere between fervid individualism and fervid communitarianism, are likewise possible. Thus, disagreements about the satisfactoriness of duties that barred aggression will persist as long as will general disagreements about the scope of individual latitude *vis-à-vis* the bonds of societal restraint and devotion. But almost everyone who takes some position or another will probably avouch that the peace-sustaining duties indeed required a certain measure of self-control and indeed attempted to bring a certain measure of public harmony. Critics who favor keen competitiveness may well deplore the smothering curbs imposed on liberty for the sake of harmony, and critics who yearn for tightly woven structures of fellowship may deplore Locke's vision of harmony as pallid and may even denounce it as obstructive of more ambitious schemes of community; but critics of Locke can join his backers in readily acknowledging that his peace-promoting duties in the state of nature were aimed at clamping down on the leeway and selfishness of persons in order to attain a degree of social discipline and cooperation.

Thus, when analysts wield the language of "community" and "individualism" to carry on the debate about the adequacy of the duties of nonaggression, they may lock themselves into boisterous disagreements, but they will at any rate have spared themselves the futility of talking past one another. Yet, should the analysts ever then resort to the language of "equality" for conducting their disputes, they well may deprive themselves of a common focus in relation to which they disagree; in short, they may be talking past one another as well as squaring off against one another. This wearisome situation is not inevitable, but it is probable.

Because the argot of "equality" sheds its independent orientation when it serves as a mere vehicle for clashes about community and responsibility, it loses much of its ability to supply a background of shared assumptions that can help to render debates more fruitful than sterile. When observers appraise Locke's duties with the categories of "individualism" and "fellow feeling," they can agree on a general characterization of the duties, although they may differ wildly about the gratifyingness or noxiousness of what they have characterized. But when observers shift to appraising Locke's duties with the categories of "hierarchy" and "equal treatment," they no longer converge on even a general characterization of the objects of their assessments. (Or, rather, this intensifying of disagreement comes about if observers shift to this latter set of concepts while studying the communitarian or anticommunitarian import of the Lockean duties. If observers instead have trained their gaze on the aspects of the duties that promote or impede equality, no exacerbation of discord will ensue. After all, the use of the language of "equality" for investigating such aspects of the Lockean duties is every bit as appropriate as the corresponding use of the language of "community" for investigating the fellowship-retarding or fellowship-encouraging tenor of those duties. When one of these languages is used appropriately by being matched with the precise concerns of investigators, it yields a small but crucial backdrop of criteria that are widely agreed upon – criteria which cannot avoid leaving room for passionate and extensive quarrels, but which can help to save the participants in the quarrels from being woefully at cross-purposes, and which thus can help to save them from badly misunderstanding one another.)

Having no independent purchase when brought to bear upon questions of solidarity-versus-individualism, the language of "equal treatment" will simply offer its terms as empty markers of positions that draw their meanings from tacit principles which the terms themselves do not specify. Thus, for instance, a Lockean who supports the duties of nonaggression as the fundaments of the "equal and independent" postures of human agents has affirmed ipso facto a conception of equal postures as equality applied to the holding of entitlements that shield against any unprovoked harm. An extreme Social Darwinist, who sneers at the duties of nonaggression and who commends fierce fighting as the process by which equality gains true effect, has clung ipso facto to a vision of equal treatment as equality applied to the holding of entitlements that permit unprovoked attacks. A less fervid Social Darwinist, who looks askance at some Lockean duties but gives assent to others, has thereby plumped for a conception of equal statuses as equality applied to the holding of entitlements that permit certain kinds of unprovoked harm while shielding against other instances of such harm. Earnest advocates of communitarianism, who not only approve of every Lockean obligation but further countenance much more sweeping obligations requiring everybody to afford plenteous sustenance to his or her fellows in recognition of the equality of all human beings, have hence proposed an understanding of equal ranks as equality applied to the holding of entitlements that allow each person to call on other people almost unstintingly for support. In all of these positions, and in the multitudes of alternative positions that one might take, the language of "equal statures" is nothing more than a shell that gets its pith from a throng of notions about the proper extent to which the members of the human race should have to concern themselves with the needs and goals and hardships of one another. Labels focused upon equality, by themselves, cannot make the slightest headway in indicating the various degrees of comradeship and commitment that are being endorsed.

Devoid of the ability to convey the modes and extent of communitarian requirements, the tags of "equality" and "equal treatment" become indiscriminately applied to disparate levels of community-focused obligations. When the argot of "equal statures" is the medium for our disputes about solidarity-versus-individualism, a proponent of the duties of nonaggression will label those duties as the keystones and safeguards of the overriding equality of human beings. Likewise, crude Social Darwinists will laud the desperate struggle of *omnium contra omnes* as the fundamental arena for expressing and upholding the norm of equality among human agents. Analysts adhering to untold other perspectives, such as that of the less belligerent Social Darwinists or that of the enthusiastic spokesmen for communitarian values, will similarly maintain that their proposals define the entitlements which befit the equal statuses held by all men and women. In short, the argot of egalitarianism lends itself to being bandied about by every side in the tussles over fellowship-versus-atomism; yet the only reason it can be so accommodating is that it carries no independent substance by which it would be more suitable for some vantage points than for others.

Ergo, when the language of "equal postures" holds sway in debates about communitarian values and anticommunitarian values, people use the same phrases to articulate wildly different perspectives. People then do not convey their divergences and clashes straightforwardly, but muddy them by voicing their discordant standpoints with largely homogeneous appeals. When everyone alike justly employs the shibboleths of egalitarianism, people will thus talk past everyone else whose outlook they do not share. Profound disharmonies will lurk beneath a veneer of cognate labels.

In sum, analysts drawing on the language of "equal treatment" while discussing the value of community will be at cross-purposes because that language can fitly garb all positions and will therefore single out none. Such a situation differs notably from quarrels over the equal or hierarchical ranks of human beings in regard to well-defined modes and sources of power. Those quarrels may themselves be murky and involuted and vehement, to be sure, but they are not as prone to sheer sterility and incomprehension as are disputes about solidarity-versus-individualism conducted in the parlance of "equal treatment." If that parlance operates as the medium of discourse in controversies about the *apportionment* of rights and privileges, it focuses our scrutiny on exactly the topics that we have to address: namely, the extent and types of uniformity among people's basic positions. As we earlier noted, decisions on these distributional topics almost always go ahead pari passu with decisions about the substance of the distributed prerogatives, in any real-life arrangements. But the fact that distributional choices and substantive choices proceed in concert and intertwine in manifold ways does not negate the fact of their separateness. Nor does it negate the fact that only the former set of choices can fruitfully be discussed in terms of "equal postures" and "equal treatment."

Of course, a reliance upon the argot of "equality" to address distributional topics will permit and indeed require the making of numerous distinctions, such as that between formal parity and substantive parity. But theorists can draw such distinctions and debate such distinctions in informative and meaningful ways by reference to the goal of equality itself, a goal which theorists understand and evaluate quite diversely. Disagreements, sharp disagreements, will forever abide; but disputants can at least retain a reasonably good sense of when and how they are disagreeing.

Now, given that the theme of equality in abstracto is an empty theme, it can even be invoked to support perspectives that would be regarded by most people as markedly elitist. To decide what counts as equality of treatment, one must employ a standard for deeming situations to be alike (and thus to be worthy of like treatment). Hence, by crafting an appropriate standard, one can classify even the most redoubtably hierarchic societies as exemplars of the egalitarian ideal. But, although one can clearly stretch the rubric of "equal treatment" to embrace all modes of society, the stretching here will have run afoul of the limitations on its plausibleness. Anyone who invokes a suitable yardstick for determining samenesses can extend the banner of "equality," without error, to describe formidable hierarchies; but the fact that such a portrayal is not strictly wrong will hardly keep it from lacking credibility. Here the constraints on what is credible will diverge pronouncedly from the corresponding constraints at work in the disputes about fellowship and individualism. In those fellowship/individualism disputes, the argot of "equal stations" can reach with plausibleness to *any* patterns of intercourse where all key entitlements are possessed by everybody alike. The theme of "parity" will apply with cogence insofar as people enjoy the same rights and privileges, regardless of how communitarian or anticommunitarian the rights and privileges are. When human beings are all entitled to display no solicitude for the needs of one another, their condition merits the label of "equality" with just as much forcefulness as when they are all required to show extensive solicitude. Precisely because the question of community as a question of substance is distinct from the question of equality as a question of apportionment, our answers to these two questions can combine in any number of ways. Therefore, by depicting the substance of entitlements in substantive terms, and by refusing to depict the substance in distributional terms (which lend themselves straightaway to being employed on every side of disputes about the question of substance), we shall have caused our disagreements to be more fertile by accentuating and thus clarifying them.

Where angels fear to tread To close this chapter, we now observe that equal ranks were not merely *insufficient* to entail duties of nonpugnaciousness or some warmer ties of mutual responsibility in the state of nature, but were also never *necessary* for harmonious ties. The reign of fellowship could endure amid pronounced hierarchies of wealth, might, and prestige. As has been demonstrated, the compatibility of equal rights and individualism punctures the notion that communitarian rights were the only rights in the state of nature that would befit human equality; here my analysis will discredit the notion that an equal sharing of rights was the only distribution thereof which could secure human solidarity and tranquility. We shall accordingly find a new reason to avoid designating the value or condition of fellowship as "equality." If the potential for the coexistence of violent selfishness and basic equality impugns such a designation, then the possible coexistence of peacefulness and hierarchy must engender a like effect. Attaching the label of "equality" to duties of nonaggression will turn out to be particularly inapt when we realize that such duties could prevail in markedly inegalitarian contexts.

Because duties of nonaggression were operative in the state of nature, each person therein enjoyed a right to be safe from unprovoked onslaughts and pillaging. For a Lockean, this entitlement and the universal holding of the entitlement resulted from the common nature of human beings as products of divine craftsmanship who had all been made in the image of the Deity. Now, whatever be the posited grounding of the entitlement, the entitlement itself and its application to everyone could scarcely betoken the comprehensive equality of the people in whom it vested. To be sure, when retained by all, that entitlement did make each person equal to everybody else in one main respect – inasmuch as no one could rightly be assaulted or robbed, except perhaps in the course of a legitimate punishment – but it clearly allowed no inferences about the general equality of persons in other respects. Although equality *could* also prevail in numerous other dimensions of people's intercourse, the entitlement to be free from harm could apply universally in a setting with deep-rooted and extensive stratification. People who were alike in their possession of the harm-averting entitlement could differ dramatically in almost every other respect.

Of course, Locke himself recognized this point when he adduced various modes of inequality that could obtain alongside the specific mode of equality on which he had trained attention. As we shall see from the following example, however, he may have understated the huge disparities that could well coexist with the aforementioned mode of equality. A harm-forbidding entitlement could perform its role among creatures who belonged to different planes of God's workmanship. Consider the story that appears at the very end of the Second Book of Samuel (and likewise in the First Book of Chronicles). After Israel's leaders had sinned by taking an unwarranted census, God punished the people of Israel by commissioning a destructive angel to spread pestilence through their land. As the angel was about to destroy Jerusalem, God abruptly ordered him to desist: "[T]he Lord repented of the evil, and said to the angel who was working destruction among the people, 'It is enough; now stay your hand'" (2 Samuel 24:16; 1 Chronicles 21:15). Having signaled that enough retribution had then occurred and that no additional punishments should take place, God re-endowed each inhabitant of Israel with the right to be left alone by the angel of destruction. Had the angel continued to afflict the Lord's chosen ones, he would thus have breached their restored entitlements to security. Even if those entitlements be regarded as mere offshoots of God's entitlement to exact obedience from His angels and other servants, and therefore even if the destructive angel's duty to stop his scourging of the Israelites be regarded as a mere offshoot of his duty to abide by the will of God, the angel could not persist in his deadly work without contravening the Israelites' renewed claims upon him.

Thus, in the wake of the Almighty's decree against further slaughter, the continued ravaging of the Hebrews would have violated the duties of nonaggression owed to them by the helper of the Almighty. Yet the fact that God's angel bore these duties of nonaggression should hardly lead us to think that angels and human beings were peers (or were almost peers). When the angel approached Jerusalem to destroy it, he was "standing between earth and heaven" (1 Chronicles 21:16) – a posture that meetly symbolized the rank of the angel, who was clearly subordinate to God and just as clearly above all human capacities. This heavenly minister who obeyed God's edicts would never "die like men, [or] fall like any prince" (Psalms 82:7); he would live forevermore and wield supernatural abilities.

All the same, despite the yawning divergences between human creatures and celestial creatures, the beings of the heavenly realm could not infringe the God-bestowed rights which the beings in the earthly realm had acquired. Angelic creatures and human creatures alike would have to show respect always for entitlements which their Master ordained. To be sure, the angelic ministers belonged to a higher precinct of God's creation than did humanity; but the gulf between the higher sphere and the earthly sphere was irrelevant to the binding force of the duties which the angels had to fulfill. What was relevant was that certain deeds – deeds of belligerence or destruction – had authoritatively been proscribed. Outlawed acts had to be shunned, regardless of the inequality or equality between the beings who would have under*gone* the acts and the beings who would have under*taken* the acts.

Now, if the overwhelming divide between immortality and mortality did not interfere at all with the curbing of immortals' discretion via duties of nonpugnaciousness, then surely the different ranks among human beings would pose no obstacles to such duties, either; after all, the disparities among people (unenslaved people, at any rate) were not as daunting as the shuddersome cleft between the supernal and the sublunary. All people in the state of nature were on the same footing by dint of their subjection to the duties of nonpugnaciousness, even while they could differ substantially from one another in countless ways that bred hierarchies. The single mode of equality could permit the hierarchic divergences, and the hierarchic divergences could permit the single mode of equality.

To describe communitarian obligations as obligations that brought about or ensured equal perches is thus grotesquely inapposite. A swallow does not a summer make, and a lone instance of parity in the state of nature would not amount to a comprehensive array of equal rankings. Just as we saw before that a regime of equality could prove direly individualistic, so we now have observed that a regime of mutual responsibility and cohesiveness could prove starkly inegalitarian. Hence, if a regime of communitarianism in the state of nature was also a regime of substantial equality, its basis for being so did not reside in the general fact of its communitarianism. Since a highly communitarian world could be profoundly inegalitarian, and thus since full-fledged equality was by no means an essential feature or element of community, the latter ideal should hardly come to be designated as the former.

Part III

Labor and property

For the Lord is a great God,
and a great King above all gods.
In his hand are the depths of the earth;
the heights of the mountains are his also.
The sea is his, for he made it;
for his hands formed the dry land. Psalms 95:3–5

Let the thief no longer steal, but rather let him labor, doing honest work with his hands, so that he may be able to give to those in need.
Ephesians 4:28

Having sought to take account of distinctions that are all too frequently overlooked, we now move to an assessment of Locke's theory of property. Here we again need to disentangle various concepts that are easily run together, but now my purpose is to highlight the problematic reversals that upend a crucial distinction which is in fact often made: the distinction between political individualism and political communitarianism. This final group of chapters will hold that Locke's theory does deserve to be labeled as "individualistic" – but just because it deserves also to be characterized as "communitarian." In setting forth the conditions for the appropriation of material goods by individual human subjects, and in hoping thus to ground the entitlements of the individual, Locke transformed all acts of appropriation into functions or consequences of humanity's needs. With his recountal of the paths by which human beings qua autonomous agents could procure things as owned possessions, he revealed quite inadvertently that autonomous agents would strip themselves of autonomy by dint of exercising it.

4 The labors of Locke: a critique

Locke's labor theory of property has won attention from a staggering range of interpreters. Some analysts have hailed the labor theory of property as the greatest feat of Locke's political writings, whereas others have scorned it as egregiously misdirected and shallow. Some interpreters view the theory as the cornerstone of Locke's *Two Treatises of Government*, while rival interpreters discount it as largely unrelated to the *Treatises*' central projects. For numerous exegetes, both friendly and hostile, the labor theory functions as the core of Lockean individualism; for others, the theory serves as the underpinning of Locke's communitarianism. Many critics and supporters of Locke have found his reasoning to be solid, but some admirers and some detractors have found his reasoning to be flimsy. Praised or derided, analyzed carefully or analyzed fleetingly, construed as bearing upon a number of other topics or construed as an isolated departure, Locke's account of human productiveness has indeed been highly productive in eliciting commentary.[1]

This latest addition to the stream of commentary diverges from all the other approaches by contending that Locke's theses are communitarian through and through *because* they are individualistic through and through. We shall start by looking in detail at the general and specific

[1] This book's citational appendix provides many references to the secondary literature on the labor theory of property. Among the works cited, the most powerful are as follows: all writings by Richard Ashcraft, Lawrence Becker, John Dunn, C. B. Macpherson, Alan Ryan, Ian Shapiro, A. John Simmons, Hillel Steiner, James Tully, and Jeremy Waldron; all essays by G. A. Cohen, Morris Cohen, Norman Geras, Mark Goldie, Ruth Grant, Peter Hulme, David Kelley, David Lyons, Thomas Mautner, Thomas Nagel, Onora O'Neill, Jeffrey Paul and Ellen Paul, Jeffrey Reiman, Cheyney Ryan, and Sibyl Schwarzenbach; all books by Steven Dworetz, James Grunebaum, John Marshall, Stephen Munzer, Kai Nielsen, Robert Nozick, Geraint Parry, Andrzej Rapaczynski, Martin Seliger, Jonathan Wolff, and Neal Wood; the 1966 essay by J. P. Day, the 1974 essay by Israel Kirzner, the 1893 book by David Ritchie, and the 1920 book by R. H. Tawney. (My commendation of someone's work as powerful does not imply that I agree with all or most of the theses therein. I disagree with almost all of the foregoing writers on certain points, and I disagree with some of them – especially Day and Tully – on myriad points.) At the time of my book's going to press, I have not yet been able to obtain a copy of Gopal Sreenivasan, *The Limits of Lockean Rights in Property* (Oxford: Oxford University Press, 1995).

themes that combine to furnish the Lockean account of appropriation – themes that are often not distinguished as tidily as they should be. After discussing some ambiguous elements in Locke's account, I shall lengthily examine its principal weak spots. Locating the gaps in his vindication of property will require very close attention to the letter and logic of his arguments. My final two chapters will proceed then to highlight the implications of the weaknesses in Locke's reasoning. As will be demonstrated, his individualistic stance partakes of an extreme communitarianism that throws all private titles of ownership into question.

At the level of generality: lording it over the earth

This first principal section will explore humanity's general entitlement and each human being's general entitlement to draw upon natural resources for sustenance in the Lockean state of nature. The second half of the chapter will then critically investigate Locke's account of the specific entitlements that accrued to people who did indeed seek to sustain themselves by laboring on particular resources.

Mastery of the bounty

Locke advanced his most famous exposition of property in chapter 5 of his *Second Treatise*, but he strewed various remarks also in his *First Treatise* and in some of his other texts. Here the *First Treatise* is of the utmost significance because of its pronouncements on humanity's general privilege to exploit the raw materials of the world. That general prerogative of humankind was the fundament of all specific claims to specific resources; clearly, were the basic activity of using the earth's abundance not acceptable, then no instances of appropriation could be acceptable. Although the abstract entitlement that was vested in the whole of humanity could never decide the form or substance of any particular claim to resources, and although it thus never fixed any limit to claims or the procedures for establishing them, it was a general and indispensable precondition for the legitimateness of each claim.

According to Locke, the fundamental dominion of the human species over the natural world derived from two chief sources: the need for the members of the species to use nature's bounty to obtain the sustenance without which they could not survive; and the express grants by God of lordship-over-the-earth to human beings. Now, the convergence of the justificatory roles of these two principal factors was hardly fortuitous. After all, according to Locke, the Deity had tailored the universe in ways most appropriate for the thriving of the creatures whom He had fashioned in His own image. Thus, if the basic needs of men and women compelled them to engage in certain activities that employed natural resources, we can know that God had authorized such activities and had therefore authorized the employment of the good things in nature. Had God not wanted the human race to enjoy dominion over the earth, He surely would not have caused the race's flourishing and indeed its very survival to necessitate such dominion. "Must" entailed "may" and even "ought," because "natural law stands and falls together with the nature of man" (ELN, 201). Hence, when we find in Scripture that "the earth [God] has given to the sons of men" (Psalms 115:16), we find what we might directly have deduced from the fact that people could not stay alive without availing themselves of the riches in their natural environment.

In the *First Treatise*, Locke initially declared in a somewhat tentative manner the prerogative of the human race to glean its sustenance from the natural plenty furnished by God: "[I]t is . . . reasonable to think, that God who bid Mankind increase and multiply, should . . . give them all a Right, to make use of the Food and Rayment, and other Conveniencies of Life, the Materials whereof he had so plentifully provided for them" (TTG, I, §41). Locke soon became more assertive, and indeed left no doubt that God had fully approved the exercise of mastery over nature by human beings. He presented this theme at greatest length in a well-known passage that should be quoted here extensively:

God having made Man, and planted in him, as in all other Animals, a strong desire of Self-preservation, and furnished the World with things fit for Food and Rayment and other Necessaries of Life, Subservient to his design, that Man should live and abide for some time upon the Face of the Earth, and not that so curious and wonderful a piece of Workmanship by its own Negligence, or want of Necessaries, should perish again, presently after a few moments continuance: God, I say, having made Man and the World thus, spoke to him, (that is) directed him by his Senses and Reason, as he did the inferior Animals by their Sense, and Instinct, which he had placed in them to that purpose, to the use of those things, which were serviceable for his Subsistence, and given him as means of his *Preservation* . . . Man had a right to a use of the Creatures, by the Will and Grant of God. For the desire, strong desire of Preserving his Life and Being having been Planted in him, as a Principle of Action by God himself, Reason, *which was the Voice of God in him,* could not but teach him and assure him, that pursuing that natural Inclination he had to preserve his Being, he followed the Will of his Maker, and therefore had a right to make use of those Creatures, which by his Reason or Senses he could discover would be serviceable thereunto. And thus Man's *Property* in the Creatures, was founded upon the right he had, to make use of those things, that were necessary or useful to his Being. (TTG, I, §86, emphasis in original)

Transparent aggregates

As one can readily infer from these quotations, Locke descried no gap between the just prerogatives of the human species and the just prerogatives of the individuals who composed that species. He did not commit a crude blunder when he shifted at times between imputing some God-bestowed entitlements to the class of all people and imputing those entitlements to each member of that class. When declaring that man enjoyed specified prerogatives which were deemed to suit his basic abilities and traits, Locke wielded "man" as a general term that pointed to the features which were shared by the individuals whom the term denoted; those features, of course, were the abilities and needs and entitlements on which Locke was training his attention. We here ought to take our cue from the *Essay concerning Human Understanding*, where Locke strove to explain how general terms carry out their functions:

That then which general Words signify, is a sort of Things; and each of them does that, by being a sign of an abstract *Idea* in the mind, to which *Idea*, as Things existing are found to agree, so they come to be ranked under that name; or, which is all one, be of that sort. Whereby it is evident, that the *Essences of* the *sorts*, *or* (if the Latin word pleases better) *Species* of Things, are nothing else but these abstract *Ideas*. For the having the Essence of any Species, being that which makes any thing to be of that Species, and the conformity to the *Idea*, to which the name is annexed, being that which gives a right to that name, the having the Essence, and the having that Conformity, must needs be the same thing: Since to be of any Species, and to have a right to the name of that Species, is all one. As for Example, to be a *Man*, or of the Species *Man*, and to have a right to the name *Man*, is the same thing. Again, to be a *Man*, or of the Species *Man*, and have the Essence of a *Man*, is the same thing. (EHU, III, iii, §12, emphasis in original)

Thus, the general word "man" conveyed the essential qualities (needs, abilities, and entitlements) which earmarked the beings who were classed by that word. To avouch that man had certain prerogatives was hence to avouch that *every* man had certain prerogatives. We hardly should be surprised, then, to come upon the following statement in the *First Treatise* just a few lines after the long remarks about "Man": "Every Man had a right to the Creatures, by the same Title *Adam* had, *viz*. by the right every one had to take care of, and provide for their Subsistence: and thus Men had a right in common" (TTG, I, §87, emphasis in original). A bit later we find that "Man" has become "a Man": "Property, whose Original is from the Right a Man has to use any of the Inferior Creatures, for the Subsistence and Comfort of his Life, is for the benefit and sole Advantage of the Proprietor" (TTG, I, §92).

To defend Locke from accusations of clumsy errors, however, we must do more than invoke his comments regarding general terms. Although some statements concerning man or mankind will reduce to statements concerning every man, a host of other such statements cannot undergo this reduction. Suppose we say that "man now resides on every continent" or that "man has lived on the earth for tens of thousands of years." In each of these statements, "man" refers to men as a group and not to every man in particular; used as an aggregational term, it brooks no reduction from the level of the species to the level of the individuals in the species. Suppose we move on to say that "man in the state of nature was vested with an entitlement to make use of nature's bounty in order to advance his survival and his well-being." Can this statement be rendered as a statement about the prerogatives of each man, or must that sort of reduction fail because the term "man" is here used exclusively as a term of aggregation?

Critics of Locke may well concede that sentences about the prerogatives of man are open to being read as sentences about the prerogatives of each man, but will also hold that such sentences do not have to be read that way. After all, in any period the species of man plainly did not depend for its survival on the survival of every man. At least some men had to be entitled to work for sustenance, of course, if their species was to have a chance of persisting; all the same, the species could long endure without the *universal* possession of an entitlement-to-strive-for-one's-sustenance. Accordingly, mankind as a whole could be endowed with a collective entitlement to look after its continued existence, while a number of individual men would not be endowed with any cognate entitlements to sustain their own lives. Locke thus blundered, or so his critics may contend, when he presupposed the equivalence of man's prerogatives and each man's prerogatives.

Here Locke could effectively have responded in two closely related ways. First, he could have pointed to his assumption, his profoundly religious tenet, that human agents all were inherently alike in their basic moral postures. If we regard the general species of man as vested with an entitlement to promote its own survival, and if further we grasp that that collective entitlement would endow at least *some* men individually with cognate entitlements (because the survival of the overarching species was clearly doomed unless *some* men from each generation survived long enough to bring about the next generation), we thus are drawn by the notion of men's equality to conclude that *every* man held an entitlement to strive for the continuation of his existence. In other words, the precept of basic moral equality would result in a fluent correlation between man's entitlement-to-quest-for-continued-life and *each* man's entitlement-to-quest-for-continued-life.

Another retort available to Locke, meshing closely again with his religious views, was that a collective entitlement-to-strive-for-adequate-sustenance which did not bestow entitlements-to-strive-for-adequate-sustenance on all persons separately was a contradiction in terms (when the terms involved had been appropriately construed, with the help of benign religious postulates). An inegalitarian vision excluding certain men from holding entitlements-to-strive-for-adequate-sustenance would commit a faux pas by excluding some men from the rank of "men." For Locke, that is, the definition of "man" or "men" comprised not only such features as rationality and animality, but also – as a consequence of the reign of a benevolent God – the station of rightful lordship over the founts of sustenance with which nature teemed. God bestowed His kindliness on men above other creatures, and He bestowed His kindliness on all men alike. While investing the human species with a prerogative to sustain itself by exploiting the abundance of nature, He had likewise conferred such a prerogative on every man individually. An endowment with that prerogative was thus an inexpungible element in a proper definition of "man," not only when "man" denoted an aggregation but also when it denoted some individual.

Locke, in sum, did not perpetrate a crude error when he swerved freely between discussing man's prerogative-to-exploit-nature and discussing the like prerogative of *each* man. Or, at any rate, he did not err flagrantly if we judge his references with a lenient eye toward the dogmas of religion that he espoused. He may have been somewhat complacent in his firm adherence to dogmas (attractive dogmas, at least when secularized persuasively), but his rigid beliefs here played a less objectionable role than in the arguments that were criticized by my third chapter. In the arguments there assessed, Locke was plainly making invalid leaps from premises to conclusions. In the passages on which we are focusing at present, by contrast, the shifts between "man" and "every man" were not directly implicated in outright speciousness; rather, they contributed chiefly to irksome vagueness and equivocality in Locke's premises. We thus can afford to grant Locke his religious tenets as the background assumptions that could warrant his inclination to run "man" and "every man" together.

Hence, we should look with unconcern on the shift that opens the *Second Treatise*'s famous chapter on property. There Locke began by proclaiming that "Men [as individuals], being once born, have a right to their Preservation, and consequently to Meat and Drink, and such other things, as Nature affords for their Subsistence." However, he immediately went on to say that God elected to give the earth "to Mankind in common" (TTG, II, §25). We should not detect in these pronouncements a surreptitious abandoning of normative individualism in favor of normative collectivism. For Locke the religious egalitarian, these pronouncements were different ways of stating the same point; to say that the world belonged to mankind in common was to say that the world belonged to all men as individuals.

Entitlements in search of specification

A crucial aspect of Locke's account of human beings' dominance over nature is what the account omits. Thus far, the quotations here have not specified the patterns of entitlements through which human beings would exploit nature's wealth. More precisely, the quoted extracts have not yet furnished a *thorough* specification of the entitlements. Let us carefully examine what has been specified and what has hitherto gone unspecified; this examination will use Hohfeld's terms strictly with Hohfeld's meanings.

A fruitful point of departure is a statement from the *Second Treatise* which we scrutinized in chapter 3 for different purposes:

> Every one as he is *bound to preserve himself*, and not to quit his Station wilfully; so by the like reason when his own Preservation comes not in competition, ought he, as much as he can, *to preserve the rest of Mankind*, and may not unless it be to do Justice on an Offender, take away, or impair the life, or what tends to the Preservation of the Life, the Liberty, Health, Limb or Goods of another. (TTG, II, §6, emphasis in original)

This extract enables us to know that Lockean people were endowed not only with *privileges* to sustain themselves, but also with *rights* against interference with their self-sustainment. Further, each individual labored under a *duty* – a duty owed to God – to preserve himself or herself with assiduousness. Everyone also had a duty to promote everybody else's survival, insofar as comforts and backing could be rendered without a breach of the prior duty of self-preservation; accordingly, everyone had a right to gain assistance from others as far as was necessary and possible. Now, because self-preservation could not succeed without the use of materials that derived from the natural world, everybody had a general entitlement and a general duty to exploit nature's resources. Conversely, everyone had a duty to accept other people's dominion over parts of the earth's abundance.

Thus, given the statement that was just quoted, and given the other general comments by Locke on the warrantedness of human beings' mastery of the world and its creatures, we can infer a number of elemental obligations and privileges and rights that accrued to everyone. But even these inferences are at a highly abstract level, and do not provide answers to more specific questions. We cannot yet say what would happen when diverse projects for survival were inconsistent with one another; nor can we yet determine which bits of nature's plenty would belong to specified human beings; nor, therefore, can we yet decide what would count as taking something away from someone else; nor, finally, do we yet have the means for judging whether or how or how extensively people could exert Hohfeldian powers in their interaction with the materials of nature. To arrive at a suitable response to any of these questions, a theory must descend from the abstract level at which the use of nature's wealth in general is vindicated, and must attain to the concrete level at which the apportionment of that wealth is specified. Enter, then, the labor theory of property.

To see the full importance of the descent from generality to concreteness, we should consider just how much was left open at the abstract level. When we look at the crucial statement quoted above, we find that under almost all circumstances no one could "take away . . . what tends to the Preservation of the Life, the Liberty, Health, Limb or Goods of another." Nonetheless, from this bare prohibition on taking things away we cannot tell which courses of conduct would amount to prohibited "takings." At this abstract stage of Locke's discussion, the only relevant principles were general authorizations and general bans – general authorizations for the use of the earth's materials, and general bans on the taking of any assets that already belonged to someone else. At this abstract stage, then, we are bereft of criteria for deciding whether any particular deed would consist in the authorized exploitation of natural bounty or in the impermissible seizing of a good from its rightful user. A person *M*'s consumption of figs and dates, for example, could qualify as a worthy use of natural resources *or* as a knavish pilfering of foods already appropriated; the acceptableness or unacceptableness of *M*'s repast would become determinate only if some standards could indicate what belonged to whom. Yet such standards could never spring from merely the general affirmations and general interdictions which we have probed so far.

For all we know at this point, the category of outlawed seizures might come close to being an empty set (at least in relation to the goods outside people's bodies). A *right* of everyone against being prevented from pursuing the aim of self-preservation could be satisfied in a legal/moral context where anyone's pursuit of that sweeping aim would give rise only to *privileges* concerning any specified group(s) of assets. In other words, although every person had a right not to be prevented from questing for his own survival, he might have nothing but a privilege to carry out the quest in some chosen way. Thus would obtain a scheme of general rights and specific no-rights, where, as long as person *M* did not interfere with person *N*'s projects to the point of excluding *N*'s hold on life, he could thwart *N*'s projects as tenaciously as his own well-being required; *N*, of course, would have corresponding privileges to impede *M*'s uses of goods, provided that *N* gave *M* enough leeway to survive. A duty to forbear from blocking a general goal would not entail a duty to forbear from blocking some specific path for reaching that goal, as long as one or more other paths were left unobstructed.

Therefore, the Lockean right to self-preservation was wholly compatible with a state of nature that was nearly as tumultuous as the state depicted by Hobbes. Unlike Hobbesian savages, people in the world-according-to-Locke would always have to avoid the unprovoked infliction of death on one another; but they could gamely strive to outwit one another for the enjoyment of particular goods. To be sure, this semi-Hobbesian state of clashes was very far indeed from the state of order that Locke envisioned. Yet until we move from the abstract plane to the concrete texture of Locke's analysis – until we move from the general entitlement-to-exploit-nature and ascertain the particular sorts of entitlements by which the exploitation would proceed – we cannot rule out the semi-Hobbesian state of turbulence made up almost exclusively of privileges without concrete rights.

Furthermore, even if we somehow can know that concrete rights would obtain along with privileges, we cannot yet tell what the duration and scope of the rights would be, especially in regard to land. Some rights over resources, usufructuary rights, endure only as long as the germane resources are being used or deliberately enhanced; other rights persist throughout the lifetime of a right-holder, even if he wholly neglects to use the relevant goods; still other rights last not merely during the lifetime of the current holder but also during the successive generations of heirs to the rights. Each of these spans and other possible spans for the duration of concrete rights could help to implement the abstract prerogative of self-conservation.

We must also seek to determine the scope or extent of the entitlements in the state of nature. Here we can understand the problem in either of two ways. On the one hand, ownership can be viewed as a single entitlement that is more far-reaching or less far-reaching in the medley of functions which it authorizes and protects. On the other hand, we can see ownership as a more inclusive or less inclusive batch of distinct entitlements that authorize and protect particular functions. Whichever of these positions we prefer, the essential point is that authoritative control over resources can embrace a varying number of capacities and protected benefits. To say that a person *Q* had proprietary entitlements concerning an asset *X* in the state of nature is to leave unspecified an array of features such as the extent to which *Q* would be entitled to take possession of any fruits or income generated by *X*, the number of legitimate means by which Q could pass the ownership of X to another person, and the range of ways in which Q could warrantedly employ X. We cannot resolve any of these matters simply by reference to the concept of property. A fortiori, then, we cannot resolve these issues merely by reference to the abstract right of self-conservation – an abstract right that would even fail to settle the choice between concrete rights of ownership and largely unadorned privileges.

Overabundance is not enough

Before we examine Locke's attempt to specify the prerogatives that human beings gained over natural assets, we ought to scrutinize an argument put forth by a host of commentators who submit that we can know the specifics of the aforementioned prerogatives as soon as we take aboard a key factual assumption (to which Locke plainly subscribed). When Locke delineated the primal state of humanity, he posited a superabundance of the natural materials with which human agents could support themselves. He expressed this assumption frequently in chapter 5 of the *Second Treatise*, with pronouncements such as the following:

> Nor was th[e] *appropriation* of any parcel of *Land*, by improving it, any prejudice to any other Man, since there was still enough, and as good left; and more than the yet unprovided could use. So that in effect, there was never the less left for others because of his inclosure for himself. For he that leaves as much as another can make use of, does as good as take nothing at all. No Body could think himself injur'd by the drinking of another Man, though he took a good Draught, who had a whole River of the same Water left him to quench his thirst. And the Case of Land and Water, where there is enough of both, is perfectly the same. (TTG, II, §33, emphasis in original)

Scarcely a page later, we come upon another renowned assertion of the theme of overabundance:

> No Mans Labour could subdue, or appropriate all: nor could his Enjoyment consume more than a small part; so that it was impossible for any Man, this way, to intrench upon the right of another, or acquire, to himself, a Property, to the Prejudice of his Neighbour, who would still have room, for as good, and as large a Possession (after the other had taken out his) as before it was appropriated. This *measure* did confine every Man's *Possession*, to a very moderate Proportion, and such as he might appropriate to himself, without Injury to any Body in the first Ages of the World, when Men were more in danger to be lost, by wandering from their Company, in the then vast Wilderness of the Earth, than to be straitned for want of room to plant in. (TTG, II, §36, emphasis in original)

Doubtless, then, Locke assumed that humankind in the early ages of its existence was confronted with a superfluity of materials on which its members drew to satisfy their needs. But could Locke join this assumption with the premise of an abstract entitlement-to-conserve-oneself and thereby single out the specific sorts of entitlements through which human beings would exert their due mastery over nature? In other words, could the postulated fact of superabundance form a bridge between the stark generality of the right of self-conservation and the concreteness of the prerogatives that were assigned to each human being as the vehicles for effectuating the general right? More than a few scholars have surmised that the appropriate answer to these queries is "yes"; in particular, the theme of overabundance – when coupled with the abstract right against being prevented from questing for one's survival – has been viewed as necessary, or as sufficient, or as both necessary and sufficient, to undergird the full rights of property for which Locke plumped.[2]

Later, we shall ask whether superabundance was a *necessary* condition for the establishment of full rights. (Throughout this volume, the words "full rights" do not betoken rights that were unrestricted. Instead, the phrase adverts to rights that were limited by natural law only.) Pertinent here is the contention that a state of overabundance was *sufficient* to render full-blown rights legitimate. Under this interpretation of Locke, human beings were endowed with powers to appropriate natural riches as their exclusive holdings whenever the riches were inexhaustible for any practical purposes. If a situation of inexhaustibleness prevailed, we can be sure that everybody had a power of acquisition to create rights of property over natural resources; after all, any acquisition in circumstances of inexhaustibleness plainly would harm no one. When *M* acquired a certain bundle of assets as his possessions from which he could exclude other people, he would leave countless other bundles waiting to be appropriated by every person who wanted one (or more). Given the lack of harmful consequences for anyone from the staking of proprietary claims amid boundless wealth, and given the basic right of each person to the possibility of securing a continued hold on life, Locke seemingly had all the premises he required in order to justify his thesis that powers of acquisition and rights of property were the fulcra by which primordial human beings gave effect to their general right of self-sustenance.

Now, as will be urged presently, this stress on superabundance is misguided. However, before we ferret out the flaws in the argument that has just been outlined, a potential source of confusion needs to be deflected. As David Hume and manifold other writers have pointed out, a full-fledged superabundance of life-sustaining goods would obviate any need

[2] For an example of this quite common approach, see Judith Jarvis Thomson, "Property acquisition," 73 *Journal of Philosophy* 664 (1976).

for the various constraints imposed by the rules and rights of ownership, *if* the goods were ready to be consumed (or otherwise employed) effortlessly or almost effortlessly. In such circumstances, a regime of bare privileges without concrete rights would hardly ever produce grave altercations. Given that the appropriation and use of raw materials for one's sustenance would require little or no work, each person would be inclined to fetch her own raw materials instead of sparking conflicts with anybody by seizing what another person had garnered. Thus, had Locke posited a felicitous state of nature in which overabundant wealth implied the absence of any need for toil, his long discussion of private property would have been gratuitous.

Not surprisingly, then, Locke proposed quite a different view of superabundance. According to him, the goods of nature were boundlessly available at the dawn of human existence in that they presented themselves without exhaustion to be consumed (or gainfully utilized) by everyone who was willing to expend the onerous labor that was normally unavoidable for the purpose; goods were not limitlessly at hand in the sense of being always or often ready for unburdensome exploitation. Some appropriative acts, such as the gathering of plentiful acorns from the ground or the drawing of water from a nearby pool, would indeed demand very little effort. But most acts of appropriation, such as the tilling and improving of land or the collecting of water from a distant pool, would bear out the Bible's declaration that people were cursed to win their sustenance in the sweat of their faces. (Among toilsome appropriations we certainly should include the picking of berries. Although some theorists describe that task as effortless, they will hardly convince anyone who has dodged thorns and wasps while picking berries under a blazing sun.)

Hence, Locke did not propound a theory that was utterly superfluous. When he portrayed the inexhaustible supplies of natural wealth, he envisioned things that were boundlessly available *to be worked upon*; he did not suggest that natural assets could fill the needs of humanity without necessitating frequently irksome labor. When he wrote that each person's acquisitions would not harm anybody else, he meant only that the acquisitions would not obstruct anyone else's opportunities to acquire goods on which labor would of course have to be bestowed. In other words, the lack of harm would consist in everybody's having left undiminished the stock of raw materials from which people could glean their sustenance through work. It did not consist in anyone's having left a copious throng of opportunities for people to gain their sustenance without work. Thus, since the lavish riches of nature had to be toiled upon extensively if they were to become serviceable, a scheme of proprietary rights was not redundant. The curbs imposed by those rights would not be necessary in relation to unimproved raw materials, but such curbs might indeed be justified with respect to the items yielded by raw materials *plus labor*. A system of proprietary restraints allotting such useful products was not inevitable, but it was far from pointless.

Let us now go back to the central thread of this short excursus. Two chief problems plague the account of natural overabundance as a sufficient source of authorization for the exercising of powers and the forming of rights. First, and more important, such an account tends to conflate rights and privileges, and thus presumes that any legal/ethical framework consisting of the latter would always consist likewise of the former. In circumstances of boundless raw materials, as we have noted, the garnering by *M* of thitherto unpossessed materials did not harm anyone. But, at the very most, all that we ever can deduce safely from the lack of harmful results is that *M* did not commit a wrong against his fellows. Since no one would incur the slightest loss from *M*'s acquisitions, no one could justly allege that *M* had encroached on any rights. In other words, *M* was privileged to take and thus enjoy all the goods from nature's abundance that his heart desired. Yet, as chapter 2's discussion of Hohfeld emphasized, privileges are not invariably conjoined with rights. *M*'s acquisition and possession of sundry goods could be privileged in a state of overabundance irrespective of whether *M*'s deeds amounted also to the exertion of powers and the attainment of concrete rights of ownership.

Save in regard to any edible items that *M* had managed already to consume, his possession of his bundle of goods could involve mere privileges without concrete rights while fully satisfying his general right of self-preservation (as long as *M* was not despoiled of his goods so thoroughly and recurrently that his prospects for survival were altogether dashed). Thus, from the fact that *M*'s attainment of useful things did not hurt anyone and was therefore privileged, we cannot automatically conclude that *M* would exercise powers and gain proprietary rights through his acquisitive exploits. Particular rights of ownership certainly *could* arise from his feats of acquisition, but they could also *fail* to arise.

A second (and somewhat less troubling) weakness in the view of overabundance as a sufficient ground for concrete Lockean rights is furthermore a deliberate weakness in the argument of my last two paragraphs. Until now in this discussion, I have accepted that a lack of physical injury would equate with a lack of moral injury. *M*'s acquisitive feats did not collide at all with the rights of anybody – and were hence privileged – because those feats had done no damage whatsoever to anyone's material fortunes. Now, though this correlation between the absence of harm to clear-cut interests and the absence of encroachments on rights is plausible and attractive indeed, it would not obtain *ineluctably*. After all, it would involve a cross-over from the sphere of nonethical concerns to the sphere of ethical matters.

Notwithstanding that a condition of superabundance was the backdrop for each person's abstract entitlement to pursue self-conservation – an abstract entitlement which meant that everyone had an entitlement to acquire unowned goods which were essential for basic sustenance – it could not ensure that every act of acquiring unowned goods was privileged (much less shielded by rights or generative of rights). A scheme of entitlements in the state of nature could bar many avenues of appropriation, even if the appropriations in circumstances of boundlessly profuse wealth would detract nary a bit from anyone's prospects for survival. Maybe, for instance, people somewhere harbored a special fondness for mice or bears or squirrels left in the wild, and hence by custom they forbade the taking of these highly edible creatures for any purposes. Somebody who acquired one of these favored animals would contravene everyone's right against the capturing of such beasts. Within this scheme of entitlements, that is, *M*'s catching of cherished mammals to supply his own basic needs was not a privileged activity. As long as people did not outlaw the acquisition of plants and minerals and animals in so sweeping a fashion that they gravely jeopardized their own lives, their prohibiting of sundry specific appropriations would not exclude their acting upon their general entitlements and duties to support themselves. Thus, even in situations with inexhaustible founts of sustenance where no acquisition of nature's plenty would intrude upon anyone's material comfort to the slightest degree, a multitude of survival-promoting acquisitions could well be banned. Not only would the reign of superabundance (in concert with everyone's general privilege to work for survival and everyone's general right which protected that privilege) fail to guarantee that all harmless appropriations were blessed by rights, but it would even fail to guarantee that all harmless appropriations were *permitted*.

The common wealth

Near the outset of chapter 5 of the *Second Treatise*, Locke proclaimed ringingly that "God . . . hath given the World to Men in common" (TTG, II, §26). Indeed, he reiterated this point with a boldness arising from his determination to impeach Robert Filmer's view that God had conveyed the world to Adam and Adam's first-born heirs in succession: "God gave the World to *Adam* and his Posterity in common. . . . The Earth, and all that is therein, is given to Men for the Support and Comfort of their being. And . . . all the Fruits it naturally produces, and Beasts it feeds, belong to Mankind in common. . . . [T]he Earth, and all inferior Creatures be common to all Men" (TTG, II, §§25, 26, 27, emphasis in original).

Our concern here is to figure out exactly what Locke implied when he wrote that people in common had received the earth and its raw materials. He certainly did not envision a scheme of joint ownership that compelled the myriad acquirers of property in the state of nature to legitimate their endeavors by winning authorization or approval from their contemporaries. In fact, a cardinal objective of his labor theory of property was to underline the absence of any need for common consent to the creation of proprietary prerogatives. "I shall endeavour to shew, how Men might come to have a *property* in several parts of that which God gave to Mankind in common, and that without any express Compact of all the Commoners" (TTG, II, §25, emphasis in original). Even before we come upon the specifics of the labor theory of property, however, we can ascertain why consent was not prerequisite to the *use* of natural bounty by individuals.

Here we should take our cue from Locke himself, who immediately returned to the question of consent after he had propounded his first main line of reasoning in support of individual ownership. He paused to take due account of an objection that might be raised against any individual's rights of property in various assets: "And will any one say he had no right to those Acorns or Apples he thus appropriated, because he had not the consent of all Mankind to make them his? Was it a Robbery thus to assume to himself what belonged to all in Common? If such a consent as that was necessary, Man had starved, notwithstanding the Plenty God had given him" (TTG, II, §28). Locke's retort to the posited objection may seem to trade on outright expediency. But, given the thesis of an omnibenevolent Designer of the world who had made a perfect match between the capacities (the desirable capacities) and the obligations of human beings – a match where "ought" entailed "can" – a reference to the limits of human capabilities and so to the impracticableness of certain requirements was morally pregnant. Because people had to take possession of natural riches to stay alive, and because people could never take possession of natural riches if they first had to gain consent from all of their fellows, and because people had a God-imposed duty to stay alive through the exploitation of natural riches, and because the benign Fashioner of the world would impose no duties upon men and women that they were utterly incapable of discharging, we can know that universal consent was not a precondition for using nature's assets in any period of human development.

Now, as we shall observe shortly, Locke tended to suppose that the wealth of nature could not be used in earliest times unless acquisitions of that wealth conferred rights of property on the people who engaged in the acquisitions. That is, he virtually equated the *use* of goods with the *ownership* of goods, when discussing the primal state of humanity. The unsoundness of this equation has already been exposed here; but, were the equation sound, it clearly thus would vindicate Locke's assertion that the establishment of proprietary rights during the state of nature did not in any way hinge on universal consent. If the use of nature's bounty was warranted in the (unavoidable) absence of consent from all people, and if any such use entailed the formation and exertion of full proprietary rights, then the formation and the exertion of such rights were manifestly not linked in any way to the garnering of consent from all people.

Here, as so often elsewhere, Locke founded his specific tenets on his theological standpoint, which was a necessary though insufficient bedrock for those tenets. When Locke insisted that private property in the state of nature did not rely for its legitimateness on universal consent, he was laying out a thesis which rested crucially on his vision of God's plan for the world and humankind: "God gave the World to Men in Common; but since he gave it them for their benefit, and the greatest Conveniencies of Life they were capable to draw from it, it cannot be supposed he meant it should always remain common and uncultivated" (TTG, II, §34). This vision of God as a loving Overseer who prompted His human creatures to be industrious was in turn an offshoot or aspect of a far-reaching premise – the premise that God deemed the continuation of humankind to be an objective of paramount importance. As we saw in a section from the *First Treatise* that was lengthily quoted earlier, the impulse of human beings to stay alive and thus their employment of the requisite proper means for staying alive were very much in harmony with "the Will of [their] Maker" (TTG, I, §86).

What did Locke imply, then, when he avouched that God had given the world to human beings in common? If the gift to humanity of the world and all its riches did not invest humanity with joint ownership of those riches, what relation between humanity and the world *did* the gift produce? My answer to this question has in fact already emerged. When Locke declared that the earth "belong[ed] to Mankind in common" (TTG, II, §26), he meant that everyone in the state of nature had both a privilege to make use of the earth's resources and a right not to be prevented from exercising that privilege. Nobody could exclude anyone from the general task of appropriating unpossessed goods that would be needed for survival and basic welfare. That is, the only right in play at the abstract level of Locke's theory was everyone's right not to be barred from the overall project of questing for survival. Whatever might be the posture of specific appropriations, no one could be excluded from the general activity of appropriating. Everyone held an underlying right of inclusion, and ergo everyone bore a duty to refrain from keeping out others (at the level of generality, where the focus was on survival rather than on specific means of survival). Inasmuch as everyone had a general prerogative to draw crucial desiderata from the natural world, and inasmuch as everybody shouldered an obligation to avoid defeating the exercise of that general prerogative by his or her fellows, the world indeed was the common pasture of humankind – a common pasture not in the sense of being under collective ownership and control, but in the sense of being available for exploitation by all and sundry. The wealth of nature was common wealth in just the way that an uninhabited and unclaimed isle was common in the seventeenth century.

At the level of specificity: the wages of vim

Having established that the general prerogative to acquire sustenance could not predetermine the specific sorts of prerogatives through which it would come to be effectuated, we shall now study the concrete verdicts of Locke's analysis. Locke developed these verdicts principally in the great fifth chapter of his *Second Treatise of Government*, but he also scattered a few germane remarks in his *Letter on Toleration* and in his *Essays on the Law of Nature*. When working out the specifics of his doctrine, he had to overcome two main points of indeterminateness surrounding the abstract right of self-preservation. We have just explored the first of these points of indeterminateness: the discontinuity between the general prerogative of self-sustainment and the specific sets of entitlements which would serve as vehicles for that expansive and fundamental prerogative. A second type of indeterminateness has largely remained implicit so far. Locke not merely had to present and justify a regime of concrete entitlements through which the right of self-preservation would be fulfilled in the primordial era of humankind, but he also needed to explain how particular portions of nature's bounty would become attached to specific individuals. Whatever were the concrete entitlements with which human beings could become vested, there had to be a way of connecting the human beings (and their entitlements) to particular goods.

With the labor theory of property, Locke essayed to ground a specific scheme of entitlements that defined the lordship which the earliest human beings exercised over nature, and he presumed as well to demonstrate how the riches of nature could be divided up into bundles that were duly linked with specified owners. While purportedly conquering the two types of open-endedness that existed during the abstract phase of his theory, Locke could also take satisfaction in two additional chief advantages of his outlook. First, he professed to show that acquisitions of nature's wealth would occur suitably without the voiced or tacit consent of anyone. Second, he argued that the primal powers of acquisition and rights of ownership were natural, in the sense that they had been authorized through precepts laid down by God rather than through precepts laid down by civil institutions or civil governors. In short, Locke assigned his labor theory of property a massive amount of work to do.

The need for labor – to satisfy needs

We can single out, as the first main step toward the concrete substance of Locke's presentation, his robust emphasis on the need for labor in the securing of any goods that promoted human survival. Even before the curse on Adam and his descendants, God had instructed men and women to "fill the earth and subdue it" (Genesis 1:28); and Locke could rarely resist a chance to underline the degree of toil that was indispensable for subduing the earth properly. Like the ancient teachers who wrote the Book of Proverbs, with their recurrent admonitions against the sluggard, Locke repeatedly sang the praises of industriousness and scorned the feckless lolling of idlers. His aversion toward sloth was due not least to his understanding of the necessity for hard labor as the means whereby the earth's riches could become useful in satisfying the wants of human beings.

Time and again Locke stressed that Mother Nature did not allow herself to be mastered easily. He made this point in his *Essays on the Law of Nature* specifically with regard to the mining of precious ores, when he was advancing an analogy between mental exertions and physical exertions:

> Careful reflection, thought, and attention by the mind is needed, in order that by argument and reasoning one may find a way from perceptible and obvious things into their hidden nature. Concealed in the bowels of the earth lie veins richly provided with gold and silver; human beings besides are possessed of arms and hands with which they can dig these out, and of reason which invents machines. Yet from this we do not conclude that all men are wealthy. First they have to equip themselves; and it is with great labour that those resources which lie hidden in darkness are to be brought to the light of day. They do not present themselves to idle and listless people, nor indeed to all those who search for them, since we notice some also who are toiling in vain. (ELN, 135)

In the first *Letter on Toleration*, Locke adverted briefly anew to the unforgoableness of toil in the human struggle to reap the bounty of nature's harvest:

> Besides his immortal soul, man has his life in this world. It is precarious and of uncertain duration, and to sustain it he needs earthly conveniences, which he either has obtained, or must obtain, by toil and industry. For the things necessary for living well and happily do not spring up of their own accord, so that on their account man is burdened with additional care. (LT, 125)

As readers ought to expect, however, the lengthiest and most numerous passages on this theme are in chapter 5 of the *Second Treatise of Government*. Perhaps the best statement of the theme is the following: "God, when he gave the World in common to all Mankind, commanded Man also to labour, and the penury of his Condition required it of him. God and his Reason commanded him to subdue the Earth, i.e. improve it for the benefit of Life, and therein lay out something upon it that was his own, his labour" (TTG, II, §32). Two paragraphs further on, Locke trumpeted this theme with a bold pronouncement which we studied above in part:

> God gave the World to Men in Common; but since he gave it them for their benefit, and the greatest Conveniencies of Life they were capable to draw from it, it cannot be supposed he meant it should always remain common and uncultivated. He gave it to the use of the Industrious and Rational, (and *Labour* was to be *his Title* to it;) not to the Fancy or Covetousness of the Quarrelsom and Contentious. (TTG, II, §34, emphasis in original)

Albeit Locke strove directly in this passage to justify the obtaining of concrete rights-of-property by the venturesome people who had labored to exploit the wealth of the pristine world, the passage lends itself also to being read more generally as a comment on the returns that labor brought. Because the drawing of ample sustenance from the earth required the expenditure of great toil and trouble, the "Conveniencies" that the natural world made possible would materialize most profusely at the hands of the diligent. Such, at least, is the message which we very plausibly can educe if we read Locke's comment with an eye toward generalization.

A similar reading is in order for his assertion that "in the beginning and first peopling of the great Common of the World . . . [t]he Law Man was under, was . . . for *appropriating*. God Commanded, and his Wants forced him to *labour*" (TTG, II, §35, emphasis in original). Locke had indicated, before this point in his discussion of property, that he construed all lawful acts of appropriation as acts that bred rights of ownership; for him, the word "appropriating" could be defined as "gaining proprietary rights (over something)." Nonetheless, the passage just quoted will become more defensible if we read it more sweepingly by opting now to define "appropriating" as plain "acquiring" – which is just how my present chapter has heretofore used "appropriating" and cognate terms.

Understood in this way, the quoted passage expresses nicely the supreme importance of work in human beings' efforts to stay alive.

Still more vivid are several paragraphs (from the *Second Treatise*'s chapter on property) wherein Locke announced that "*labour makes the far greatest part of the value* of things, we enjoy in this World" (TTG, II, §42, emphasis in original). Having signaled the basic tenor of these paragraphs with a slightly earlier comment that "the extent of *Ground* is of so little value, *without labour*" (TTG, II, §36, emphasis in original), Locke protractedly argued that refinements and transformations induced by toil should receive overwhelming credit for the conveniences that served human wants. Let us glance at only a single extract from his lengthy discussion:

> For 'tis *Labour* indeed that *puts the difference of value* on every thing; and let any one consider, what the difference is between an Acre of Land planted with Tobacco, or Sugar, sown with Wheat or Barley; and an Acre of the same Land lying in common, without any Husbandry upon it, and he will find, that the improvement of *labour makes* the far greater part of *the value*. I think it will be but a very modest Computation to say, that of the *Products* of the Earth useful to the Life of Man 9/10 are the *effects of labour*: nay, if we will rightly estimate things as they come to our use, and cast up the several Expences about them, what in them is purely owing to *Nature*, and what to *labour*, we shall find, that in most of them 99/100 are wholly to be put on the account of *labour*. (TTG, II, §40, emphasis in original)

Throughout the discussion from which this passage has been excerpted – a discussion that admittedly followed, rather than preceded, the exposition of the labor theory of property – Locke declared the pre-eminence of labor in furnishing "the great part of what [man] applyed to the Support or Comfort of his being" (TTG, II, §44). Without hard toil, human agents could never manage to live well; and indeed they could never manage to live, period.

The specifics of Locke's theory

We come at last to the detailed working out of Locke's justificatory project. To be sure, Locke expounded his labor theory of property before he delivered most of the passages in the *Second Treatise* that present labor as the vital sine qua non of human flourishing; and indeed he marshaled those passages for the retrospective bolstering of his theory. But those passages become stronger when read as very broad statements without univocal or automatic connections to specific schemes of entitlements. Whereas the positing of ineluctable ties between the general necessity for human labor and particular latticeworks of entitlements is delusive,

Locke's abstract observations on the key role of labor – when construed as too sweeping to carry definite implications for the choice between privileges-with-rights and mere privileges – are highly credible (in their outlines, at any rate). That is, we improve Locke's standpoint by interpreting very broadly his reflections on the productiveness of labor, and thus by interpreting those reflections as analytically prior to his arguments in favor of property.

As we now begin to plumb the more detailed texture of the Lockean theory, we know that everyone at the dawn of humanity had a general privilege to draw upon the bounty of nature and a general right which protected that general privilege. We know further that people's toil would undoubtedly have to play a crucial part in effectuating that abstract privilege and that abstract right. Pointing to these primal conditions, Locke had to grapple with the two thorny topics that we noted earlier. First, he had to fix upon an array of concrete entitlements that would appositely connect human beings to the bountiful resources of nature. In addition, he had to show how specified things from nature's bounty could come to be associated with particular persons. And, we now may add, he also needed to fix upon an apt role for labor in the structuring of entitlements.

We shall in turn consider each of the main attempts by Locke to argue in favor of a structure of private property as the natural answer or the best answer to the cruxes which he had to address. Each strand of his arguments will exhibit profound weaknesses. After we have explored in depth the shortcomings in Locke's positions, we shall go on to see how problematic those shortcomings are.

The equation of rights of use and rights of ownership

Locke's first chief line of argument, made up of several contentions quite different in their degrees of subtleness, collapsed the general right-not-to-be-prevented-from-employing-the-wealth-of-nature into specific rights of property over any assets employed. Locke pushed together the concrete and the abstract by supposing that the effectuation of human beings' general prerogatives would simply have to take place through the establishment of myriad concrete rights. We discover the crudest instance of this conflation near the outset of chapter 5 in the *Second Treatise*:

> The Earth, and all that is therein, is given to Men for the Support and Comfort of their being. And though all the Fruits it naturally produces, and Beasts it feeds, belong to Mankind in common, as they are produced by the spontaneous hand of Nature; and no body has originally a private Dominion, exclusive of the rest of Mankind, in any of them, as they are thus in their natural state: yet being given for the use of Men, there must of necessity be a means *to appropriate* them some way or other before they can be of any use, or at all beneficial to any particular Man.

The Fruit, or Venison, which nourishes the wild *Indian*, who knows no Inclosure, and is still a Tenant in common, must be his, and so his, *i.e.* a part of him, that another can no longer have any right to it, before it can do him any good for the support of his Life. (TTG, II, §26, emphasis in original)

This passage echoes the natural-law conception of the personal sphere or *suum* – but in a strangely muddled fashion. We can understand this extract in two main ways, each of which will pose severe difficulties. Before we look at each of the two interpretations, however, we should notice that Locke indeed was attempting here to vindicate rights of property. As he himself suggested, his goal was to explain how individual persons could achieve "private Dominion [over various things], exclusive of the rest of Mankind." Hence, when he insisted that everyone would "no longer have any right" to food that nourished an Indian, he was using "right" in a non-Hohfeldian manner that embraced not just Hohfeldian rights but equally Hohfeldian privileges. Had Locke abided by Hohfeld's patterns of usage, the above characterization of the Indian's food would clearly have left open the possibility that another person or set of persons had a privilege to eat the food. In such circumstances, the relations among people would have been privilege/no-right rather than right/duty; and thus, at least in regard to this particular batch of food, proprietary rights would have been as notably missing as in the Hobbesian state of nature. But since we know that Locke was trying to demonstrate exactly "how Men might come to have a *property* in several parts of that which God gave to Mankind in common" (TTG, II, §25, emphasis in original), we can be quite sure that he was not painting a scene devoid of all Hohfeldian rights. That is, we can very safely conclude that he employed the term "right" more sweepingly here than he would have done if he clairvoyantly had adopted Hohfeld's guidelines for usage. (We scarcely can reproach Locke for having failed to anticipate a subtle and precise argot developed in the twentieth century.)

According to the first of our two readings of the passage under consideration, Locke was not submitting a thesis about digested food when he held that "Fruit, or Venison, which nourishes the wild *Indian*, who knows no Inclosure, and is still a Tenant in common, must be his, and so his, *i.e.* a part of him, that another can no longer have any right to it, before it can do him any good for the support of his Life." Instead, the premise that the food had to be "a part of [the Indian]" was a premise referring to the Indian's *suum* – his sphere of personality, which comprised his belongings as well as his body and mind. Interpreted in this way, the passage as a whole amounts to a declaration that concrete rights of property were essential for implementing the general right of self-conservation, a general right attaching to everybody. The Indian had to gain proprietary control over his food before he could satisfy his needs with it ("before it c[ould] do him any good for the support of his Life"). More generally, likewise, there always had to "be a means *to appropriate* [desirable assets] some way or other before they c[ould] be of any use, or at all beneficial to any particular Man." Recall here that Locke wielded "appropriation" and cognate terms to denote specifically the gaining of rights of ownership – rather than to advert to the gaining of possession *tout court*, with or without such rights. (Hereafter, we shall follow his usage.) In our first reading of the excerpt under consideration, then, we have found the positing of an ineluctable link between the quest for survival and the acquisition of private property.

So construed, Locke's argument is deeply unsound – for reasons that have already surfaced. It conflates possession and ownership, or enjoyment and exclusive dominion. Stated in the vocabulary of Hohfeld, Locke's position ill-advisedly presupposes that rights and powers must accompany privileges. As was explained earlier, people in the state of nature could readily survive without owning any goods, so long as they all had privileges to use and consume the goods. In order to stay alive, people had to take possession of useful things from the world of nature; yet the possession did not have to be proprietary. Someone acting on the basis of concrete privileges to use certain portions of natural wealth would thereby be drawing sustenance from the wealth as gainfully as would someone using those particular portions on the basis of concrete rights of ownership. Unless a person chanced to be plundered of his goods so exhaustively and recurrently that his life fell into grave danger, everyone's general right against others' thwarting of his or her quest for survival would be respected in a scheme of privileges-without-powers-and-without-concrete-rights. After all, even in the nasty and brutish turbulence of the Hobbesian state of nature – where anticipatory murders were privileged deeds – most savages did survive for a while, though perhaps not for very long.

Under our first reading, Locke's argument has foundered because it scants the dissimilarities between rights and privileges. A second reading allows the argument to avoid that specific misstep. But, as will presently be observed, this reinterpretation does not save Locke's reasoning from being utterly problematic. We here shall assume that Locke indeed was referring to digested victuals when he described the Indian's nourishment as "a part of him." In an obvious and important sense, the Indian did have to digest his food "before it c[ould] do him any good for the support of his life." In addition, and somewhat more to the point, whenever food had become incorporated into the body of the Indian through digestion, it clearly had become his exclusive property. Given that every human being within the state of nature had a right to the fundamental integrity of his or her body, and given that the extracting of digested food would involve gross violations of this right to integrity, the process whereby food passed through someone's gastrointestinal system was a process that yielded a right. Human beings appropriated their food by making it indivisible from their bodies; each human being's right to the exclusion of all other persons from his body was ipso facto a right to the exclusion of all other persons from the victuals that had become the stuff of his body.

This second reading of Locke's position has endowed that position with a healthy regard for the distinctness of rights and privileges. But three or four major problems afflict this reading. Most glaring among these problems is the fact that Locke himself undermined this interpretation. Shortly after the argument on which we are focused now, Locke insisted that proprietary rights over edible things accrued to people before the things were digested or devoured:

> He that is nourished by the Acorns he pickt up under an Oak, or the Apples he gathered from the Trees in the Wood, has certainly appropriated them to himself. No Body can deny but the nourishment is his. I ask then, When did they begin to be his? When he digested? Or when he eat? Or when he boiled? Or when he brought them home? Or when he pickt them up? And 'tis plain, if the first gathering made them not his, nothing else could. (TTG, II, §28)

We shall return more searchingly to this passage later. For the present, we merely ought to observe how it belies the notion that Locke regarded digestion as the catalyst or keystone of rights of property.

Another shortcoming in the second interpretation of Locke's standpoint is that the standpoint so recast will have told us nothing about inedible goods which human agents needed and used. If digestion was the process that founded rights of ownership, then things such as land and shelter and garments must presumably have forever gone unowned. Or, if indeed they were fully subject to ownership – as Locke emphatically thought they were – they must have lent themselves to appropriation in ways not pointed out by an argument concerning digestibles.

Furthermore, Locke's argument as portrayed by our second reading is not only deficient in its blanket exclusion of many goods from its scope, but is deficient also in its complete failure to tell us the predigested standing of food and drink. Inedible assets are omitted entirely from the argument, but even comestibles undevoured are wholly left out as well. If people within the state of nature did not own their supplies of nourishment before having eaten them, those supplies until the point of consumption were on a par with all inedible goods (in being strictly unowned). Or, if sources of nourishment could indeed be owned while still uningested – as Locke explicitly thought they could – they must have lent themselves to appropriation in ways not pointed out by an argument dealing only with foods already eaten.

A final weakness in the second interpretation of Locke's comments about the Indian's food is that the interpretation makes those comments seem faintly ridiculous. After all, among the numerous hazards that arose in the state of nature, efforts to compel human beings to disgorge food were almost certainly not too prominent. Edible items drenched with the gastric juices of people's stomachs presumably carried very little appeal for anyone. And when those items had evolved through digestion into being the components of human bodies – a stage at which the various items would appeal only to someone of cannibalistic tastes – a prohibition on seizing the items was superfluous. Just as Shylock could not remove any pound of flesh from Antonio without impermissibly shedding blood, the would-be cannibals in the state of nature could not eat any fully absorbed nutrients without infringing the constant right of someone to the integrity of his or her body; and thus the existence of that basic right was enough to bar that undesirable conduct, with no need whatsoever for restraints on the eating of metabolized food. In short, the proprietary rights contemplated by our new reading of Locke's argument were redundant. Either the protected "goods" were rebarbative and hence safe without protection, or they enjoyed ample protection on general grounds without having to be guarded by special rights.

Under our first main reading and our second main reading, then, Locke's comments on the Indian's food were misdirected. Some of Locke's other arguments in this general vein were not preposterous but were ultimately no more convincing. Take, for example, the following remarks set forth slightly later in chapter 5 of the *Second Treatise*:

> [I]n the beginning and first peopling of the great Common of the World, . . . [t]he Law Man was under, was . . . for *appropriating*. God Commanded, and his Wants forced him to *labour*. That was his *Property* which could not be taken from him where-ever he had fixed it. And hence subduing or cultivating the Earth, and having Dominion, we see are joyned together. The one gave Title to the other. So that God, by commanding to subdue, gave Authority so far to *appropriate*. And the Condition of Humane Life, which requires Labour and Materials to work on, necessarily introduces *private Possessions*. (TTG, II, §35, emphasis in original)

To some degree, here we find again the conflating of possession and ownership. A general privilege and a general duty to take possession of nature's wealth, along with a general right protecting the general privilege, could not preordain the scheme of focused entitlements that would concretize and flesh out those generalities. A command to subdue was not perforce the same as a command to appropriate, because the subduing could occur via concrete privileges without powers and concrete rights.

As long as people had privileges to use and retain the good things of nature's bounty, their survival did not depend on their procuring of concrete rights. Human beings could live and indeed could thrive by employing various assets in a world where all assets were forever strictly unowned.

To the extent that the latest passage quoted above has confused the general quest for survival and the concrete ownership of desiderata, it should draw the same criticism that was leveled against the passage on the Indian's nourishment (under our first reading). But Locke was now invoking his labor theory of property as well – a theory inserted with the statement that the labor of each man "was his *Property* which could not be taken from him where-ever he had fixed it." Hence, were the labor theory of property a successful theory, we might have to give credence to Locke's pronouncement that "the Condition of Humane Life, which requires Labour and Materials to work on, necessarily introduces *private Possessions*." Thus, until we detect the fundamental unsoundness of the labor theory of property, we shall have to suspend full judgment on the passage quoted above; let us say temporarily that at best the passage is dubious and misleading.

More sophisticated and somewhat more germane in the present context are passages where Locke contended that the institution of private property in the state of nature was the only means (or the surest means) to win the highest level of welfare for humankind. In these passages, the conferral of rights of ownership is not really portrayed as an utter sine qua non for the ability of human agents to live at all, but it is pictured as a sine qua non for optimal human flourishing. Understood in the current language of economics, these passages commend private property as the most efficient vehicle for apportioning wealth.

Locke believed that God had adjured human beings not only to subsist but also to thrive. Human prosperity was an integral part of God's design for the world, a world that had been given to people "for their benefit, and the greatest Conveniencies of Life they were capable to draw from it" (TTG, II, §34). Having thus proposed that the Deity intended human agents to flourish rather than to live poorly, Locke could vindicate private ownership if he somehow could establish that such ownership was the best means for achieving human affluence. Although Locke never tried to affirm this point directly, we can find it lurking implicitly in some portions of the *Second Treatise*'s chapter 5.

Across several paragraphs that we earlier very briefly reviewed, Locke emphasized the powerful creativity of labor in its adding of value to the earth's raw materials. He argued at length that human toil produced nearly all of the desirable features of desirable goods. "[*L*]*abour makes the far greatest part of the value* of things, we enjoy in this World" (TTG, II, §42, emphasis in original). In a section shortly before these paragraphs, Locke had underlined the productive role of labor in quite a similar way:

> [H]e who appropriates land to himself by his labour, does not lessen but increase the common stock of mankind. For the provisions serving to the support of humane life, produced by one acre of inclosed and cultivated land, are (to speak much within compasse) ten times more, than those, which are yeilded by an acre of Land, of an equal richnesse, lyeing wast in common. And therefor he, that incloses Land and has a greater plenty of the conveniencys of life from ten acres, than he could have from an hundred left to Nature, may truly be said, to give ninety acres to Mankind. For his labour now supplys him with provisions out of ten acres, which were but the product of an hundred lying in common. I have here rated the improved land very low in making its product but as ten to one, when it is much nearer an hundred to one. (TTG, II, §37)

Crucial for our present discussion is the conflating of use and ownership at the outset of the passage just quoted, where productive exploitation of natural riches is summarily deemed to be appropriation. In fact, this misstep pervades the passage, with a roughhewn divide between enclosed land and common land – a divide that runs together "inclosed" with "cultivated," and "common" with "wast[e]." Having again equated profitable possession and exclusive possession, Locke might appear to be as overconfident as when he wrote about the Indian's meal. But perhaps we here can extenuate his apparent glibness by uncovering a silent presupposition to which he cleaved.

In the passage currently being scrutinized, Locke could well have thought that the most efficient uses of nature's bounty would not occur unless there was private ownership of the bounty. He probably accepted a view that has figured saliently in political thought since ancient times – perhaps most renownedly in Aristotle's scorn for collective ownership (*Politics*, 1263a). According to that view, individuals tend to shower more care and toil on assets from which they reap all the benefits, and are less inclined to exert themselves when they have to share the fruits of their labors with their fellows. If the earliest human beings had lacked powers to acquire rights of property in the natural assets they employed for their upkeep, they would still have done whatever was necessary for survival; but they would not have strained to employ the natural riches as fruitfully and far-sightedly as possible, since each worker's hold on any given bundle of riches would have been highly precarious. Only with the prospect of a secure stream of benefits from worked-on materials, would each person be prepared to expend the time and drudgery needed for the maximizing of total output. And because the institution of private property was the lone regime of apportionment that would channel the benefits of labor entirely to the people who had produced them, it was the sole array of concrete prerogatives that furnished the correct incentives for people to bring about the highest level of manufactured "convenien-cys." Hence, given that God had charged humanity to prosper as well as to survive, the only route for fulfilling God's decree to the utmost was the origination of private ownership.

We shall look again at this argument about efficiency after we have studied the labor theory of ownership. But even at present we can challenge the argument on a number of grounds. Least important, but not completely insignificant, is the matter of human urges. As sketched above (with exaggeration), the line of reasoning about the efficiency of private ownership has implied that human beings in the state of nature were driven wholly or predominantly by selfish grasping. Such a line of reasoning presumes that people were so voracious and acquisitive that they would refuse to work extensively unless they reaped all the material profits and advantages from their sweat. Yet such a depiction can appear hyperbolic even to analysts who do not agree with a goody-goody vision of human agents as selflessly communal and sacrificing. People's selfishness might indeed be more tempered with communal concern and sympathy than is generally acknowledged by the argument about the maximizing of output through prerogatives of exclusive dominion.

Furthermore, a thesis of unalloyed human selfishness does not have to emerge as a thesis of unalloyed devotion (by human beings) to material wealth. Obtrusively egoistic agents might strive for the esteem and deference of one another much more than for the exclusive enjoyment of the goods they had made. In that case, each person would do his best to create as many desirable things as possible, not because he would expect and want to keep all the things himself, but because he would endeavor to win the awe or admiration of others for his abilities. Respectful acclaim for the proficiency of one's toiling, rather than sole dominion over the items made by that toiling, thus would serve as the prime desideratum impelling toilers to maximize their productive efforts. No system of chiefly private ownership – assigning creations to the people who had created them – would be necessary to encourage maximal output, even in a world of self-centered hogs.

Another main weakness in the efficiency-centered argument is its blithe assumption about the greater security of holdings in a regime of concrete rights-to-exclusive-enjoyment (versus a regime of privileges without concrete rights). In humankind's natural state, a system of private property could hardly ensure that everyone would possess in safety the goods produced by his or her toil. As Locke himself strongly emphasized, the principal drawback of the state of nature was the terrible insecurity of persons and holdings. The primeval stage of human existence was a stormy time "full of fears and continual dangers" (TTG, II, §123). Hazards marring the state of nature threatened proprietary rights with special acuteness, given the pervasive impulse of human beings to avoid honest industry and to opt for plunder: "[M]en are so dishonest that most of them prefer to enjoy the fruits of other men's labour rather than work to provide for themselves" (LT, 125).

Of course, any such consideration is irrelevant when one seeks to justify the advent of private ownership on a strictly deontological basis. If one's justification along those lines can succeed, then rights of ownership would be justified regardless of their effectiveness or ineffectiveness. But here the attempt to vindicate a structure of private property is consequentialist through and through. An argument heaping praise upon the efficiency of private ownership will lose its force if individuals' retained holdings in the state of nature would diverge substantially from the holdings that belonged to the individuals by dint of their proprietary rights. After all, in those circumstances the much-vaunted incentives for efficient production would not obtain, and thus the mere fact that people had come to be endowed with proprietary rights – ineffective rights – would scarcely promote the maximizing of output. Unless all or most of the prescriptions laid down by a regime of property would indeed become operative in the state of nature, arguments hailing those prescriptions are curiously beside the point (when our focus is on the state of nature).

While the assertions about the efficiency of private dominion have overlooked the potential insecurity of that dominion, they have also slighted the possible security of holdings based on stark privileges. If people in the state of nature lacked powers to invest themselves with any proprietary rights, the control they wielded over the goods they used was founded only on privileges. Ought we, then, to infer that such control must have been exceedingly unstable and tenuous? A flatly affirmative response to this question will have confusedly run together two distinct lines of conduct, which relate to each other as a class and a subclass: the set of actions that people *could* legitimately perform, and the set of actions that people *would* legitimately perform. If no one had any concrete rights covering the possession and use of things within the state of nature, then everyone could legitimately despoil other persons of the items they had acquired. But, especially in a context marked by superabundant raw materials, human beings might very likely opt to obtain their sustenance by working together or in solitude rather than by seizing the fruits of the work of their fellows.

To have a privilege was not perforce to exercise that privilege, and thus the universal retention of a privilege-to-invade-people's-holdings might generate hardly any invasions. Although each human being in the primordial state of nature might well have had a privilege to snatch the goods made by other people, each human being likewise retained a privilege to expend his own efforts on profuse raw materials. We can hardly say with stout confidence that people would avail themselves of the former privilege more frequently than of the latter; and indeed we can hardly say with stout confidence that people would avail themselves of the former privilege very often at all. Possessions based just on privileges could stay as secure de facto as possessions based on full rights. And therefore the privileges could match the rights in yielding robust incentives for the maximizing of total output.

Suppose we grant for now that a structure of privileges without concrete rights would leave possessions exposed to substantial insecurity. Suppose we accept further that a scheme of proprietary rights would issue in considerable security. Must we consequently avouch that an array of stark privileges would fail to induce maximal production? And hence must we conclude that rights of ownership were essential for the achieving of efficiency in the state of nature?

To see that the answers to these queries are negative, we have to impugn a basic premise that has hitherto gone unchallenged in the current discussion. That basic premise runs as follows. A general state of security for one's holdings could promote ambition and industriousness by guaranteeing that fruitful labor would principally redound to the benefit of those who performed the labor. When people felt confident that productive toil would bring advantages first and foremost to the toilers themselves, they would obviously be inclined to engage in toil. Had the link between fruitful efforts and rewards significantly diminished, people would be reluctant to undertake any truly arduous efforts or any efforts that paid off only during the longer term.

Now, the perceived conjunction between reliable benefits from toil and willingness to engage in toil is scarcely to be dismissed. If such a conjunction were entirely implausible, it would not so easily get presupposed. But this putative tie between security and efficiency was not inevitable. In times of disquietude when human agents felt insecure about the prospects of keeping their possessions, they might work all the harder – to accumulate so many possessions that their stocks of various items could withstand frequent seizures, or to replenish goods that had already been lost to spoliation. Whenever people were confident that some of their fruitful labor would bring them *some* rewards, the absence of *full* rewards for the labor (an absence caused by pillaging) might inspire a lot of people to work with extra sedulity in order to amass the comforts that could be gained with much less sweat in a system of full rewards. If manifold human beings wished to keep a high level of consumption more than they wished to keep a high level of relaxation or play, and if they therefore would react to expected thievery by working longer to maintain their high levels of consumption, then a social environment with fairly significant thievery and insecurity could maximize the output of useful goods. Given these underlying preferences, whereby people valued their wealthy lifestyles more than they valued leisure, a context of great security would induce people to spend less time on the production of riches than they otherwise would have spent.[3]

Of course, nothing preordained the existence of a link between insecurity and optimal productivity. Any number of human agents could harbor preferences that would result in a lower output when disorderliness prevailed. Yet, if the drawing of connections between insecurity and maximal productivity should hardly pretend to be conclusive, it can show at any rate that the connections between *security* and maximal productivity were likewise not automatic. Here my challenge to efficiency-focused arguments does not proceed as a definitive refutation or overthrow of its target, but simply as an exposure of inconclusiveness therein.

In this respect, my latest line of attack against the notion of the peculiar efficiency of private dominion has resembled my other lines of attack against that notion. None of the criticisms offered here has purported to strike an irretrievably crushing blow. Each criticism has dealt with possible paths that human conduct and human urges could take; such matters are far too open-ended and variegated to permit any unequivocal resolution. Instead of making bold to devise some irrefragable proofs, my ripostes to the efficiency-focused arguments have merely sought to reveal a number of possible ways in which the institution of private property within the state of nature might prove to be inefficient.

Having seen that the case for the output-maximizing results of private ownership is far less compelling than it may seem at first, we now should remark a salient aspect of the efficiency-focused arguments – an aspect that later will receive our sustained attention. Though some efficiency-focused arguments are more perceptive and convincing than others, they all share an additive or agglomerative impulse. That is, they applaud the institution of private ownership by adverting to the good of the human species considered as a whole (or to the good of some geographically isolated subset[s] of humankind). Such arguments direct their attention to the overall quantity of material output and material welfare achieved by

[3] In order to make my point clearly, I pass over many complexities that could arise from reversals and discontinuities in the structures of people's preferences. For example, whereas insecurity might stimulate productive endeavors so long as it remained at a fairly moderate level, it would discourage such endeavors if it grew severe.

human agents *en masse*, rather than to the quantity of output or welfare associated with each individual.[4] Construed within this orientation, rights existed as functions of collective well-being.

Of course, a focus on aggregates or collectivities does not in all circumstances rule out a focus on the postures of separate agents. For example, as was earlier argued, Locke believed that "Man's" broad entitlement to use natural resources was a basic entitlement belonging to humankind as a species *and* to individual persons. With regard to that key entitlement, there existed no cleft between the status of the overall group and the statuses of the group's members. But in the present context a rupture between the good of humanity and the good of various human agents would persistently lurk.

On the one hand, the gap between the welfare of individuals and the welfare of collectivities should not be exaggerated. If an efficient scheme of concrete entitlements had emerged, then many people would stand to profit, and perhaps most people would stand to profit. Furthermore, *every*body would stand to gain from an output-maximizing scheme of entitlements in very infrequent situations, where the desires and talents of particular human beings were universally in accord with the collective aims and requirements of the human species. And we should scarcely flinch from acknowledging that just about everyone would suffer if human interaction was regulated by a grotesquely inefficient array of concrete entitlements.

On the other hand, the efficiency-focused arguments cannot support any sweeping verdicts about the benefits that accrued to *all* individuals from the maximizing of gross production. For ease of reference, we may assume throughout this paragraph that proprietary rights during the state of nature were indeed a sine qua non for generating the highest levels of output overall. We may further suppose here that the proprietary rights were seldom or never breached. And we also may confine our examination of benefits – benefits for human beings and for the human species – to nothing but the raw levels of material goods. Even with these sweeping assumptions, we can detect a yawning gap between collective well-being and individual well-being. To insist on a full transparence or correspondence between the plane of the individual and the plane of the collectivity, one will have to invoke some unbelievable premises about human skills and aspirations. One will have to maintain that every person within the state of nature had just the talents and likings that would cause him to get more wealth in a scheme of private property than in any scheme of privi-

[4] Although this statement will undergo a partial qualification in chapter 5, my present point will remain entirely unweakened.

leges with few or no proprietary entitlements; however, such a contention will be ludicrously far-fetched. Even though we have avouched for the sake of argument that the scheme of mere privileges would have generated a somewhat smaller measure of output on the whole, we should not infer that *every* person fared better in the scheme of proprietary rights. People possessed of certain qualities – like physical brawn and vigor, an abiding penchant for risks, a wanderlust or some other mode of restless vitality, and adroitness in removing wealth from the grip of people who had acquired it – would stand a very good chance of doing better within a world of bare privileges than within a world full of concrete rights. In theory, of course, everyone at a given time in the state of nature might have had none of the aforementioned qualities. Hence, in theory, everyone at a given time in the state of nature could quite conceivably have benefited from a structure of property (in comparison with any structure devoid of concrete rights). But, in practice, the likelihood that no people at some specific time would partake of the aforementioned attributes was dauntingly slim. Lower still was the likelihood that no people with the aforementioned attributes would ever crop up throughout the entire period of the state of nature. Plainly, then, we should not confidently presuppose a total absence of people who could profit from a regime of unadorned privileges; such an absence was an exceedingly remote possibility. We therefore may conclude that, although the maximizing of overall welfare could sometimes occur through the maximizing of every individual's welfare, it would often have to occur quite differently.

Efficiency-focused arguments, then, cannot rely on a neat congruity between the interests of separate persons and the interests of humankind. Such arguments, which pose their theses as theses about overall production, must refer to the good of humanity rather than to the good of all persons qua individuals. Instructive here will be a comparison between the reasoning about efficiency and the reasoning about a general human entitlement-to-use-nature's-resources. With regard to that entitlement, some of Locke's chief premises – his premise about the right-protected privilege of the human species to continue itself as such, and his premise about the fundamentally equal statuses of all persons – could effect an unbroken match between the posture of individuals and the posture of the whole species, as was earlier shown. Given that at least some of the members of the human species would have to be entitled to employ natural riches if the species was to survive at all, and given that *every*one would hold such an entitlement if *any*one did, the basic prerogative of the species to exploit natural riches would entail the vesting of everybody with that exact prerogative. In regard to our present topic, however, the unfailing concurrence of interests between the aggregate and the individidual in the state of nature could not be ensured (and was in fact singularly unlikely). There were no starting points that combined to yield a seamless correlation between the highest level of assets for humanity and the highest level of assets for each person.

The efficiency-focused writers' only contention is that the production of material goods by humankind in the state of nature would reach its maximum when governed and channeled by a system of private property. Such a contention leaves plenty of room for gaps between the position of the species and the position of any particular member of the species. Whereas nobody could survive without making use of natural resources, any number of people could do better in a regime of bare privileges-without-concrete-rights than in a regime of private property. As has just been argued, people endowed with certain characteristics would be apt to secure more goods in a state of nature unmarked by any proprietary rights than in a state of nature bestrewn with such concrete rights; people so endowed could clearly exist in principle and would almost surely exist in fact. Thus, whereas we could assume safely that what was authorized and essential for humanity (the employment of the bounty of nature) was authorized and essential for every living person as well, we cannot assume that what was desirable for humanity (a web of rights of exclusive ownership) was desirable for every person as well.

In short, even when we have pretermitted the sundry leaps of faith that detract from the persuasive power of the efficiency-focused arguments, we should not presume that those arguments can uphold their recommendations with tributes to the inherent primacy or unyielding sanctity of the individual person's welfare. An efficiency-centered line of justification for private ownership must advance its refrain in a collectivist key, by pointing to the implications of private ownership for the common weal and by having to disregard the implications of private ownership for the standing of each person considered separately. Because the good of an individual in the state of nature might diverge from the common good of the human species, an argument that lays its prescriptive stress on the common good of the species will accordingly have obliged itself to approve the subordination and overriding of individuals' interests whenever necessary. Efficiency-oriented reasoning can account for the bestowal of rights of property on the earliest human agents, *not* because such rights were integrally promotive of the welfare and wishes of every agent, but because the rights were integrally promotive of the welfare of humankind. In other words, such reasoning assigns people their rights as functions of collective goals and demands. (Nothing said here is incompatible with the slightly complacent assertion that "a King of a large and fruitful Territory [in the undeveloped expanse of the New

World] feeds, lodges, and is clad worse than a day Labourer in [highly developed] *England*" (TTG, II, §41, emphasis in original.) Myriad analysts have seized upon this statement by Locke and have found there a proposition that everyone in a land with private ownership would be more wealthy than everyone in a land devoid of such ownership. We here may note *en passant* that this commonly accepted reading is somewhat glib; the quoted words, after all, do not encompass out-and-out vagabonds in highly developed England. More important, however, are the differences between Locke's comparison and the chief comparison drawn here. Whereas Locke was underlining a contrast between the lot of anybody in primitive conditions and the lot of anybody in an advanced society, here the central comparison has focused on two main types of primitive settings. Although Locke's famous contrast between the king and the laborer was indeed a contrast between a situation marked by the absence of private ownership and a situation marked by the sway of private ownership, it was much more importantly a contrast between the indigence of undeveloped societies and the affluence of developed nations. That additional key component or dimension of Locke's example has not figured at all in the analysis put forth here, which pertains only to different structures of primitive arrangements and which has no bearing on advanced societies. We have compared a state of nature involving private property and a state of nature involving little or no such property. Either version of the primordial state of humankind would be economically undeveloped, and thus our comparison of the two versions will never light upon the extreme disparities that Locke underscored when opposing England to the Americas. If society *J* is an enormously productive civilization that has won ascendance over much of the natural world, and if society *K* is a group of savages whose economic achievements have furnished them with barely more than a hand-to-mouth existence, we can infer quite plausibly that every hearty person in *J* who is not a shiftless tramp will be wealthier than every person in *K*. But if we now submit that *J* and *K* are essentially on a par as two variants of a crude and prepolitical state of nature, our inference loses whatever plausibleness it had.)

The workings of individualism: the labor theory of property Thus far in our examination of the specifics of Locke's reflections on private ownership, we have observed the following three main points. First, his tendency to equate possession (legitimate possession) and ownership led to outright blunders, with a failure to distinguish between the general aim of survival and a specific mechanism for structuring that aim. A latticework of proprietary rights could never win by default over a latticework of privileges without concrete rights, because a regime of naked privileges could impel and undergird the quest for survival as appropriately as any matrix of full-fledged rights. Second, we can glean from Locke's arguments a more sophisticated position focused on the aggregate output of humankind. That position, however, has revealed itself to be highly inconclusive. Third, if we leave aside how dubious the sophisticated position is, we can see that it accounts for people's rights of ownership entirely by reference to the needs of humanity as a whole. According to such a stance, individual rights in the state of nature would gain their justification solely as the vehicles of collective enterprises.

Thus far, then, we have probed the consequentialist side of Locke's endeavor to vindicate the existence of proprietary entitlements in the state of nature. We have found a thoroughly specious vein of argument that depicts such entitlements as the only means by which human agents could exploit natural riches in order to survive at all, and we likewise have unearthed a dubious vein of argument belauding proprietary rights as the only means for ensuring the efficiency of production in the aggregate. As readers of Locke can hardly fail to notice, however, he did not restrict himself to consequentialist tacks. In most of his discussions about the concrete rights that people would acquire over natural assets, he took a deontological approach – an approach that has come to be renowned as his labor theory of property.

With the deontological frame of reference, Locke not only could marshal an alternative basis for proprietary dominion but could also address a grave shortcoming in the consequentialist style of argument. Even if his conflating of possession and ownership or his rough appeals to efficiency had managed somehow to justify the girding of individuals with full dominion over various parts of nature's bounty, he still would not have managed to justify the specific links between persons and the products which they had shaped. That is, the consequentialist skeins of argument would not provide any grounds for the specific structure of ownership whereby people were entitled to nothing more and nothing less than the concrete fruits of their labor. If the effects sought in the presocietal scheme of ownership were security and proper incentives, then any human agent *could* be entitled to exactly the things that she herself had produced, but clearly she never *had* to be entitled to exactly those things. Products at least as good as her own would serve at least as well to bring about the fitting incentives and satisfaction.

Were the institution of private property acceptable only inasmuch as it could endow everyone with means to survive, then useful objects that were equally gratifying could substitute for one another without restriction. Everybody would be entitled to a certain level of welfare, fixed by the basic needs that everyone had to satisfy or fixed by the amount of wealth that each person generated by toiling; but no one would have an automatic entitlement to keep the specific goods that he himself had created. After all, the function of promoting survival could just as well be discharged by other goods of similar quality. Likewise, were the institution of private property acceptable only inasmuch as it could ensure efficient productiveness, then useful objects equally capable of arousing the apt incentives could substitute for one another without restriction. While everybody would be entitled to a measure of assets that would fluctuate in accordance with the size of her contribution to the overall output of humankind, no one would have an automatic claim to the goods that she herself had produced. Incentive-stirring rewards for fruitful efforts could just as well be supplied by other goods of similar quality.

Thus, because the consequentialist arguments denude particular items of their particularity by focusing on the items' general effects, the goals recounted in such arguments could never assign specific things – specific interchangeable things – to specific persons. A fortiori, then, those goals could never assign to each person the exact items that he or she had created. To knot the specific ties between producers and their own products, Locke needed something more than a consequentialist approach. With the labor theory of property, he aspired to fill this gap as well as to demonstrate that the links between workers and their respective creations would be links of proprietary prerogatives.

A compendium through extracts Intimations of Locke's chief theory of property occur in some of his texts apart from the *Second Treatise of Government*. In a passage quoted previously herein from the *Letter on Toleration*, for example, Locke fumed that men "are so dishonest that most of them prefer to enjoy the fruits of other men's labour rather than work to provide for themselves" (LT, 125). Locke proceeded again along these lines in the *Essay concerning Human Understanding* when he denounced the wickedness of "taking from others, without their Consent, what their honest Industry has possessed them of" (EHU, IV, iv, §9). To the same effect – at least in the context of our present discussion – Locke several times referred in his *Essays on the Law of Nature* to the dominion gained over entities and materials by the fashioner from whose hands they had issued (ELN, 157, 183, 185, 187). Nonetheless, Locke there always had in mind the Deity's prerogatives over the universe which had come about by virtue of His designs and craftsmanship. Accordingly, Locke neglected there to present his remarks (on rights acquired through creation) as remarks with a bearing on the projects of human toil. Only in chapter 5 of the *Second Treatise* did he fully articulate the connections between the process of human labor and the forming of proprietary rights.

Having announced that God imparted the world to human beings in common, Locke had to provide a theoretical ground from which he could derive the apposite individuation and distribution of natural bounty. He introduced such a ground in the most important and celebrated paragraph of his disquisition on property:

Though the Earth, and all inferior Creatures be common to all Men, yet every Man has a *Property* in his own *Person*. This no Body has any Right to but himself. The Labour of his Body, and the *Work* of his Hands, we may say, are properly his. Whatsoever then he removes out of the State that Nature hath provided, and left it in, he hath mixed his *Labour* with, and joyned to it something that is his own, and thereby makes it his *Property*. It being by him removed from the common state Nature placed it in, it hath by this *labour* something annexed to it, that excludes the common right of other Men. For this *Labour* being the unquestionable Property of the Labourer, no Man but he can have a right to what that is once joyned to, at least where there is enough, and as good left in common for others. (TTG, II, §27, emphasis in original)

By and large, the rest of the labor theory of property does little more than refine the crucial verdicts of the paragraph just quoted. Hence, before we study that paragraph in detail, we should take notice of the major portions of Locke's analysis that serve as a commentary thereon.

Locke proceeded with his amplifications straightaway, by means of some questions and replies which we noted earlier in a different context:

He that is nourished by the Acorns he pickt up under an Oak, or the Apples he gathered from the Trees in the Wood, has certainly appropriated them to himself. No Body can deny but the nourishment is his. I ask then, When did they begin to be his? When he digested? Or when he eat? Or when he boiled? Or when he brought them home? Or when he pickt them up? And 'tis plain, if the first gathering made them not his, nothing else could. That *labour* put a distinction between them and common. That added something to them more than Nature, the common Mother of all, had done; and so they became his private right. (TTG, II, §28, emphasis in original)

Locke multiplied his pregnant examples, and included some situations gleaned from the modern era:

Though the Water running in the Fountain be every ones, yet who can doubt, but that in the Pitcher is his only who drew it out? His *labour* hath taken it out of the hands of Nature, where it was common, and belong'd equally to all her Children, and hath thereby *appropriated* it to himself.

Thus this Law of reason makes the Deer, that *Indian's* who hath killed it; 'tis allowed to be his goods who hath bestowed his labour upon it, though before, it was the common right of every one. And amongst those who are counted the Civiliz'd part of Mankind, who have made and multiplied positive Laws to determine Property, this original Law of Nature for the *beginning of Property*, in what was before common, still takes place; and by vertue thereof, what Fish any one catches in the Ocean, that great and still remaining Common of Mankind; or what Ambergriese any one takes up here, is by the *Labour* that removes it out of that common state Nature left it in, *made* his *Property* who takes that pains about it. And even amongst us the Hare that any one is Hunting, is thought his who pursues her during the Chase. For being a Beast that is still looked upon as common, and no Man's private Possession; whoever has imploy'd so much labour about any of that kind, as to find and pursue her, has thereby removed her from the state of Nature, wherein she was common, and hath *begun a Property*. (TTG, II, §§29–30, emphasis in original, paragraph number omitted)

Locke went on to make clear that any individual's ownership of land would emerge by very much the same route as any individual's ownership of portable items:

But the *chief matter of Property* being now not the Fruits of the Earth, and the Beasts that subsist on it, but the *Earth it self*; as that which takes in and carries with it all the rest: I think it is plain, that *Property* in that too is acquired as the former. *As much Land* as a Man Tills, Plants, Improves, Cultivates, and can use the Product of, so much is his *Property*. He by his Labour does, as it were, inclose it from the Common. Nor will it invalidate his right to say, Every body else has an equal Title to it; and therefore he cannot appropriate, he cannot inclose, without the Consent of all his Fellow-Commoners, all Mankind. God, when he gave the World in common to all Mankind, commanded Man also to labour, and the penury of his Condition required it of him. God and his Reason commanded him to subdue the Earth, *i.e.* improve it for the benefit of Life, and therein lay out something upon it that was his own, his labour. He that in Obedience to this Command of God, subdued, tilled and sowed any part of it, thereby annexed to it something that was his *Property*, which another had no Title to, nor could without injury take from him. (TTG, II, §32, emphasis in original)

In a passage that we already have scrutinized for a different purpose, Locke declared that the right-creating power of human toil was the link between the general entitlement to self-preservation and the concrete entitlements of individual ownership:

[I]n the beginning and first peopling of the great Common of the World, . . . [t]he Law Man was under, was . . . for *appropriating*. God Commanded, and his Wants forced him to *labour*. That was his Property which could not be taken from him where-ever he had fixed it. And hence subduing or cultivating the Earth, and having Dominion, we see are joyned together. The one gave Title to the other. So that God, by commanding to subdue, gave Authority so far to *appropriate*. And the Condition of Humane Life, which requires Labour and Materials to work on, necessarily introduces *private Possessions*. (TTG, II, §35, emphasis in original)

After emphasizing that human labor accounted for almost all the value of useful things, Locke reaffirmed his key premise that the sole dominion of every human being over herself and her abilities was the fundament of proprietary rights:

From all which it is evident, that though the things of Nature are given in common, yet Man (by being Master of himself, and *Proprietor of his own Person*, and the Actions or Labour of it) had still in himself the *great Foundation of Property*; and that which made up the great part of what he applyed to the Support or Comfort of his being, when Invention and Arts had improved the conveniencies of Life, was perfectly his own, and did not belong in common to others. (TTG, II, §44, emphasis in original)

Within every man and woman abided the foundation of property, which endowed each person with exclusive control over a share of nature's wealth as a consequence of employing his or her own capacities. By being his or her own, a human agent could be an owner of material riches.

We may suitably drop the curtain on this flurry of extracts with the rose-colored peroration from Locke's remarkable chapter:

And thus, I think, it is very easie to conceive without any difficulty, *how Labour could at first begin a title of Property* in the common things of Nature, and how the spending it upon our uses bounded it. So that there could then be no reason of quarrelling about Title, nor any doubt about the largeness of Possession it gave. Right and conveniency went together; for as a Man had a Right to all he could imploy his Labour upon, so he had no temptation to labour for more than he could make use of. This left no room for Controversie about the Title, nor for Incroachment on the Right of others; what Portion a Man carved to himself, was easily seen; and it was useless as well as dishonest to carve himself too much, or take more than he needed. (TTG, II, §51, emphasis in original)

Even if we were to endorse the general justification that Locke expounded, his final paragraph would appear sentimental. That paragraph will seem especially inadvisable as we focus on the lacunae which put his justification into doubt.

Four false trails Before we turn our attention to the pitfalls in Locke's approach, we should glance at four misdirected charges that have frequently been hurled by critics of Locke. Although these charges have surfaced in a number of expositions, and although they should consequently attract some notice here, they have all been quashed at various times by other analysts. This excursus will hence remain brief.

First among these false trails is the contention that Locke stumbled by ascribing self-ownership to each human agent while insisting also that human agents were God's "Property, whose Workmanship they are" (TTG, II, §6). Some analysts writing in defense of Locke on this point have given salience to a distinction drawn in the *Essay concerning Human Understanding*: a divide between men and persons (EHU, II, xxvii). In chapter 5 of the *Second Treatise of Government* – we now should remember – Locke did not maintain that every human being had a proprietary right in his or her body. Rather, he specifically stated that "every Man has a *Property* in his own *Person*. This no Body has any Right to but himself. The Labour of his Body, and the *Work* of his Hands, we may say, are properly his" (TTG, II, §27, emphasis in original). We can thus presume from these words that men and women were owned by God while they themselves owned their sundry accomplishments and initiatives. God enjoyed the exclusive rights to what He had made, and people enjoyed exclusive rights to what they had made.

Now, although the view of self-ownership as an encroachment on God's prerogatives will prove to be ill-advised, the response just outlined is less than satisfactory. Even if we accept that Locke was sufficiently consistent to wield the same "person"/"man" dichotomy in the *Second Treatise* as in the *Essay concerning Human Understanding*, and even if we overlook certain problems and ambiguities in the *Essay*'s distinction (of which a thorough analysis would take us too far afield), we ought to see that the foregoing riposte has not done justice to God. Here the relevant point can be expressed in two chief ways, the first of which very closely approximates the point that I highlighted with the aid of *The Winter's Tale* in chapter 3. Given a belief in an all-encompassing God, a God who "shows Himself to us as present everywhere" in a universe where "our being and our work depend on His will" (ELN, 109, 183), we scarcely can deny God His rights of ownership in human accomplishments – accomplishments which He fully drove and sustained. If human beings had "first been made and also [we]re constantly preserved" by the divine Craftsman (ELN, 185), then He held the same entitlements-through-creation in regard to their feats and their endeavors as He held in regard to their lives and limbs.

Further, even if one disregards the omnipresence of the Deity, one still can insist that His proprietary prerogatives would extend at least as far as those of His human agents. According to Locke, the ownership of productive assets by anyone would pertain not merely to the assets themselves but likewise to the fruits or yields of the assets. As Locke declared with reference to land and to the products of land, whatever someone "tilled and reaped, laid up and made use of, before it spoiled, that was his peculiar Right; whatsoever he enclosed, and could feed, and make use of, the Cattle and Product was also his" (TTG, II, §38). Indeed, Locke could even write that "the Grass my Horse has bit [and] the Turfs my Servant has cut . . . become my *Property*" (TTG, II, §28, emphasis in original). If human agents were so clearly entitled to the output of their productive holdings, why would the Lord of all the earth not enjoy the same entitlement? And, if the Deity did possess that very entitlement, what grounds could there ever be for denying Him full ownership of the exploits and accomplishments that were carried out by the people whom He had made?

Happily, we need not rely on the division between persons and men in order to brush away the objections to the prospect of double ownership. At hand is a more straightforward reply. As Locke himself argued, and as several commentators have aptly noticed,[5] the rights of men and women would be operative solely in the mundane realm of interpersonal dealings – not in the metaphysical realm inhabited by the Lord. People would assert their rights *vis-à-vis* one another only; *vis-à-vis* God, their rights had no force. Locke said as much when he observed in his *Essays on the Law of Nature* that "goods . . . are never so much ours that they cease to be God's" (ELN, 203). He was even more emphatic and more explicit during his onslaught on Filmer's absolutism in the *First Treatise*: "[H]owever, in respect of one another, Men may be allowed to have propriety in their distinct Portions of the Creatures; yet in respect of God the Maker of Heaven and Earth, who is sole Lord and Proprietor of the whole World, Mans Propriety in the Creatures is nothing but that *Liberty to use them*, which God has permitted" (TTG, I, §39, emphasis in original). These statements about the ownership of external goods apply also to the ownership of oneself. Each human being had rights of property over his person, but only in relation to all his fellows. In relation to God, a human being enjoyed no rights to physical safety or to anything else, for God was the unchallengeable "superior who has right and authority over [people]; for who will deny that the clay is subject to the potter's will, and that a piece of pottery can be shattered by the same hand by which it has been formed?" (ELN, 157.) Yet the absence of any rights for people against the impositions of God did not curtail the strength of their rights against the impositions of one another. God's ultimate ownership of each person at the metaphysical level would entirely square with the ownership of each person by herself at the mundane level of human intercourse. Only if exegetes collapse these distinct levels will they worry at all about the simultaneous ownership of each person by herself and by her Creator.

For Locke, of course, the metaphysical realm was hardly a realm devoid of normative implications. Presiding over that realm, he thought, sat a King whose goodness was absolutely impeccable. God the King laid duties upon all men and women, some of which were directly and exclusively owed to Him, and some of which were directly owed by people to one another (as well as indirectly to Him). Hence, the relationship

[5] See, e.g. Jeremy Waldron, *The Right to Private Property* (Oxford: Clarendon Press, 1988), 177–8.

between the metaphysical sphere and the mundane sphere in regard to proprietary control over persons was the relationship between natural law and individuals' right-protected liberties. God exerted His proprietary dominion over His human creatures by generally requiring them to embrace some patterns of conduct and to forbear certain other patterns of conduct; people exerted their proprietary dominion over themselves by choosing for themselves their specific paths of compliance with the basic decrees of God while being morally safe from the gratuitous interference of other people.

As was noted parenthetically earlier, all full-blown rights of property would have to emerge as rights that were subject to the peace-engendering confines of natural law. In other words, the simultaneous ownership of people by themselves and by their benevolent Craftsman was the state of affairs wherein the rights of each human agent could appropriately exist as rights in harmony with the rights of his or her fellows. Few if any analysts think that the full-blown rights held by persons *vis-à-vis* one another were pseudo-rights, notwithstanding that everybody vested with rights would have to tailor his actions to avoid infringing the cognate rights of everyone else. Few if any analysts, then, should feel that God's ownership of persons was somehow inconsistent with the self-ownership of each person.

A second dubious criticism of Locke has concentrated again on his presumption that every human being would possess rights of property in herself. With arguments that go back at least to Kant, the objection urges that the whole idea of self-ownership is utterly specious. Ownership, we are told, can never obtain as a reflexive relation; people can never own themselves or their conduct.[6]

Once again the person/man dualism can be marshaled for a defense of Locke. Since we are told in the *Second Treatise* that each *man* had rights of property in his own person, rather than that each *person* had rights of property in himself, the ownership of oneself was not as starkly reflexive as it might seem at first. But, because this retort is somewhat strained, and because of problems and ambiguities in the person/man distinction (at least with respect to the role of that distinction here), we should opt again for a more straightforward reply. Complaints about the very idea of owning oneself are silly dogmas. Essential components in the varied bundles of entitlements that made up ownership could apply as much to a person and his abilities as to any external goods.

[6] I have in mind here especially the following two articles by J. P. Day: "Locke on property," 16 *Philosophical Quarterly* 207 (1966); and "Self-ownership," 20 *Locke Newsletter* 77 (1989). For Kant's view, see Immanuel Kant, *Lectures on Ethics* (London: Methuen, 1930) (Louis Infield trans.), 165, 166.

Although Locke was not too clear and careful about identifying the entitlements that he regarded as essential to ownership, we can fasten on two major ingredients (or two major groups of ingredients). One cardinal element of proprietary possession was the right of exclusion – the right, within the limits of natural law, to be free from seizures and invasions. As Locke asserted in a much-discussed paragraph, a keynote of property was "that *without a Man's own consent* it *cannot be taken from him*" (TTG, II, §193, emphasis in original). When one attained ownership of an asset, one's dominion "exclude[d] the common right [and privilege] of other Men" (TTG, II, §27). Another integral feature of proprietary possession was the privilege to control – the privilege, within the limits of natural law, to use and arrange one's holdings as one saw fit. As Locke declared, the goods in which human agents had rights of property were "*their own, and at their own dispose* . . . or else it is no property" (TTG, II, §194, emphasis in original). In the state of nature, human beings were always free to "dispose of their Possessions, and Persons as they th[ought] fit, within the bounds of the Law of Nature" (TTG, II, §4). People with proprietary dominion over assets would exercise "the Right [i.e. the privilege] they thereby have, to dispose of them, as they please" (STE, §105).

Both of these central aspects of property could mark the relationship between anyone and himself, as plainly as they could mark the relationship between anyone and his goods. There was nothing mysterious about the right of each human agent to be free from encroachments upon his physical or mental integrity. Such a right to noninterference, which serves to guard every human being against unwanted invasions of the faculties of body and mind, is now a commonplace element of tort and criminal law. Likewise, the moral/legal capacity of an individual to select and pilot the course of her own behavior was scarcely very strange, much less inconceivable. When Locke proclaimed that "[e]very Man is born with a . . . *Right of Freedom to his Person*, which no other Man has a Power over, but the free Disposal of it lies in himself" (TTG, II, §190, emphasis in original), he was not advancing an unintelligible position. A human being could have a moral/legal entitlement to choose and direct the pathways of her conduct, within the bounds of the law of nature, just as obviously as she could have an entitlement to choose and direct the ways in which her external goods were to be employed (within the bounds of the law of nature).

Here the critic of the idea of self-ownership might respond by arguing that at least the will of any person could not be owned by the person whose will it was. After all, the essential characteristics of proprietary dominion both involved the exercise of the will, in order to control and exclude. But – so we might be told – the will could not steer itself; to say that the will could guide itself is as ludicrously redundant as to say that we believe propositions by believing that we believe. Hence, given that the enjoyment of rights of property entailed the exercise of the will, and given that the will cannot bring itself to bear on itself, the notion that a person could enjoy rights of property over his own volition is muddled.

This seemingly attractive riposte contains at least three basic weaknesses, the first two of which can only be mentioned in passing. First, any response like the one above must unwisely take for granted the choice theory of rights, over the interest theory. Such a preference is unsupported and largely unsupportable. In addition, the posited rejoinder has smugly dismissed the Spinozist threat of inescapable backslides in perception and knowledge, by discounting the topmost plunges within the backslides as nonexistent and ludicrous. Infinite regresses of volitions that must get willed and beliefs that must get believed can hardly be overcome by being ignored.

Of somewhat more direct relevance to the present discussion, however, is the mistakenness of the posited argument (by the critic of Locke) in the reaching of its conclusion. Even if we temporarily allow that the choice theory ought to be preferred to the interest theory, and even if we grant that the will cannot apply its thrust and its helmsmanship to itself as the means of sparking its present drive, we aptly can refuse to accept that human agents in the state of nature did not enjoy proprietary dominion over their wills. Anybody could exercise dominion over his will, by choosing to keep his will from falling under the sway of other people, and by thus securing his prospective capacity to do as he pleased (although his pleasing was always regulated by natural law). A person could effectively lose control of his will in two chief ways. For the Locke of the *Two Treatises of Government*, overweening coercion was enough to deprive someone of any genuine freedom of the will. People were justified in resisting any efforts to overpower their wills through brute compulsion, for anyone who tried to enslave them "ha[d] no lawful Authority, whilst Force, and not Choice, compels them to submission" (TTG, II, §189). Indeed, in the world of Lockean liberalism (rather than in the world of neo-Lockean liberalism), no one could rightly alienate his or her entitlement to be free from brute duress, since the full proprietary lordship of every competent person over his or her own will was never legitimately for sale:

> This *Freedom* from Absolute, Arbitrary Power, is so necessary to, and closely joyned with a Man's Preservation, that he cannot part with it, but by what forfeits his Preservation and Life together. For a Man, not having the Power of his own Life, cannot, by Compact, or his own Consent, *enslave himself* to any one, nor put himself under the Absolute, Arbitrary Power of another, to take away his Life, when he pleases. (TTG, II, §23, emphasis in original)

Another way in which the agency of a human being could slip from the control of the human being himself was the complete overriding of that agency, through electronic implants or through drugs (or through any other effective means). What has here been said with regard to the coercing of people's wills must apply to the suppression or replacement of people's wills a fortiori. Human agents were always justified in resisting any efforts to lead them into functioning as automatons. And, in the world of Lockean liberalism, a human being never could rightly cede control over her will. Just as no one could agree to become a slave, no one could agree to become an empty puppet.

Warding off the undue coercion of the individual will and the utter displacement of the individual will, each human being would thus assert the proprietary right to be free from intrusions. By way of focused defiance, and by way of general unreadiness to abjure the faculty of volition, each human agent would exclude her fellows from directing her will – in much the way that she would exclude them from seizing hold of the material assets over which she enjoyed proprietary prerogatives. And, even if we avouch that the will could not apply its management to itself for the purpose of controlling its *current* projects and surges, we can perceive that its exclusion of outside dominance enabled it to control its future (by keeping open any number of possibilities that would otherwise become closed, and by closing or delaying some possibilities that would otherwise become actual).

Of course, the will might fail in its striving to preserve its integrity and autonomy; either by its choice amid desperate circumstances, or by the overwhelming rapaciousness of other wills, it could lose its freedom and independence. But such a failure – a failure in the exercise of the right of exclusion – could happen with regard to any owned things. Extortion and theft and vandalism could indeed occur. In short, though a person's will could successfully be invaded and overpowered, the same was true of all material goods in which a person had rights of property.

Before we leave the second unwarranted criticism of Locke, we should reflect here on its doubts about the owning of actions. As was earlier suggested, the target of these misplaced doubts is Locke's assertion that "[t]he *Labour* of [a man's] Body, and the *Work* of his Hands, we may say, are properly his" (TTG, II, §27, emphasis in original). Now, in concert with the critics of Locke, we heartily can affirm that references to the ownership of one's actions are often ill-advised and misleading, and that such references should therefore often be dropped in favor of references to the ownership of one's broad capacity for productive exploits. In the Marxist idiom, we frequently should advert to the ownership of one's labor-power and not to the ownership of one's labor. On the other hand, this partial concession offers very meager assistance to the analysts who deride all talk about the ownership of oneself. Not simply is the concession just a partial concession, but it lacks any bearing on the problem of the ownership of oneself.

To make the above concession – to agree that we often should refer to the ownership of capacities or abilities rather than to the ownership of activities[7] – is not to say that all references to the ownership of activities are wrong in a flagrant manner. Consider the following scenario. A person *M* and his comrades choose to pay a substantial fee for a renowned poet to deliver a reading of her works in their presence. The poet accedes to their request, and performs quite brilliantly in return for their payment. Unquestionably, one way to view the reading of poetry is to see it as a rental of the poet's capacities by *M* and his chums. Such a description is indeed highly persuasive and may very well be the best account of the whole transaction. But far from thoroughly inadmissible is the view that *M* and his comrades gain proprietary rights in some of the poet's acts (the set of acts involved in her reading, obviously). According to this interpretation, the paid-out money has bought her reading of poetry itself as a marketable performance, instead of having rented her ability to produce the reading. *M* and his chums have purchased a stretch of conduct, in largely the same fashion that they might purchase food at a restaurant. Just as the title to the food at the restaurant will have lodged in them whenever they pay therefor, the rights in the poet's reading will have attached to them whenever the poet indicates her acceptance of their offer. The ephemerality of the poet's performance is entirely consistent with the performance's being owned, much as the ephemerality of the food at the restaurant is wholly consistent with the food's being owned. When *M* and his comrades pay the bill for their food, the title will have passed to them – whether they have eaten the food before they present their money, or whether they devour the food immediately thereafter, or whether they decide to bring the food home with them for consumption by themselves and their pets. Similarly, the rights in the poet's reading will have passed to the buyers when the poet accepts their offer; the fact that her recitation will have forever disappeared after being performed is not a whit more disturbing in the current context than is the disappearance of the restaurant's victuals after being consumed.

This characterization of the poet's performance and the events surrounding her performance – the characterization of the performance as an activity that is bought, rather than as a product of capabilities that are

[7] Here and everywhere else, I use "abilities" (or "ability") as a term interchangeable with "capacities" (or "capacity"). No attempt is made to narrow the former term by applying it to only those capacities that have been developed or cultivated.

rented – is hardly indisputable. As I have stated, the transaction between the poet and her admirers can perhaps more fittingly be viewed as a transaction of rental than as a transaction of purchase. Nevertheless, the view of the transaction as an instance of purchasing is far from unintelligible or foolish. Moreover, that view can bear *mutatis mutandis* on a wide range of services, from hair cuts to operatic performances. When a particular service is discrete and clearly defined (rather than continuous and somewhat free-floating), a payment for the provision of it can be classified readily as a buying of the service itself. Such a classification yields no decisive advantages that effectively debar anyone from viewing the payment as a rental of the ability to supply the service; but neither are there any conclusive disadvantages to be suffered.

Yet let us grant, for the sake of argument, that all references to people's ownership of activities are wrong. Let us assume that we should always refer instead to the ownership of capacities or abilities. Such a concession lends not the slightest aid to scholars who ridicule the idea of self-ownership. After all, if we cannot rightly speak about the ownership of actions, then we never can rightly speak about the ownership by *A* of *B*'s actions, any more than we can correctly speak about the ownership by *A* of *A*'s actions. In other words, objections to the perceived ownership of conduct lack any specific relevance to debates about the possibility of self-ownership. Challenges to the possibility of reflexive ownership can proceed without impugning the possibility of the ownership of conduct, and challenges to the possibility of the ownership of conduct can well proceed without impugning the possibility of reflexive ownership. Even if someone insists that people's actions in the state of nature were never subject to proprietary dominion, he or she can grant that self-ownership was possible in the sense described here; and even if someone brands as absurd the idea of self-ownership, he or she can grant that actions were sometimes ownable. In short, since a person *Q* could enjoy proprietary possession of her mind and body without owning any of her actions (if her actions were completely unowned by anyone), and since *Q* could enjoy proprietary rights in somebody else's actions without owning herself (if she was not owned at all by anyone), neither a refutation of the principle of self-ownership nor a refutation of the idea of ownable actions is sufficient or necessary for the other.

Let us now move to the third false trail which some critics of Locke have pursued. One of the most recurrent gripes about the labor theory of property is that it overlooks basic aspects of production and life in modern social arrangements (and indeed in nearly all social arrangements). This reproof can emerge in several key forms. One allegation is that the labor theory of property fails to do justice to the social embeddedness of work. Not only do countless people labor in groups to fashion products that are thus not ascribable to any one person, but the persons themselves are molded crucially by collective practices in myriad ways. Through education and through many other varieties of social intercourse, human beings emerge as human beings. Likewise, almost all the tools and machines that human agents employ in their productive enterprises are manufactured collectively. And those enterprises always have to draw upon background services such as fire protection and law enforcement and transportation networks. Fanciful and irrelevant, then, is the labor theory of property – a theory which presumes that individuals are solely responsible for their exploits and talents and achievements.

Another main target of this third false objection is the paucity of resources that are left in common to be appropriated. In almost any developed nation, the vast majority of desirable things belong to private or public owners. Even the assets that remain in common to some extent – most significantly the air that everyone breathes – are regulated by governments at numerous levels. Locke's theory of property hence seems wildly inadequate, for it takes as given the availableness of natural wealth. If an industrious human being cannot get access to common raw materials (materials that belong to no one), he can hardly exert his power to enclose such materials under his dominion through labor; yet access to common raw materials has almost completely disappeared in advanced societies. The Lockean recipe for procuring ownership therefore appears again to be ridiculously beside the point, when judged against harsh truths of our modern age.

Closely connected to the unavailableness of ample resources are the marked inequalities among persons in their economic and social ranks. Whereas the Lockean picture of humanity's natural state implies that persons within that state were blessed with equal freedom to use their labor as they saw fit – a type of equality, to be sure, which did not entail equality in the holding of material goods – the circumstances of any civilization are circumstances of hierarchy and straitened freedom. Because almost every valuable thing is owned, and because the distribution of the valuable things is far from egalitarian, some persons have very narrow leeway to choose how they should expend their toil. Some human agents own scarcely anything besides themselves and their personal talents; they must earn their bread by working for individuals or corporations with rights of property in essential goods and capital. To a considerable extent, these toilers cannot determine how they should work or what the proper remuneration is to be for their work. They generally have to do whatever they are told by their bosses, and they generally have to take whatever they can get for their wages. In contrast with the halcyon state of nature as depicted by Locke, where everyone retained extensive control over the disposition of her capacities and over the recompense to which the exerting of those capacities would lead,[8] the prevailing social orders in nearly all times and places have restricted the opportunities for such control by the members of the toiling classes. Indeed, even the members of the *middle* classes enjoy far less control over their lives and earnings than the Lockean perspective might seem to suggest. To our modern era, replete with human agents of sharply cabined autonomy and discretion, the labor theory of ownership appears to have very little to say.

Each of these variants of the third fallacious objection is largely wrong and wholly inapposite. In the initial variant, the objection errs by assuming that the labor theory of property cannot take account of the interpersonal formation of things and human beings. At least in principle the Lockean theory can provide for the collective shaping of skills and goods, by insisting only that everyone should garner rewards in line with what he or she has contributed to societal welfare through the employment of his or her productive capacities. (For the assessment of contributions, many factors – factors such as the length of time spent on work, the amount of energy devoted thereto, the proficiency of one's labors, the value of the created goods, and the risks that one has borne – can all be of relevance.) Elaborated along these lines, the theory still can affirm that people own what they have produced. But now it also more sophisticatedly will avouch that, in circumstances of collective production, the achievements of everybody have to be understood as shares of an enterprise's overall output rather than as specific items or parts of items.

Complaints about the present-day absence of goods in common, and about the present-day hierarchies of wealth and strength, have also erred by charging the labor theory of ownership with an inability to account for settings that it indeed accommodates pretty well. In advanced societies, with little or nothing left any more in common for everybody's taking, the distribution of wealth can run along exactly the course which the labor theory of property envisages. Any person who owns some capital or some goods in modern times has amassed those things by removing them from their common state via labor, or by acquiring them – perhaps through multitudinous intermediaries – from someone else who took things out of their common state. Of course, theft is one chief means by which goods and capital can move to a particular person from another. To the degree

[8] Throughout the last three chapters of my book, in line with Locke's own patterns of usage, I employ "disposition" and "dispose" and "disposal" with a broader sweep than is sometimes characteristic of those terms. Those cognate words here extend not merely to one's power of reassignment or conveyance or transfer, but likewise to one's general control over the standing and the functions of any asset. Someone authorized to determine the "disposition" of any assets is someone authorized to elect the basic roles that the assets are to perform. (For Locke's own pattern of usage, see TTG, II, §§4, 190, 194.)

that anyone's current holdings have stemmed from the infringement of anyone else's rights, the holdings cannot deserve the countenance of the labor theory of property. In fact, that theory must call for the negation or correction of any holdings based upon wrongful transfers, to the largest extent feasible. But holdings unsullied by direct or indirect pillaging are in tune with the prescripts of the labor theory of property.

Albeit any such holdings may fail to leave "enough, and as good . . . in common for others" (TTG, II, §27), and albeit such holdings therefore may eliminate opportunities for subsequent people to extract riches from the bosom of Nature for themselves, the holdings are still acceptable – if they have avoided any infractions of the Deity's cardinal law, which requires the comfort and preservation of everybody as far as possible. Precisely which conditions or circumstances have to obtain for the avoidance of such infractions is an abiding and contentious query in the disputes surrounding neo-Lockeanism. Yet, while virtually unanimous agreement on the specifics of a germane proviso is scarcely reachable, the labor theory of ownership can invoke the general standard of a preservation- and comfort-guaranteeing proviso all the same. Existent holdings which satisfy the demands of the proviso, and which have not been tainted by past or present wrongs, can receive the stamp of approval from the Lockean theory. In sum, the labor theory of property does indeed amount to a touchstone for evaluating and analyzing the modern schemes of proprietary possession, insofar as it amounts to a touchstone at all. It affords a criterion for separating legitimate from illegitimate holdings, and it explains why people cannot get holdings any longer by certain paths.

Here the critics of Locke may reply that their assaults on the apparent irrelevance of the labor theory of ownership have not been aimed at the inability of the theory to account in the broadest terms for the fundaments of our present holdings. Rather, they have aimed at the inability of the theory to describe in moderately specific terms the routes by which holdings have evolved since the advent of any complex societies (and the routes by which holdings should evolve now). Though such a response is fair enough on its own, it highlights the irrelevance of the critics' attacks much more than the irrelevance of Locke's theory. After all, Locke repeatedly underscored the limited application and usefulness of his theory. Time and again he emphasized the distinction between humanity's state of nature and humanity's civilized regimes.

Locke observed, for example, that his labor theory of ownership set forth the "original Law of Nature for the *beginning of Property*," and he remarked intentionally by contrast that "the Civiliz'd part of Mankind . . . have made and multiplied positive Laws to determine Property" (TTG, II, §30, emphasis in original). In a like vein, he pointed out the gap between the set of highly restrictive rules for taking from the commons "in *England*, or any other Country, where there is Plenty of People under Government, who have Money and Commerce," and the set of much more relaxed rules "in the beginning and first peopling of the great Common of the World" (TTG, II, §35, emphasis in original). Similarly, Locke realized that although "*Labour*, in the Beginning, *gave a Right of Property*, where-ever any one was pleased to imploy it," the emergence of social frameworks involved a more complicated approach to distribution:

> [A]fterwards, in some parts of the World, (where the Increase of People and Stock, with the *Use of Money*) had made Land scarce, and so of some Value, the several *Communities* settled the Bounds of their distinct Territories, and by Laws within themselves, regulated the Properties of the private Men of their Society, and so, *by Compact* and Agreement, *settled the Property* which Labour and Industry began. (TTG, II, §45, emphasis in original)

In these and other passages, Locke proclaimed the very point which his critics fault him for having overlooked. He explicitly intended his theory to be etiological or foundational rather than directly pertinent to the modern arrangements for the creation and exercise of proprietary dominion.

None of this is to say, of course, that no connection exists between the rights of property earned in the state of nature and the rights of property that should prevail in subsequent times. As will later be discussed, the rights that Locke sought to justify with his labor theory of ownership would bear (in some important respects) upon the entitlements that people deserve now. Originary gains and prerogatives would not disappear or lose all their force in the transition from the state of nature to more advanced and organized schemes of life. Yet, as Locke often stressed, the rules and specific bounds of property would unavoidably change on quite a number of fronts. Radical metamorphoses would not occur, but notable alterations would. Because of such alterations, the rules determining ownership in humankind's natural state would be partly irrelevant – though far from wholly irrelevant – to any determination of rights thereafter. This partial irrelevance Locke acknowledged gladly indeed; to highlight such irrelevance undeceivingly or accusingly is hence to push at an open door.

Fourth, and most sophisticated, among the false trails of animadversions on Locke is the frequent jeering at his statements that a worker "mixed" or "annexed" or "joined" her labor with raw materials when she worked.[9] Critics retort that sundry kinds of labor would not involve any

[9] I especially have in mind here Jeremy Waldron, "Two worries about mixing one's labour," 33 *Philosophical Quarterly* 37 (1983); Waldron, *Private Property*, at 184–91. (I am distancing myself from only some aspects of Waldron's worries about "mixing." Other aspects of his remarks on this topic strike me as perfectly sound.) For a highly sophisticated defense of Locke's notion of "mixing" – amounting to a re-elaboration thereof – see A. John Simmons, *The Lockean Theory of Rights* (Princeton: Princeton University Press, 1992), 265–77.

physical transmutations that are normally regarded as "annexing" or "mixing." Suppose, for example, that a person retrieved a walnut from the ground and put it into a nearby shed that was used for storing walnuts (and other lasting foodstuffs, perhaps). Such an action or set of actions would doubtless qualify as an instance of labor, but would hardly result in any transformative occurrences that can credibly be described as "mixing" or "annexing" or "joining." This basic point emerges even more clearly in the following example. Suppose that a person built his hut in proximity to a massive oak, which would furnish ample shade and which would also lend some protection from the wind and from storms. Thitherto, the oak and all the constituents of the hut had gone unpossessed by anyone. While the erection of the hut certainly would count as labor that engendered proprietary rights in the hut itself, it might well count also as an instance of labor that engendered proprietary rights in the oak. Surely, however, no one will profess that the untouched tree was mixed with the hut-builder's labor, in any usual senses of the word "mixing."

Now, on the one hand, terms like "mixing" and "joining" and "annexing" are scarcely optimal as tags for the interchange between human labor and natural assets. Those words are especially inapposite if we hold that Locke was adverting to activities, rather than to capacities or energy, when he wrote about the labor that joined or mixed with the raw materials. On the other hand, the Lockean words present no insurmountable difficulties when we interpret them as some colorful though misleading ways of describing the transformations rendered in natural bounty by human toil. When human labor mixed or joined itself with the world's materials, it altered them by employing them for the satisfaction of needs and desires. Generally, the alterations occurred through outright adjustments in the shape or composition or whereabouts of the very assets which someone thus was using for the direct fulfillment of certain wants. Sometimes the alterations occurred instead through adjustments in the environs of particular assets; although the oak in the example above was not changed in its form or matter or siting, it procured new functions as a consequence of the changes in its surroundings (i.e. as a consequence of the building of the hut). Such alterations, of form or content or position or functioning, were precisely the events to which the Lockean argot of "annexing" and "mixing" referred, at least when understood generously. By and large, then, as here construed, the Lockean words amount to some acceptable shorthand for the deliberate incorporation of useful items into the projects of human beings who were questing for their own survival and comfort.

Nothing in my main challenge to the labor theory of property will depend on a challenge to the much reviled terms of "mixing" and "annexing" and "joining." My critique will invoke those terms without caviling at them. Instead of dwelling upon the infelicitousness of some of Locke's expressions, I devote my scrutiny to the drift or tenor of Locke's arguments. An exposure of fundamental snags in the arguments can achieve greater force if it has exercised some interpretive generosity while proceeding.

The theory undone Having stepped aside from the four false paths which have led some critics of Locke astray, we now are better positioned to discern the true weaknesses in his theory. Let us look again at the crucial paragraph in his argument:

> Though the Earth, and all inferior Creatures be common to all Men, yet every Man has a *Property* in his own *Person*. This no Body has any Right to but himself. The *Labour* of his Body, and the *Work* of his Hands, we may say, are properly his. Whatsoever then he removes out of the State that Nature hath provided, and left it in, he hath mixed his *Labour* with, and joyned to it something that is his own, and thereby makes it his *Property*. It being by him removed from the common state Nature placed it in, it hath by this *labour* something annexed to it, that excludes the common right of other Men. For this *Labour* being the unquestionable Property of the Labourer, no Man but he can have a right to what that is once joyned to, at least where there is enough, and as good left in common for others. (TTG, II, §27, emphasis in original)

Two brief clarificational remarks are in order. First, given the objectives of the critique that follows, we can refrain from insisting on any single sense of the term "labour." We may assume that Locke was referring to activities or capacities or energy, but we ought to shrink from fixing on any one of those referents to the exclusion of the others. Second, in line with what was earlier noted, we should hardly blame Locke for using his moral/legal idiom with far less exactitude than is now achievable in the wake of Hohfeld. Clearly, when Locke affirmed that "no Body ha[d] any Right to [a man's own person] but [the man] himself," he meant that no one had a right *or* a privilege in regard to anybody else's person. Likewise, when he announced that labor spent on a natural asset "excludes the common right of other men," he was obviously using "right" in a fashion that embraced privileges as well as true rights. Much the same can be said for the contention that "no Man but [a laborer himself] can have a right to what [his own labor] is once joyned to." In other words, we should interpret Locke's pronouncements as constituting a labor theory of *property*. We should not weaken his arguments smugly and gratuitously by holding them to criteria of semantic precision which they never ventured to meet.

Now, we of course shall grant that each human being in the natural epoch retained exclusive rights and exclusive privileges in relation to his own body's labor. Such a premise, alas, does not support the conclusion drawn by Locke; indeed, the very role of the premise as a premise is what debars it from giving support to the Lockean position. Locke's premise fails to authorize his conclusion, exactly because of the line of reasoning that connects the two.

Although we cannot be sure whether Locke used "labour" to advert to actions rather than to energy or capacities, we can say with confidence that he wielded the term in one or more of those ways. That to which everyone in the state of nature had a right was her own ability as a worker or her own activity as a worker or the energy she applied to her work. Each of these things would lie in each human agent as a potential or as a component or as a set of dynamic states. When labor operated qua ability or force or activity, it interacted with the world by changing various objects therein. (Any particular change in the natural materials might be exceedingly small – perhaps amounting to a slight adjustment in their location, for example.) Locke referred to the interaction of labor with raw materials as "mixing," and referred to the changes in the relevant objects as the "joining" of labor with the objects. Transformed by a human agent's exertions, a particular item thus had "something annexed to it, that excludes the common right [and privilege] of other Men." Alterations that Marxists tend to describe as the "materializing" of labor were described by Locke as "annexing" and "joining."

Locke astutely chose his expressions. To maintain that modified riches had been "annexed" to labor or "joined" with labor was to imply quite firmly that the labor had kept its posture and its identity throughout its productions. In reality, however, the terms of Locke's argument cannot but express the gaps they try to efface; and the reason that those terms cannot but express those gaps is precisely that the terms are terms of an argument. Labor qua energy or process or ability must always remain detachable from labor qua effected improvement. The labor emerging through the initiatives of the subject must forever remain detachable from the labor concretized in the object. If we wished, we could here advert to the practices of our legal institutions and economic institutions, where the disjoinability of these modes of labor is acknowledged in any number of ways. But, for purposes of the current critique, we probably are better advised to go instead through Locke's reasoning more closely than ever. Specifically, we should note that the reasoning does in fact amount to a line of reasoning.

In the crucial paragraph above from the *Second Treatise*, Locke began with a declaration that every human being in the state of nature had "a *Property* in . . . [t]he *Labour* of his Body, and the *Work* of his Hands." Locke then explained that somebody who improved an unowned item through work "hath mixed his *Labour* with [it], and joyned to it something that is his own." Straightaway, Locke delivered his encouraging verdict that the toiler "thereby makes [the improved item] his *Property*." Locke next attempted to underline his view of the interaction between labor and raw materials, and to reaffirm his conclusion, when he wrote that any worked-upon object "being by [the laborer] removed from the common state Nature placed it in, it hath by this *labour* something annexed to it, that excludes the common right of other Men." Finally, he recapitulated his argument – his premise about self-ownership, his premise about the joining of labor to materials, and his inference about the ownership of materials – in a ringing assertion: "For this *Labour* being the unquestionable Property of the Labourer, no Man but he can have a right to what that is once joyned to."

As we have just seen, Locke began by positing that anyone's labor qua activity or ability or energy belonged exclusively to the man or woman who labored. This postulate was the premise about self-ownership which we here have presupposed for the sake of discussion. Locke did not begin with an underived principle to the effect that labor qua accomplished improvements in raw materials belonged exclusively to the specific person whose toil had brought about the improvements. Had Locke opened with such a principle, he would not have needed to devise an argument which would issue in that principle as a demonstrated conclusion. He would have flatly insisted that any labor qua achieved enhancement in unowned resources should lie in the exclusive possession of the man or woman responsible for the enhancement. And he hence would not have derived such proprietary dominion – the proprietary dominion over the achieved enhancement – from the ownership of one's labor-qua-capacity-or-activity-or-drive. Instead of having been *founded* thereon, the ownership of one's labor-qua-realized-enhancement would be flatly *equivalent* to the ownership of one's labor-qua-capacity-or-activity-or-force, or otherwise would be logically *parallel* thereto. (Of course, Locke would still have had to explain why an entire asset, as opposed to just the change in the asset, should belong to the toiler who had produced the change; but he could have slyly skirted this problem, had he contended that such a pattern of ownership was an axiomatic ground of his theory.)

Locke did in fact submit an argument, with the premises and the verdict described above. From his employment of the term "thereby" when he stated that somebody who worked on a natural asset would "thereby make . . . it his *Property*," we indeed can tell that he was drawing an inference. And from the final statement in his key paragraph, as well as from the rest of that paragraph, we can verify that he derived the ownership of one's labor-qua-effected-improvement from the ownership of one's labor-qua-activity-or-ability-or-energy. The labor that would exist as the "unquestionable Property" of each human being was her labor qua activity or ability or force, which then served to ground the ownership of her labor-qua-effected-transformation because "no [one] but [the laborer] can have a right to what [labor qua activity or capacity or force] is once joyned to." In sum, the proprietary possession of the labor concretized in the object would ensue from the proprietary possession of the labor that carried on through the initiatives of the subject. Between these two aspects of labor ran the process of "joining" – the joining of any human subject's labor to the materials in which the labor thus became concretized. As a bridge and an intervention between the two modes of labor, that process would undo any efforts to equate those modes.

In Locke's discussion, then, his thesis about the joining of labor to materials was the wedge that would prise open the gap of nonidentity between his initial thesis about the ownership of labor-qua-potential-or-act-or-drive and his conclusion about the ownership of labor-qua-achieved-transformation-of-goods. In other words, the thesis about "joining" was what made his discussion into a full-fledged argument (a philosophically interesting argument), and was therefore what would block his discussion from confirming the sheer identity between the labor within the subject and the labor within the object. If those two types of labor had indeed been flatly identical, Locke's argument would have been both needless and devoid of significance. Yet, because Locke advanced his argument and so recognized the need for it – an argument not empty and pleonastic, but suitably meaningful and endowed with content – we can rightly observe that he committed himself to holding that the labor within the subject and the labor within the object were not identical. And, given that his argument had to be invalid unless those two kinds of labor were identical, he thus committed himself to holding that the conclusion of his argument was unwarranted. By apprehending the unforgoability of his argument as a link between his initial tenet and his desired verdict, and by consequently engaging in the argument, he could not help revealing its unsupportableness and speciousness. To propound his line of reasoning was perforce to invalidate it.

Let us recapitulate this critique in a slightly more formal manner. Locke began in effect with the following premise:

1. In the state of nature, the labor of each person *P* belonged exclusively to *P* himself.

In this initial premise, the referent of "labor" is the labor within the subject – i.e. labor as an activity or a capacity or a flow of energy. Locke then added the following premise:

2. Each person *P* who improved some unowned assets by working on them had thereby mixed his labor with them.

Once again, the referent of "labor" is the labor within the subject. Locke then drew his renowned inference:

3. In the state of nature, the labor of each person *P* belonged exclusively to *P* himself.

In this conclusion, the referent of "labor" is the labor within the object – i.e., the transformed state of the worked-upon assets that was brought about by *P*. If "labor" here referred to the same thing as "labor" in the first premise, then that opening premise and the ultimate inference of Locke's argument would be wholly indistinguishable.[10] In that event, there would have been no need whatsoever for Locke to construct an argument. By recognizing that he did have to construct an argument to justify his conclusion, Locke confirmed that the labor singled out by his initial premise was not identical to the labor singled out by his eventual inference. He thus unwittingly confirmed that his argument was invalid; after all, the argument could not be valid unless the two kinds of labor were identical, since their separateness would leave room for the possibility that various true statements about one kind of labor were false when advanced about the other kind. In sum, Locke's very putting forth of an argument ensured that its conclusion was unsustained.

[10] Consider the difference between Locke's argument and the following argument: (1) All men are mortal. (2) Socrates is a man. (3) Therefore, Socrates is mortal. In this shopworn syllogism, the word "mortal" in the major premise bears precisely the same meaning as the word "mortal" in the conclusion, without rendering the conclusion a simple restatement of the major premise. We cannot say the same about the word "labor" in the two relevant steps of Locke's argument.

5 Once more unto the breach

Our critical investigation of Locke's theory of property has uncovered the failure of his theory to justify its conclusions. Although his attempt to reach those conclusions had to rely on the full equivalence of labor within the subject and labor within the object, the very undertaking of the attempt showed that any such equivalence was strictly disallowed. Severed by a process of "joining," which Locke's articulation of his theory inevitably highlighted, the active labor proceeding from the subject and the expended labor bestowed upon the object could never be reduced to each other. The *Second Treatise*'s argument, which had to collapse those modes of labor into a single phenomenon, tried to establish their identity by appealing to a premise that underscored their distinctness (i.e. a premise about the joining of active labor to raw materials).

Nonetheless, even if Locke's endeavor to justify his theory of ownership has foundered, his champions may seek to salvage his theory with some different routes of justification. We now shall explore the cardinal routes of justification that indeed have been broached. As will become apparent, none of those routes can fare any better than the justification that was marshaled by Locke himself. After having confuted the attempts to redeem Locke's theory, we shall probe the worrisome implications of the theory's undoing.

Ownership shall make you free?

One common tack for justifying anew the conclusions of the labor theory of property is to maintain that the theory's distributive guidelines had to be followed as the essential means of doing justice to the self-ownership of each human being in the state of nature. According to a bold version of this defense, a seizure by person *Q* of goods made by person *R* would entail the thralldom of *R*, albeit a temporary thralldom. Such a seizure would compel *R* to toil for *Q* rather than for himself. It would thus deprive *R* of his basic freedom to employ his capacities for production as he saw fit. Any such rapine would infringe the self-ownership of *R* and would violate his natural equality with *Q* (and everyone else).

A milder version of this approach does not construe plunder as temporary enslavement, but insists that proprietary rights were apposite consequences of fruitful toil in the state of nature because such rights served the profounder right of each human being to self-direction. Had people lacked full dominion over the things which they themselves had produced, they could not have planned their lives with any assurance. Everyone's long-term projects would have been persistently at the mercy of his fellows, and even his short-term projects would have met with grave dangers frequently. No one could have had much confidence concerning his own latitude to determine how and when his productive capabilities should be plied. Had each person's belongings lain open to be snatched and looted by everybody else, no one could have harbored many firm expectations in regard to the free disposal of his own belongings. And since the free disposal of one's possessions was prerequisite to the free disposal of oneself, any general failure to reward productivity with rights would have precluded meaningful self-determination. Such a failure would thus have jarred with the natural entitlements of all human beings "to order their Actions, and dispose of their Possessions, and Persons as they think fit, within the bounds of the Law of Nature, without asking leave, or depending upon the Will of any other Man" (TTG, II, §4).

The bold apology countered

Let us deal first with the bold response. Theorists who describe pillaging as the temporary enslavement of the dispossessed person(s) have committed some of the errors highlighted at various other points in this book, and have committed further missteps as well. We straightaway should note the unwiseness of attacking plunder as an infringement of equality rather than as a mere infringement of self-determination and liberty. If no one attained proprietary prerogatives in the state of nature, then no one had a right against anybody else's seizing of assets. Everybody of course retained a *privilege* to obstruct such seizures, but no one held a right that would be transgressed by other people's marauding. Hence, the plundering by *Q* of goods made by *R* was nothing more than a path of permissible conduct open to everyone. Although *Q* was privileged to despoil *R* of the things which *R* had produced, *R* was likewise privileged to despoil *Q* of the things which *Q* had created. A privilege-to-maraud attached to everybody alike, and thus the use of that privilege did not contravene the prevailing scheme of formal equality. Anyone who chose to act on that privilege was merely doing what everybody else was perfectly free to do. Any person *R* when deprived of fruits of his toil would clearly suffer a partial loss of his ability to determine his own future, but the equality of his stature *vis-à-vis* his fellows would remain unimpaired. (Of course, the formal equality of a situation structured by privileges without concrete rights would tend to promote substantive inequalities. Strong and dexterous and crafty people would almost surely fend for themselves better in a context of privileges-without-rights than would maladroit and weak and slow-witted people. But the criterion of formal equality is the proper focus of our attention here. After all, as has more than once been observed, the network of equal rights and privileges in Locke's state of nature would yield a strictly formal equality that allowed a host of substantive inequalities to obtain [TTG, II, §54]. If Locke could stress the *equality* of formal equality while thereby playing down the manifest inequalities of the ever substantive world, the argument herein replying to Locke's defenders can do the same in very good faith indeed.)

Another weakness in the heavy-handed defense of Locke is that it fails to explain why everyone in the state of nature would own exactly the set of goods on which he or she had worked. We lack grounds for presuming that the initial rights of each person over external goods would cover all of his or her products and only those products. If the need to endow people with rights of property arose from the objective of giving each person *P* the benefits yielded by his work, that need could readily be fulfilled by conferring on *P* a batch of goods which were made by some other person(s) but which were as valuable as the goods that *P* himself had created. Once we partly shift our focus from the standing or nature of particular items to the role of those items in ensuring some desirable consequences, we leave room for the substitution of other items that would bring about the same consequences.

Suppose that two people in the state of nature, *Q* and *R*, created similar goods of similar quality while working close to each other. If we try to vindicate rights of ownership by contending that they helped to guarantee that each person would get the sustenance for which she had successfully labored, then we have to remain indifferent between the following outcomes: (1) *R* enjoyed ownership of the things created by *Q*, and *Q* enjoyed ownership of the things created by *R*; (2) *R* enjoyed ownership of the things created by *R* herself, and *Q* enjoyed ownership of the things created by *Q* herself. We shall likewise have to remain indifferent between those outcomes and any blend of those outcomes. (A blend along these lines would involve *R*'s ownership of some of the varied goods created by *Q*, and also *Q*'s ownership of some of the varied goods created by *R*. Such a state of affairs would be entirely fitting as well in circumstances where only some of *R*'s productions and some of *Q*'s productions were interchangeable.) Having recommended the labor theory of property as a theory designed to guard against servitude, the bold defense of Locke has unfastened the conceptual/moral tie between the laborer and the products of her own labor. In other words, the defense of Locke has disconnected the tie that Locke so gamely aspired to knot.

Thus far, the mistakes in the incautious defense of Locke are akin to some blunders which my previous chapters have addressed in other contexts. More serious is an error hitherto unexplored. What the bold champions of Locke maintain is that violent seizures of anybody's possessions in the state of nature would amount to the temporary infliction of servitude on the dispossessed man or woman; those seizures would force the victim to carry out his toil for the culprits rather than for himself. Here, however, the supporters of Locke have failed to note a crucial divide. To take advantage of somebody's accomplishments, through predation, is not the same as steering somebody's present and future actions.

A plunderer's ravaging extends to what has been done and made already; a slavedriver's commands relate to what must be done and made at present (and in the future). A free human being in the state of nature who was the victim of spoliation had not been forced to undertake the exertions that gave rise to the pillaged goods. Although plunder deprived the victim of the opportunity to dispose of any assets that the raider had seized, it did not compel him to produce the lost assets in the first place. Robbed of the ability to dispose of the captured goods thenceforward, the victim nonetheless had had leeway to dispose of his productive energies as he wanted when creating the looted goods in the past. So long as the victim retained his independence, he retained his freedom to dispose of his productive capacities.

Anybody in servitude, on the other hand, not merely lacked control over the disposition of the things he had shaped, but also lacked control over the disposition of the productive energies that he employed when shaping those things. Unlike the free person who was victimized by a foray after having expended his or her labor discretionarily, a slave would have to submit to external instructions and demands from the outset. A slave could indeed be said to work unwillingly for somebody else, because he had to do as his owner pleased from the start to the finish. To be sure, he would tend to have very little say in deciding what should be done with his products – a state of powerlessness he shared with the free victim of depredations – but he would likewise tend to have very little say in deciding what should be done with his own laboring capacities.

Thus, if we ignore the other flaws in the heavy-handed defense of the labor theory of ownership, we still must reject its underlying analogy between enslavement and looting. An eventual loss of some goods on which one has freely worked is quite distinguishable from any wholesale loss of one's latitude to work freely. A precept affirming the right-protected freedom of everyone in the state of nature to elect the uses of his or her laboring capacities – a precept that is understood here as an insistence on the need to prevent bondage – would therefore not have weighed at all against the perpetration of looting. Somebody unenslaved whose products were pillaged had experienced no curtailment of his freedom to orient his own faculties for toil in whatever ways he thought best. Depredations had not obliged the victim to produce anything; nor had they debarred him from any type of production or activity in the future.

Here, however, the devotees of Locke may adduce a seeming counterexample. Suppose that a victim of marauding found that certain assets were far less likely to be despoiled than were various other assets. (Maybe the safer things were less desirable to the lurking plunderers, or perhaps they were easier to protect.) Although the victim did not relish the more secure creations as much as the less secure things, she chose to expend her energies on them in the hope of keeping most of the items which she had made. That is, she channeled her labor into routes adopted not on the basis of her personal predilections, but in response to threats of forcible seizures. Would this channeling effectively operate as a mode of subjugation whereby the victim had surrendered her freedom to elect her own pursuits?

We should here reply in the negative, for two reasons. First, the comparison between the victim's maneuvers and the obedience of a slave does not withstand close investigation. Second, even if we temporarily grant that the comparison works as far as it is supposed to go, it does not go far enough to salvage the strong defense of Locke.

Some elements of the victim's reactions to marauding were possible in a situation of outright servitude but were far from probable; and one key element of those reactions would not occur at all in the situation of bondage. To a much greater degree than a typical slave, the person whose goods were pillaged would retain discretion to choose among a number of options for the plying of her productive faculties. Though sometimes masters might extend to their slaves a bit of leeway in choosing the appropriate means and ends of production, they would almost always decline to gird their slaves with the breadth of discretion still enjoyed by the victim of the marauding. Likewise, the threat of rapine to which the victim responded by adjusting the course of her behavior was less immediate and certain than the punishments usually inflicted on recalcitrant slaves. Pillage could loom of course as a highly pressing danger indeed, but generally it would stay more remote and indistinct and confined than the severe disciplinary actions which a slaveholder would stand ready to take against an unruly bondsman. In addition, the worker trying to outsmart ransackers would usually enjoy a much more plentiful range of opportunities to protect herself than would a slave in fending off punishments for contumacy. Servile revolts could happen, but the harsh constraints imposed on people in bondage would tend to cause submission – however grudging – to be the far more frequent route of servile behavior. Someone warding off pillagers, on the other hand, would normally have more space and resources to devise new means of "revolt" (that is, new means of security for her handicraft).

Even more important here is the prime respect in which the analogy between plunder and servitude breaks down altogether. Though a slave who complied with the demands of his owner might ipso facto spare himself any penalties, he did not ipso facto endow himself with any entitlement to his products or any control over them. Everything belonged to his owner, as a matter of right and as a matter of fact. A free person who staved off plunder, by contrast, would indeed retain an entitlement to her output and furthermore would retain actual control over it. She constantly held a privilege to keep all the items that she had made, as she did not work for any master who bore a right to the control of her products; and, if her efforts to avoid rapine proved successful, she herself was then able to decide how her goods ought to be disposed. When a raider seized her things, he did so not because the things had accrued to him by right, but because he thereby exerted a privilege – namely, the privilege to take those things – which was held, ex hypothesi, by him and her and every one of their fellows. Whereas a slave who sought to dispose of any goods that he fashioned would thereby flout his owner's rights, an unenslaved worker who disposed of any goods that *she* fashioned would not thereby violate the rights of potential plunderers or anyone else.

In sum, pillage arising from the absence of rights of ownership in the state of nature would not bring about the subjugation of victims by predators, even if the victims changed the patterns of their production to enhance the security of the fruits of their labor. But suppose for the moment that the correspondences between looting and enslavement were undiminished by the problems reviewed thus far. Even so, the analogy between the two cannot serve the purpose for which the defenders of Locke cite it. The analogy does not rescue the labor theory of ownership, because its two compared elements – looting and enslavement – do not reach widely enough. Fundamental limits had to prevail in any Lockean state of nature, and those limits must belie all pronouncements that concrete rights of ownership were the indispensable guardians of personal autonomy and integrity.

As was discussed earlier, a state of nature earmarked by privileges without concrete rights would be governed still by the abstract right of each human being to self-sustainment. No one would bear specific rights to specific assets, but everyone would retain the general right against being prevented from questing for his own survival. Thus, while specific raids on specific holdings might generally be allowable exercises of privileges, they became impermissible when they clearly jeopardized the life and basic well-being of any person who was their target. No one had a right to be altogether free from despoliation, but every victim enjoyed a right to be free from seizures so extensive and chronic that they posed an acute threat to his ability to survive. While a person *B* owed no stable and concrete duties to shrink from snatching the goods of any person *A*, he owed *A* the general duty to refrain from imperiling *A*'s life; and, in circumstances where *A*'s possessions had been plundered repeatedly and exhaustively, *A*'s overall right to basic welfare would turn *B*'s privilege-to-snatch-*A*'s-goods into an obligation-to-shrink-from-snatching-*A*'s-goods-at-present.

Thus, even in a state of nature containing no particular rights of ownership, everyone always held a general right against being thwarted by other people in the satisfaction of his basic needs. No one could justly be despoiled of his assets, if the marauding then would leave him unable to continue his grip on life. Whenever necessary, the sweeping right of each person *C* to self-preservation would suspend the ordinary privilege of each other person to ransack *C*'s goods. In other words, the Lockean state of nature without the institution of private ownership would guarantee the essential human right which Locke so emphatically proclaimed – the essential right of basic security denied to slaves only, in the Lockean scheme of things (TTG, II, §23). A free and well-behaved human being, while inhabiting a Lockean world that excluded private ownership, would retain always his right to fundamental security against attacks on his person and against life-threatening raids on his goods. And therefore, because the lack of that cardinal right was the hallmark of subjugation, a free and well-behaved human being would never undergo legitimate bondage.[1]

Defenders of Locke may answer now that, even if the bare right to

[1] Through a line of reasoning basically akin to that which has figured in the last few paragraphs, we can question Robert Nozick's assertion that "[t]axation of earnings from labor is on a par with forced labor." Robert Nozick, *Anarchy, State, and Utopia* (New York: Basic Books, 1974), 169. As Nozick himself recognizes, the levying of an income tax can be confined to the portions of one's earnings that are "above the amount necessary for basic needs" (ibid.). In light of such a restriction on the applicability of income taxes, however, the comparison of taxation to enslavement loses its pertinence. Indeed, when Nozick proceeds to complain about the tendency of an income-tax system to favor lovers of sunsets over lovers of movies (ibid. at 170), he is presenting an argument that can quite credibly support an extension of income taxes – an extension that would take account of the value of leisure.

self-sustainment would be tolerably protective in the absence of private ownership, a regime of such ownership would procure a greater level of human comfort. That possible line of argument has received a fair amount of attention already in this book, and we shall soon examine it again. Here, however, it is thoroughly out of place. It proceeds with a starkly consequentialist focus on productive efficiency rather than with deontological/consequentialist concerns about slavery; indeed, it puts aside the matter of slavery in order to pursue a quite different point. Proposals for maximizing the welfare of human beings are not at odds with proposals for avoiding subjection, but are plainly distinct therefrom.

The moderate apology countered

Let us now scrutinize the milder defense of Locke, which submits that proprietary rights within the state of nature were prerequisites of each individual's self-direction. We first should notice that this subtler apology exhibits most of the shortcomings that weaken the brasher apology. For example, the milder defense is similarly unable to explain why everyone in the state of nature deserved to own the very items that he or she had made, as opposed to any surrogate items that would yield the same measure of satisfaction. Because the moderate apology, like the bolder apology, has endeavored to vindicate the labor theory of ownership with a partly consequentialist tack, it has duly licensed the substituting of assets for one another on the basis of their apparent efficacy in bringing forth the desired consequences.

Other shortcomings are new. Let us ponder, for instance, another important way in which the milder defense of Locke must fail to account for the specific ties between every person and the fruits of his or her labor. Because the subtle apology reinterprets the labor theory of ownership as a theory aimed at maximizing the room for individuals to dispose of themselves and their productive capacities as they wished, it leaves unexplained why only successful work would garner proprietary prerogatives for the worker(s). If such prerogatives got assigned to people in order to facilitate the self-determination of everyone, then there were ample grounds for rewarding people on the basis of their exertions rather than on the basis of their output.

That is, people who toiled with diligence and care in the state of nature would deserve rights of property over various assets, even if they had few results to show for their pains. Or, at least, they deserved such rights if their failures to produce many goods stemmed from misfortunes that could not reasonably have been anticipated; the merits of their claims would perhaps be far weaker if their unproductiveness had derived from stupid or reckless blunders. Of course, even when dismal productivity ensued from nothing more than bad luck, the claims of luckless people to goods would hardly be incontestable. Nothing in the abstract ideal of "self-determination" could ground an utterly irresistible case for satisfying those claims. Yet, although the reasons in favor of using diligence rather than success as the touchstone for apportioning rights might not be inexorably dispositive, the reasons against that mode of apportionment would not be unanswerable, either.

A luckless person could plausibly maintain that a scheme of ownership would fall far short of advancing everyone's self-determination if it did nothing to reward assiduous human beings whose toil had proved ineffective through no substantial fault of their own. If such people came away with no rights of ownership from their efforts, then they had hardly received encouragement to pursue the worthy projects that they found most attractive (as opposed to the worthy projects that entailed very meager risks). Through mishaps they had been deprived of the fruits of their labor, as severely as people who were divested of the fruits of their toil by raiders. If the ideal of personal self-direction militated against allowing the ravages of plunder to ruin anyone's projects, then it likewise should deal with the ravages of misfortune that could not be averted by an attentive prudence. In other words, people victimized by bad luck could argue poignantly that their own control of their lives would not be meaningfully preserved unless they could share in the sundry goods created by people who had been more fortunate and hence more productive.

Though transfers of goods from lucky people to conscientious but ill-starred people might curtail the self-governance and autonomy of the lucky, their loss could be outweighed by the bolstering of the ill-starred persons' self-governance and autonomy. After all, if sheer industriousness became the central factor for allotting proprietary rights, industrious persons who had managed to succeed in their labors could expect to enjoy dominion over numerous things which they themselves had crafted. Their nonretention of their remaining products would therefore not unduly abridge their self-determination, whereas it could strongly enhance the self-assurance of the otherwise despondent and luckless toilers who acquired those remaining goods.

Far more was here at stake than a right to charity like the right of each human being "to so much out of another's Plenty, as will keep him from extream want, where he has no means to subsist otherwise" (TTG, I, §42). Such a right to charity operated as a departure – a thoroughly principled departure, yet a departure – from the established norms of ownership, which generally pointed to very different considerations. In the present discussion, however, we are looking not at exceptions to the general standards, but at the general standards *tout court*.

If we focus on the self-determination of human beings, we can discern a strong though inconclusive case for a scheme of property that distributed rights entirely with reference to the careful exertions undertaken by people, rather than with reference to the accomplishments yielded by those exertions. Insofar as that strong case prevailed in the state of nature, the fundament of proprietary assignments was earnest diligence as opposed to the fruitfulness of such diligence. Instead of serving as a mere deviation from the touchstone of fruitfulness, the touchstone of diligence would have altogether supplanted it. (Of course, to say that the one criterion would supplant the other is not to overlook the possibility that the two of them would coincide with regard to manifold particular outcomes.)

Thus, if the keystone of distribution in the state of nature was enterprising sedulity, the so-called transfers of products from the lucky to the unfortunate were not transfers at all – if "transfer" indicates a movement of goods away from the titled holder thereof. Within such a scheme of distribution, a creator of useful things would not have any privilege to enjoy the portion of his overall output that belonged to venturesome people whose exertions had chanced to end in failure. Someone who insisted on retaining all her products at any stage would thereby contravene the rights of her ill-starred fellows.

Before we move on to another difficulty, we should briefly note why this latest problem would apply only to industrious people rather than to sluggards as well. If the right to self-determination was the distributional linchpin in the state of nature, why would indolent human beings not receive a share of the goods produced by hardworking people, so that the self-determination of each indolent person would be kept afloat? If lazy men and women could not pursue their inactive tendencies with confidence that they would avoid starving, were not their rights to self-direction unfairly cabined? Would not the slothful have precisely the same entitlements as the venturous to dispose of their own productive abilities as they wanted?

These questions are not as telling as they might initially seem, for they have disregarded the fact that proper self-determination in any Lockean state of nature was always self-determination constrained by the precepts of natural law. Though every person enjoyed a right-shielded privilege to dispose of himself and his capacities in the ways he deemed to be fit, the right and privilege terminated at the point where breaches of natural duties began. And because God "bid Mankind [to] increase and multiply" and had "commanded Man . . . to labour, and . . . to subdue the Earth, i.e. improve it for the benefit of Life" (TTG, I, §41; II, §32), each person had to shoulder a duty to engage in persistent toil. Because everyone "is *bound to preserve himself* and . . . when his own Preservation comes not in competition . . . *to preserve the rest of Mankind*" (TTG, II, §6, emphasis in original), no one had a privilege to adopt an idle and decadent mode of life that would contribute nothing at all to the pursuit of humankind's material sustenance. Everyone bore an obligation to work extensively, as work and nonbelligerence were the only means by which anybody could foster the preservation of himself and his fellows. Hence, idle persons could not warrantedly invoke the right and privilege of self-direction in order to demand a share of the assets that industrious people made. Quite as much as the author of the Second Epistle to the Thessalonians, Locke believed that diligent laborers owed no duties to provide for the well-being of chronic sluggards. As he observed in a famous passage that has previously been quoted herein:

> God gave the World to Men in Common; but since he gave it them for their benefit, and the greatest Conveniencies of Life they were capable to draw from it, it cannot be supposed he meant it should always remain common and uncultivated. He gave it to the use of the Industrious and Rational, (and *Labour* was to be *his Title* to it;) not to the Fancy or Covetousness of the Quarrelsom and Contentious. (TTG, II, §34, emphasis in original)

In short, one's right-shielded privilege of self-determination was one's right-shielded privilege to choose one's patterns of industriousness. One's privilege did not permit a frequent abstention from all industrious projects.

Having noted the limits of the first important new problem that afflicts the milder defense of Locke, we can better apprehend the force of this problem. The norms distilled in Locke's labor theory of ownership, when refocused on individual self-determination, would not bestow approval on accidie but would indeed allow a sweeping shift in the fulcrum for the distribution of wealth – a shift from the factor of successful exertion to the factor of sedulous exertion. Whether the focal point for the distribution of property was the *outcome* of earnest toil or the *undertaking* of earnest toil, the distribution would give due effect to the divine imperative that called for assiduous striving. Hence, if the labor theory of ownership was construed by Locke as aiming to guarantee the self-piloting of individuals, he could not use the rationale of his theory to select either one of the aforementioned bases of distribution in preference to the other.

Even more grave is a second new difficulty. When the subtle defense of Locke extols the principles in the labor theory of property as guidelines for facilitating the self-governance of persons, it overlooks the reciprocality of obligations and rights. We are asked to think that proprietary rights were crucial within the state of nature as guardians of autonomy and free choice. Without proprietary entitlements, the reasoning goes, each human agent would lack confidence in the basic security of her ventures, and so she would feel inhibited from pursuing any number of projects that she would otherwise have elected to carry out. Such a line of reasoning is not flatly wrong, but it is thoroughly one-sided and is therefore deceptive.

When a person *Q* gained proprietary rights in the things on which she had labored, she enhanced her ability to conduct herself as she pleased; but she thereby curbed the prerogatives of her fellows to conduct *themselves* as they pleased. For anybody who would have sought to take advantage of an entitlement to snatch *Q*'s possessions, the endowment of *Q* with proprietary rights to her goods could not but serve as a check on unimpeded self-governance. Connected integrally with *Q*'s autonomy-bracing rights were the autonomy-circumscribing duties which those rights laid on other people. Hence, a tribute to rights of property as the buttresses for individuals' self-direction can just as well take the form of a complaint about rights of property as the barriers to individuals' self-direction.

Defenders of Locke can retort here in several ways. Perhaps they will recall that the right and privilege of self-determination could only extend to the point where natural duties commenced. Beyond that point, the right and privilege would submit to the reign of the duties. Locke's proponents can thus maintain that a route of individual self-direction involving plunder was always to be condemned because it conflicted with the requirements of natural law. At odds with the titles of ownership that people established when they worked, depredations were an activity to be deplored. Far from being *unjustly* overridden by competing avenues of self-governance, a course of despoliation would have clashed with the fundamental imperatives that defined what was just.

This initial response that might be offered, which delegitimates plundering by reference to the established rights which the plundering would invade, has egregiously begged the question. If analysts invoke the ideal of self-determination as their mainstay for justifying the institution of property, they have to explain why toilers who gained proprietary rights to specified assets would be favored above potential looters in their respective claims to full self-determination. Insofar as proprietary dominion was based upon the furthering of self-governance, and insofar as proprietary dominion was only one important mode of self-governance that jarred with some other such modes, people scarcely could be content with pointing to the proprietary dominion as the grounds for resolving any clashes between routes of self-governance. After all, the very questions to be decided here, in light of the overarching value of self-determination, were why and whether the self-determination of the aspirant owners would trump the self-determination of the aspirant pillagers; no one could ever trade on "established" rights of ownership when dealing with those two queries, for the rights could not be established till the answers to those queries were settled.

Supporters of Locke may therefore seek to modify their initial riposte in ways that can avert any flagrant begging of questions. For example, they may re-emphasize the unyielding obligation of industriousness in the state of nature. Everyone's natural right and privilege of self-direction would fail to authorize looting, not because of "established" rights of property in the looted goods, but because acts of looting were inherently unproductive and were perpetrated by loafers who exploited the diligence of their fellows. A life of rapine breached a person's God-imposed duty to engage in efforts that were intended to foster the material well-being of humankind. Barren of productivity, deeds of plunder occurred as desperate corollaries of the sin of idling – rather than as creative ventures that could satisfy the requirement of industrious toiling.

This revised parry does indeed stay away from begging the question crudely, but it founders at any rate. We can begin by observing that banditry was not perforce unproductive. Especially in the state of nature, where markets and highly organized commerce did not develop for quite a long time (until the introduction of money, which greased the wheels of primitive bartering), raids of despoliation could sometimes be the most efficient means of transferring assets to their optimal uses. In addition, the raids could swell the overall output of humanity by inspiring quite a few of the robust victims of despoliation to work more diligently than ever. As I earlier argued, people stripped of their hard-won goods might respond by making even more goods in order to compensate for any loss of their material riches. If the productivity-enhancing effects of plunder outweighed its productivity-retarding effects – if the impulse to achieve and maintain a level of comfort overpowered the disincentives spawned by the likelihood of sometimes failing to reap what one had sowed – then numerous deeds of plunder could serve the goal of output-maximization.

More important, the revised parry assumes that people who undertook marauding would undertake little else. Even if we grant arguendo that the marauding would yield no beneficial results per se, we clearly are not bound to infer that the marauders did nothing beneficial when not engaged in plunder. Nor are we bound to infer that the marauding issued in detrimental results. People who snatched the goods of their fellows could be highly productive and assiduous toilers who performed the looting to supplement their own toil rather than to obviate it. Perhaps such people would want to expand their comforts beyond the level gained by their own fruitful exertions, or perhaps they would seek to overcome the poverty in which they had been left by the fruitlessness of their own exertions (a fruitlessness caused by various misadventures, not by insufficient striving or care). Whatever was the motive or set of motives for the pillaging, the fact that the pillagers indeed carried out true labor would mean that they had followed the natural mandates which required industriousness. The role of a person as a brigand would not exclude his role as a conscientious worker.

But let us now submit arguendo that people who resorted to marauding did not ever perform any productive labor at all. Must we thence conclude that their predatory acts flouted the obligation of industriousness? Here the correct answer is plainly "no," since brigandage itself did not clash with the obligation of industriousness; what did clash with that obligation was the idleness of the brigands. Whenever someone who indulged in looting was idle in various other respects, the idleness rather than the looting was the component of behavior that breached the natural-law requirement concerning diligent work. When the plunderers were not also loafers, they complied with the natural-law requirement very nicely.

Of course, the plunder committed by the generally slothful people allowed them to loaf scandalously, because it furnished them with adequate sustenance. To enable something, however, was decidedly different from necessitating it. Plunder and fruits of plunder could as easily combine with sedulous toil as they could render possible the lethargy that replaced honest toil. Furthermore, just as plunder did not necessarily give rise to loafing, so loafing did not necessarily occasion plunder. Idlers could draw their sustenance from alms instead of relying on the involuntary transfers wrought by predations.

In short, the duty to perform steadfast toil would not suffice to establish the illegitimacy of rapine. If marauding was not forbidden on other grounds, it was not forbidden, period. Champions of Locke may respond now by asserting that a strict ban on thievery in the state of nature would strongly reinforce individuals' self-direction because the only maneuvers thereby outlawed were maneuvers in which no one would ever need to engage. With depredations proscribed, everyone could feel secure in the holding of her possessions and could thus build up her general stock of things to a point where she would be thoroughly self-reliant. (Of course, each person nonetheless might participate in voluntary exchanges of items with the people around her, whose autonomy would equal her own.) Since nobody depended at all on any seizures of goods from others, no one would feel too straitened if those seizures were prohibited flatly. Everyone would merely be barred from actions which she had no inclination to do. In sum, given that a regime of private property would encourage maximal independence for everyone, and given that that regime would consequently forestall the pressures which might drive people toward brigandage, it would bolster the self-determination of everybody while clamping only the mildest of restrictions thereon. Everyone would gain enhanced latitude under such a regime, and no one or almost no one would experience the regime's constraints as constraints. So might argue the devotees of Locke in a final effort to save his theory of property as a theory of human self-direction, while appropriately taking account of the reciprocality of duties and rights.

This latest argument in defense of Locke neglects the possibility of unforeseeable mishaps that could buffet the self-reliance of anyone; therefore, its picture of natural harmony among autonomous agents is hyperbolic and rose-colored. More important, it has missed the basic point which it seeks to counter. Suppose for the moment that the state of nature included functional rights of property, and suppose as well that every human being in that state was largely or fully self-reliant. Under such circumstances, the rights of property would still place checks on the leeway of everyone, precisely by girding everyone with functional barriers against everyone else. Would these effective barriers and restrictions pose no real obstacles to any person's self-governance, because no person would have to draw on anyone else's goods for survival? If we answer this query in the affirmative, we shall have collapsed the general right and privilege of self-determination into the general right and privilege of self-conservation. And then the factors that worked against the deducing of concrete rights-of-ownership from the general prerogatives of self-conservation must apply equally to the general prerogatives of self-disposition.

An affirmative answer to the last paragraph's query attaches little or no importance to the curbs on each person's conduct that did not palpably interfere with the basic quest for survival. If we hold that the achievement of full autonomy in procuring daily sustenance was an unrestricted freedom *tout court*, we disregard any trammels which would not preclude that achievement. We therefore shall have attributed no protective strength to the general right and privilege of self-determination that was not already provided by the general right and privilege of self-conservation. And so, given that the latter set of prerogatives was unable to ground a system of concrete rights of ownership, we have disallowed the basing of such a system on the former set of prerogatives.

If, on the other hand, we avouch that prerogatives of self-direction pertained to actions beyond those which indispensably figured in the quest for survival, we cannot exclude acts of plunder. Or, at any rate, we cannot exclude them without begging the question. When we grant the Lockean proposition that everyone's right and privilege of self-determination covered all deeds within the bounds of the natural law, we then must sanction all deeds of looting which stayed within the bounds of that law. One cannot retort by branding all deeds of looting, qua deeds of looting, as inherently violative of natural law; the very point in contention here is the status of such deeds. Having failed to prove the thesis that acts of plunder would collide with basic imperatives of natural law, one cannot now prove it by merely reasserting it with gusto.

Now, the most recently posited argument in support of Locke has ventured to bolster its position by asserting that people in the state of nature would not feel confined by the restraints which proprietary prerogatives imposed. If this assertion amounts to saying that nobody would ever want to do more than what was requisite for survival, it again has crudely collapsed the scope of self-determination into the drive for self-sustainment. And, again, the insurmountable difficulties in grounding a scheme of property on the latter must apply as well to the former. Perhaps, however, the assertion conveys a different understanding of people's putative lack of interest in committing plunder. Perhaps the reason for everyone's abstention from pillaging within the state of nature was not that the pillaging was unnecessary for the continuation of his existence, but that it was seen as undesirable. Although human beings would almost certainly endeavor to carry out a number of projects that were not key components of their quests for survival, they would never perceive rapine as an appealing activity. Thus, prohibitions on looting would not cause anyone to feel deprived of self-governance; such prohibitions merely banned conduct that enticed no one. People as they exerted their own capacities would freely choose to abstain from pillaging, and would therefore undergo no loss of their self-direction if the pillaging was ruled out.

Construed in the way just broached, the latest line of argument in defense of Locke does not reduce self-determination to self-preservation; but it almost surely is false. While it invokes a reasonable and important distinction, it applies the distinction in a highly unpersuasive manner. To grasp how unconvincingly the distinction has been applied, let us first look at the distinction in general by examining very quickly some of the dietary taboos laid down in the Torah.

As nearly everyone with some knowledge of Judaism will be aware, the Hebrew Scriptures pronounce certain animals to be inappropriate for consumption by the people of Israel. Among the germane taboos, which are chiefly found in Leviticus 11:2–47 and in Deuteronomy 14:3–20, some edicts outlaw the ingestion of varied animals that are prized by numerous people in the modern West as significant and attractive sources of food. Doubtless, the most celebrated of the proscribed creatures are pigs and lobsters and hares and crabs. In the present-day West, taboos on eating those animals strike most people as full-blown curbs on any individual's range of choices – which, of course, is one major reason that the taboos are so spottily observed. Other bans in the Torah's dietary restraints, however, do not appear even slightly burdensome or confining to most inhabitants of most Western nations today. For example, God has barred His people from eating lizards and mice and bats and many winged insects. Some people in some of the advanced Western countries may regard flies and mice as splendid delicacies – and therefore some people may deplore as onerous a restriction on the eating of all such animals – but the thought of consuming those vermin is shuddersome for most of us. In the eyes of anyone who indeed does blanch at the prospect of eating vermin, the directives which forbid the savoring of them will hardly loom as crushing intrusions on each person's self-governance. Those directives outlaw vile patterns of consumption that would not have been adopted in any case, and so the directives keep intact the self-disposition of each human agent (i.e. each human agent who is not inclined to devour rats and flies).

Put flippantly, then, the basic question at hand is whether deeds of looting bear a greater resemblance to flies and bats than to lobsters and pigs. That is, would people within the state of nature tend to classify deeds of looting as repellent and undesirable conduct or as enticing and expedient conduct? And, in turn, would they smile on the prohibition of looting – as a demand with which they could comply effortlessly – or would they instead regard it as an irksome demand for their abstention from gratifying behavior? And hence, in turn, would the prohibition of looting interfere not at all with the self-direction of people, or would it interfere significantly with their self-direction by closing off choices that would otherwise have been taken up?

No incontestable answers to these queries are possible, of course, but we certainly can adduce strong reasons for holding that the option of plunder would attract many people in the originary stages of humankind. Marauding would quite clearly resemble pigs and crabs more than it would resemble lizards and mice. After all, some people would produce things far better than would all or most of their counterparts, and they thus might provoke acts of plunder motivated by jealousy or avarice. Someone noting the prolificacy or excellence of the goods made by someone else would perceive rapine as highly tempting indeed. Furthermore, even if we take no account of differences among people's creative skills, we should recognize the allure of rapine as a supplement to persistent toil. As my fourth chapter has already discussed, the primal superabundance of wealth in nature was a superabundance of raw materials and was not a superabundance of finished goods. Most raw materials had to be worked upon considerably in order to become useful items that could satisfy needs. Accordingly, even an industrious human being might often benefit handsomely from an act of pillage, to compensate for his lower-than-expected production or to increase his affluence beyond the healthy level obtained by his own productive exploits. In sum, given the enduring appeal of predatory acts in the state of nature, any ban on such acts would pare the scope of self-determining latitude for just about everyone.

But, the defenders of Locke may retort, this discussion of the reasons for the attractiveness of marauding is acutely tendentious. It has focused entirely on the perspective of someone contemplating a deed of pillage, and has therefore disregarded the victim's perspective. To be sure, the victim of a larcenous deed could become the perpetrator of such a deed; but the fact that everybody was sometimes a perpetrator and sometimes a target would scarcely remove the difference between those roles. (In the bizarre *How It Is* by Samuel Beckett, the role of each torturer as a victim stands in clear contrast with the role of each torturer as a torturer.) Thus, in light of the crucial differences between a target of rapine and a perpetrator of rapine, an assessment flowing exclusively from the standpoint of the perpetrator is one-sided and thoroughly misleading.

Locke's supporters can further argue as follows. Granted, seizures of useful products were enticing and beneficial when viewed from the perspective of someone who was aiming to carry out seizures. But they were rebarbative and injurious when viewed from the perspective of anyone who underwent seizures. Moreover, the harm and dread that were suffered by every person qua victim would loom larger than the gains enjoyed or anticipated by every person qua culprit. In the state of nature, then, people would submit to a latticework of proprietary rights as supportive of everybody's free self-directedness – notwithstanding its unavoidable imposition of the duties that would accompany the rights. Security stemming from the rights would undoubtedly be more important than the options which the duties would take away. Everyone, if asked to consider carefully, would plump for social arrangements that included proprietary rights. Only through the sway of such rights could everybody's basic pattern of preferences attain due fulfillment, with security favored over liberty-to-maraud. In sum, only thus would the self-governance of each person come to be realized.

For reasons that were explained earlier in a slightly different context, this hypothetical retort by Locke's defenders cannot withstand scrutiny. Since the general privilege and right of self-determination were always held by everyone (i.e. everyone unenslaved), the retort by Locke's defenders must make its assertions about everyone. If the central thesis of the retort applies to only some human beings and not to others, it cannot sustain an argument that focuses on universal privileges and rights of self-direction. Yet that basic thesis does indeed apply to only some persons and not to others.

Human agents blessed with characteristics such as brawn and venturesomeness and cunning and nimbleness and a hardy penchant for danger could thrive within a state of nature that was devoid of all ownership. They were quite likely to achieve more than they would within an aboriginal network of concrete rights. They not only were apt to succeed famously when trying to ransack the possessions accumulated by other people, but also were apt to guard skillfully against being despoiled of their own possessions. For these people, a world of privileges without concrete rights would breed a host of attractive opportunities for gain, at a cost that they would readily shoulder. If asked to make an informed and careful choice, these people would justly opt for a state of nature where pillaging was allowed. A state of nature with rights of ownership would impede their self-direction by giving them security which they gladly would trade for liberty-to-maraud; the benefits of having their rights would not fully counterbalance the duties laid upon them by others' rights. Thus, even if we accept arguendo that a state of nature with rights of property would establish potent shields for each individual against the forays of others, and even if we likewise avouch that any state of nature equipped with no rights of property would engender considerable turmoil, we can never warrantedly conclude that such rights were either adequate or essential to further everybody's self-governance.

Great expectations and just deserts

Having failed to salvage the labor theory of ownership by adverting to putative connections between property and autonomy, the champions of Locke may resort instead to the *expectations* that ruled the minds of primitive people. Any such maneuver can join with arguments concerning autonomy, like those which have just been criticized; or it equally well can join with arguments concerning efficiency, like those which were challenged earlier and which will shortly be challenged anew. Whatever the alignments among these stances, the appeals to expectations evolve by focusing on the outlooks and the raw conceptions of justice that prevailed among the earliest people. When bound up with arguments concerning autonomy, the appeals to expectations insist that human beings in the presocietal age could claim dominion over their products because they had expected to receive dominion when they made the products, and hence because it was the only arrangement that could give effect to their self-determined pursuits and goals. When bound up with arguments concerning efficiency, the appeals to expectations insist that human beings in the presocietal age could claim dominion over their products because their efforts to make the products had been impelled by the belief that dominion would ensue therefrom, and because the granting of dominion was therefore the best way of maximizing the long-run output of humankind. In either of these scenarios, the fact that people looked forward to the accrual of proprietary entitlements is understood as a major reason for the vesting of such entitlements.

According to this approach, human beings expected naturally to keep the fruits of their toil; and their very expectations would count decisively in support of their claims to keep those fruits. Satisfying their expectations would entail the scotching of certain privileges – privileges to carry out plunder – but would not entail the breaching of any rights. Thus, because the fulfillment of the expectations would not involve any wrongs whatsoever, and because it would give people the things they plainly desired, it nicely met the demands of justice and of sound policy. It promoted, as well, the aims of individual self-direction and overall efficiency.

Appeals to expectations have figured as essential components of appeals to the deserts of individuals – appeals which arise in numerous discussions of property. Desert-focused arguments seek to justify people's retention of the fruits of their labors, on the ground that their toil had made such retention their due. Having engaged and succeeded in productive exploits, laborers would deserve to reap benefits from the good that they had done. Just as everyone deserved to be punished when responsible for misdeeds, so everybody deserved to be enriched when responsible for creating wealth.

Now, developed only as far as in the preceding paragraph, the arguments focused on deserts will manifestly have come to nought. They partake of all the shortcomings that besmirch the labor theory of ownership, for they bluntly rearticulate that theory (although they abstain from dubious contentions about the "mixing" of human labor with the raw materials of the natural world). Save by begging the question crudely, those arguments cannot explain why proprietary prerogatives were the fitting rewards for labor. Should the defenders of Locke affirm that such prerogatives in the state of nature were requisite for the security of the holdings that were people's rewards, their stance will not merely beg the question – the question dealing with the appropriateness of various rewards, or any rewards, for toiling – but also must overconfidently assume that concrete rights in the ungoverned state of nature would yield security, and that privileges without concrete rights would result in continual depredations. Moreover, the desert-focused arguments cannot begin to explain why rights of property qua deserved rewards would apply to *all* of the unowned assets on which a person had expended his labor, or why the rights would bear on *only* those assets and not on equally desirable products that could function as worthy surrogates. Nor can an emphasis on deserts manage to justify the rewarding of successful labor alone, without comparable rewards or any rewards at all for ill-starred projects of labor.

If lines of reasoning expressed in the argot of "deserts" do not by themselves enhance the labor theory of property, can they bolster that theory when combined with appeals to expectations? Ought we to say that an industrious toiler would deserve all the fruits of his toil if he expected to receive them? An affirmative response to these queries will run afoul of three major problems, at least two of which are hopelessly insurmountable.

Least knotty among these problems is the elaborateness or preciseness of the expectations that are being invoked. If expectations were to serve as the cornerstones for the distributional scheme envisaged in the labor theory of ownership, they had to call for exactly such a scheme. Laborers would have to expect to gain full-fledged rights in all the goods that they fashioned, and in only those goods. They could not expect merely an appropriate level of *remuneration* or *welfare*; nor could they expect to gain full-fledged rights in only some of their products. Insofar as the expectations of people did not meet the conditions that have just been described – insofar as their expectations pointed toward distributive schemes that would depart from the standards in the labor theory of ownership – the expectations could not remedy the faults in the labor theory.

A more devastating problem that must subvert the role of expectations as underpinnings of the labor theory of property is the moral indeterminateness or openness of the expectations themselves qua bare expectations. Because people might anticipate the occurrence of some wicked pattern(s) of conduct or some morally neutral pattern(s) of conduct, their anticipation per se would not generate any moral leverage. A judgment concerning the moral force of expectations cannot advert only to their posture as expectations; we always must inquire about the substance of the expected acts or events. If everyone anticipated monstrous treatment at the hands of his fellows and expected in return to treat his fellows monstrously, the string of abusive acts would scarcely become virtuous by dint of everybody's having foreseen them.

In the current context, where we focus on expectations dealing with rights of property as rewards for toil, we presume arguendo that the acquisition of such rights over unowned things in the state of nature would not intrude on any established rights. In other words, the primeval acquisition of such entitlements would breach no duties and therefore would occasion no wrongs. But we cannot yet say whether the acquisition of such entitlements within the state of nature would be commendable; it might be ethically neutral and thus not worthy of praise. To determine whether the expectations dealing with rights of property were estimable, we must determine whether the rights themselves were laudable.

Here the only evident move for the supporters of Locke is to connect the earliest rights of property with one or more desirable aims – aims such as individual self-governance and collective efficiency. After all, given that any expectations qua expectations cannot decide the worthiness of the acts or events with which they deal, our focus on people's expectations of proprietary rewards in the state of nature will lead us to ask about the suitableness of those rewards; and, given the failure of the Lockean emphasis on self-ownership and "mixing," the sole available lines of reasoning which might somehow vindicate proprietary rewards are arguments that will highlight factors such as autonomy and output-maximization. Yet a renewed dependence upon those lines of reasoning is extraordinarily problematic. Not only have the flaws in those lines of reasoning become apparent already, but the arguments unearthing the flaws have mostly taken for granted that people by and large would expect to gain dominion over the sundry fruits of their labors. All or most of the criticisms set forward here against output-maximizing theories and autonomy-focused theories have allowed that expectations of proprietary rewards for toil – expectations that could be accurate or inaccurate – would figure prominently indeed in the state of nature. Hence, the invoking of expectations now will do nothing to redeem the criticized theories.

In short, expectations as expectations are like the rain in falling indiscriminately upon the just and the unjust. People's expecting of proprietary rewards in the state of nature must leave us with the task of determining the obligatory or nonobligatory status of the rewards. When carrying out that task, we cannot settle on a positive verdict except by resorting to argumentative routes that have been discredited. And, because my discrediting of those routes has not denied the possible abundance of expectations focused on proprietary rewards, one's noting of the expectations cannot shore up the discredited arguments. Expectant outlooks, which were themselves unable to confer an authoritative blessing on the proprietary rewards, would likewise fail to contribute any backing to other routes of authoritative endorsement.

But let us concede for now that efficiency-focused arguments or autonomy-focused arguments can advert with fruitfulness to the expectations that arose in the natural state of human existence. By invoking those expectations of proprietary rewards, we shall assume, the aforementioned arguments can advance a telling case for the proprietary rewards themselves. Should we then conclude that the expectations indeed could fill the gaps in the labor theory of property? Could the expectations serve as the keystones or the underpinnings in such a theory? We now have come to the third main problem that stymies any bedrock appeal to expectations.

Expectations always arrived too late to act as the fundaments in a theory that would account for private property by tracing it to its origins. People anticipated what the norms and the regularities within their environs had led them to anticipate; their anticipation thus could never serve as the grounding for the norms and regularities. When the labor theory of property relies upon expectations as its keystone, it puts the attitudinal cart before the distributional horse. It seeks to ground a pattern of distribution by adverting to outlooks that could not form until the distributional pattern had begun to make itself felt. Anticipatory outlooks could not fulfill their role as foundations, since they had to derive their shape from the norms which they ostensibly had to found.

Taking pains

Locke suggested another route by which the labor theory of property might be salvaged, when he sneered at indolent and covetous thieves in the state of nature who "desired the benefit of another's Pains, which [they] had no right to" (TTG, II, §34). If the labor theory of property could not achieve its ambitions by construing labor in a positive light, perhaps it could fare better by emphasizing the wearisome and painful aspects of human toil. Locke never hesitated to recall that human beings had been condemned to work by their angry Maker, whose own exertions had not produced obedient men and women; and this view of work as a punishing ordeal could connect with the labor theory of property by way of a renewed focus on what people deserved. Given that labor was so time-consuming, burdensome, and frequently dreary, anyone who carried it out should get the benefits of her pains. Elementary considerations of fairness would demand that the fruits of toil must belong to toilers as recompense for their drudgery, at least when nobody else was thereby harmed. When human agents went to the trouble of creating or transforming various items, any distributional scheme that withheld their output from them would show a flagrant lack of respect for their humanity and their industry.

Alas, this new appeal to deserts does no better than the appeals examined above. Even if we assume that people had to be rewarded for the pains they incurred when laboring, we hardly need to accept that they would draw the exact rewards prescribed by the labor theory of ownership. Once again we can ask why rights of property were the fitting rewards for the expenditure of one's sweat, why the rights of property would align each toiler with nothing more and nothing less than the whole agglomeration of goods that he himself fashioned from the thitherto unowned resources of nature, and why exertions that had met with ill luck and thereby had come to grief would earn no remuneration (or only meager remuneration). Furthermore, why would someone with little prowess in laboring get the shoddy goods that he struggled to produce, while someone with greater skill would get the high-quality goods that *he* produced in a relatively relaxed manner? To evade these questions by answering them along the lines set forth in the labor theory of property is not to salvage that theory with new veins of argument, but is staunchly to reaffirm it without improvements.

Besides, even the assumption that human agents had to be recompensed for the hardships they underwent when toiling is an assumption easily challenged. Of course, everybody held a general right protecting his or her general privilege to take possession of the resources that were needed for survival; but the general right and privilege amounted to more *and* less than a policy of rewarding people with concrete rights for the painfulness of their exertions. The general right and privilege obtained as more than any such policy because they applied to human beings who were strictly unable to perform hard tasks with their minds or bodies. And the general right and privilege obtained also as less than any scheme of distribution expounded by the labor theory of ownership, because they did not ensure that every specific project of irksome and successful toil would bring benefits to the man or woman who had carried the project out. Unless someone had been deprived of assets so sweepingly and recurrently that his life would be in danger if he again were plundered, he could not invoke against plunderers his general right against being thwarted by other people in his quest for survival. After all, that general entitlement could just as suitably square with a regime of privileges-unconnected-to-rights-of-ownership as with a regime containing such rights.

Given that the general prerogative of survival could not per se demand that particular benefits should go to all toiling people in remuneration for the sheer arduousness of their endeavors, can champions of Locke find another basis for deeming such a policy the only fair policy? (Fairness is the concern here; this chapter will soon look separately at possible arguments involving output-maximization.) To understand why a system of rewards would not be the only fair policy, and therefore to understand why any argument declaring a system of rewards to be the only fair policy is invalid, we should highlight the ways in which an instance of dreary labor would and would not fulfill an overriding imperative.

On the one hand, projects of industrious labor would of course tend to satisfy the duty-to-undertake-assiduous-and-productive-ventures, imposed by God upon everyone. In this respect, the labor did not arise from wholly free choices dealing with issues that were irrelevant to God's demands and to primal obligations. On the other hand, an act of toil would emerge in its concreteness from free decisions that were bound not by duties but by various practical considerations (at most). Qua careful and earnest striving, the act of toil directly responded to the cardinal precepts of God; but qua striving invested with a specific content, the toil proceeded from the inclinations and aptitudes of the toiler. In the state of nature, at least, no human being was under a divinely imposed or civilly imposed duty to opt for any specified pathways of industrious conduct in distinction from other such pathways. Decisions about concrete ways of living up to the obligation of hardworking sedulity were left to the judgment of individuals. (For reasons that will be examined in my next chapter, the view expressed in the last four sentences must ultimately be modified. But we should accept that view for the moment, in order to contend with the labor theory of property on all conceivable fronts. A qualification of this paragraph's view about the specific content of human toiling will certainly not enhance the position of Locke and his followers in any way.)

Now, inasmuch as projects of labor met an essential duty, *and* inasmuch as projects of labor went ahead without restraint or compulsion, they did not unimpeachably deserve any rewards. Let us briefly highlight in turn the duty-bound facet and the unconstrained facet of productive endeavors.

Fulfilling an obligation can frequently avert punishments rather than procure benefits. Someone who abides by the natural duty and civil duty to forbear from slaying anyone else will thus have kept herself out of prison, but will not have thereby earned any great rewards. In a like fashion, someone who conforms at a decent level with the requirements of basic social courtesy will thus avoid ostracism, but will not usually earn special benefits. To be sure, in the situations just noted and in the sundry other contexts that are analogous, the discharging of the relevant obligations *can* trigger rewards; but it never *has* to trigger rewards, and very frequently it does *not* trigger them. Although indeed one can picture any number of circumstances in which the heeding of some specified duties will elicit remuneration or plaudits frequently, those circumstances are paralleled by myriad situations in which the heeding of some specified dictates will normally go unremunerated.

What is crucial here is that the concept of fairness would not determine whether the heeding of the duty-to-carry-out-laborious-work should garner special rewards for anyone in the presocietal stage of humankind. Although we can perceive the fulfillment of that duty as deserving of some rewards, we equally well can think that any acts fulfilling the duty were the minimal acts required for everyone who wished to avoid divine punishments (punishments inexorably imposed – despite the failure of Dante to include a place for the slothful among the shades in perdition, and his consequent siting of their woes on a terrace of Purgatory). Quite defensible, though not irresistible, is the view of arduous toil as nothing more than "doing one's duty" along lines that warranted no particular recompense.

While the fundamental activity of strenuous labor answered a divinely ordained summons, the concrete modes of that activity derived not from duties but from the preferences of the people who embarked upon the activity. (Or so we may assume for the present.) Here again we find no grounds for conceding that the pains undergone by toilers merited indemnification. With arguments akin to those offered by Rousseau and Proudhon, we need to ask why someone who voluntarily undertook exertions would have a justifiable claim to be rewarded for the exertions – when (ex hypothesi) the sole basis for any reward was the unpleasantness or painfulness of the exertions.

Everyone in the state of nature who chose this or that avenue of production did not have to reach his choice by virtue of any obligations owed to anyone else.[2] His free predilections, rather than the behests of his fellows, accounted for the pathways of industrious striving that he pursued. Why, then, should his productive exploits make him deserving of indemnification? By performing some exploits and forgoing others, he conducted himself in line with his own impulses and desires. No one ordered him to do what he did, and no one barred him from doing what he declined to do. Although his projects of assiduous toiling might accord with the wishes of his contemporaries, the accord would result entirely from the fact that the wishes of his contemporaries matched his own. In short, because all the concrete tasks that anyone carried out in the state of nature were functions of his own proclivities and objectives, he could hardly claim indemnification on the ground that he had had to comply with the bidding of other people. No one in the state of nature would

[2] In line with what I indicated in the postscript to chapter 1, I am ignoring familial obligations. If I took account of such obligations here, my basic points would remain unaffected.

merit indemnification for the pains involved in specific acts of production that he or she opted to undertake – because people never deserve to be indemnified for doing just what they want. If the sole basis for any rewards was the unpleasantness of the endeavors that led to them, people scarcely deserved to be rewarded for having done as they pleased.

Now, one can of course shift one's focus from people's *outlooks* to the *consequences* of their exertions. Although everyone in the state of nature did engage in only the concrete acts of toil that she wanted to carry out, and although no one thus deserved any *indemnification* for her striving, the salutary effects of toiling might warrant the *remuneration* of toilers as such. A focus on those salutary effects might fare better as a justification for rewards to laborers than has the pain-indemnifying justification. However, far from shoring up the pain-indemnifying position, the remunerational focus displaces that position with an alternative rationale. Instead of being salvaged, the indemnificatory argument will have been abandoned. (Note further that the alternative rationale has to explain why the rewards to laborers would match the rewards prescribed by the labor theory of property. Any attempt to explain that point will encounter the major difficulties which we have already explored.)

Let us ponder some other complaints that might be marshaled against the argument in my penultimate paragraph. One such criticism might stress that any person within the state of nature could choose to satisfy the wishes of someone else when engaging in productive endeavors. Given that anyone could attend to the needs of anybody else, will not an argument pointing to people's self-indulgence have missed its mark? This objection is clearly otiose, for it ill-advisedly equates freedom with self-indulgence. Everyone in the state of nature could indeed elect to pursue the satisfaction of anybody else's desires; but, in adopting such a course of behavior, a person would be doing what she wanted to do. Her decision to cater to the preferences of another person or set of people would not proceed from any duties obliging her to make that decision. After all, no person within the state of nature owed such duties to anyone beyond his or her family. (Recall, once again, that some of the discussions in my next chapter will cast doubt on this statement about extrafamilial duties. Here the absence of such duties is simply presupposed for the sake of argument.) Thus, except in the presence of illegitimate force, complaisant conduct emerged as freely chosen projects that would advance the welfare of others. Far from demonstrating that people in the state of nature did not choose to please themselves in their productive enterprises, complaisant acts instantiated their full liberty to do so. For anyone obliging and generous, no firm correlation held between freely willed acts and selfish acts.

To confront a more important but equally unsuccessful attack, we should concentrate on the physical needs and limitations that would underlie human toil. Someone in favor of rewards for the arduousness of toil can insist that nobody in the state of nature was truly free to make meaningful decisions about working. Human creatures had to derive their sustenance from the bounty of nature by performing work on it, and the avenues of work that were feasible at a given time were shaped and often tightly restricted by the natural surroundings. Hence, because of the general need to fashion goods from the raw materials of nature, and because of the concrete bounds on the opportunities posed by natural conditions, people did not enjoy much liberty to determine their fate.

This new objection fares no better than the last objection. Insofar as it succeeds in questioning the latitude for individual self-determination during the prehistoric period, it returns us to asking whether the fulfillment of duties should elicit any rewards. In light of human beings' dependence on goods produced by labor and natural resources – a dependence which the new attack underscores – we can know that the survival of human creatures *en masse* depended on productive exertions carried out by most or all of those creatures. Furthermore, in light of the divinely imposed duty to sustain oneself and one's fellows, and in light of the fundamental equality of human beings, we know that everyone had an obligation to perform useful work. And we know that the performance of useful work proceeded in a variety of conditions, some of which could severely narrow the range of choices open to workers who were pondering how they ought to apply their skills. Given all of these factors, then, we indeed may wish to de-emphasize the freedom of each person to choose the concrete paths of his or her toil. However, any such move will straightaway bring us back to the problem of deciding whether the reimbursement of toilers for the pains of obligatory efforts would be warranted. As we have observed, that problem does not give rise to any conclusive answers; we can easily regard a person's compliance with the obligation-of-industriousness as "merely doing his basic duty," or we can regard it as more praiseworthy conduct that would deserve recognition.

In other words, to re-emphasize the dutiful character of people's productive exploits is to reinstate the uncertainty and indeterminateness that reign when we attempt to find solid grounds for deciding whether those exploits would be rewarded. Because a stress on the duty-laden aspects of toil can yield a case against a policy of rewards as well as in countenance thereof, we have leapt from the frying pan back into the fire. With the obligatoriness of toil in the foreground, some important but less-than-decisive factors would weigh in *support* of the remuneration of toilers, and some important but less-than-decisive factors would weigh *against* such remuneration. A renewed concentration on the imperativeness of work must pull us back to a field of underdetermined choices.

Whenever someone insists that laborers in the state of nature deserved reimbursement because labor was a necessity, there is a confusion between the deserts of each human being qua human being and the deserts of each human being qua laborer. Every person qua person, every person qua creature whose survival the Lord demanded, would enjoy a constant entitlement to a share of natural bounty that was sufficient to preserve his life and sufficient to keep intact his basic well-being. In that respect, every man and woman within the state of nature did deserve a "reward." But, insofar as everyone had a claim to such a "reward," he held the claim by virtue of being human and not by virtue of laboring.[3]

A policy of reimbursement for the hardships attendant on productive accomplishments would distribute assets in ways that would almost certainly prove both needless and insufficient for the purpose of assigning to everybody the "rewards" that attached to membership in the human species. Whenever the hardship-indemnifying scheme of distribution

[3] This paragraph has deliberately used the language of "deserts" quite expansively, and has forborne from distinguishing between deserts and entitlements. When the contrast between deserts and entitlements is drawn, somebody is said to deserve a given thing only if he has engaged in efforts to produce it or attain it. Somebody does not deserve a thing when he enjoys an entitlement to it solely as a consequence of his status. Activity or deliberate forbearance, rather than the bare occupation of a role or membership in a group, is a precondition for the engendering of deserts. Hence, although a person has a moral entitlement to everything he deserves, he also very frequently has moral entitlements to any number of things that he does not deserve.

In the paragraph to which this note is appended, the deserts/entitlements distinction has clearly gone by the wayside (at the level of terminology); the tag "deserts" has embraced both halves of such a distinction. But that slighting of differences in terminology is meant to flag the germane substantive differences. After all, the cardinal objective of the argument in that paragraph and the next paragraph is to insist on the unequatability of what was due to human beings qua human beings and what was due to human beings qua workers. By highlighting the affinities between those unequatable standards, we can grasp how they are so easily confused. Little wonder is it that confusion emerges when the benefits due to human beings qua human beings can be recharacterized so smoothly as their "deserts." Given the Lockean belief that sundry entitlements belonged to each human being qua human being, the activities by which anyone sustained himself can be viewed as efforts by which he *deserved* the general entitlements that belonged to him qua human being. Furthermore, such activities would not be confined to the modes of conduct that we ordinarily designate as "labor." Those activities included as well the passive and active measures whereby each person avoided any potential harm from his fellows, and also the passive and active measures whereby each person kept himself from committing suicide. The full assemblage of his acts and omissions that redounded to his basic welfare could qualify as acts and omissions through which he deserved his general human entitlements. Thus, although behavior that preserved human entitlements was not flatly identical with behavior that procured the entitlements connected to full-blown toil, both types of behavior can be classified as good conduct that generated deserts; and so they readily can be run together by sloppy analysts.

reimbursed anyone more handsomely than was needed for survival and basic welfare, it operated along lines unnecessary for safeguarding the deserts of each human being qua human being. And whenever such a scheme of distribution reimbursed anyone less handsomely than was needed for survival and basic welfare, it operated along lines insufficient to guarantee the deserts of every human being qua human being. (Locke himself understood this point about insufficient force when he wrote that obligations of justice had to coexist with obligations of charity. Although everyone had a duty to respect the proprietary rights of everyone else, the holders of such rights had a duty to acknowledge the principle that "*Charity* gives every Man a Title to so much out of another's Plenty, as will keep him from extream want, where he has no means to subsist otherwise" [TTG, I, §42, emphasis in original].) In sum, the arguments which highlight the role of work as the indispensable means of human survival and well-being can push us readily toward the inference that people's work would not properly attract any compensation as such. Instead, the obligation of everyone to carry out industrious projects would exist alongside the distribution of goods to people qua people rather than to people qua laborers. Such a conclusion is not irresistible, but it indeed is plausible when we concern ourselves with the fundamental needs of the human race and of individual human beings.

Thus, an attempt to rescue the labor theory of ownership by underlining the arduousness of labor must run afoul of two severe difficulties. First, it cannot explain credibly why fair remuneration for toilsome exploits would coincide with the remuneration envisaged by the labor theory of property. Quite feasible were countless variations in the depth and scope of the entitlements that could operate as rewards for the hardships of productive exertions. Second, this attempt to redeem the labor theory of ownership cannot even establish firmly that labor was a proper basis for rewards at all. Not only will a focus on the burdens and drudgery of work have failed to pin down the nature of the appropriate recompense therefor; it likewise fails to show that the carrying out of work would per se warrant the assignment of recompense in *any* form or amount.

The realization of possibilities

Defenders of Locke can also seek to shore up his labor theory of property by directing attention to the role of labor in the actualizing of possibilities that would not have become actual otherwise. When a human being produced useful goods, she brought forth items that would never have materialized if her work (or corresponding work by someone else) had not proceeded. Only insofar as people applied their energy and skills to creative tasks, did wealth emerge and accumulate beyond the level of nature's raw materials. Without the application of the energy and skills, the potential wealth would never be realized. Hence – can argue the champions of the labor theory of property – someone who had made useful things would aptly gain full dominion over his or her output, which had come into being only as a result of his or her efforts. If we leave aside instances of joint production, no one except a laborer himself was responsible for the things he created. No one else deserved blame if the laborer's products were injurious, and nobody else deserved credit if the products satisfied human needs. Valuables should flow only to him or her whose industry had brought them into existence; because the valuables could not have developed in the absence of someone's industry, they belonged to the human agent whose productive capacities had been their sine qua non.

This latest defense of Locke exhibits too many shortcomings to be taken very seriously. We straightaway should observe how close its argument is to earlier arguments that have proved unsuccessful. It verges on being a bland rehearsal of the labor theory of ownership, bereft of the assertions about the "mixing" of natural assets with labor. It also resembles closely the arguments about deserts and about the onerousness of toil. To the degree that it collapses into those arguments which we have previously explored, it shares their faults and non sequiturs.

Even more plainly than the earlier arguments, the line of reasoning here examined has perpetrated an "is"/"ought" transition. It highlights a certain fact about the indispensableness of labor in producing myriad goods, and thence it aims to derive the prescript that toilers ought to get full dominion over the fruits of their productive endeavors. This crossover from the actual to the normative, a crossover from the fact of responsibility to the norm of responsibility, begs a number of questions. For example, the line of reasoning here assessed must show at a minimum that nobody other than a laborer *L* (and his family) could have a natural right to *L*'s products. Instead of demonstrating that point, however, the argument under scrutiny has treated it as a given. By taking that point for granted, the argument has begged one of the major questions at issue; after all, until we know whether anyone besides a specific laborer could possess a natural right to the laborer's output, we shall never know if the laborer himself would hold an exclusive natural right to his output. Defenders of Locke cannot advert merely to the fact that any number of particular goods arose only through the efforts of laborers. That putative fact indeed was a fact, but clearly it was not the sole fact that could be vested with moral weight in this context.

The fact that each human agent needed a certain amount of goods in order to survive was another fact that could be vested with normative significance. This fact about needs, colored with the proper normative hue, could undergird a need-based distributive arrangement combined with a scheme of duties-to-perform-diligent-work. Of course, many other webs of entitlements were also conceivable, with justifications centered on the ascribing of moral weight to various other facts. Like every transfer from "is" to "ought," the crossover from facts of human toil to norms governing the output of human toil could go ahead in a myriad of sensible ways that were all far from conclusive. To posit only one route for the crossover from those facts to those norms is to beg key questions rather than to submit a theory with appropriate and rigorous groundings.

Furthermore, even if the aspiring vindicators of Locke can show decisively that everyone in the state of nature did not hold any original rights to the goods transformed or produced by someone else, they will not have thereby shown that the people who transformed or produced the goods were themselves endowed with rights to those goods. Each person within the state of nature might retain nothing more than a raw *privilege* to exercise control over his own output, and each would thus have a privilege to exercise control over anyone else's output. In that situation, no one would hold a right to anyone else's products; but no one would hold a right to his or her own products, either. Such a state of nature would markedly diverge from the one depicted in the labor theory of property.

Indeed, even if Locke's supporters can establish rigorously that no one other than a laborer *L* could have a natural entitlement (a natural right *or* a natural privilege) concerning the disposition of *L*'s products, they will not have thereby shown that *L* would have rights to all her products. Given that no one other than *L* had any natural entitlement to use *L*'s products, and given that *L* did not have any natural entitlement to use the products of other people, and given also that *L* enjoyed a general right to her basic well-being and a general privilege to pursue her basic well-being, she indeed would have concrete rights to any of her products that she required for the fulfillment of her general right. If she made no products beyond the things she needed for her fundamental welfare, then she would have a right to the totality of her output. But if she created some additional things – things that quite readily could be used by her, yet plainly as luxurious items rather than as the means of satisfying her basic wants – her posture in regard to those things was not as clear-cut. The premises stated in this paragraph do not in themselves enable us to determine whether she would win full rights in those additional things; the premises do not rule out her attainment of full rights, but they certainly leave open some other possibilities.

For example, instead of gaining rights in the extra goods, *L* might gain and wield a power of assignment thereover. She herself would not be entitled to keep the goods for her own projects and purposes, but she would enjoy a power to select the recipient(s) of the goods, who thus would become endowed with full rights thereto. Although each laborer *L* would have a duty to exercise her power, she would not bear a duty to give her surplus things to any specific human agent(s) ahead of others. Before *L*'s assignment of the things to somebody or some group of people, no one would have a claim on the things, and no one would have a privilege to seize them. Hence, the rights that would lodge in anyone who obtained a surplus item from *L* would be nonoriginary and mediated instead of being primal and natural. And so a thesis of excluded entitlements – a thesis that no one held any natural entitlements to anyone else's products – can allow situations wherein people had rights to only some of the things which they themselves had produced.

In a setting like the one just hypothesized, the indispensableness of labor in the production of the surplus assets would have received acknowledgment through the generating of powers only, and would therefore not have resulted in the *direct* formation of any rights to the assets. What a laborer earned for the expenditure of his toil was not a right to the surplus riches, but the entitlement to say who should get those riches. In other words, the pattern of rights and powers in such a setting would differ unmistakably from the pattern commended by Locke's theory of ownership. (Let us briefly observe that the hypothesized framework of entitlements would not perforce decrease people's productive undertakings. Here the most notable weaknesses in efficiency-focused arguments can be left unhighlighted, as two chief considerations stand out. First, although powers of assignment would for most toilers be less attractive rewards than proprietary rights, each rewarded person would in any event bear the God-imposed obligation of industriousness. Would that key obligation be flouted? Recall that the efficiency-centered arguments must suppose that people would conform by and large with natural duties such as the duty to respect proprietary prerogatives. Without such conformance, after all, there could never be a link in the state of nature between private ownership and prosperity-encouraging peacefulness. Hence, an efficiency-prizing Lockean will be treading on somewhat dangerous ground if he affirms that people would tend to comply with the natural obligation of industriousness only when compliance would suit their grasping ambitions. Second, in the hypothesized regime of entitlements, a person giving effect to his powers of assignment could often hope for some reciprocal favors from the people chosen to take his extra goods. To be sure, the people who got his things would confront no out-and-out duties of neat reciprocation when they themselves had extra goods to bestow; ex hypothesi, no one wielding a power of allotment would ever be bound by a duty to confer goods on a specific person or set of people rather than on somebody else. But, as David Hume emphasized when he pointed out the collaboration between two men who pulled the oars of a boat [*Treatise of Human Nature*, book III, part II, §ii, ¶10], activities could be planned and quite well coordinated without the intercession of promises and duties.)

As has been noted, all or most of the pitfalls in the latest attempt to rescue Lockeanism are very much the same pitfalls that have turned up in previous attempts. For example, given the central thesis that *A*'s products would not exist without *A*'s endeavors, why should *A* be rewarded with proprietary rights in her output? Moreover, why should the rights pertain exclusively and exhaustively to *her* output? We can close this discussion by reviving another query that has surfaced before: why should remuneration of any type belong to *A* as a worker (in distinction from *A* qua human being)?

To approach this question, we should think about the obligatory aspects and voluntary aspects of human work. In the line of reasoning on which we are now focused, the voluntariness of work can move to the fore on some occasions. That is, the latest defense of Locke can submit that each worker made a free choice to carry out the work which she then performed. She ought to be recompensed because her products would never have emerged if she had not chosen to create them and had not effectuated her choice. This version of the argument raises two prime difficulties. First, insofar as the underscoring of voluntary choices is justified, it engenders an inconclusive struggle between an emphasis on freely elected projects and an emphasis on achievements. While the emphasis on freely elected projects will lead us to query why people would be rewarded for doing just as they pleased, the emphasis on achievements will lead us to think that rewards for laborers were warranted because of the good which the laborers had done. Since we here encounter a clash of intuitions – intuitions in favor of the reimbursement of people for creating goods that were highly useful, and intuitions against the indemnification of people for conducting themselves exactly as they wished – we must live with a certain irresolvableness that can be transcended only by leaps of faith.

A second main difficulty in highlighting the voluntariness of production is that the voluntariness would consort with strict obligatoriness. When we say that *B*'s products would derive their existence from the freely chosen labors of *B*, we ipso facto presume that *B* was capable of productive ventures. But, under Locke's chief assumptions, we are therefore committed to the notion that *B* had to shoulder an obligation of industriousness. Once we recognize that *B* bore such an obligation, we should reconsider our premise deeming his productive exertions to be voluntary. Perhaps he did not have a duty to create the precise things that he created, but he manifestly had a duty to create *something* useful.

Thus, when anyone argues for remuneration to toilers on the ground that the products fashioned by any toiler *B* would never have come about if *B* had declined to make the products, the argument overstates the breadth of *B*'s freedom to avoid work. His output served as the concrete fruits and fulfillment of his general obligation to toil assiduously. Potential variations in the specific composition of his output did not detract in any way from its serving as the fulfillment of a general imperative. And so we can very aptly declare that *B* could not have elected to refrain from coming forth with his products; we lack a sturdy basis for highlighting the concrete variability or optionality of his output and for de-emphasizing the general requisiteness thereof. Understood at the level of specificity, his output depended on his choices and could quite properly have been different from what it was. Understood at the level of generality, on the other hand, his output did not depend on his choices and could not rightfully have been withheld. If *B* had opted not to make the specific goods that he fashioned, he would have been required to make other goods of comparable utility. We are no more warranted in slighting this general state of compulsion than in slighting the ample scope for toilers to choose among the many specific paths whereby the compulsion could be heeded.

Perhaps because of the problems that have just been examined, the arguments about the unforgoableness of work in the production of countless assets have tended not to concentrate on the subjectivity of the person who produced some specific asset(s). Instead, they have focused on the standing of each producer's fellows in relation to each producer's output. Those arguments have been less preoccupied with establishing the deserts of each creator of goods than with insisting on the lack of justifiable claims by other people to the created goods. According to the implicit tenor of this approach, a laborer won his rights to his output by default more than by the strength of his own deserts.

Unfortunately, such an approach leads straightaway to irksome snags (which have already been explored herein). It commits an "is"/"ought" conflation as it moves from facts of causative responsibility to precepts of remunerative deserts. Although the facts of causation could receive a normative glow that would let them serve as supports for the germane precepts, a host of other facts could likewise be given normative roles that would enable them to support very different precepts. Moreover, even if Locke's champions are permitted to beg the question by avouching that everybody other than person *A* would not hold a natural right to *A*'s products, they will have yet to show that *A* had any right to those products;

everybody, including *A*, might have only a natural privilege to possess and exploit the items that ensued from *A*'s labors. In that event, rights did not accrue to *A* ineluctably by default. Indeed, even if we grant now that everybody other than *A* would not have a natural right *or* a natural privilege concerning the disposition of any items that *A* produced, we have not thus conceded that *A* herself would have rights to everything that flowed from her toil. As was demonstrated a little while ago, *A* conceivably would enjoy natural rights in only a certain share of her output (and accordingly would have fewer rights, under those conceivable circumstances, than the labor theory of property would ordain). In short, whether the voluntariness or the mandatoriness of labor be highlighted, these efforts to rehabilitate the labor theory of property – through appeals to the unforgoableness of work in the creation of useful things – will have foundered.

Incentives for productivity

We now train our scrutiny on the final prominent effort to redeem the labor theory of ownership. This purported rescue lies in the efficiency-focused arguments which we studied just before we turned to the labor theory itself. As was shown in the earlier discussion, Locke indeed laid stress on the privilege and obligation of humankind to procure the most extensive possible comforts from the God-given wealth of nature. When Locke proclaimed, near the outset of his chapter on property in the *Second Treatise*, that "God, who hath given the World to Men in common, hath also given them reason to make use of it to the best advantage of Life, and convenience" (TTG, II, §26), he was sounding a theme to which he returned often.

Very closely connected, and supportive of a focus upon efficiency, are the passages where Locke emphasized the role of labor in subduing and domesticating the environment. Not only did human work transform the materials of nature into usable products and increase the availability of those raw materials, but it more profoundly remade the world by causing human agents to feel at home therein. Whereas the undeveloped earth was intimidating and largely inscrutable, the developed earth embodied the goals and striving of the people who shaped it. Instead of being subservient to untamed environs, people who exploited the earth with cleverness and sedulity had taken command of their surroundings to a considerable extent; and they fashioned those surroundings into a mirror that supplied human agents with a reflection of themselves and their ends. To overcome as far as possible the divide between humanity and the workings of nature, then, each person had to keep his output of useful goods at the highest levels that he could yield. By doing one's utmost to effectuate human lordship over the natural world, one did one's utmost to make that world an objective counterpart of human capacities.

Hence, whether the cardinal aim for the people in a Lockean universe was the maximizing of comforts and conveniences or the sharpening of humankind's imprint on nature, the pursuit of efficiency would indeed commend itself strongly. When people maximized their productive exploits, they thus fulfilled the role prescribed for the human species by the Lockean God. Alas, however, some daunting problems emerge when the ideal of efficiency is perceived as militating unequivocally in favor of the institution of private ownership. Even more dubious is the notion that that ideal would ordain the exact patterns of individual ownership described by the labor theory of property. In the present discussion, we shall first review the main difficulties that plague all efforts to invoke the goal of wealth-maximization as a grounding for private property in abstracto; because chapter 4 has plumbed those difficulties at length, my review here will be terse. We shall then investigate some additional problems that arise when the wealth-maximization credo is called upon to buttress Locke's labor theory of ownership.

Arguments lauding the efficiency of private ownership may indeed exaggerate people's selfishness and rapaciousness, and they overlook the potential for the gratifying of selfish impulses through forms of remuneration other than material riches. Moreover, when such arguments profess to be dealing with conditions that would characterize the state of nature, they also go amiss with implausible assumptions about the advantageous security that a network of concrete rights would offer. To insist on the wealth-maximizing solidness of proprietary entitlements in the state of nature is doubtless to overreckon the likely impact of such entitlements, and is furthermore to scant the stability and peace that might flourish in a regime of privileges without concrete rights. For reasons which this book has adduced at length, the effectiveness of proprietary rights in the state of nature was doubtful in the extreme. If people were so intent on grabbing the goods of others that they would delightedly have availed themselves of any open privileges-to-grab, then they presumably would exhibit meager deference to rights of ownership when infractions of those rights could easily go unpunished. Conversely, the perils seemingly raised by privileges-without-rights were not at all a foregone conclusion. If people were so restrained about the snatching of one another's wealth that they would have shrunk from violating the rights of one another in the absence of any central authority, then they would furthermore be inclined to shrink from making much use of any open privileges-to-snatch. What is more, even if proprietary rights would indeed engender security in humankind's natural state, and even if privileges-without-concrete-rights would indeed have engendered *in*security, we ought to shrink from glibly concluding that a framework of proprietary prerogatives would maximize wealth. Until we know the importance that people placed on having certain levels of material comfort (as opposed to certain levels of relaxation or play), we cannot know whether their productive accomplishments would be dampened or stimulated by bouts of plunder-occasioned insecurity.

These weaknesses that spoil the efficiency-focused arguments for the institution of private property may not be absolutely fatal but are indeed grave. Theorists who want to sing the praises of individual ownership as the fount of incentives for efficient production have posed themselves a formidable task. But if the general case to be made for private ownership as wealth-maximizing is doubtful at best, the case for the wealth-maximizing role of the particular scheme of ownership recounted by Locke is still more dubious. Apart from the problems that have just been summarized, three main difficulties block all attempts to salvage the labor theory of ownership through appeals to wealth-maximization.

The irrepressibleness of substitutibility

First, like other arguments with consequentialist bearings, the appeals to wealth-maximization cannot explain why Locke insisted on tying workers to their own products and why he failed to leave room for substitutions of assets. If the links between laborers and the fruits of their labors in the state of nature were approached wholly as a matter of securing the fit incentives for optimal productivity, then the underlying goal could be met in circumstances where no one ever obtained the fruits of his or her own work. So long as everyone was rewarded with items that were as pleasing as the items which he himself had made, the apt incentives would come about. Should appropriate arrangements for substitutions of products have emerged, then the substituted products could fully satisfy the rights of the toilers who received the products as compensation for their endeavors. After all, ex hypothesi, the rights of each toiler would consist in his being owed whatever remuneration could best advance the wealth-maximizing cause; and here the streams of remuneration composed of the substituted assets would spawn and reinforce the incentives that were deemed to be necessary for the maximizing of wealth.

Yet any patterns of recompense involving surrogate goods were at odds with the pattern that was defended by the labor theory of property. For Locke, the output of worker *A* could never be interchangeable with the output of worker *B* in regard to the establishment of primary rights (though *A* and *B* could exchange their products after making them and attaining primary rights to them, of course). Interchangeableness would not apply at the point when goods were originally appropriated from the bounty of nature, since the fundament of original appropriation was the "mixing" or "joining" of someone's work with specific natural resources. When anybody expended her labor on particular unowned assets, she did not thereby garner rights to the measure of well-being afforded by the assets; she garnered rights to the assets themselves. Those assets, and those assets alone, were "mixed" or "joined" with the work that brought her titles of ownership.

For efficiency-focused theories, by contrast, interchangeableness must always apply to any fruits of work at the stage of primal acquisition (whenever feasible practically). Such theories uphold proprietary connections between particular human agents and particular goods, but not because the goods and the agents are perceived as integrally conjoined. Rather, the theories hail the proprietary conjunctions solely on the instrumental ground that the conjunctions would spur the maximizing of wealth. Hence, such theories unavoidably suggest that any particular matrix of proprietary connections in the state of nature would have to be abandoned if some alternative arrangements would better promote efficiency. And, even more important, such theories likewise always leave open the possibility that any person's primal rights to goods involved goods other than the person's own products.

Locke disallowed the notion that any person *X* could ever hold original rights to products fashioned by any person *Y* who was not *X*'s servant or slave or child, and he disallowed equally the notion that people who were not servants or slaves or children could fail to hold original rights over products which they could use and which they themselves had formed with unowned materials. Yet an argument that pursues wealth-maximization can very readily call for toiler *A* to have original rights over products fashioned by toiler *B* (and vice versa); if a pattern of proprietary entitlements along those lines would enhance the overall output of goods by human beings in the state of nature, the entitlements were to be so arranged. Because the principal focus of wealth-maximizing theories is trained upon the goal of wealth-maximization itself, those theories cause every scheme of ownership to be worthy of consideration *and* subject to dismissal. For theorists bent on the maximizing of wealth, proprietary relationships in the state of nature were pure means rather than ends. For Locke, proprietary relations were the means to survival and basic welfare, but were also ends rooted in the self-ownership of each person.

Incentives to try and try again

Another potent obstacle to the reconstruing of the labor theory of ownership as a theory of incentives for maximal productivity is the troubled situation of people who were careful and hardworking but luckless. Within the labor theory of ownership, a toiler earned nothing for his unsuccessful exertions, no matter how much care and diligence he had shown. Undeflectable misadventures stripped the toiler of any rightful claim to be reimbursed for the projects that had failed.

To be sure, a human agent in desperate straits because of unavertible setbacks would enjoy a natural entitlement to some alms from his fellows. However, in five chief ways, the alms were quite different from the rewards that would accrue to successful ventures.[4] For one thing, natural entitlements to alms did not become operative unless the mishaps suffered by any person *M* had dragged her down into beggary. Save when reduced to poverty, she could not lay claim to charitable relief at all. Thus, the dispensation of help was far from straightforwardly connected to the amount of someone's work. If a person *M* had slid into destitution as a result of damage to her crops from an early blizzard, and if a person *N* had also undergone massive losses from the blizzard but had retained a decent income through other exploits, then only *M* would get charitable assistance; yet *M* and *N* alike had devoted a substantial amount of labor to the growing of crops.

Furthermore, in a system of entitlements built on Lockean principles, each person's power to seek support from charity would not gain any effect unless the potential donor had amassed a surplus of goods. In some well-known pronouncements that were earlier partly quoted herein, Locke thrice made reference to a crucial condition that would have to be met for the incurring of any responsibility to afford relief:

> God the Lord and Father of all, has given no one of his Children such a Property, in his peculiar Portion of the things of this World, but that he has given his needy Brother a Right to the Surplusage of his Goods . . . since 'twould always be a Sin in any Man of Estate, to let his Brother perish for want of affording him Relief out of his Plenty . . . . *Charity* gives every Man a Title to so much out of another's Plenty, as will keep him from extream want, where he has no means to subsist otherwise. (TTG, I, §42, emphasis in original)

[4] For a recent historical debate concerning Locke's views on charitable relief (as well as some other issues), see David Wootton, "John Locke and Richard Ashcraft's *Revolutionary Politics*," 40 *Political Studies* 79 (1992); and Richard Ashcraft, "Simple objections and complex reality: theorizing political radicalism in seventeenth-century England," 40 *Political Studies* 99 (1992).

Strictly speaking, this quoted passage per se does not entail the conclusion that the giving of alms was mandatory solely when people who were called upon for the giving had accumulated some extra goods. After all, the passage states merely that a person with goods above a minimum level was required to furnish sustenance to the needy; the passage does not state expressly that a person with goods below the minimum level was *not* required to succor the needy. But once we here recall that no one was bound to strive for the preservation of other people unless "his own Preservation c[ame] not in competition" (TTG, II, §6), we can see that the famous passage quoted above does highlight an essential limit on eleemosynary demands. Anybody who lacked a "Surplusage of . . . Goods" did not have to offer alms to the indigent. Yet, in light of this clear restriction on the purview of charity, the entitlement of a luckless toiler to relief from his straitened circumstances was very different indeed from rights of ownership obtained through successful work. At least in the state of nature as envisioned by Locke, the rights procured by someone through fruitful industry were not reliant at all upon the affluence of anyone else. A person's rights that were conferred by charitable relief, on the other hand, did directly hinge on the prosperousness of her contemporaries.

Moreover, rights that sprang from charitable support were derivative, in the sense that they applied to items already owned. Those rights therefore diverged starkly from the rights achieved through someone's expenditure of labor on natural riches thitherto unpossessed. Rights of the latter kind, pertaining to specific goods, did not depend on anyone's holding of antecedent rights to those goods; in fact, the rights of labor only originated in goods to which no antecedent rights were held by anyone. Rights ensuing from alms, by contrast, extended solely to things over which some benefactor(s) had previously gained proprietary dominion. These derivative rights came about through transfers of assets from the current owners to needy recipients. Whether the transfers proceeded voluntarily or involuntarily, they had to occur if rights from alms were duly to take effect. No such transfers played a part in the vesting of the rights that attached to fruitful toiling, because those rights involved original acquisitions rather than rearrangements of acquisitions.

Apart from being subordinate (both chronologically and logically, though not ethically), the rights gained through alms were more confined – on the whole – than rights won through sweat. With regard to the latter group of rights, in a primal state of superabundant raw materials, the lone curb on one's appropriative discretion was a ban on the waste or spoilage of anything within one's control (TTG, II, §§31, 37, 38). Even before the introduction of markets into the state of nature, someone toiling could secure his dominion over items as manifold as he and his dependents could use for any warranted purposes. (After the introduction of mechanisms for exchange, which operated first with barter and then with monetary transactions, the essential bounds on appropriation were neither diminished nor enlarged *in the abstract.* But markets increased the range of normal uses for any products; specifically, the markets allowed at first the trading of goods for other goods and then the trading of goods for money, which could be stored in nearly limitless quantities without spoiling. Once markets enabled goods and services to be treated as objects of exchange, each person was then at liberty to produce far more things than he himself could employ in satisfaction of his present desires and needs. So long as the additional things were put to use by being exchanged for money or alternative items, the prohibition on waste and spoilage was not transgressed.)

Contrasting sharply with the potential abundance of the rights attained through work was the meagerness of the rights attained through alms. Whereas rights of the former sort could apply to luxuries as well as to basics, rights of the latter sort would only apply to basics. Locke affirmed that rights of the latter sort would merely fulfill the "pressing Wants" of the beneficiary, who would thus be kept "from extream want" (TTG, I, §42). One's power to demand charitable assistance, in other words, was a power to save oneself from starving but was not a power to get conveniences and comforts beyond the modest level required for one's continued survival. While work could endow a human agent with rights over all the things he wanted to use for any unprohibited purposes, charity would endow a human agent with rights over only the things he had to use for the preservation of his fundamental welfare.

A countervailing discrepancy between the full rights attained through charitable assistance and the full rights to one's own products is that the rights attained through assistance were "remuneration" for anybody qua person, while the rights to products of one's own labor were remuneration for anybody qua toiler (qua successful toiler, that is). A conscientious person in poverty would have an entitlement to basic aid, not because he had succeeded in his productive efforts, but because his efforts had come to naught. Even when a physical handicap or mental handicap precluded someone from performing any labor, he or she would have an entitlement to alms from anyone who enjoyed a surplus of goods. A power to demand for oneself the gaining of charitable relief was a power held by everyone – or at least by everyone who was not a willful malingerer – regardless of anybody's capacity to work. In order to retain such a power, one had to do one's best to comply with the obligation of steadfast industry; but one never had to be a successful worker. If deeds of genuine work were beyond one's capability, one could even remain aloof from work altogether. Although one's standing as a member of humankind was an indispensable precondition for exerting the power to obtain charitable support, one's standing as a laborer was dispensable.

Now, given these key divergences between the power to get proprietary rights through donations and the power to get proprietary rights through one's toil, the place for alms in Locke's theory must leave a gap between the entitlements of ill-starred toilers and the entitlements of their luckier counterparts. According to the labor theory of ownership, a careful and industrious worker would receive a more niggardly return for his efforts when he ran afoul of mischances than when he shared the pleasant fate of God's people, who "shall long enjoy the work of their hands. They shall not labor in vain" (Isaiah 65:22–3). Perseverance and watchfulness were not sufficient to yield the medley of rewards that accrued when perseverance and watchfulness were accompanied by good luck. Someone who had met with misfortune in his labors would also meet with misfortune in his recompense.

Such a situation, when judged by efficiency-focused standards, would be highly dubious because it would very likely fail to bring about the correct incentives for the maximizing of wealth. If people knew that they would be penalized quite severely for mishaps not foreseeable or escapable through earnest precautions, they would tend to adjust their patterns of behavior in ways that ran athwart the objective of efficiency. Such reactions were not inevitable, but they were probable. One form that such reactions could take was overcautiousness. Aware that the victims of disasters and misadventures would find nothing more than scant relief from those hardships, people might devote a great deal of time-consuming effort to warding off the disasters and misadventures. Productive energies that could be employed in creating valuable things would instead be used for the adoption of countless safeguards, to preserve the valuables already made and to ensure that the making of further valuables would go ahead smoothly. Most or all of the safeguards would function as useful items only inasmuch as they would operate to protect truly useful items; in the absence of this protective function, most or all of the safeguards would not have any utility. Most or all of them would carry no intrinsic pleasurableness or desirableness. Ergo, if the existence of more generous arrangements for hardworking but unfortunate people would inspire a shift of their output from excessively burdensome precautions to agreeable assets, then a structure of primal rights that offered the more generous remuneration would be more efficient *ceteris paribus* than a structure of primal rights that furnished the paltry level of remuneration envisaged by Locke.

One way, then, in which any number of fairly risk-averse people might adapt to Lockean principles regarding ill-fated toil was to expend an inordinate amount of their time and strength on the development of cautionary devices and procedures. Apart from a debilitating surfeit of cautiousness, however, an undesirable result of the Lockean principles might be substantial underproduction of truly valuable goods. Dismayed at the abiding potential for a low return on careful and assiduous labor, people might decide to work far less than they would if they were assured of being healthily compensated for all their efforts. Of course, each person would still produce as many goods as he needed in order to stay alive, and doubtless he would choose to create more goods than the minimum required for his basic needs; yet people might well opt to devote less energy to productive pursuits than in a context where one's exerting of one's abilities was itself a ground for full rewards when undertaken with proper care and diligence. When people felt insecure about the extent to which their careful striving would ultimately pay off, opportunities for leisure became more attractive. Insofar as conscientious work was perceived as an unreliable source of general welfare, the alternatives to work – such as theft and indolence – grew more enticing. To the degree that parsimonious ways of dealing with the ill-starred projects of laborers would discourage people from toiling as enthusiastically as they otherwise would, the parsimonious treatment would cut against the goal of wealth-maximization. A blending of insecurity and risk-aversion would foster dismal results.

All too easily, then, the Lockean approach to the mischances of zesty toilers could retard the development of efficient production. But, as some of my arguments in earlier portions of this book attest, the inefficiency of the Lockean approach was not a foregone conclusion. If people were risk-preferring instead of risk-averse, they might relish the importance of sheer luck in the distribution of entitlements. They might relish the large disparities between the unfortunate and the fortunate in the Lockean scheme of rights, and they would subscribe gladly to the notion that the successful braving of risks was quite as proper a ground for the determining of rewards as were skill, alertness, and industriousness. Furthermore, even when the human agents residing in a Lockean world did not take pleasure in risks as sources of excitement and as good opportunities to test mettle, they might react to risks in ways that contributed to the maximizing of wealth.

As this book has observed more than once, people might be so desirous of certain goods (or certain degrees of comfort) that they would quickly respond to actual or potential losses by producing a greater flow of goods than they would produce in conditions of substantial security. Even if hardly anyone treasured sundry risks for the sake of risks, a lot of people could act upon their unease by intensifying their work in order to give themselves ample margins of safety that would cause the risks to be less worrisome and destructive. If people derived keen happiness from maintaining their lavish lifestyles and were even prepared to toil quite strenuously therefor, they well might opt to exert themselves with special vigor when they grasped that some of their toil would almost certainly go uncompensated. To remain in place with their material comforts, they would have to run faster; and they might be inclined to do what they had to do. In such circumstances, where people were intent on maintaining their prosperity, a scheme of modest remuneration for worthy but ill-starred projects could help to maximize the total output of goods. (Of course, if the insecurity became severe, its productivity-stimulating effects would doubtless be overtopped by its productivity-retarding effects.)

Like my previous challenges to efficiency-centered arguments, then, the current challenge is less than fully decisive. Although the Lockean guidelines for the treatment of unfortunate workers could impede the maximizing of wealth in certain contexts, they could support wealth-maximization in other contexts. We cannot pin down the most probable results of those guidelines, till we know workers' attitudes toward risk and their attitudes toward wealth *vis-à-vis* leisure. Yet, notwithstanding that this most recent criticism of the wealth-maximizing version of Locke's ideas will join the earlier criticisms in being inconclusive, the cumulative effects of those overlapping criticisms are wide-ranging indeed. No challenge on its own is a lethal thrust, but the challenges together come close to inflicting such a thrust. At the very least, our sustained perusal of efficiency-focused arguments has revealed that those arguments themselves are limp and inconclusive as means of rescuing the labor theory of property.

Selective dutifulness

A final important difficulty that plagues the wealth-maximizing arguments in this context is the question of the dutifulness of people when confronted with natural-law demands. Central to the wealth-maximizing arguments is the contention that human beings would not elect to trouble themselves very much with toil if they stood to gain few direct benefits therefrom. According to efficiency-focused doctrines, people were so averse to laboring that they had to have prodigious incentives if they were ever to become trusty workers; and the only incentive strong enough to induce work reliably was the prospect of obtaining the fruits of one's endeavors. If human beings were not entitled to all the fruits of their successful exertions, they would be loath to undertake exertions very diligently or frequently.

Now, as I have remarked, the paramount problem with this efficiency-focused stance is that it pays no attention to the constant mandate directing people in a Lockean world to go about their lives industriously. An obligation to toil as diligently as possible would pertain to everyone inhabiting such a world. In light of that general duty, however, the creation of a profitable incentive to work was needed only if some or all of the natural-law requirements did not evoke trustworthy obedience on their own. If all the behests of natural law would elicit firm compliance by dint of their status as natural laws, and thus if the prescript calling for assiduous labor would attract firm compliance on its own, then institutions aimed at bringing about compliance would be starkly superfluous. Therefore, because efficiency-centered arguments have stressed the need for enticing people to honor the natural-law mandate that required diligent labor, the propounders of those arguments have ipso facto presumed that that mandate would not by itself win respect.

In short, the efficiency-focused arguments have emphasized that the obligation of industriousness would tend to be flouted in the absence of a remunerative scheme that supplied everyone with straightforwardly selfish grounds for heeding the obligation. Theorists who are bent on efficiency have assumed that obligatoriness would have to fuse with expedience in order to gain a purchase on human life. Alas, what is so dangerous about their piquant assumption is the implausibility of confining its scope to only a single norm. Insofar as we accept the likelihood that the obligation of industriousness would go unfulfilled when not combined with incentives that appealed to selfish urges, we can draw some arch inferences about the standing of other obligations. Although such inferences do not follow necessarily, they indeed do follow persuasively; if we never can know with certitude (on the basis of efficiency-focused arguments alone) whether our extrapolations are justified, we can feel some confidence nonetheless.

Since the natural obligation that called for steadfast industry did not by itself go very far toward ensuring that everyone would work hard, we ought to doubt whether the other precepts of natural law fared any better. Specifically, we have to raise some tough questions about the natural duty of everyone to abstain from interference with the proprietary holdings of others. In the state of nature, devoid of punitive mechanisms of government that could bring to bear overwhelming violence against anyone responsible for infractions of rights, the general duty of noninterference would suffer disregard. After all, as Locke himself frankly noted, the "greater part" of humanity were "no strict Observers of Equity and Justice" in the primeval stage of human affairs (TTG, II, §123). If people were not disposed to act in accordance with the obligation of industriousness, then they probably were not disposed to act in accordance with their other essential obligations, either. Uninclined to act virtuously, and unimpressed by the natural-law moorings of the duty to perform toil, people would hardly feel intense scruples about violating the natural-law prohibition on plunder.

To be sure, even someone residing in the state of nature would have to shrink from committing deeds of rapine in certain circumstances. Yet this reluctance would ensue from naked self-interest rather than from any nonprudential concern for heeding one's obligations – at least if the basic point of the efficiency-focused theories is to be believed. Moreover, given the lack of centralized enforcement for the rights held by everybody within the state of nature, there would very frequently not exist any prudential reasons for the eschewal of theft. On the manifold occasions when no prudential grounds for desisting from larceny were present, human agents like those envisioned by the efficiency-oriented reconception of the labor theory of ownership would almost certainly take scant notice of the duty borne by each person to respect the proprietary prerogatives of everyone else.

Thus, by underlining the need to reinforce natural duties through strong incentives, the efficiency-focused arguments have proclaimed the selfishness and recalcitrance of human beings. According to such arguments, people in the state of nature were moved far more by advantage than by obligatoriness; alone, the binding weight of a natural law had no significant effect on behavior. Yet, if this highlighting of people's disregard of natural mandates has pointed to the advisableness of giving some inducements for individuals to conform with the obligation of steadfast work, it also suggests that natural rights of ownership would afford little security when not yet backed by disciplinary institutions with reliable punishments. And, since the favoring of rights above privileges has tended to dwell on the security offered by full-fledged rights, this exposure of the rights' *in*solidity casts doubt upon their very desirableness.

In other words, the efficiency-focused arguments have gone a long way toward undercutting their own objectives. Such arguments have aimed to establish that proprietary entitlements were essential as the basic security-promoting vehicles for industriousness in the state of nature. However, the arguments unfold via a line of reasoning which suggests quite strongly that those entitlements would yield no greater security than would unembellished privileges.

What remains of efficiency

Earlier, this book delivered two chief verdicts on efficiency-focused doctrines. First, we have seen that the institution of private property in the state of nature was scarcely guaranteed to be more efficient than webs of entitlements involving few or no concrete rights. Second, even if the institution of private property was indeed the most efficient way of allotting various assets, it could only be justified on collectivist grounds – because some people within the state of nature would have fared better in a world of privileges-unattached-to-concrete-rights.

In the current chapter's approach to the efficiency-centered stance, we have found that the arrangements derivable from the labor theory of ownership would not embody the ideal of efficiency. This observation, of course, largely parallels and extends the first of the two main points that have previously been advanced. We move now to a discussion that parallels and extends the second of the previous points. This discussion will generalize that point by showing that no efficient matrix of rights and privileges was justifiable except on communitarian grounds.

Here the analysis will evolve by highlighting some tensions in the goal of efficiency. However, we shall not now stop to address a host of complicatedly technical and far-reaching difficulties, some of which relate to the ordering of people's desires, and others of which relate to the costs of the prospective transactions among people. Those problems, which have frequently been explored in writings that take the "law-and-economics" movement to task,[5] render numerous situations optimal in regard to the pursuit of efficiency. That is, those arcane but redoubtable problems make the goal of efficiency a partly indeterminate goal by allowing it to be realized through a plurality of diverging routes.

In spite of the aforementioned problems, which to a pretty large extent are ineliminable, the champions of Locke have good reason to align themselves with the overarching effort to maximize people's output of goods and services. After all, efficiency is a basic value that harmonizes quite

[5] Among the multitude of critiques of the law-and-economics theories, the most powerful contribution is still Duncan Kennedy, "Cost–benefit analysis of entitlement problems: a critique," 33 *Stanford Law Review* 387 (1981).

well with various pronouncements by Locke on the essential duty and privilege of human beings to gain the greatest possible sustenance – the highest possible level of comforts and conveniences – from the world. When we recall that "God . . . hath given the World to Men . . . to make use of it to the best advantage of Life, and convenience" and that "God gave the World to Men . . . for their benefit, and the greatest Conveniencies of Life they were capable to draw from it" (TTG, II, §§26, 34), we discover an outlook that should incline its modern proponents to endorse the quest for efficiency. If human flourishing was the cardinal end that everyone was required and allowed to serve, then the aim of maximizing the overall production of useful things was virtually a corollary.

Moreover, apart from squaring substantially with a number of Locke's explicit observations and recommendations, the bench mark of efficient productiveness can fill the gap left by the undoing of the labor theory of ownership. In light of that theory's arrant invalidity, the defenders of Locke must find alternative bases for the distribution of wealth. If they want to justify some particular scheme(s) for the apportionment of goods in humankind's natural state, then they have to search among Locke's other tenets and arguments. The labor theory of ownership provides nothing except an ersatz justification. Thus, not only can Lockeans quite warrantedly assert that the drive for efficiency is a drive which can be associated with the *Two Treatises of Government*; in addition, they *need* to employ the standard of efficiency as the lone available standard – or the best available standard – that can underpin a Lockean theory of property.

To be sure, the touchstone of efficiency in the state of nature would not normally prescribe a distribution of useful items that would be precisely similar to the distributional pattern commended by the labor theory of ownership. (Undoubtedly, the efficient patterns of distribution would usually converge with the labor theory's prescribed pattern in certain respects; however, the agreement would tend to be far from total.) Yet the norm of efficiency would at least confer a stamp of approval on *some* networks or arrangements of asset-holding and not on others. And, unlike the labor theory of property, it can be elaborated with arguments that are not entirely invalid.

Let us proceed to highlight, then, a basic disjuncture in the norm of efficiency. Heretofore, the discussions of efficiency in this volume have used the label "wealth-maximizing" as a synonym for "efficient." For the purposes of the arguments hitherto, this usage has been unproblematic. But now we must notice that the tag of "efficiency," in its general usage, has a somewhat broader sweep than the phrase "wealth-maximization." The concept of efficiency divides into two main parts – with various branches, most of which will go unrecounted here – and only one of those two chief parts is usually described as "wealth-maximization."[6]

On the one hand, the touchstone of efficiency can obtain in forms that are thoroughly aggregational. Expounded along these lines, the criterion of efficiency relates to the overall amount of wealth that ensues from the collective and individual projects undertaken by members of the human race (or any relevant subdivision of humankind). When the additive impulse of this orientation rules the day, distributive questions are completely subservient to the need for attaining the largest possible total quantity and value of goods. Insofar as structures of distribution affect the worth and level and quality of the aggregate output of desirable things, those structures clearly must be taken into account – but only as factors that can help to ensure the opportunities and incentives that will lead to the maximizing of total wealth. Productivity trumps fairness; or, rather, productivity is the measure of fairness.

On the other hand, a basic alternative approach to efficiency retains the objective of enlarging the total output of goods and services, while not pursuing that objective at the expense of what is commonly viewed as fairness. Although this widely espoused conception of efficiency can proceed along many paths, the path that has been most often traveled in recent decades is the one that carries the name of Pareto. Under this approach to efficiency, current institutions are not justified unless there is no available means of causing an improvement in someone's welfare without adversely affecting the position of someone else; and proposed institutions should not be adopted unless they will improve the well-being of a person or set of people without detracting from the well-being of anyone else. In short, the maximizing of wealth is here no longer strictly transindividual. Instead of being purely agglomerational, the maximizing of wealth goes ahead within the limits thrown up by the entitlement of each

[6] Several other distinctions, such as the often slighted difference between a person's fondness for a batch of goods and the person's readiness to pay for the goods, will surely have a bearing on the remarks that follow. Nonetheless, those distinctions are not here sufficiently important to make worthwhile an investigation of them and their complexities. Such an investigation would leave the gist of the following remarks intact, and would introduce a bevy of needless tangles. We now are looking primarily at the fostering of incentives for the production of the largest array of goods and services that was possible in the natural state of the human species, with constraints of distribution attached or not. And although one's conception of the largest feasible output would become more sophisticated and multiform if one took account of certain distinctions not posed here – such as the divide between the proclivity to gain satisfaction from certain goods and the willingness to pay the requested price of the goods – the basic problem of furnishing apt incentives for the stimulation of human productivity would persist in its general contours. Ergo, having to strike a balance between comprehensiveness and lucidity, the present discussion blurs some contrasts that might be honed and explored to good effect in various other arguments.

person to get the largest amount of goods achievable by someone in his or her position. Only in this respect do labels about the "maximizing of wealth" have pertinence – which doubtless is why such labels are hardly ever invoked as tags for this criterion of efficiency.

When we lend our countenance to this second version of efficiency, we must ask new questions about frameworks of entitlements. Under the aggregational approach to efficiency, the question to be resolved is how entitlements should be structured to elicit the most extensive and valuable medley of useful products from all the exertions of human beings (taken together). Under Paretian guidelines for the measurement of efficiency, by contrast, the question that comes to the fore is how entitlements should be structured to avoid placing anyone in a worse position than he or she would occupy in the absence of the chosen entitlements. To withstand the Paretian test, the availability of a class of entitlements must improve the holdings and welfare of some person(s), and it must not diminish the possessions and comforts that would otherwise be enjoyed by anybody else.

We here have looked at two broad conceptions of efficient productiveness: the wealth-maximizing version, which trains its focus primarily or exclusively on the aggregate output in any setting, and which thus casts very few glances at distributive problems; and a fairness-upholding version, which guards less against the constricting of the overall wealth of humankind than against the curtailment of any individual's wealth. Now, our purpose here is not to evaluate these conceptions of efficiency or other possible standards of efficiency on their merits. Nor shall we try to judge which conception tallies more persuasively with Locke's standpoint in his theory of property. After all, even if we highlight the tendency of Locke to conflate the use of "man" as a term for humankind and the use of "man" as a term for each particular human agent, we shall not have secured any clinching guidance on the matter at hand. Our noticing of his tendency will have cut in both directions for any choice that we have to make between the two general understandings of efficiency. If we view Locke's conflation of the individual and the species as a subsumption of the moral bearings and dignity of the former into the moral bearings and dignity of the latter, then we quite likely shall be disposed to read Locke's championing of prosperity as his firm adherence to the wealth-maximizing ideal. If on the other hand we see Locke's conflation of the individual and the species as a reduction of the moral posture of humankind to the moral posture of everyone who belonged to humankind, then we might well be disposed to read Locke's commendation of prosperity as his advocacy of the Paretian credo (or any doctrine basically similar).

Each of these interpretations can find substantial support within

Locke's texts. When we note in the *Second Treatise* the privilege of every human agent to place his or her survival ahead of the survival of anybody else, we buttress the attempt to classify Locke as a proleptic follower of Pareto. When we think instead of the importance attached by Locke to the preservation of humanity as a whole, we buttress the attempt to classify him as an exponent of the wealth-maximizing creed. Locke wrote, for instance, that "*by the Fundamental Law of Nature, Man being to be preserved*, as much as possible, when all cannot be preserv'd, the safety of the Innocent is to be preferred" (TTG, II, §16, emphasis in original), and he likewise avouched that laws should "tend to the preservation of the whole [of humanity or society], but cutting off those Parts, and those only, which are so corrupt, that they threaten the sound and healthy" (TTG, II, §171). These sentiments, while far from dispositive of our current question, do show at least that the aggregational tenor of the wealth-maximizing ideal was partly foreshadowed in the *Second Treatise of Government*. Locke's work can thus be cited by votaries of that ideal as well as by votaries of Paretianism.

Rather than dwelling upon the substantive flaws and virtues or the degree of faithful Lockeanism in the two wide-ranging conceptions of efficiency that have been outlined here, we shall focus upon the unlikelihood of a perfect coincidence between those conceptions in their recipes for economic arrangements. Each of them will classify sundry schemes of entitlements as efficient, while deprecating various other such schemes for their inefficiency. Yet the touchstones for these appraisals differ notably from the one conception to the other, as we have observed. Whereas the wealth-maximizing principle must decree the apportionment of some asset *X* to some human agent *Q* whenever this distributive pattern can indeed help to maximize the total output of goods and services, the Paretian principle disallows the assignment of *X* to *Q* unless the impact of the assignment will not lower anyone's welfare.

Of course, each of these two guidelines for distribution can warrant manifold regimes of entitlements. Moreover, some bundles of entitlements that feature in many wealth-maximizing regimes will doubtless coincide with some bundles of entitlements that feature in many Pareto-efficient regimes. But to accept the strong probability of overlapping elements in the two broad conceptions of efficiency is not to declare that those conceptions nearly always converge. Although in principle the determinations of optimality and suboptimality can differ hardly at all between the wealth-maximizing standpoint and the Paretian standpoint in a specific context, this result is certainly not preordained and in fact is close to being unimaginable. Far more probable is a rather wide divergence between the standpoints.

Given that a wealth-maximizing project in most conceivable circumstances has to avoid a throng of distributional outcomes which a Paretian project demands, and given likewise that a Paretian project must eschew a host of wealth-maximizing outcomes in virtually any setting, the chances are remarkably slight that every person will benefit at least as much from wealth-maximizing prescripts as from Paretian prescripts. And, of course, the chances also are remarkably slight that every person will benefit at least as much from Paretian prescripts as from wealth-maximizing prescripts. Some men and women will gain more assets in a web of entitlements devoted to the maximizing of wealth, and others will gain more assets in a web of entitlements devoted to Paretian objectives. To be sure, we cannot define at an abstract level the types of human agents who stand to profit from either one of these distributional schemes as opposed to the other. The relevant variables, connected partly to the structures of people's inclinations or preferences and partly to the existent modes of wealth, are far too complicated and abundant to allow any sweeping predictions. Yet, if the complexities of the variables must block almost every wide-ranging prediction, then they also practically exclude any full convergence between the distributional outcomes of a wealth-maximizing world and the distributional outcomes of a Paretian world; and, with much the same force, they practically exclude a scenario in which either of those worlds totally surpasses the other (by being advantageous for every person).

In sum, the patterns of holdings and entitlements in a context that has been governed by a starkly wealth-enhancing ideal will almost always diverge from the patterns of holdings and entitlements in an otherwise similar context that has been guided by Paretian objectives. Equally, there is no more than the slimmest likelihood that either the wealth-maximizing standard or the Paretian standard will yield outcomes that are superior to the alternative standard's outcomes for all people alike. Given the sheer variety of ways in which the one ideal or the other can prove to be advantageous, the possibility is remote indeed that one of the ideals will have more beneficial consequences for every member of humankind.

At any rate, the two chief contentions that have just been urged – the thesis about the noncoincidence of Paretian outcomes and wealth-maximizing outcomes, and the thesis about the nonattainment of universal preferability by either the wealth-enhancing dictate or the Paretian dictate – do not have to highlight the acute improbableness of the scenarios which they controvert. More important is the *possibility* of contrary scenarios, in which the Paretian outcomes and wealth-maximizing outcomes diverge, and in which neither set of outcomes is unalloyedly more attractive. When grasping that the basic states of affairs presented by those contrary scenarios are bound in most instances to hold, we grasp with helpful vividness that those states of affairs *can* hold. Illuminating indeed is the fact that Paretian norms and wealth-enhancing norms remain distinct from each other in almost every possible context, and illuminating as well is the fact that neither array of norms is universally superior to the other in any credible context; nonetheless, what is truly decisive is that Paretian norms and wealth-maximizing norms *can* diverge, and that neither broad set of norms can ever be *assured* of comprehensive superiority over the alternative set.

Now, before we ponder the implications of the divergences between wealth-maximization and Paretianism, and before we ponder the implications of the fact that neither standard is universally superior to the other, we should more fully take account of the openness that characterizes the principle of efficiency. Not only are there myriad concrete differences between the wealth-maximizing project and the Paretian project, but there are differences as well within each of those projects. Each of those two approaches to efficiency can yield a number of distributional options. When wealth-maximization is our goal, we encounter a host of divergent pathways for achieving the best production of goods against quite a steady background of individuals' preferences; and we encounter a further host of divergent pathways for achieving the best levels of sundry goods in light of the changing configurations of preferences which the goods help to shape and reshape. Likewise, when Pareto-optimality is our goal, we encounter many potential networks of distribution that can satisfy our objective. Countless schemes of distribution allot goods and services in ways that will each leave no room for improving anybody's position without harming the position of someone else. Any such scheme *D* is Pareto-optimal in the sense that a move away from *D* is disallowed flatly by the Paretian ideal of efficiency. But a Pareto-optimal scheme of distribution cannot trump any other Pareto-optimal distributional scheme, since a move from the latter to the former is just as strictly barred by Paretian guidelines as is a move from the former to the latter.

Like the competing claims advanced by wealth-maximizing norms and Paretian norms, the competing claims of the diverse options within each set of norms will prevent any option from improving *every*one's welfare in comparison with the welfare yielded by some or all of the other options. This point can be grasped quite easily in regard to the many structures of distribution that qualify as efficient under Paretian standards. After all, if a certain structure can make everyone better off than can any alternative structure, none of the alternative structures is Pareto-optimal; only the one best structure deserves to be classified that way.

Almost as clear is that this point about the lack of a universal supremacy will extend to the host of distributional frameworks that can serve as vehicles for the maximizing of wealth. After all, if one framework can lift everybody's wealth above the highest levels that would be fostered by any of the other frameworks, then only that one best framework can rightly be said to maximize the total prosperity of the human race. Because the race's wealth consists of all wealth embodied in individuals' holdings and in the benefits accruing to individuals from collective holdings, an arrangement that can bestow more riches than any other arrangement on every person will result ipso facto in the largest possible quantity of overall wealth. Thus, once we recognize the potential for a multiplicity of arrangements that can maximize wealth – a potential that must abide in nearly all conceivable circumstances – we knowingly or unknowingly affirm that each such arrangement will for some people be inferior to competing arrangements that can also maximize wealth.

In short, when one takes account of the open-endedness or indeterminateness in the ideal of efficiency, one should grasp that any efficient web of entitlements is bound to place some people in less desirable positions than they would occupy under other efficient matrices of entitlements. Given the enduring conflicts between Paretian and wealth-maximizing goals, and given the myriad of routes by which either set of goals can be realized, the fulfillment of either set of goals will nearly always involve a scheme of distribution that fails to promote the welfare of many people as much as other efficient schemes would. Most structures of distribution that are efficient will render optimal the positions of *some* people, yet no such structures will render optimal the position of *every*one. We must thus infer that the rules which would govern the apportioning of assets in a Lockean state of nature could never be justified except on communitarian grounds. Unable to ensure an optimal result for each person, and therefore unable to draw support from individualistic principles, the norms of distribution would have to stem from collective grounds as the lone available supports. Whether those grounds were Paretian principles or wealth-maximizing principles, they would justify norms by reference to an overall state of affairs – and not by reference to the distinctness or inviolability of each human subject. The specific grounds and norms would enable some human agents to realize the objective of procuring maximal comforts for themselves, while other human agents might fall far short of that objective.

Here a recapitulation, with some clarification, is in order. Because of the dead ends in the labor theory of ownership, the champions of Locke must sift through his cardinal postulates for guidance on distributive matters. As has been remarked, the fundament of the Lockean state of nature consisted in the duty and the right-protected privilege of every human agent to quest for the satisfaction of his or her basic wants. Although that fundament could square with manifold regimes-of-concrete-entitlements that were mostly at odds with one another quite sharply, it would yield some context-specific guidance toward the best methods for allotting various assets. When expanded into a call for outright flourishing and hence for a maximum of conveniences and comforts – an expansion quite clearly undertaken by Locke – the end of human survival would attain still more determinacy in its guidance. Further context-specific prescriptions could thus emerge.

Now, whatever the exact recommendations that issue from any focus on human wants and interests and prosperity, the recommendations must all be consequentialist. They all impart their advice by reference to the conditions needed for promoting human welfare and affluence; in other words, those recommendations stand or fall in accordance with their ability to promote the goal of efficient production. Yet nothing in this teleological focus can guarantee a consentaneity between the welfare of the collective and the welfare of any specified person. An institution that brings about the maximal well-being of humankind can have failed to maximize the well-being of some particular member(s) of humankind. Whether the fulfillment of consequentialist aims at the level of humanity occurs along Paretian lines or along the lines of stark wealth-enhancement, it can place some people in worse positions than they would have occupied if the species-wide aims had been effected by alternative routes. As has been observed, a pattern of outcomes that is optimal for the human race can consist easily of outcomes that are suboptimal for any number of persons separately. Thus, since the only relevant touchstone for Paretian arguments and wealth-maximizing arguments is the optimality of collective patterns, and since that touchstone can never guard against suboptimal outcomes for particular people, those arguments cannot furnish any individualistic grounding for the schemes of entitlements which they advocate. Efficiency-focused standpoints, when not allowed to stray from their own criteria, have to view the fate of each person as a normatively subordinate element in the fate of humankind.

Let us now consider one or two brief objections. Why does the discussion in the last paragraph ignore opportunities for individualistic modes of justification? After all, because there forever lurks the possibility that some means of giving effect to Paretian or wealth-maximizing principles will eventuate in the most desirable outcome for every person, there ipso facto remains the possibility that a splendid network of outcomes can indeed justify itself on the basis of each person's individualistic entitlement to the amplest possible measure of well-being.

This objection misunderstands the central problem examined here, for it ignores crucial arguments that were presented a short while ago. There is indeed always a possibility, however remote, that circumstances will develop wherein the best arrangement of distributive outcomes for humanity is also a pattern which endows every human being with the largest amount of wealth that he or she can accumulate through any efficient structure of holdings (in the context of the prevailing limits on the abundance of resources). Under those conditions, as has here been explained, only the one best structure of entitlements will be efficient. But such conditions are hardly sure to arise, and in fact will almost never arise. A theory that depends on such circumstances for the truthfulness of its appeals to "the sanctity of the individual" cannot rightly engage in those appeals; it can never come close to guaranteeing the actuality of the conditions that are essential for the pertinence of any individualistic lines of justification. Thus, to the extent that we can succeed in justifying an efficiency-focused theory's general recommendations and results (as opposed to some extremely special cases that might somehow emerge within the general scope of the theory's principles), we have to avoid relying on moral individualism and have to trade upon the moral collectivism that amounts to the theory's lifeblood. A wealth-maximizing or Paretian goal is communitarian, in the sense that its drive for optimal well-being eventuates in overall arrangements or patterns that are linked merely by chance to the optimal well-being of every individual.

This response to the first objection leads to a follow-up objection. Why do appeals to individualism crumble just because no framework of entitlements can manage to profit *every*body more than other such frameworks? Why should we chafe at granting the validity of the individualistic appeals if we allow that a host of frameworks of entitlements will include maximal benefits for *some* people (who can never be singled out beforehand)? And why should not the primal status of everyone as a holder of entitlements be enough to ground individualistic appeals, which can define the sanctity of the individual in terms of that primal status?

Confronted with this objection, posed in three rather different ways, we can opt for two chief rejoinders. First, and much less important, the objection has gone astray by assuming flatly that an efficient web of entitlements is bound to bring optimal results for some people (although not necessarily for all people). In fact, one can easily hypothesize a configuration of natural assets and human preferences that yields an efficient matrix of entitlements from which no one gains as much as he or she would have gained through certain other efficient webs of entitlements. Optimality for the whole of humankind, as judged by Paretian standards or by pure wealth-promoting standards, can involve sub-optimality for everyone in the species.

Far more important is a second reply, in which the major divergences between individualism and collectivism need to be highlighted. Efficiency-focused doctrines take as their defining objective the establishment of the greatest feasible quantity of wealth and welfare, although such doctrines tend to differ about how starkly aggregational the pursuit of wealth-enhancement should be. Whether a given theory trains its attention exclusively on the overall amount of goods, or whether it sets Paretian limits on the enlarging of that amount, it firmly seeks the augmentation of wealth in order to promote human flourishing. Efficiency-centered theories do not rule out altogether the attainment of maximal well-being by everyone, but they neither guarantee nor try to guarantee such an outcome. To be sure, they demand that outcome on any of the negligibly few occasions when it is possible; for, when possible, it does uniquely serve to maximize wealth and to realize a Pareto-efficient scheme of holdings. But those theories hardly strive to pursue that outcome on other occasions, since a posture of maximal well-being for every person is not then prerequisite to the maximizing of wealth or to the construction of Pareto-optimal schemes of holdings. Save in the exceedingly rare conditions where the attainment of maximal well-being by everyone has become feasible, it is not essential by any means for compliance with efficiency-centered standards.

In other words, though an efficiency-focused theory calls for the channeling of the largest possible quantity of riches to every person, it does so only when such a course is available and hence when that course is necessary for the accomplishment of the theory's principal aim – the aim of maximizing humankind's total output or of establishing a Pareto-efficient structure of entitlements. Projects for assigning to anybody an individually optimal share of riches are dispensable and subordinate, and are undertaken only if they will be of service to the optimality of collective outcomes and patterns. When an efficient scheme of entitlements has allotted to any person a batch of assets at least as good as the batch attainable by that person in every other efficient scheme, the apportioned assets have flowed to their new possessor merely as a product or function of the overarching ends of the human species. Were the vesting of those assets in that recipient not promotive of the species-wide ends, the vesting would not conform to Paretian standards or to wealth-maximizing standards and would thus not take place in any efficient scheme of things.

In short, the creed of Paretianism and the creed of wealth-maximization offer their proposals in a collectivist key, to which the outcomes of individualistic doctrines are fortuitously connected at most. Those creeds do not advance theses about the putative right of every individual to the maximizing of his or her welfare – a right which all legitimate frameworks of entitlements must preserve. Instead, the efficiency-focused creeds pursue objectives relating to humanity as a whole, and they do not justify the endowment of any specific person with an optimum of well-being unless that endowment tends toward the realization of the humanity-wide objectives.

Of course, most efficient frameworks of entitlements will indeed confer maximal benefits on some people. By and large, that is, each of those frameworks will bless a number of people with holdings which exceed or match the holdings that would be extended to those people by any other efficient framework of rights and liberties. But the fact that most of the efficient assemblages of entitlements will give maximal amounts of wealth to some people, and the fact that on rare occasions an efficient assemblage of entitlements will even give a maximal amount of wealth to every person, cannot inflict the slightest damage on my arguments here. Any number of communitarian policies or arrangements can serve the interests of particular people by allowing them to receive more wealth than they otherwise would receive; and, at truly exceptional junctures, some communitarian policy or arrangement may serve the interests of everyone by making everyone better off than would any alternative arrangements or policies. In other words, the decisive question here is not whether efficient matrices of entitlements can bring optimal advantages for some people, nor whether the ideal of efficiency can bring optimal advantages for *every*one in extremely rare situations. Rather, the telling questions are how the efficient matrices of entitlements have had to be justified and how they impose restraints (or how much they impose restraints) on the self-interested projects of individuals.

In this response to the second of the two main objections that were hypothesized above, we have heretofore probed the kinds of *justification* which efficiency-centered theories must adopt. Those theories elaborate their proposals by adverting to the requirements and the aims of a collectivity, and by treating persons' assigned holdings as mere offshoots or aspects of the collectivity's enterprises. Let us now proceed to explore the curbs which those theories place on the self-interested projects of individuals.

With regard to wealth-maximizing doctrines, the relevant limits are quite apparent. Each person *Q* is obligated to show respect for the rights that are bestowed on others by a wealth-maximizing system, whether or not the system has accorded *Q* the most generous batch of assets which he can gain from any feasible structure of possessions that is wealth-maximizing or Pareto-optimal. For the sake of boosting the total output of humankind (or an apposite subdivision of humankind), each person must submit to the trammels posed by the rights which other people enjoy. The need to procure optimal results at the level of the community or the species will supply the crucial grounds for the sacrificing of optimal results at the level of specific persons; to any extent necessary, the enlarging of aggregate production will trump every individual's freedom to advance his or her own interests.

With regard to Paretian doctrines, the imposing of checks on the advancement of selfish interests is perhaps less striking at first. After all, the Paretian standard forbids the diminution of anyone's welfare for the sake of aggregate output. Everybody in a Paretian world enjoys a type of secureness (bearing upon her interests and her accomplishments) that is totally unavailable in a wealth-maximizing world. But only an astounding one-sidedness can prompt someone to depict this type of security as the means of endowing individuals with the greatest possible wealth or welfare. What the Paretian guidelines really protect is not so much the holdings of individuals as the general patterns and limits which the guidelines decree. As was emphasized in my earlier discussion of Hohfeld, any right belonging to a person *Q* entails the shouldering of a duty by someone other than *Q*. Rights and obligations are connected reciprocally, and hence all rights to secureness must involve obligations to abide by those rights. Thus a Paretian right, which shields its holder against the worsening of his status, always comes with a duty borne by everyone else to shrink from committing any deeds which will harm that status. Just as the maximizing of an individual's riches in a world of pure wealth-enhancement must operate within curbs laid down by the maximizing of a collectivity's riches, so the enlargement of anybody's riches in a world of Paretian buffers can only go ahead within the confines of those buffers (which leave room for shifts among ranks). Anyone who aspires to improve her lot can legitimately do so only if her improvement will cause no harm to the standing of any other person(s); if harm indeed will ensue, her wishes to expand her own comforts and conveniences will have run afoul of somebody else's right to security from the harm.

To be sure, Locke carefully avoided suggesting that people's basic entitlements to preserve their lives and to seek prosperity were full-blown "meal tickets" which could guarantee that all human agents would flourish by being given the items necessary for flourishing. The entitlement to self-conservation and the entitlement to pursue the means of flourishing were only entitlements to *quest* for survival and prosperity. They were not assurances that the quests would succeed; even more clearly, they were not assurances that prosperity and survival could be gained with little or no toiling. (These concessions, made here willingly for the sake of argument, will have to undergo modification when we see the profound import of Locke's failure to devise a valid theory of property. As will become apparent in chapter 6, the theses which Locke intended to suggest do not always coincide with the theses to which his arguments are committed.) However, none of the concessions in this paragraph is inconsistent with my present analysis.

As has here been argued, the workings of Paretianism and the workings of wealth-maximization circumscribe in any number of ways the latitude of people to promote their own interests. Constraints imposed by the efficiency-centered doctrines are not merely constraints on the degrees and kinds of individual flourishing that anyone may enjoy. Such constraints also close a multitude of pathways by which the flourishing can be sought. When a person *Q* holds a right to be secure from all harm engendered by the acquisitions of other people, each other human agent not only is debarred from effecting an acquisition that will redound to the injury of *Q*, but also is barred from even trying to carry out such an acquisition where the detriment to *Q*'s interests is reasonably foreseeable. Like other proprietary rights, the rights allotted in furtherance of wealth-maximizing goals or Paretian goals are entitlements that shield their bearers against infractions and attempted infractions. In order to keep the aggregate production of goods as high as possible, or in order to sustain the levels of welfare that Paretian guidelines serve to protect, the leeway of individuals to strive for the satisfaction of their own wants will suffer abridgement.

Let us look, finally, at the notion that individualistic justifications for efficiency-centered norms are indeed available because of each person's standing as someone qualified to procure entitlements. Should we concede that wealth-maximizing and Pareto-optimal structures of entitlements can aptly bedeck themselves with the garb of individualism by defining the sanctity of the individual as nothing but a moral capacity for holding entitlements? The chief problem with such a tack is that it too glibly wipes away the disjuncture between collectivism and individualism. Although cogent critiques of that disjuncture are feasible and desirable, they have to exhibit more subtlety than the question just asked.

To portray a scheme of entitlements as individualistic by describing every person's bare membership in the scheme as the crucial hallmark of its atomistic tenor is to construe the notion of individualism as purely formal. If we merely know that everyone occupies the status of an entitlement-holder in a certain regime of privileges and rights, we know nothing about the substance of the regime or about the substance of anybody's posture therein. Our knowledge, relating to the formal membership of each person in any system of entitlements, cannot distinguish between heavily communitarian and strongly individualistic entitlements; the people governed by communitarian norms are members of their communitarian network, quite as much as the people governed by individualistic norms are members of their individualistic network. Thus, if we are inclined to grant that the sheer participation of each person in a framework for the assigning of entitlements will have rendered the framework individualistic, we ought to recognize that that "individualistic" framework can be communitarian through and through. We have clearly not ruled out the prospect that the "individualistic" system of entitlements will need to be justified in terms that must concentrate upon the ends of humanity as a whole. We likewise have failed to rule out the prospect that that network of entitlements will involve the clamping of numerous restrictions on every individual's pursuit of selfish concerns. In short, we might soon discover that a wholly abstract individualism has nothing more in common with a full-fledged individualism than the will of Spinoza's God had in common with the will of a human being. They "have no point of agreement except the name. They could be no more alike than the celestial constellation of the Dog and the dog that barks."[7]

What has just been disparaged as a clumsy attempt to override the dichotomy between individualism and communitarianism is very much akin to clumsy attempts that might emerge from the opposite direction. Faced with a sternly individualistic matrix of entitlements, perhaps largely along the lines of the matrix envisioned by extreme Social Darwinists, a hopeful observer might contend that the bloodshed and the leeway for piggishness everywhere around him are solidly communitarian. This jaunty analyst might explain that a social system with entitlements which make brutal grasping a near-inevitability has thereby oriented itself toward the collective goal of fostering the very conditions that encourage the brutal grasping. Such an analysis has reduced collectivism to a glaringly empty shell that can be filled with the substance of *every* social arrangement, including every arrangement that is horrifyingly atomistic. If social arrangements are communitarian just by virtue of being social arrangements, then the tag of "communitarian" has entirely lost its distinctive significance. With this evacuation of meaning and specificity, the pseudocommunitarian approach to obvious individualism aligns itself with the pseudoindividualist approach to patent collectivism. For each approach, the reinterpretation of social life cannot work except by flagrantly disregarding substantive features and by giving exclusive pride of place to an infinitely elastic form. Hence, the reinterpretations undertaken by such approaches will have no impact on the arguments that have been presented in this section; after all, my arguments highlight *substantive* problems dealing with restrictions on conduct and with avenues of justification.

[7] Baruch Spinoza, *The Ethics*, in *The Ethics, Treatise on the Emendation of the Intellect, Selected Letters* (Indianapolis: Hackett, 1992) (S. Shirley trans. and S. Feldman ed.), 45 (Scholium to proposition 17 of part I).

6 The drawing of consequences

Having explored the invalidity of Locke's attempt to justify private ownership, and having seen that his labor theory cannot be rescued through alternative rationales or grounds, we move finally to the consequences of his lack of success. Because the labor theory has foundered, and because there are no direct substitutes for that theory which might reaffirm its prescriptions, the most salient underlying axiom in the Lockean state of nature – the axiom of humanity's privilege and duty to seek the prospering of all human agents and the prospering of humankind as a whole – had to yield criteria that could fill the gap left yawning by the dissolution of the labor theory. Locke's central postulate had to provide not just an abstract basis for humankind's obtention of sustenance, but also the more specific precepts that would direct the apportioning of the sustenance.

The labor theory was here to stay

Yet, before we investigate the revamped elaboration of Locke's perspective, we ought to grapple briefly with a preliminary question. On the one hand, nothing in this book's arguments about the labor theory of property rests on the thesis that the rights of ownership amassed in the state of nature would continue to hold their force as rights after the transition from humanity's presocietal stages to societal intercourse and conventions. My critique of Locke can apply in full to his search for origins, irrespective of the obligatoriness or nonobligatoriness of natural proprietary rights within civil society. On the other hand, the critique presented here will have delivered an even more telling verdict if its chief target – the natural apportionment of desirable things to owners – served as a fundament of property not only during the primeval phase of human life, but also during the era which replaced that phase. Insofar as Locke believed that the labor theory of ownership was a durable and resilient doctrine with an important bearing on the frameworks of rights and privileges that occurred in full-fledged societies, a critique of the labor theory can have momentous implications indeed. We therefore are well advised to ask if any of the distributional patterns proposed within that theory would be transferred from the primal circumstances of human beings to the contexts of civil regulation.

Let us be quite precise here about what we need to investigate. As was indicated in chapter 4, we should not fritter away time by inquiring whether Locke avouched that the labor theory of ownership delineated all of the rules which fashioned the legitimate proprietary arrangements in any commonwealth. Although a surprising number of analysts have upbraided Locke for putting forward a model that in certain ways was irrelevant to the highly complicated conditions of advanced societies, he himself expressly affirmed and underscored that partial irrelevance; he thus ought not to be charged with having failed to descry it. Locke did not hesitate to observe that, once the institutions of civil governance had arrived on the scene, the natural standards expounded by the labor theory of property would lose a share of the leverage which they enjoyed as the crucial norms for the conferring of ownership. Locke devised his labor theory to unearth the *roots* of property. He never professed to be recounting the full array of criteria that shaped the distribution of products in a civil society. Rather, he merely aspired to adduce the norms that would decide the apportioning of riches in circumstances where much of nature's bounty had yet to be acquired by anyone. He thus could hardly decline to grant that those original norms would have to undergo some elaboration and some modifications when useful items had nearly all become tied to owners:

> [A]fterwards, in some parts of the World, (where the Increase of People and Stock, with the *Use of Money*) had made Land scarce, and so of some Value, the several *Communities* . . . by Laws within themselves, regulated the Properties of the private Men of their Society, and so . . . *settled the Property* which Labour and Industry began. (TTG, II, §45, emphasis in original.)

In sum, Locke clearly did not expect the natural bases of distribution to carry over into civil society without being attenuated or supplemented in any way. However, if he plainly did not suppose that the natural *criteria* of distribution would operate in civil society with as much force as in the primal era of humankind, he did suppose that the natural *rights* which accrued to people under those criteria would retain their validity even after the primal phases of humankind had settled into the past. Locke noted frequently and emphatically that the chief objective which impelled human agents to create civil institutions was the bolstering of proprietary rights. A horde of passages in the *Second Treatise* convey this view of society and government. For instance, Locke famously asserted that the "great and *chief end* therefore, of Mens uniting into Commonwealths, and putting themselves under Government, *is the Preservation of their*

Property" (TTG, II, §124, emphasis in original). We meet with this view as well in the *Letter on Toleration*:

[M]en are so dishonest that most of them prefer to enjoy the fruits of other men's labour rather than work to provide for themselves; therefore, to protect their possessions, their wealth and property, and also their liberty and bodily strength, which are their means of livelihood, they are obliged to enter into society with one another, so that by mutual assistance and combined forces each man may have secure and private possession of the things that are useful for life. (LT, 125)

Now, the obvious reading of these passages and the numerous similar passages is that rights of ownership procured in the state of nature would remain completely or very largely intact throughout the processes of conversion from that primordial state to all legitimate schemes of government. If natural rights did not keep their force as rights, and if no one thought that such rights would keep their force, we are bound to feel puzzled by Locke's insistence that human beings erected social frameworks in order to preserve their rights duly. If people stood to become curtailed of all their natural proprietary rights through the very advent of civil governance, then they undertook the "preserving" of those rights in a ludicrously inept manner. Hence, uninclined to pronounce Locke guilty of indulging in stark absurdities, we should now conclude that he depicted the natural rights of ownership as entitlements that extended past the state of nature without dissolution.

Yet, however straightforward and inviting is the position just advocated, it has won no esteem in certain quarters. In recent years, some analysts have contended that Locke envisioned the natural rights of ownership as way stations that were left behind whenever the natural circumstances of humanity (in a given area) had been superseded. According to this interpretation, Locke's references to social and political institutions as preservers of rights were concerned only with rights established by civil laws.[1]

Once a government with its rules of property had supplanted the state of nature, it indeed had no Hohfeldian power to negate the rights which its own rules conferred. A holder of any rights established by civil laws was persistently immune from the nonconsensual changing of those

[1] As should be plain, my references in this chapter to "civil laws" and the "civil law" do not focus on the civil-law/common-law divide. Instead, the relevant separation here is between the civil law and the *natural* law – between the law in an organized society and the law in the state of nature.

For the most notable exposition of the view of Lockean natural rights which this section of my final chapter is combatting, see James Tully, *A Discourse on Property* (Cambridge: Cambridge University Press, 1980), chapter 7. For some early criticism of Tully on this point, see John Mackie, "Book review," 32 *Philosophical Quarterly* (1982), 91, 93; Jeremy Waldron, "Locke, Tully, and the regulation of property," 32 *Political Studies* 98 (1984).

rights. In this respect, legitimate governments did surely *preserve* rights. But, we are told now, such governments at their origins were not similarly disabled with regard to the proprietary entitlements that had been achieved in the natural stages of the human condition. Quite the contrary. Anyone who was endowed with natural entitlements of ownership had had to relinquish them, as soon as he or she left the state of nature by opting to join a realm of social interaction and governmental authority. That is, the inception of society and its norms entailed the voiding of natural rights and the reallotment of people's holdings on the basis of conventional standards (as opposed to originary standards that anteceded conventions). Of course, nothing *precluded* a wholesale or nearly wholesale coincidence between the natural webs of assigned rights and the conventional webs thereof; however, by the same token, nothing *guaranteed* a blanket convergence. To any extent allowable under the restrictions of natural law, the conventionally determined rights could differ notably from the rights amassed in the state of nature. Likewise, the conventions themselves could plainly differ in numerous respects from the right-bestowing norms that had reigned throughout humanity's primal era.

In other words, or so this recent approach to Locke contends, the institutions of government preserved human beings' rights in two central ways while not preserving them in another crucial way. A legitimate government in a Lockean scenario always had to wait for consent from owners before rescinding any rights of the owners that the government had itself established. Thus, the proprietary entitlements created by civil laws would generally be preserved against abrogation (though voluntary transfers of the entitlements were allowed, of course). In addition, obviously, the government would protect the rights of each human agent from the thievery of his fellows. Not only did such rights stand in need of preservation from any redistributive fickleness on the part of the government that had granted them, but they likewise had to be preserved from all deeds of plunder that might be carried out by any person or set of people within society at large. This latter species of preservation, the preserving of rights against the evils of criminality through good law-enforcement, was the very essence of government in a Lockean world.

By contrast, a third species of preservation – the preserving of natural rights of ownership – did not come about, at least not de jure. Legitimate governments were not obligated to treat the natural proprietary endowments of people as the bedrock units on which the workings of civil law had to ground themselves. Instead, the natural rights of ownership had to fall by the wayside. Dominion over all goods became collective dominion, as society through its government hence received the power to define and distribute each right of ownership on the basis of conventional rules.

Insofar as people retained the holdings that they had garnered in their presocietal state, they did so merely because their natural rights of property chanced to be coextensive with the rights assigned to them by the pertinent civil laws. The reason for the continuity of their holdings was not that their original entitlements somehow had been preserved. Although governments indeed were bound strictly to preserve *conventional* rights of ownership, the very sustaining of conventional rights involved the superseding of natural rights.

In reply to this new interpretation of Locke's ideas, we probably should begin by conceding that the interpretation is not so outlandish that it ought to be dismissed straightaway as void of any support. Though formidably tendentious, the verdicts expounded by the new approach are not flagrantly and directly at odds with the relevant pronouncements and arguments of the *Second Treatise*. One should not confuse the implausibility of a reading with the impossibility thereof. In every part of the *Second Treatise* where Locke extolled the formation of society as a means for the "preserving" of rights, he may indeed have sought to suggest no more than the "preserving" of *civil* rights of ownership (along with the natural rights to bodily integrity and to freedom and to the general quest for one's sustenance and welfare). That is, he may never have had in mind the carrying over of any natural rights of property into the regimes of legal entitlements that emerged as successors to the primal conditions of the human race. We can appositely impugn such a reading of Locke's intentions, but we cannot rule it out unequivocally on the basis of his wording alone.

All the same, even if the new approach does not clash unmistakably with the words of Locke's text, it leaves itself acutely vulnerable to criticism. It relies on giving "preserve" (and any cognate forms of "preserve") a thoroughly forward-looking sense; it declares that the sole proprietary entitlements due to be preserved were entitlements created *after* the instituting of preservative mechanisms and measures. Less strained readings, which opt to define "preserve" in harmony with typical usage, will understand the phrasing of Locke's account as quite a manifest signal that the role of government in sheltering property would apply retrospectively as well as prospectively. We shall more convincingly take account of the Lockean emphasis on "preserving" if we avouch that the people who began the institutions of government were thereby aiming to keep the rights of ownership which they held as they established those institutions.

A bad argument

More important than any tussles over the best way to construe specific phrases and terms, however, is the quality of the arguments that have been propounded as supports for the unconventional reading of Locke's text. Even if that reading were less implausible as an understanding of particular sentences and passages, it would lack much force in trying to square itself with broader strands of Locke's theory. Among the flimsy arguments put about in justification of the unconventional reading is a line of thought partly similar to one of the four false trails that we examined in chapter 4. In such a line of thought, the strategy is to highlight the labor theory's presumed irrelevance and insignificance with regard to any setting where all exploitable land had been appropriated. Within such a setting, people could not find unowned assets on which to toil, and therefore the prevailing scheme of entitlements excluded any further obtention of proprietary prerogatives through one's work. Hence, either a continued endorsement of the labor theory's standards would disallow some human agents from exercising their general right to procure sustenance, or it would eventuate in conflicting titles to goods. Bereft of any ability to yield determinate guidelines that would do full justice to every person's indefeasible natural rights, the labor theory could no longer hold sway. And, because the labor theory ceased to enjoy any application, the rights bestowed in accordance with its criteria were doomed to lapse. Civil law, which emerged as the replacement for those criteria, became the lone source of rights of property.

The argument just rehearsed has gone amiss in two chief ways. First, as we have explored in depth, the laments about the irrelevance of the labor theory of property – an irrelevance that came about as society and government were established – are mostly unsupportable and unwise. Although the labor theory runs aground upon a variety of deep problems, the transition to social governance (from the state of nature) is clearly not one of them.

Let us momentarily overlook the labor theory's manifold weaknesses. In a setting where usable plots of land had all been appropriated, then, riches would be assigned to people by exactly the routes set forth in the labor theory. Remember that that theory prescribed the distribution of unowned assets to anyone who had worked upon them. Such a principle of distribution would not be violated by the proper workings of people's entitlements in any context where nothing was unowned and hence where nothing at all was left to be originally acquired. Furthermore, not only would the principles of the labor theory go untransgressed, but they would likewise go untranscended; after all, they included principles of exchange that would operate in a context where the owners of fertile land (and other means of production) coexisted with people who owned nothing aside from their respective capacities for toil.

In the state of nature as sketched by Locke, the batch of entitlements that rewarded any individual's toil was partly constituted of powers dealing with the transfer of goods. Many familiar elements of the Lockean natural state, such as the remunerating of servants for their endeavors, relied on powers-of-transfer through and through. If people did continue to hold the full array of their natural prerogatives of ownership when they joined themselves to the structures of a civil society, they continued to hold the powers that enabled various transfers of their possessions. Thus, if natural prerogatives of ownership extended into the jural frameworks of societies, then the reimbursement of toilers through the payment of wages could go ahead as a matter of routine within those societies. As a result, the fact that all exploitable land had undergone appropriation was not a threat to the well-being of landless people. By exercising powers of transfer, human agents with dominion over productive forces could convey the necessities of life (or the means of acquiring them) to workers in exchange for the workers' productive activities. Since everyone held the natural Hohfeldian power to alienate temporarily her capacity for labor – or to alienate the services she performed – and since the proprietors of material riches held natural Hohfeldian powers to alienate the sundry components of their wealth, everyone with a fairly sound constitution would be able to keep herself alive by toiling for others in a world where every parcel of land had been appropriated already. (Fundamental duties of charity would impel the handing over of sustenance to people who were not able-bodied.) Only if landless persons had been disqualified completely from exchanging their toil for cash or for other kinds of reimbursement, would they have been precluded from surviving in regions where there was no more land unpossessed. But because human beings were entitled to make exchanges during the primal epoch before the advent of civil institutions, and because our hypothesis here has been that the entitlements of the primal epoch carried over subsequently to the age of civil laws, we have to conclude that the acquiring of every portion of land throughout any area would not prevent landless people from giving due effect to their basic rights.

Locke, of course, not merely believed that all-encompassing swarms of acquisitions would pose no threat to anyone's basic rights; he assumed as well that the all-embracing sweep of ownership would in fact redound to the *benefit* of nonowners. Since the spread of human dominion over the entirety of the earth would involve the spread of a benign exploitation of the earth's riches, the outcome of that spread would enhance the fortunes of everybody. Somewhat like the Deity's filling of the earth with the glorious knowledge of Himself as envisaged by Isaiah and Habakkuk, the filling of the world with the enterprise and talents of human owners was a situation that blessed all people. Locke often made this point by contrasting the impecuniousness of the American Indians with the comforts of the highly developed land of the English. "For I aske whether in the wild woods and uncultivated wast of America left to Nature, without any improvement, tillage or husbandry, a thousand acres will yeild the needy and wretched inhabitants as many conveniencies of life as ten acres of equally fertile land doe in Devonshire where they are well cultivated?" (TTG, II, §37.) In a much-discussed passage, Locke asserted even more explicitly that the spread of labor and ownership throughout a country was a boon to all people, to nonowners as well as owners. Having declared firmly that "'tis *Labour* indeed that *puts the difference of value* on every thing" (TTG, II, §40, emphasis in original), he proceeded to the following observation:

> There cannot be a clearer demonstration of any thing, than several Nations of the *Americans* are of this, who are rich in Land, and poor in all the Comforts of Life; whom Nature having furnished as liberally as any other people, with the materials of Plenty, i.e. a fruitful Soil, apt to produce in abundance, what might serve for food, rayment, and delight; yet for want of improving it by labour, have not one hundreth part of the Conveniencies we enjoy: And a King of a large and fruitful Territory there feeds, lodges, and is clad worse than a day Labourer in *England.* (TTG, II, §41, emphasis in original)

In short, far from serving to undermine the ability of people to obtain sustenance, the extending of proprietary dominion to every usable plot of land was the surest means of strengthening that ability – for those who remained landless as well as for the landowners. Once all the earth and the earth's bounty had been appropriated and parceled out, a typical laborer might indeed have very few opportunities to become an owner of land, at least in the short term; still, he would enjoy ready access to a greater supply of comforts and conveniences than was ever within the reach of any landowner during the presocietal stage of humankind.

Now, as was earlier remarked, the principles of the labor theory of ownership could never ordain the multitudinous paths by which they would be effectuated in specific regimes of law. Those basic principles, and the throngs of entitlements which they had established, surely could not prescribe the myriad specificities of contract law or indeed any other body of law. Nor could the general principles of the labor theory determine the extent to which natural rights and powers had to be limited for the sake of bringing about a legal structure that would preserve those exact rights and powers. But such observations, however unexceptionable, are starkly beside the point as a criticism of my current analysis. Here the sole point at issue is whether natural proprietary prerogatives emerged intact from the state of nature when human beings entered civil society. We can affirm that everyone's prerogatives carried over into civil society, without attempting to deduce all the nuts and bolts of societal arrangements from those prerogatives in themselves or from the chief criteria that engendered those prerogatives. For purposes of dealing with many of the nuts-and-bolts questions of a society, the fundaments of the labor theory were doubtless of little help; yet those fundaments were crucial in setting out the baseline positions which the nuts and bolts were intended largely to fortify.

Let us now presume arguendo that analysts are correct in avouching that the norms in the labor theory of ownership were utterly irrelevant and obsolescent as soon as frameworks of civil laws had emerged. Despite what has just been argued, we shall grant for the moment that the relation between the civil laws and the natural principles was one of pure superseding rather than one of buttressing and consolidating. In other words – according to our briefly adopted assumption – not only were the labor theory's directives incapable of serving as guides for all the branches and involutions in laws concerned with the apportionment of wealth, but they also were unable to serve as guides for even the general drift of those laws. Yet, in spite of becoming saddled with this temporary hypothesis, we should hardly feel obliged to conclude that human beings' earliest rights of ownership did not endure the transition from the state of nature to the authoritative control of civil governance. After all, the rescinding of particular norms as guides or touchstones for future acquisitions of goods would scarcely have to involve the nullifying of any previous acquisitions made on the basis of those norms. A thoroughgoing refusal to abide any longer by the labor theory's principles could conjoin with a thoroughgoing refusal to discard any outcomes which those principles had theretofore yielded. A prospective repeal would not inevitably ordain a retroactive annulment.

We can think more vividly about the disjunction between past and future results by going back to the image of the labor theory's norms as the "roots" of ownership. In general, the trunks of trees grow in ways quite different from the ways in which the trees' roots grow; the roots are subterranean and horizontal and very frequently downward-pushing, while the trunks are above ground and are typically upright. In these respects, the principles of a trunk's development notably diverge from the principles by which its roots develop. All the same, the trunk can never detach itself from its roots except by bringing its own viability to a close. It preserves what its roots have done, and it builds itself upon their growth even as its own growth proceeds along a sharply contrasting vector. Supplementation and incorporation, not cancelation and undoing, mark the overall ties between the roots and the trunk.

In a like manner, the posited divergence between the touchstones of distribution in a full-fledged society and the corresponding touchstones within the state of nature would leave copious room for the persistence of natural rights and powers in the society. Even if we have arguendo held that the precepts of distribution in civilized regimes not only would be *underdetermined* by the norms of the labor theory but also would unfold as outright *departures* from those norms, we have scarcely held that the civilized regimes would abolish the entitlements that had been established by the primeval norms. A far-reaching transmutation of distributive guidelines could occur without scotching the rights and powers that had come into play before the transmutation. To be sure, by contrast with the upper part and the lower part of a tree, an altered framework of distribution could sever itself completely and viably from the elements of the framework that anteceded it. Originary entitlements could abruptly lapse. But the altered framework of distribution would never *have* to uproot or override those entitlements just by dint of being an altered framework; and, in a Lockean scheme of things with requirements for the preservation of natural rights and powers, a shift in the criteria for apportioning goods indeed would *not* result in the canceling of originary entitlements. Such a shift would not entail anything athwart the Lockean focus on the need to preserve natural rights.

Another bad argument

A second faulty argument in this area is closely related to a strand of the first argument. Here attention moves to the people in control of the earth and the earth's riches at the dawn of society. Because the holdings of these people extended to all nonhuman assets, and because everyone had a general right not to be prevented from using nature for sustenance, the presocietal owners of natural bounty were obligated to relinquish their wealth in order to avoid massive infringements of the general rights of nonowners. (Or so we are asked to believe.) If the natural proprietary prerogatives of the owners had remained intact, then their duties to facilitate the survival of their contemporaries would have gone alarmingly unobserved. Nothing less than a surrender of assets to communal dominion would ensure proper compliance with those duties; had that surrender not occurred, the ability of the landless people to satisfy their most pressing needs would have disappeared.

Like the previous argument, this second bad argument has erred by drawing far too bold conclusions and by disregarding certain entitlements that were taken for granted in the labor theory of property. Perhaps the supersession of natural entitlements and the reassignment of holdings by a newly fashioned society would allow the needs of the landless to be met, but those needs could also be met in ways anticipated by the Lockean labor theory. After all, as was noted in response to the first bad argument, the ownership commended by Locke's theory was a set of prerogatives that included the power to convey goods or money in return for a laborer's performance of useful acts. Thus, insofar as the owners of the earth and the earth's fruits at the outset of civil life were in need of help for the enhancement of their possessions, some opportunities for employment awaited anyone with a reasonably sound mind and body. That is, healthy people who owned no capital could sustain themselves by toiling for wages or by carrying out services for fees – whenever a demand for the toil or the services existed. Such people could stay alive quite comfortably without owning any land or other nonhuman factors of production. Indeed, as has here been emphasized, Locke maintained that landless workers in a productive society would live better than the most flourishing landowners in the primal stage of human development.

If healthy people among the landless could secure their well-being through reciprocally beneficial exchanges with the owners of the earth and its fruits, landless people who were infirm could also retain a hold on life, through the operations of charity. As has been pointed out, everyone with sufficient resources in the state of nature and in subsequent times was duty-bound to relieve the plight of the indigent. According to Locke, who underlined this duty throughout a well-known passage that was quoted at length earlier, "*Charity* gives every Man a Title to so much out of another's Plenty, as will keep him from extream want, where he has no means to subsist otherwise" (TTG, I, §42, emphasis in original). Although people who were both landless and physically decrepit or mentally decrepit had no usable factors of production at their disposal, their ability to remain alive would not suffer hazardous neglect in a world informed by the principles of the labor theory of ownership. Just as the batches of entitlements prescribed by that theory would include powers of transfer which made wages and fees possible, so those batches would come with duties of alms-giving which safeguarded the interests of the debilitated. Such duties, moreover, would address the needs of the healthy when productive employment was not available. Like handicapped men and women who could not perform work, an able-bodied but landless person who could not find an opportunity for selling his or her services was then entitled to receive aid.

In short, a system of entitlements governed by the axioms of the labor theory would provide for the basic welfare of people who did not own any means-of-production outside themselves. Because the owners of land and capital had the power to exchange fees or wages for the toil of their fellows, and because they likewise had duties to assist any of their fellows who could not reasonably support themselves, the overall network of entitlements proposed by the labor theory would obviate the need for a transfer of people's assets to communal dominion. Landowners merely had to abide by obligations to furnish jobs or alms for nonowners; they did not have to cede their rights of property altogether.

A third bad argument

Another dubious argument has focused attention on particular passages in the *Second Treatise*. These passages have been thought to suggest that the creation of any commonwealth entailed the relinquishing of proprietary prerogatives by individuals to collective control. Chief among these passages is the following discussion of the route by which people entered into society:

> [E]very Man, when he, at first, incorporates himself into any Commonwealth, he, by his uniting himself thereunto, annexed also, and submits to the Community those Possessions, which he has, or shall acquire, that do not already belong to any other Government. For it would be a direct Contradiction, for any one, to enter into Society with others for the securing and regulating of Property: And yet to suppose his Land, whose Property is to be regulated by the Laws of the Society, should be exempt from the Jurisdiction of that Government, to which he himself the Proprietor of the Land, is a Subject. By the same Act therefore, whereby any one unites his Person, which was before free, to any Commonwealth; by the same he unites his Possessions, which were before free, to it also; and they become, both of them, Person and Possession, subject to the Government and Dominion of that Commonwealth, as long as it hath a being. (TTG, II, §120)

Equally telling, in the eyes of some analysts, is a later remark dealing with the cession of "Natural Power" by the human agents who formed societies:

> Men unite into Societies, that they may have the united strength of the whole Society to secure and defend their Properties, and may have *standing Rules* to bound it, by which every one may know what is his. To this end it is that Men give up all their Natural Power to the Society which they enter into, and the Community put the Legislative Power into such hands as they think fit, with this trust, that they shall be govern'd by *declared Laws*. (TTG, II, §136, emphasis in original)

A closer look at these excerpts will reveal, however, that they do not proclaim the doctrine ascribed to them. The first of these passages does not say anything about the wholesale renunciation or cancelation of original rights. Rather, it wields such terms as "annexed," "unites," and "submits." With this parlance, it adverts to the two main kinds of modification that originary entitlements had to undergo when human beings erected their societies: limitation and elaboration.

As Locke contended, and as has been acknowledged freely herein, the founding of society could not but impose some new restrictions on the natural prerogatives and choices of individual agents. Rights of property, like rights to liberty and security, did not disappear or come to be overridden and null; but their boundaries were tightened in order to make the operations of government feasible. Each person exiting from the state of nature and moving into civil society would have to part "with as much of his natural liberty in providing for himself, as the good, prosperity, and safety of the Society shall require: which is not only necessary, but just; since the other Members of the Society do the like" (TTG, II, §130). The intensified constraints on the natural leeway and rights of persons fell far short of obliterating those natural prerogatives. Not only did the more pronounced trammels cause no crushing harm to the sets of rights and powers they limited, but the process of their development arose from "an intention in every one the better to preserve himself his Liberty and Property" (TTG, II, §131). For the sake of buttressing natural entitlements, people chose to accept all the curbs that were needed to promote the conditions of stability and safety by means of which the entitlements were buttressed. Fortification, not cancelation, was the chief objective.

In addition to undergoing some new restrictions, natural rights and powers received much more elaboration and specificity once they had assumed the role of elements in a legal structure. As has been mentioned, the gnarled details of contract law and various other bodies of law in any given society did not take their shape from natural prerogatives alone; *au contraire*, the involutions of law enabled those natural prerogatives to acquire a fine degree of exactitude that could not be obtained in pre-societal dealings. For purposes of implementation and identification, with regard to entitlements both natural and civil, the rules of any legal framework evolved along paths too intricate to be deduced from the bedrock powers and rights which people earned in the days before the advent of civil law. Compared with natural prerogatives, the rights and powers at work in legal systems were complicatedly ramified and precise.

Hence, the first of the supposedly damning extracts which we are studying has shown itself entirely consistent with the view that Lockean natural rights and powers retained their basic force in civil society. When that quoted passage describes possessions as "submitted" or "annexed" or "united" to a community, it describes them merely as subject to the limits and the elaboration that have just been recounted here. As the passage reminds us, people entered a commonwealth in order to attain "the securing and regulating" of property; and the securing and regulating proceeded through the imposition of curbs and through the specification of particular elements. Such steps aimed to fortify and uphold natural prerogatives, and certainly did not venture to do away with them. People who united or annexed or submitted their holdings to commonwealths were simply letting their natural rights and powers "be regulated by the Laws of the Society." Far from having yielded the ownership of all assets to the clutches of a community, each person attempted to consolidate his individual ownership by putting his assets under an efficacious system of governmental constraints. The submitting and the annexing of one's goods to the jural ambit of a community were measures designed to make proprietary prerogatives more stable and more exact by bringing about new limits on them. Annexation was not abandonment, and submission was not surrender.

Let us turn to the second of the long quotations above. There the crucial wording is that "Men give up all their Natural Power to the Society which they enter into." Distortively taken out of context, this wording does imply that the human beings within the state of nature could not attach themselves to any society except by ceding their resources and abilities to the society. If every person had to assign the whole of his "Natural Power" to the community that he joined when leaving the natural state of human existence, he effectively had to transfer the ownership of himself and his assets to the community. Prerogatives that had thitherto been held by private owners would thereafter reside within the grasp of the community. Having absorbed the "Natural Power" of everybody in toto, governments in societies would hence enjoy a full "Natural Power" concerning the disposition of all assets and the exclusion of all persons therefrom (not least the persons who had formerly owned the assets). We thus seem forced to conclude that each government within the precincts of its domain functioned as the owner of everything.

Once we set Locke's phrasing in the context of the *Second Treatise*'s sustained remarks on the beginnings of government, we can highlight the fallacies of the interpretation just summarized. The words "Natural Power" do not convey a meaning as broad as any such interpretation supposes. Though Locke did not define the word "power" with a strict Hohfeldian scope,[2] he plainly did use it here in a specific and rather technical fashion. Shortly before he mentioned everyone's "Natural Power," he announced that "in the State of Nature . . . a Man has two Powers" (TTG, II, §128). He furnished a concise account of these powers: "The first is to do whatsoever [a man] thinks fit for the preservation of himself and others within the permission of the *Law of Nature* . . . The other power a Man has in the

[2] In this present discussion, I follow Locke's usage rather than Hohfeld's.

State of Nature, is the *power to punish the Crimes* committed against that Law" (TTG, II, §128, emphasis in original).

Locke went on to explain that every sensible person clearly renounced these powers for the sake of gaining admission to a commonwealth. Each entrant into civil society had to yield the first of the two main powers "so far forth as the preservation of himself, and the rest of . . . Society shall require" (TTG, II, §129). We have noted as much already, when observing that proprietary entitlements would have to partake of new restrictions as human beings sought to transcend the state of nature. Much more sweeping was the abandonment of the second principal power that Locke outlined. Upon leaving the state of nature, each man "wholly *gives up*" the "*Power of punishing* . . . and engages his natural force, (which he might before imploy in the Execution of the Law of Nature, by his own single Authority, as he thought fit) to assist the Executive Power of the Society" (TTG, II, §130, emphasis in original).

To be sure, despite the categorical tenor of the statement just quoted, the second power did not *completely* shift from each person in society to the government at the helm thereof. As Locke had earlier argued, anyone could avail herself of the prerogative to fend off wrongdoers when the punishments inflicted by law would manifestly arrive too late:

> [F]orce, or a declared design of force upon the Person of another, where there is no common Superior on Earth to appeal to for relief, *is the State of War*: And 'tis the want of such an appeal gives a Man the Right of War . . . against an *aggressor*, though he be in Society and a fellow Subject. Thus a *Thief*, whom I cannot harm but by appeal to the Law, for having stolen all that I am worth, I may kill, when he sets on me to rob me, but of my Horse or Coat: because the Law, which was made for my Preservation, where it cannot interpose to secure my Life from present force, which if lost, is capable of no reparation, permits me my own Defence, and the Right of War, a liberty to kill the aggressor, because the aggressor allows not time to appeal to our common Judge, nor the decision of the Law, for remedy in a Case, where the mischief may be irreparable. (TTG, II, §19, emphasis in original)

Nevertheless, if the renunciation of the punitive power was not wholly unconditional, it certainly was extensive. We can pretty safely characterize this sweeping renunciation as total, in regard to most of the settings and encounters that formed the everyday lives of human agents.

Returning now to the extract which contains the words "Natural Power," we can see that that phrase refers specifically to the power of retribution. In the paragraph of the *Second Treatise* from which the extract comes, Locke was dealing with the problems of law-enforcement that arose in the state of nature. He dwelt on some crucial difficulties pertaining to the lack of a central mechanism for detecting and punishing violations of natural law:

For the Law of Nature being unwritten, and so no where to be found but in the minds of Men, they who through Passion or Interest shall mis-cite, or misapply it, cannot so easily be convinced of their mistake where there is no establish'd Judge: And so it serves not, as it ought, to determine the Rights, and fence the Properties of those that live under it, especially where every one is Judge, Interpreter, and Executioner of it too, and that in his own Case: And he that has right on his side, having ordinarily but his own single strength, hath not force enough to defend himself from Injuries, or to punish Delinquents. (TTG, II, §136)

Having enumerated the drawbacks associated with the highly decentralized administration of justice that obtained before the development of civil society, Locke pointed to society itself as the cure for the ills engendered by the natural state of diffuseness. He sounded this theme in statements that included the statement about the total cession of "Natural Power":

To avoid these Inconveniencies which disorder Mens Properties in the state of Nature, Men unite into Societies, that they may have the united strength of the whole Society to secure and defend their Properties, and may have *standing Rules* to bound it, by which every one may know what is his. To this end it is that Men give up all their Natural Power to the Society which they enter into, and the Community put the Legislative Power into such hands as they think fit, with this trust, that they shall be govern'd by *declared Laws*, or else their Peace, Quiet, and Property will still be at the same uncertainty, as it was in the state of Nature. (TTG, II, §136, emphasis in original)

Placed in context, the wording of this quotation is more precise and narrow than some interpreters have believed. As this passage contends, the flagrant weaknesses in the originary method of law-enforcement were the difficulty of ascertaining or identifying transgressions and the difficulty of bringing sanctions to bear against the people who had committed wrongs. To get around the first difficulty, the difficulty of ascertainment, people opted for expressly declared laws and for established judges. To get around the second grave difficulty, the difficulty of marshaling appropriate force, each person had to transfer to the community the whole or nearly the whole of his entitlement-to-punish-malefactors. Each person "engaged[d] his natural force . . . to assist the Executive Power of the Society" (TTG, II, §130). With a pooling of individuals' capacities for inflicting sanctions, a government could mobilize enough brawn to "defend [people] from Injuries, [and] to punish Delinquents" (TTG, II, §136). By way of such a pooling, the government would "have the united strength of the whole Society to secure and defend. . . Properties" (TTG, II, §136).

This centralizing of the prerogatives of enforcement, then, was very much what Locke had in mind when he affirmed that people "give up all their Natural Power to the Society which they enter into" (TTG, II, §136). Ponder once more the last of the long quotations above. There we find a description of two chief needs that confronted any societal arrangement: the need for combined strength and the need for smoothly ascertainable laws. Straightaway, we find a description of the routes by which those chief needs were met. The first need was satisfied through the blanket relocation of "Natural Power" from individuals to their social unit, while the other important need was met through the founding of a legislature to enact and promulgate decrees. And because the satisfaction of the first need would involve the reassignment of everybody's punitive power, the response to that need involving the reassignment of everyone's "Natural Power" was focused on the carrying out of punishment. That is, Locke here employed the words "Natural Power" to denote retributive powers only.

Ergo, comments about the wholesale renunciation of "Natural Power" do not suggest the canceling or renunciation of proprietary entitlements (apart from the entitlement to engage in punitive measures). We should hardly be surprised to learn that the former sort of renunciation would not entail the latter; recall that human beings gave up their "Natural Power" of punishment – and also agreed to certain limits on their other proprietary prerogatives – in order to bring about the institutions that would set private ownership on a solid footing. Instead of marking the *termination* of private ownership, a central disciplinary mechanism emerged as the *reinforcer* thereof. By striving to create such a mechanism, people sought to "preserve their Lives, Liberties and Fortunes" (TTG, II, §137).

Thus, having looked closely at a couple of passages which are sometimes adduced as evidence for the view that natural rights of property ceased to function when human beings left the state of nature behind, we have discovered that those passages lead us to quite a different conclusion. In those passages we have found two acceptable and harmless positions. First, everybody who wanted to enjoy a secure place in a community had to let her entitlements of ownership be restricted in ways that went beyond the restrictions of natural law. Furthermore, everyone within a community had to abdicate her prerogative-to-visit-punishments-upon-knaves, and had to allow the centralizing of that disciplinary role (through the assignment of the role to authoritative enforcers). Neither of these observations can constitute the slenderest backing for the verdict that the transition from nature to society involved a far-reaching supersession of private rights of ownership by communal rights. On the contrary. Both the acceptance of some curbs on a number of proprietary prerogatives and the wholesale surrender of the punishment-inflicting prerogative were choices made in order to strengthen private titles of ownership.

One more dubious argument

To close this discussion of the relationship between rights of property within the state of nature and rights of property within legal systems, we should explore another passage that may seem to tell against the independent validity of natural prerogatives in regimes of civil law. This passage is especially striking because its cardinal theme is at variance with what might appear to be the message of the specific clause that will attract our attention. Shortly after making the arguments on which we have just been focusing, Locke again adverted to the high degree of protection that a jural system ought always to bestow upon individual rights of property:

> The *Supream Power cannot take* from any Man any part of his *Property* without his own consent. For the preservation of Property being the end of Government, and that for which Men enter into Society, it necessarily supposes and requires, that the People should *have Property*, without which they must be suppos'd to lose that by entring into Society, which was the end for which they entered into it, too gross an absurdity for any Man to own. *Men* therefore *in Society having Property*, they have such a right to the goods, which by the Law of the Community are theirs, that no Body hath a right to take their substance, or any part of it from them, without their own consent; without this, they have no *Property* at all. (TTG, II, §138, emphasis in original)

Now, so long as we disbelieve the far-fetched view that the "preservation" of ownership applied exclusively to the rights engendered *after* the founding of societal institutions, we shall read this excerpt as underscoring the continuousness of natural prerogatives and civil prerogatives. We have come upon a bold expression of the axiom that governments should exist for the preservation of property, and have likewise come upon a stern admonition which condemns the taking of any goods without the approval of their owner(s).

The complications of consent Before we consider one apparently vexing element in this latest quotation, we should briefly take account of the importance that Locke attached to consent. Here and elsewhere, Locke made consent an unforgoable precondition for the taking of property. And, as readers of Locke can scarcely fail to have noticed, he assigned an equally vital place to consent in the originating of governmental authority. Not only did he argue that the particular arrangements and institutions in each society must emerge by way of consent – consent received from the people living therein – but he avouched recurrently that the general step of abandoning the presocietal phase of human life was a choice that needed consent as well from everybody who took that step. To be sure, people had to enjoy an opportunity to select the type of governance that would reign in the aftermath of the state of nature; yet everyone first had to decide whether to eschew the state of nature at all. As Locke insisted, no one could rightly be compelled to forswear the natural state of the human species. "*Every Man* [is], as has been shewed, *naturally free*, and nothing [is] able to put him into subjection to any Earthly Power, but only his own Consent" (TTG, II, §119, emphasis in original). People were entitled to choose the paths by which they would depart from the state of nature, and were entitled also to choose whether they should indeed depart from that state.

Having observed that Locke insisted upon the need for voiced or tacit consent to the formation of sovereignty and to the renouncing of human agents' primal condition, we can discern close connections with his paragraphs on the need for the consent of owners to any taking of their goods. As has been pointed out, the move from the state of nature to the security of civil law resulted in the imposing of many new constraints on everyone's rights of property. Though the advance beyond the primeval era did not destroy the titles of ownership that had been acquired thitherto, it surely did place some curbs on numerous aspects of those titles. Hence, to this limited degree, the transition from the state of nature to full-fledged government took away some proprietary prerogatives. And since Locke emphasized that no one could ever justly take "the whole or any part of [somebody else's property], without [the proprietor's] consent" (TTG, II, §139), the shift from the natural state of the human species to a state of civil order could not proceed except by garnering the consent of everybody who made the shift. Consent figured crucially not only because it authorized and legitimated the narrowing of personal freedom, but because it authorized and legitimated the narrowing of people's entitlements to control their own wealth. However far the narrowing was from a complete effacement of primal rights and powers, it was sufficiently constraining and burdensome to induce a need for consent.

If the imposition of sundry checks and trammels on proprietary prerogatives counted as a "taking" that required the consent of anyone who had earned the prerogatives, then the outright canceling of all those prerogatives would amount to an even clearer instance of "taking." Such an outright canceling is envisioned, of course, by the interpretations of Locke that are here impugned. According to those interpretations, the rights of property gained by people in the state of nature would lapse throughout a region as soon as all of the exploitable territory had come under the sway of owners. People's entitlements would expire, as dominion over all land would thus vest completely and directly in a new commonwealth.

Because the aforementioned interpretations of Locke have described a sweeping transfer of ownership from individual human agents to societal institutions, and because Locke repeatedly insisted that goods could not be "taken" without the approval of their owners, we should expect here a noteworthy place for such approval in the exegeses of Locke's work which point toward a wholesale reassignment of land and other riches. We find, however, the opposite of what we expect. Within those dubious interpretations, the duplex role of consent has shrunk to a unitary role. On the one hand, according to those recent interpretations, people forming communities were indeed entitled to choose the modes of government that would prevail; in the determination of the course of civil society, the need for consent loomed large. On the other hand, those dubious interpretations allow no role for consent at the initial stage of deciding whether humankind's natural lot should be abandoned at all. While the question of the specific paths for leaving the state of nature was a question to which the justifiable answers always had to be grounded in people's consent, the prior question about having to leave the state of nature was not a question to which the answer hinged in any way on consent. People could choose *how* they were going to depart from the state of nature, but they could not choose *whether* they should depart therefrom. Such, at least, is the tenet which certain scholars have imputed to Locke.

These scholars, who perceive a sharp split between the proprietary rights during the state of nature and the proprietary rights under communities, have slighted the role of consent because they derive the natural/social rupture from human agents' cardinal prerogative and duty – the prerogative and duty to quest for survival. Mistakenly fearing that the spread of individual ownership to every usable plot of earth would foreclose all opportunities for the landless to keep themselves alive, these readers of Locke have held that only a blanket supersession of natural rights and natural powers by civil rights and civil powers would permit every human being a fair chance to preserve herself. In the eyes of these scholars, the abandonment of the state of nature through the reassigning of wealth from individuals to communities was not an option which people could elect to forgo. Consent or a lack thereof was beside the point, since no one could ever justly countenance the elimination of anybody's fair opportunities for survival. Thus, while people had latitude to select the jural and economic and political institutions that would supplant the state of nature, they had no leeway in deciding whether their primal state should indeed be left behind and transformed. They were thoroughly obligated to effect the repeal of all their natural rights and powers of ownership.

In sum, the interpretations oppugned herein have committed Locke to allowing that a legitimate expropriation of property could take place without any consent from the affected owners. People who had earned rights of ownership in the natural state of humanity could not obstruct the taking of all those rights as soon as the proper moment came for the transition to schemes of full-fledged society and governance. A massive transfer of ownership would proceed, regardless of how unwilling were all or most of the owners to endorse such a transfer. Somewhat like the Year of the Jubilee recounted in the Book of Leviticus, this far more extensive reallotment of owners' titles would not depend on the winning of approval from anybody harmed by the reallotment. With much the same peremptoriness that characterized God's written commands pertaining to the observance of the Year of the Jubilee, His natural-law imposition of a duty on each person to facilitate the survival of everyone in the human species would require people to abandon the state of nature when that state precluded the fulfillment of that duty. Fundamental imperatives of the Deity outweighed and extinguished the prerogative of each owner to withhold her or his consent.

In other words, the view just outlined has stripped all natural proprietary rights of their character as proprietary rights (insofar as such rights are understood in Lockean terms). Instead of having been merely *limited* by duties of fellowship and almsgiving, those rights were completely *overcome* by those duties. And instead of having procured titles that could not be flatly taken away without consent, the owners of riches in the natural era of humankind would see their goods confiscated whether they approved of the confiscation or not. This peculiar arrangement, we are asked to believe, was what Locke ventured to describe when he wrote about the primal condition of the human race.

Presently we shall find indeed that the argumentative bearings of the *Second Treatise* must make the originary rights of ownership highly problematic – far more vexingly problematic than has heretofore been suggested. But, for purposes of recounting Locke's attempted portrayal of humanity's natural state, we are well advised to reject the thesis of a profound cleft between the rights of ownership within the Lockean state of nature and the rights of ownership within civil society. By eschewing that thesis, we can eschew the version of that thesis which slights the role of consent and choice with regard to the dispossession of owners during the final period in the state of nature.

If we accept now that the formation of society involved only a *limiting* of natural prerogatives as opposed to an outright *voiding*, and if we further hold that the advent of society came about in order to improve human beings' safety and comfort rather than to keep anyone from starving, we can join with Locke in highlighting the significance of consent and choice as always prerequisite to any "taking" of goods. Once we dismiss the notion that the transcending of the primal lot of the human species was a life-saving occurrence which followed willy-nilly from the entitlements of the landless to preserve themselves, we can see that nothing overwhelmed or outweighed the crucial role of consent in any transfers of property which lifted human beings above their primal lot. Before people submitted any of their natural holdings to civil regulation, they would have an opportunity to decide not just how the scheme of regulation was to be crafted, but also whether they wanted a scheme of civil regulation at all.

Since everyone in pretty good health could earn his keep regardless of the decision to move ahead or to forbear from moving ahead with the creation of governance, and since anyone handicapped could invoke his right to charitable relief in the state of nature as well as in societies, the obdurate reluctance of people to give consent to the founding of societal institutions would not imperil anyone gravely. Thus, the cardinal duty and the right-protected privilege of self-sustainment would not have the effect of trumping owners' entitlements to choose the apt circumstances under which their possessions would be partly or entirely relinquished for the sake of engendering a community. Given that no disastrous harm would arise if people failed to consent to the formation of a community, the prerogative of withholding consent would stay in everyone's moral arsenal. That prerogative would abide as long as the only factor capable of removing it – a serious prospect of acute harm to landless people – did not emerge.

To clarify is not to cancel Let us now return to scrutinizing the long quotation from the remarks on consent and property in section 138 of the *Second Treatise*. As we observed, the quoted passage tends to support one's perception of a substantial continuity between rights of ownership within the Lockean state of nature and rights of ownership within civil regimes. However, a clause in one of the sentences from that passage may strike some readers as troubling. Locke wrote there that people in a society "have such a right to the goods, which by the Law of the Community are theirs, that no Body hath a right to take their substance, or any part of it from them, without their own consent." The noteworthy clause, for present purposes, is "which by the Law of the Community are theirs." From this phrasing a reader will perhaps jump to the conclusion that the entitlements of owners, such as the entitlement to be free from nonconsensual transfers, were completely derivative of the laws that governed the assignment of wealth in each community. That is, a reader may think that rights and powers of property acquired in the state of nature would cease to function after the demise of that state.

This inference proceeds through two main steps, the first of which is attractive, but the second of which is highly doubtful. First, the inference assumes that the array of laws which defined ownership for any given society were exhaustive, in the sense that everything owned was owned because some law(s) classed it as being so. If (once the state of nature had disappeared) a resource *X* failed to count as a thing to which some person(s) held a proprietary entitlement under civil law, then it failed to count as a thing to which some person(s) held a proprietary entitlement of any sort. Now, this first major link in the inferential chain can pass without controversy, as it synopsizes the chief respect in which the primal phase of humanity differed from the subsequent phases. Natural ownership was at a remove from civil ownership precisely because the latter was determined by civil dictates whereas the former was determined by pre-societal dictates.

Much more dubious is the second basic assumption that impels the undesirable interpretation of the clause on which we are focusing. To declare that Locke's words implied the voiding of natural rights and powers of ownership by civil societies, a reader has to maintain that laws within just societies were not bound to give effect to those natural rights and powers. Only if this latest assumption is indeed true, can the modifier "which by the [just] Law of the Community are theirs" ever be incompatible with "which by the Law of Nature were theirs." Yet this key assumption has here been challenged at length. Moreover, it receives no clear-cut support or vindication from the clause which we now are studying; rather, that clause can most persuasively be read as pointing in quite a different direction. With an eye toward Locke's frequent emphasis on the aim of "preserving" natural rights and powers of ownership, we should read the modifier "which by the Law of the Community are theirs" as referring not to the *supersession* of natural rights by civil rights, but to the improved *identification* of the natural rights by means of the civil. Sharpened ascertainableness, instead of nugatoriness, was the outcome when civil law arose to preserve and supplement natural law.

Once again we must think about a passage in the context of antecedent passages from the same discussion. Locke began the *Second Treatise*'s chapter on "the ends of political society" by adverting to several major defects within the natural system of law-enforcement (where each person was entitled and obligated to punish any infringements of natural law as well as he could). Chief among those shortcomings were the absence of a "settled, known *Law*" that could easily be consulted, and the absence of "*a known and indifferent Judge*, with Authority to determine all differences according to the established Law" (TTG, II, §§124, 125, emphasis in original). To repair these marked inadequacies, governmental institutions had to emerge. Such institutions would "*dispense Justice*, and decide the Rights of the Subject *by promulgated standing Laws, and known Authoris'd Judges*" (TTG, §136, emphasis in original). By enacting and promulgating a set of laws, and by furnishing some impartial judges to resolve any disputes that might arise, a system of governmental authority would afford the means for the exact identification of entitlements. The erection of government allowed the ascertaining of rights and powers to be accomplished with levels of precision and clarity that were not achievable in the state of nature.

With regard to exactitude and authority in the identifying of ownership, then, the rules that functioned during the state of nature were quite distinct from the rules that subsequently evolved. But the heightened exactitude and authoritativeness were scarcely the earmarks of a thoroughgoing transformation; on the contrary, they were preservative factors that enabled the reinforcement and continuation of natural entitlements in any just society. To be sure, those natural prerogatives would not remain completely unaltered during the transition from humanity's primal state to civilized regimes. As has already been discussed, natural rights and powers of ownership had to undergo elaboration and limitation in the course of becoming civil rights and powers of ownership. Nevertheless, the limitation and the elaboration hardly constituted nullification. The imposing of sundry checks on the natural rights and powers, and the fleshing out of those rights and powers with many detailed provisos, served overall to endue those rights and powers with more vitality and secureness.

In other words, having stated that people's goods were "by the Law of the Community . . . theirs," Locke was taking the same view which he expounded in his chapter on property when he wrote that peoples through their governments "settled the Bounds of their distinct Territories, and by Laws within themselves, regulated the Properties of the private Men of their Societ[ies], and so, *by Compact* and Agreement, *settled the Property* which Labour and Industry began" (TTG, II, §45, emphasis in original). Each community, in relation to all other communities as well as in relation to all the individual owners whom each community embraced, was bound to preserve the owners' natural powers and rights as civil powers and rights by defining them with enforceable exactness. Certainly the new definitions incorporated new restraints and new guidelines, and thus we shall here do well to observe again that the consequence of those new restraints and guidelines was not the superseding of any natural entitlements, but the preservation of them. New constraints and guidelines were needed for upholding natural entitlements in a system of regulated security.

In sum, the remark about "the Law of the Community" does not warrant any conclusion that the shift from the state of nature to the law and order of civil governance involved the supplanting or undoing of natural rights by jural rights. Although the transition from the state of nature did proceed through a comprehensive reclassifying of ownership as ownership in accordance with civil laws, a just reclassification had to accommodate and protect the originary patterns of holdings. Not merely could the exhaustive transformation of natural rights into civil rights *permit* the sustained effectiveness of the natural rights, but, insofar as the transformation was just, it served *perforce* to continue the effectiveness of those rights. In contrast with the age of redemption as described by Paul in his Second Letter to the Corinthians, the coming of the new did not here entail the passing of the old. Indeed, the coming of the new preserved better the constituents of the old. Though the shift from humankind's natural state to the law and order of a community did proceed through the imposition of curbs and the development of ramifications, those curbs and those ramifications did not add up to any sort of annulment. In fact, as has repeatedly been explained, those new controls and specifications were the means of upholding the entitlements on which they impinged.

Let us close with a caveat. This interpretation of a specific passage from the *Second Treatise* – like the other interpretations of that text which have been presented in this discussion of the continuity between natural prerogatives of ownership and civil prerogatives of ownership – is not indisputable. As was conceded near the outset of this discussion, there are no absolutely clinching arguments in favor of the perspective advanced here. On the one hand, the virtues of this perspective and the drawbacks of the contrary view should not be discounted. Far-fetched is the notion that Locke's insistence on the need for the preservation of rights and powers of ownership was meant to apply exclusively to the rights and powers attained after the institutions of government had been formed; and weak or invalid are the arguments which have been adduced to shore up that understanding of his insistence. On the other hand, the flimsiness and implausibility of that view do not amount to an utter indefensibleness. One should not purport to have demolished that view altogether, in a bid to highlight the merits of the interpretation espoused here. After all, as was stated earlier, this book's critique of the labor theory of property will yield its unsettling effects regardless of the verdict for which we opt when pondering the force of natural rights of ownership within civil society.

The thoroughgoing communitarianism of individualism

In what, then, do the unsettling effects of this book consist? Why is the slippage in the labor theory of property a grave threat to the coherence of Locke's *Two Treatises*? Why should not the individual rights and powers of ownership in a Lockean world be deemed the outgrowths of political individualism, despite the gaps in the labor theory? And why would not the tenets of individualism call for such rights and powers straightforwardly?

As we attempt to work out the answers to these various questions, we shall go down paths that may appear to conflict with what has just been argued about the continuation of natural entitlements in regimes of civil law. In fact, however, the conclusions reached here will not be in tension with the foregoing arguments. The main purpose of those arguments was to show that Locke believed in the enduring and binding force of natural proprietary prerogatives – a force that did not disappear or ebb when the state of nature had been transcended. Throughout those arguments, the view impeached was the notion that Locke had held the ending of humankind's natural state to be the ending of any rights and powers of ownership won therein. Here the target and thus my purpose are very different. No longer are we looking chiefly at the explicit conceptions and pronouncements which Locke articulated; rather, we now are focused on implications of his arguments which he failed to espy. Indeed, the point of departure for our perusal of those implications is the collapse of the labor theory of property. Needless to say, that collapse went unrecognized by Locke.

Hence, given that we have just traced part of the surface logic of the *Two Treatises* at face value, and given that we now shall be probing some of the deeper cracks that lurk beneath the surface, there are no vexing inconsistencies between the two general groups of arguments in this chapter. Nor, indeed, do we have to stop at pointing out that no irksome incompatibility obtains. As was asserted near the beginning of this chapter, my arguments that have focused on Locke's explicit theses should serve to strengthen the impact of the present cluster of arguments. Precisely because Locke stressed the continuity between natural rights of ownership and civil rights of ownership, a critique impugning the basis of the natural rights will also have questioned the basis of the civil rights.

In other words, the preceding arguments in this chapter have sought to underscore the persistence of the primal rights of ownership not in order to affirm the unproblematic efficaciousness of those rights, but in order to reveal that the daunting problems which disrupted those rights would fully bear as well on the rights of ownership established by governments in a Lockean world. If the distributional axiom expressed in the labor theory of ownership could not ground the originary entitlements that joined persons to things, then neither could it ground those entitlements when they were reclassified as civil entitlements. Because the underpinnings of natural rights of property and the rights themselves would keep almost all their force when the state of nature had vanished, any flaws in those underpinnings would carry their effects into every jural framework that succeeded the natural state.

In the critical reflections that form the current part of this chapter, we to some extent shall resuscitate the view of civil entitlements that has been opposed in the first half of the chapter; but the partial correctness of that view will be attributed to factors strikingly different from those which have been invoked by scholars who adhere to that view. Although the distribution of goods in every full-blown society indeed took its shape from standards fixed by the reigning government, the authority of the government in this matter did not ensue from any revocation of erstwhile rights and powers of ownership. Similarly, although the countless entitlements that joined persons to goods in the state of nature did not constrain or predecide the patterns of holdings that emerged in any community, the reason for this lack of constraint was not that the originary entitlements had been earned in accordance with criteria which ceased to prevail.

Instead, the decisive role of governmental authority was due to the fact that public agents were implementing the same general criterion which grounded allotments during the presocietal stage of the human species. That is, governments carried out the role that had formerly been discharged by individual persons in their judgments relating to the guidelines of natural law. And since there was no change in the basic precept of distribution – the basic precept of natural law which required that distributional outcomes be selected to maximize the flourishing of the human race – the altering of distributive patterns could go ahead at any time as boldly as necessary for the observance of that precept, without having been occasioned by departures or shifts therefrom. Governments operated with no less freedom and no more freedom to adjust holdings than individuals had had in the state of nature. And, finally, because governments had inherited the task of ensuring proper conformance with God's demand for the thriving of the human species as far as possible, they had likewise inherited the myriad difficulties which surrounded that task. (Moreover, the things discussed by this paragraph amount to various implications which Locke presumably never saw in the arguments of the *Second Treatise*. By contrast with the approach to Locke that has been assailed throughout the initial part of this chapter, the approach developed here will concentrate not on stances that he sought to defend, but on the stances to which his arguments committed him *malgré lui*.)

While highlighting the implications of Locke's theory of property, my analysis splits into two chief sections. We first shall plumb Locke's theory in light of God's general mandate requiring the preservation of humankind and each human being. A second main section will then complicate the first by drawing attention to a special feature of God's demand for the promotion of human flourishing and survival. Specifically, we should notice that no one apparently was adjured or even allowed to treat everybody on a par. Although the basic duty to foster the survival of human creatures generally would be at odds with the favoring of anyone over anyone else, each person was arguably entitled and obligated to pursue his or her own welfare above the welfare of others. Each had to abide by an imperative to lend sustenance to his fellows only when doing so would leave himself with adequate sustenance. As will be seen, some strange consequences would follow from the privilege and duty of every person to put his self-sustainment ahead of the sustainment of other people (considered either jointly or severally). This endorsement of self-concern would alleviate or sidestep a few nagging difficulties, but would bring along some equally formidable snarls.

Individualism as epiphenomenal and dispensable

The present discussion will expand and re-emphasize the points that concluded my earlier discussion of efficiency. What is challenged here is the common view that Locke presented the welfare of the community as a mere restriction or check on the prerogatives of each owner. According to that still widespread view, the obligations of charity and the obligation to avoid causing unprovoked harm indeed established some salutary bounds on owners' discretion; but communal concerns did not perform any role apart from setting those bounds. Even analysts who reject such a view, and who squarely emphasize the importance of humanity-wide interests as the bedrock of people's *general* entitlements to use the bountiful earth, have tended not to regard *specific* rights and powers (over specific things) as products of humanity-wide objectives. On the one hand, in the eyes of these exegetes, the welfare of the whole human species was the essential desideratum that justified and impelled the exploiting of the earth. On the other hand, the collective welfare did not determine the assignment or identification of particular holdings that would be acquired.

To be sure, a handful of exegetes have gone further. They have declared that individuals' holdings were assigned by rules which in turn were chiefly warranted as the means of giving effect to people's abstract rights of self-preservation.[3] By enabling the manifold riches of the earth to be suitably allotted among the countless persons who were entitled to make use of them, the criteria of apportionment served to realize the goal for which the general prerogative-to-exploit-the-riches had been granted by the Deity all along: the goal of clearing the way for humankind and individual human beings to flourish. However, because the analysts who adopt this more sophisticated position have remained content with expounding what they see as the overt logic of the *Two Treatises*, they fail to undertake any challenges to the labor theory of property. Indeed, these interpreters have done markedly less to aid a tough-minded exploration of the philosophical merits of the labor theory than have some analysts whose views are more traditional in other respects. Ergo, the far-reaching profundity of Locke's communitarianism – the profundity of the downright communitarianism to which Locke bound himself unknowingly in his texts – has gone unglimpsed.

Here, as has been stated, my analysis proceeds by mulling over the ruins of the labor theory of ownership. Far from taking the virtues of that theory for granted, this discussion will take for granted what was earlier demonstrated at length: the invalidity of the theory. After having scrutinized Locke's cardinal justification for the principles of the labor theory, and after having scrutinized some other modes of justification that can plausibly be distilled from his texts, we now know that we shall have to look elsewhere for apposite guidelines that could deal with the problems of distributive justice.

The labor theory of property supplies no real answers to any of the key distributive questions (each of which can be broken down into numerous smaller questions). It cannot prescribe how the lavish bounty of nature would be carved up into shares or holdings for individuals, either before or after the expending of human toil on parts of the bounty. Nor can it justify the forging of any links between particular human agents and particular lots of goods. Nor, finally, can it prescribe the composition or nature of the links between the shares of wealth and the individual human agents, even if it could somehow align each element in the set of shares with an element in the set of individuals. That is, the labor theory cannot determine whether the ties between goods and people would consist of full rights along with privileges; and, equally, it cannot determine the central features of any rights for which it presumes to call.

We thus are forced to retreat apace from the labor theory of ownership, in a search for other potential founts of guidance on distributive matters.

[3] I here have in mind especially Tully, *A Discourse on Property*, at part II.

However, because this book aspires to be an interpretation of Locke's political philosophy, our retreat from the labor theory cannot involve a shift of attention from his writings. We have to substitute a criterion of apportionment from Locke's texts, rather than from somewhere beyond them. And within his texts the only criterion that truly supports his basic aim – the aim of promoting human survival, with a maximum of conveniences and comforts – is precisely that aim itself. We have to fall back directly on the principle which the labor theory was designed to supplement and uphold.

Were the labor theory valid, we would have to countenance its guidelines of distribution as the essential paths for the self-sustainment and prosperousness of humankind. After all, we here are endorsing Locke's basic premises for the sake of argument, and thus we here are endorsing (for the sake of argument) his insistence on the self-ownership of each person. Hence, if Locke could somehow have derived the conclusions of the labor theory from the principle of self-ownership, we now would have to extend our blessing to those conclusions. We would have to accept the labor theory's distributive proposals as the vehicles for effectuating the abstract entitlement of each person to procure sustenance.

But in fact the labor theory of ownership has proved completely unsound. We therefore are not confronted with anything that would intrude between the choice of distributive arrangements and the central objective (the objective of human thriving) which the choice of arrangements had to further; we have done away with the notion that the webbing of concrete rights and privileges commended by the labor theory would necessarily follow from any of the Lockean starting points. Instead of having to bow to the demands of that theory, human beings would orient their specific distributional frameworks to the general demands of human flourishing, as far as possible. To be sure, prescriptions pretty much along the lines of the labor theory's prescriptions might indeed emerge in numerous contexts, through the periodic adjusting of distributive outcomes to the requirements of communal prosperity. But, whenever the labor theory's instructions did prevail, they prevailed as epiphenomena. They could not present themselves as foundations on which all other aspects of human intercourse had to be built.

Now, before taking a closer look at the implications of our newly direct reliance on the goal of human well-being, we should glance at an ineliminable feature of that goal (and of our reliance). Although the discomfiting of the labor theory has removed all the operative theorems from the space between the primary purpose and the specific substance of allotments, that space would not itself disappear. The abstract mandate concerning the sustenance of humankind would leave a variety of choices unresolved. In part, this openness obtained because of the yawning gap between the sheer generality of the mandate and the knotted specificity of the choices that were posed. Contingencies of multiple kinds debarred a smooth and foreordained journey from the tier of abstraction to the tier of concreteness. Another reason for the multifariousness of the paths between those tiers was the dearth of uniformity among people's standpoints (and among their levels of knowledge). Throughout humanity's state of nature, in which everybody had to enforce the natural law, the divergences among people's viewpoints were especially troublesome. Yet even after the arrival of full-fledged institutions of civil governance, the enforcement of proprietary prerogatives lay in many hands. Officials from the major branches of government all contributed to the shoring up and defining of such prerogatives; and the outlooks of those officials, even within one branch, could sharply collide.

In short, the goal of maximizing humanity's comforts and conveniences was very far from univocal in its sundry applications. To say as much, however, is not to say that that goal was utterly indeterminate and that it yielded no guidance at all. We certainly can discuss in general terms the mandate regarding the promotion of human flourishing, and we also can educe some specific consequences from it. Let us, then, begin by observing that the demise of the labor theory of ownership has revealed that all proprietary entitlements in the state of nature were functions of collective pursuits and needs. Having charted the undoing of the labor theory, we now can understand that the rights and powers of property in the state of nature had to be founded on the general decree from God requiring the preservation of humankind. By the same token, the absence of such powers and rights would always have to be grounded on that general decree. Whether the relations between particular human beings and particular assets were composed of rights and powers or solely of privileges and immunities, the relations were never justified except by being properly tailored to the weal of the human race (or to the weal of a subdivision of the race in a certain expanse of land).

Not only could each person invoke the principle of human well-being as the ground for a *general* entitlement – the entitlement to quest for the thriving of oneself and one's fellows – but each person would also have to rely upon that principle as the basis for every *concrete* right and power of ownership. Instead of constituting merely a capacious framework or a set of capacious frameworks with broad restrictions and buffers, the pursuit of human prosperousness determined every answer to every question that arose in each framework. When Jesus told his disciples that every hair of their heads was numbered and that sparrows never fell to the ground without the will of their Father, he described a pervasive force with a reach somewhat akin to that enjoyed in economic affairs by our prime distributive touchstone. This touchstone worked its effects immediately or through the mediation of lesser principles (including those put forth in the labor theory of ownership). Even when the narrower principles were at work, however, the basic mandate to promote human flourishing was the chief determinant of every result. It prescribed the adoption of the narrower principles in any context where its own ends were thereby furthered. In any context where a lesser principle would not serve the ends of the basic mandate, the lesser principle could not justifiably hold sway. Intermediate bench marks, quite as much as specific outcomes, had to stand or fall in accordance with the fundamental criterion.

Note the difference between the role of intermediate guidelines sketched above and that role as understood in the labor theory of property. As construed here, such guidelines were completely epiphenomenal in the state of nature and in every subsequent age. They lacked any measure of legitimacy unless their varying operations secured the wealth and comfort of humankind at levels that would otherwise not be reached. For proponents of the labor theory, the stature of the intermediate guidelines was very different. Locke presumed in fact that the labor theory's standard was not an intermediate standard at all; he presumed that his labor theory acknowledged a fundamental imperative that flowed automatically from the basic right of self-ownership. From his perspective, the rule announced by the labor theory was no more discardable than the bedrock entitlement of which that rule was supposedly a necessary aspect or implication.

Once we recognize the labor theory's invalidity, we see that all distributive norms between the cardinal objective of humanity's welfare and the concrete holdings attained by specific persons were governed by the frequently changing batch of requirements which the cardinal objective posed. With talons that reached down all the way, the cardinal objective held particular outcomes and intermediate rules alike in its grip. And therefore we now can see that every pattern of individualism in the state of nature and in full-blown societies was a product of communitarianism through and through. (Here and everywhere else in this discussion, we are reflecting on the nature of a Lockean world or community where justice would reign. Given a world or a community tarnished by injustice, there could always emerge a host of institutions and practices that failed to support the cause of human well-being. Such institutions and practices, however, are not of any concern here. In chapter 5 of the *Second Treatise*, Locke endeavored to outline the conditions that would inform a just arrangement of property; having grasped that Locke's theory is indefensible, we now are exploring the conception of natural justice and property entailed by his basic points of departure. In other words, having sustained a challenge to some of Locke's *conclusions* about justice, I replace those conclusions with a different model which has acquired its shape from his deepest *premises* about justice. And so the lone conceivable world or set of worlds with any bearing upon my project is the world or set of worlds marked by justice in a Lockean sense. Statements here about unavoidable practices are statements about the practices that were unavoidable *in any such world[s].*)

As has here been argued, the cornerstone of all specific entitlements and of the criteria for bestowing entitlements was a cornerstone suffused with collectivism. Particular results, and the norms that brought the results, emerged only insofar as they could enhance the weal of the human species. To be sure, as this chapter will discuss quite extensively, Locke tried to leave some room for each human agent to satisfy her own basic needs in preference to the fulfillment of others' needs. What is more, Locke trusted that the good of the human species would normally coincide with the good of everyone in the species. As was noted earlier, Locke believed that the entitlement of humankind to quest for plentiful comforts would necessarily involve the entitlement of every member of humankind to quest for his or her own well-being. Nonetheless, on occasions when the good of the human species clashed with the good of certain individuals, the collective good had to take priority. No person was free to strive for comforts and conveniences when the routes of her striving were a danger to the collective weal.

As Locke proclaimed: "For *by the Fundamental Law of Nature, Man being to be preserved*, as much as possible, when all cannot be preserv'd, the safety of the Innocent is to be preferred" (TTG, II, §16, emphasis in original). We come upon such pronouncements often: "[T]he *first and fundamental natural Law*, which is to govern even the Legislative it self, is *the preservation of the Society*, and (as far as will consist with the publick good) of every person in it" (TTG, II, §134, emphasis in original). Indeed, even when emphasizing the limits on the punitive role of government, Locke made clear that a rift between the welfare of any person(s) and the welfare of societal structures would have to be resolved in favor of the communal interest:

> [T]he *end and measure of . . . Power*, when in every Man's hands in the state of Nature, being the preservation of all of his Society, that is, all Mankind in general, it can have no other *end or measure*, when in the hands of the Magistrate . . . but [should be] a *Power to make Laws*, and annex such *Penalties* to them, as may tend to the preservation of the whole, but cutting off those Parts, and those only, which are so corrupt, that they threaten the sound and healthy. (TTG, II, §171, emphasis in original)

Thus, given that the dismantling of the labor theory of ownership must leave all proprietary entitlements rooted in the basic moral imperative obliging each person to enhance the wealth of his species or his community, we know that any pattern of individualistic entitlements in the Lockean state of nature would directly flow from that prime communitarian mandate. Prerogatives of ownership that encouraged rapacity and harsh self-concern were nothing but vehicles for the implementation of communal objectives. When such prerogatives held sway, they did so because of their effectiveness in serving the fundamental requirements of the human species. Had the prerogatives not been suitable for filling the needs of humankind, they would not have held sway at all (in a Lockean world free of injustice). If possessive individualism characterized the state of nature, its predominance stemmed from its ability to promote communitarian ends.

Hence, no matter how individualistic were the rules in the state of nature that defined any entitlements to resources, they were pure functions of collective needs and constraints. When individualism surfaced, it surfaced as a mode and a product of communitarianism. But now we have to inquire about the extent to which the rules for the specification of entitlements could take individualistic forms. Since everyone was always under a duty to add as much as possible to humankind's wealth, the latitude for gross self-indulgence might appear highly straitened. If every person had to take constant notice of the preferences and needs of others, how could anybody retain the smallest bit of discretion to ignore those preferences and needs?

The status of production Here we ought to distinguish several matters. Let us first explore the *production* of goods and services. Except for people with severe handicaps, no one in the Lockean state of nature had a privilege to shirk the toil of production. Everyone bore an obligation to do her best to raise the overall output of desirable things. If anybody in decent health had enjoyed a privilege to be lazy and idle, then everybody would have had such a privilege, and therefore Locke could not have been warranted in deeming the "preservation of all Mankind" to be "every one's Duty" (STE, §116); although the preservation of humankind would perhaps have gone ahead all the same, it would no longer have been obligatory for anyone. In short, our granting of Locke's main premises has forced us to grant as well that no one without an incapacitating malady could enjoy a privilege to be unproductive and indolent.

Everyone in the state of nature, then, would have to devote himself to augmenting the output of goods and services for the human race. But what types of goods or services would any specific human agent have to produce? Grappling with this latest query, one cannot furnish a reply that is comprehensive and unequivocal. A plain reason behind one's hesitation, of course, is that the opportunities for production would acquire their shape largely from the natural resources and the human talents that were available; and thus, given the crucial role of those factors, the specific content of the duties of production would vary markedly from one setting to the next. More important still is the fact that we cannot give a sure response to this latest query even when we stay at a rather high level of abstraction. To be sure, at a lofty level of abstractness we justifiably can declare that each person had a duty to bring forth goods or services in a manner most appropriate for sustaining the wealth and comfort of humankind. Yet, as soon as we come to grips with this question on a slightly lower plane of abstractness, we are faced with uncertainties.

On the one hand, we may very well be disposed to submit that each person had to manufacture the things or grow the foods or perform the tasks for which his capabilities were best suited. So long as each of the goods produced or services done was valued by any human agent(s), the maximizing of the sheer quantity perhaps would go further in bestowing riches on humankind than would other ways of proceeding. Nonetheless, we only have grounds to say that that result would *perhaps* occur. Maybe, instead, the welfare of humanity would receive the greatest boon from a somewhat different course of exertions. Each human being possibly would do well to focus her productive talents on things that were especially treasured, rather than on the items of which she could produce the largest amounts (because of her particular skills). That is, if everyone strove to make the items that were most needful and valuable – instead of the items which she had a true flair for making – the general prosperousness of humankind might increase more than from any other pattern of conduct. (Obviously, the needfulness and valuableness of one's products would depend on what was being made by one's fellows. Some degree of coordination would have to take place in order to avert the overproduction or underproduction of any particular good.)

We cannot be sure a priori, then, whether people had to confine themselves to the tasks which they could do most proficiently, or whether they had to confine themselves to the tasks that bore the most esteemed fruits. Besides, the two alternatives just mentioned were very far from being exhaustive. People could effect myriad combinations of those extreme alternatives – combinations whereby they would focus in part on tasks which they best could do, and in part on tasks that separately were most fruitful. Any one or any set of those combinations would perhaps most strongly support the flourishing of humanity; and the desirableness of the specific combinations would almost certainly change from time to time. We should note in addition that the extreme alternatives were themselves not mutually exclusive in every context. Certain people could doubtless make certain keenly valued goods more proficiently than all other items.

In short, once we allow our gaze to descend from the sweeping generality of God's cardinal prescript, we begin to encounter murkiness. We meet with questions that had to be resolved in context-specific ways – questions that sometimes would preclude univocal answers, even within one context. Yet, amid the uncertainty and the open-endedness, we know that God's cardinal prescript stood as the point of reference for determining the justifiableness of anyone's work. To the degree that any pattern or arrangement of toil was somehow appropriate, it was so because it contributed demonstrably to the realization of human thriving.

The status of distribution Let us shift our attention now to the matter of entitlements. Given that everybody had to fulfill an obligation to promote the comfort of humankind as far as possible, what sorts of entitlements would best conjoin things to persons? And how would the apposite entitlements come to be procured by their holders?

To answer these questions fully, a respondent will have to specify two main points and any number of additional points. We have outlined these points before. First, we shall have to settle the extent to which people's privileges and immunities would be supplemented and displaced by various rights and powers. That is, a respondent has to say how the chief Hohfeldian classes of entitlements would be blended to form the proper junctions between individuals and goods. Probably we ought to assume that the germane clusters of the entitlements would differ notably among diverse kinds of goods.

Second, we have to decide who would hold an entitlement to what. Whereas the point in the last paragraph relates to the nature or composition of the entitlements, this second key point concerns the placing or positioning of the entitlements as the routes that would attach acquirers to the things they acquired. Knowing how much control the bearer of a certain entitlement would have in regard to any things covered by the entitlement, we still must ask who the bearer was and what the things covered by the entitlement were. On a pretty high plane of generality, we must learn how people managed to qualify for the gaining of control over any assets, and we need to learn what defined the boundaries of each person's control. In discerning the configuration and formation of entitlements, we thus ascertain the norms by which the entitlements became vested in people.

Now, although we have just reviewed these prime aspects of entitlements separately, the separation is of course purely analytical. In the state of nature and in every age afterward, all the problems that surrounded entitlements had to be addressed together. Each of the two main aspects of entitlements bore upon the other in crucial ways, and hence neither aspect could be developed in isolation. Moreover, anybody addressing either aspect would also have to take account of numerous ancillary matters – such as the longevity of entitlements and the range of functions which the entitlements allowed or protected. Answers to all these questions would impinge upon the advisability of the answers to our two overarching questions (dealing with the kinds of entitlements and the positioning of entitlements). Ergo, ways of tackling these matters were perforce ways of tackling simultaneous equations.

Indeed, the interaction among the problems mentioned here was undoubtedly more far-reaching than has just been implied. Not only did responses to questions about entitlements bear on one another extensively, but they also bore weightily on responses to questions about productive toil. As was argued a little while ago here, every person *M* had a duty to cater to the preferences of anybody who would employ or consume the goods that flowed from *M*'s productive activity. Whether *M* engaged in tasks at which he was best, or whether he engaged in tasks that would yield especially prized results, he had to accommodate the desires of all the people to whom his products would accrue. He could not disregard the wishes of any people whom he could reasonably expect to gain entitlements over some or all of his output; rather, he had to choose the productive exploits that would most fittingly meet those wishes. And therefore we now can see that matters relating to entitlements were closely bound up with matters relating to production. After all, because the weaving together of the various facets of entitlements would decide who ought to possess which goods – and because every human being had to tailor his products to the needs and inclinations of anybody who was entitled to possess or use the products – the facets of entitlements all played key roles in determining what should be created. Solely through the lodging of the entitlements would people know whom they were required to please with their toil, and thus solely through the lodging of the entitlements would people know what they were required to produce. (Observe, by the way, that nothing in this paragraph has ruled out the possibility that every human being within the state of nature could justifiably use her toil to please herself only. If the relevant scheme of distribution endowed each human agent with a right to everything she produced, each then had to cater merely to her own preferences. We cannot affirm a priori that such a distributional scheme obtained at any point, but equally we cannot affirm a priori that such a distributional scheme would not obtain ever.)

Conversely, the nature of the specific opportunities for productive undertakings would help to ordain the answers to the questions about entitlements. To a large degree, the success of any pattern of entitlements in promoting human welfare would hinge upon the talents and raw materials that lay ready for productive utilization. Hence, just as the pathways of productive exertion would be crucially shaped by the entitlements that fixed where the pathways led, the bestowing of the entitlements would be crucially affected by the availability of specific resources of production. Arrangements for the *generation* of goods and services had a heavy impact on arrangements for the *distribution* of goods and services, quite as much as the latter had upon the former.

Complicatedly interweaving with productive potentialities, the myriad facets of entitlements would congeal into distributive systems – systems that could frequently change – throughout the Lockean state of nature. Of vital importance for our present discussion is the fact that the networks of entitlements which arose could be strongly individualistic in their surface manifestations. On the one hand, of course, the classifying of frameworks as communitarian or individualistic is not an endeavor free of problems. We can pretty smartly tag a world of collective rights-to-resources as "communitarian," and we can pretty smartly tag a world of privileges-without-rights (a world akin to the Hobbesian state of nature or the utopia of extreme Social Darwinists) as severely "individualistic," at least in its formal structuring; but we cannot so readily tag a world of individualized rights. When we concentrate on everyone's duty to respect the rights of everyone else, a world of individual rights can seem communitarian. Yet when our focus lies on the right of everyone to be free from everybody else's intrusions and demands, the world of individual rights can seem highly atomistic. Moreover, any world in compliance with the basic principle of the *Second Treatise* would almost always contain a blending of distributional matrices. To label such a heterogeneous world as "individualistic" or "communitarian" is problematic indeed.

On the other hand, we do not encounter very grave difficulties in classifying some of the key webs of entitlements that could form within the Lockean state of nature at certain points. What is more, a heterogeneous scheme encompassing all the major webs of entitlements would hardly ever combine those arrays of entitlements in closely balanced proportions. Such a scheme nearly always would tilt in one direction or the other of the communitarianism/individualism axis, and would often do so quite sharply. Thus, we need have no qualms about acknowledging that the state of nature could develop some patterns of entitlements that were clearly individualistic.

However, what must be emphasized again and again here is that the unmistakable patterns of individualism were as roundly communitarian as the more equivocal patterns and were indeed as roundly communitarian as the unmistakable patterns of communitarianism. Recall that every just distributive scheme within the Lockean state of nature acquired its justness by promoting the cause of human thriving. If and only if a framework of distribution best advanced the prosperity of humankind as a whole, it tallied with the fundamental criterion of justice that we have discovered in the *Two Treatises*. And since we here are taking account of only those distributive frameworks that would meet the Lockean standard of justice, we can warrantedly submit that frameworks would not arise except by satisfying a deeply communitarian norm. Whenever a pattern of acutely individualistic entitlements prevailed in the Lockean state of nature, it prevailed because it thus satisfied a deeply communitarian norm – that is, because it thus served the goal of humankind's flourishing more effectively than any competing matrix of entitlements, at least for a certain period. Such an individualistic pattern of entitlements would emerge because its clear-cut individualism was profoundly communitarian. The reason for its ascendance was the same as the reason for the prior or later ascendance of a pattern of entitlements that was stoutly communitarian on its face.

For the bleakly individualistic set of entitlements, as much as for the overtly communitarian set, the communitarian promotion of humanity's interests was the overriding imperative and thus the prime mover. That overriding imperative accounted for all the elements of every distributional pattern, either by ordaining the pattern and its results directly or by having ordained them indirectly through a medium-level norm which flowed in turn from the overriding imperative directly. Everybody's holdings served the communitarian end of human flourishing, immediately or through the mediation of rules which served that end immediately; every holding gained its justification by reference to that paramount end, immediately or mediately. Justification could never come from anywhere else. No allotment of goods had any independent moral validity, and no medium-level guidelines had any independent moral validity. Validity attached to allotments and subordinate guidelines only insofar as they were the most effective means for the realization of humanity's interests.

Think, for example, of the holdings assigned by the criterion that Locke recommended in his chapter on property. Whenever that criterion governed the distribution of assets in the state of nature, it performed such a role because it was needed for the thriving of humankind. Nothing else could vindicate the adoption of it. And thus the holdings apportioned on the basis of that criterion were due not at all to every human agent's self-ownership, but were due instead to the fitness of the criterion for shoring up the weal of the human species. As earlier sections of this book have argued at length, the premise of every human being's self-ownership would never warrant conclusions like those advanced by the labor theory of property. That premise did not justify such conclusions, because it did not bridge the gap between labor within the object and labor within the subject. Very much in contrast with the impotence of the claim of self-ownership was the justificatory strength enjoyed by the goal of promoting humanity's welfare. Although the mission of improving the weal of humankind would almost never escape substantial indeterminateness, it generally would have enough selective force to call for *some* matrices of entitlements in preference to others.

Whereas Locke in his labor theory of ownership had to rest his verdict on unsupportable connections of deontology between laborers and labored-on riches, the connections between the paramount goal of human flourishing and the rules or outcomes which served that goal were thoroughly instrumental. Those instrumental relations were far from wholly univocal and determinate, but they were not utterly vaporous, either. Arguments pointing out those relations could well prove sound in any number of contexts. And thus, whereas the ownership-of-oneself-by-oneself would not carry implications for the ownership or nonownership of any items external to oneself, the good of humanity would indeed bear such implications (though the implications would shift from time to time and from place to place, because of divergences among particular settings). Insofar as the ownership or nonownership of any thing(s) by a person *B* supported the interests of humankind, the obligatory pursuit of those interests would demand *B*'s ownership or nonownership of the thing(s). Unlike the norm of self-proprietorship, the norm of collective welfare could ordain the proprietary or nonproprietary status of everything; the reach of that norm embraced the earth and all the fullness thereof.

In fact, the reign of the collectivist norm was so expansive that it extended to the self-ownership of each human being. Like all other proprietary prerogatives, the ownership-of-oneself-by-oneself was encumbered with all the relevant restrictions of natural law. Yet, as has here been emphasized, the chief duty imposed by natural law was the duty to enhance the overall comfort and security of the human race with all one's heart and with all one's soul and with all one's might. Therefore, each person had to exercise the prerogative-to-dispose-of-one's-own-capacities by engaging in toil that would best advance the well-being of humankind. Self-proprietorship, which here has gone unchallenged as one of the foundational elements in Locke's theory, had to operate in conformity with the natural-law insistence on the collective good of humankind. Each human being's privilege to determine his own endeavors was thus a privilege to heed communitarian obligations.

Both of the major strands of self-ownership – the general privilege to employ one's abilities, and the general right against encroachments by one's fellows on the integrity of one's person – were governed fully indeed by natural law's communitarian impulse. Let us first consider here the prerogative of everybody to be free from others' intrusions. Very safely we may assume that any valid enforcement of that prerogative would accord with the fundamental requirement of natural law (i.e. the requirement that everyone should promote the good of humanity). After all, the set of valid exertions of that prerogative would not include efforts to resist appropriate sanctions for one's breaches of natural law; it would only include efforts to resist *improper* attacks and burdens. Such defensive maneuvers would almost certainly redound to the profit of the whole human race – because they discouraged deeds of wanton aggression, and because they enabled the completion of worthy and legitimate tasks. Ergo, not merely would resistance to abuses against one's person be plainly authorized by the norm of self-ownership, but it was obligatory under the cardinal precept of natural law. Had that cardinal precept instead required submission to most attacks on one's mind and body, the prerogative to rebuff such attacks would then have doubtless had to give way. (Recall again that self-ownership was always self-ownership in strict accordance with the behests of natural law. And recall likewise that the present discussion has refrained deliberately heretofore from taking into account the entitlement of everybody to satisfy his own needs ahead of all other people's needs.) Fortunately, however, the defensive reactions authorized by the principle of self-ownership would clash very rarely or not at all with the promotion of humanity's welfare.

Equally subject to the foremost imperative of natural law was the other strand of self-ownership. Every human agent, as the proprietor of himself and his own capacities, had a privilege to elect how those capacities would be used; but, to be acceptable, any actions ensuing from that privilege had to meet the demands imposed by the law of nature. Thus, any such actions had to contribute more to the flourishing of humankind than would any alternative patterns of conduct. In other words, every course of human behavior had to follow the paths required by the God-decreed objective of human thriving. The entitlement to dispose of one's abilities was hence an entitlement to conduct oneself along preordained routes.

And, as has been discussed, one's exercise of one's abilities in line with the mandatory pursuit of human welfare could involve catering to other people's desires and wants. Suppose that the needs of humankind entailed the vesting of any share of person *B*'s output in any person(s) other than *B*. In such a context, *B* was obligated to tailor her productive exertions to meet the wishes of everyone who was due to receive her goods. Only through such tailoring of her work would *B* contribute as much as possible to the quest for human thriving.

In any case, whether *B* could justly retain the whole of her output, or whether she was obligated to furnish much of her output to one or more of her fellows, the communitarian sway of natural law determined who would acquire *B*'s products; and thereby it determined whose preferences *B* had to indulge. In doing so, it determined which products *B* was obliged to make. And so we find that the natural law held in its communitarian grip the choices that ostensibly followed from the self-ownership of persons. Though everybody had a privilege to expend her own toil within the confines of natural law for purposes that would gratify her most, the confines were so intrusive that they largely or entirely collapsed the privilege into the obligations which the privilege accompanied. Everyone had a duty to engage in persistent work, and everyone had to focus all of her labor on the goods and services that were needed for the flourishing of humanity. Communitarianism ruled the ownership-of-oneself-by-oneself that formed the heart of individualism. (The remarks in this paragraph have not overlooked the frequent indeterminateness of the ideal of human flourishing at the level of concrete implications. For reasons that have already been explained, such indeterminateness would not derogate from the scope of natural law's chief objective as a principle that governed every realm of human exertion. We should remember that the indeterminateness would prevail in only some contexts. Furthermore, even when it did prevail, it was not so sweeping as to elide all bases for the drawing of differences. Within some range of options, the imprimatur of natural law could apply with roughly equal force to any position; but the range would exclude far more options than it would comprise. Most important, whether or not a range of tenable choices did emerge in any specific setting, the course of action that anyone took up would have to be justified by reference to the weal of the human race. Actions could not partake of justice if they could not be presented credibly as optimal contributions to the drive for humanity's well-being. People had to orient their behavior to the good of the human species, and always had to eschew every other pattern of conduct. Albeit such an orientation would often involve choices among alternatives, it invariably would predecide which alternatives would count as permissible. Though room for discretion did exist in quite a few contexts, the discretion always had to limit its sweep to paths carved out by the overriding goal which allowed the room for discretion in the first place.)

Bad luck, carelessness, and torpor One Lockean premise that goes unchallenged here is the premise of a superabundance of materials for productive activity in the state of nature. In the presocietal stage of human life, everyone could draw unstintingly on a plethora of natural assets while always leaving more than enough for everybody else. But, as this book has noted already, the abundance of resources throughout the primal era of humankind was hardly an abundance of finished products. Rather, the inexhaustible plenitude consisted almost wholly of things that needed to be labored upon in order to become useful goods (or in order to give rise to some useful goods). Without work that could frequently be extensive, few portions of the natural bounty would provide sustenance for a human being. To attain even a scanty modicum of the finished goods that were requisite for survival, human beings had to exert themselves in toil that very often could be quite arduous. Locke recurrently made this point.

Now, given the paucity of natural assets that could serve people's needs without having undergone significant changes through human work, two broad types of developments were acutely distressing for anyone who lived in the state of nature. One of these, a type of development which this book has explored already from quite a different angle, was the occurrence of misadventures. Anyone in the presocietal era could heed the obligation under natural law to toil steadily, and likewise could heed the obligation under natural law to expend his efforts on bringing forth the goods and services most conducive to humanity's thriving, and might nonetheless accomplish very little. Because reasonable precautions to avert mishaps were never utterly fail-safe, no one could be assured of generating an output that would adequately reflect his prowess and his persistence. Between any exertion and its results there lay manifold opportunities for things to go awry, even when the performance of an exertion was meticulous in its care and skill. Moreover, what could happen to any single laborer could happen as well to many people at once (particularly if catastrophic outcomes were due to natural disasters such as earthquakes or hurricanes). And so the human agents who lived in the primordial epoch could encounter marked shortages of the goods they required for their survival and well-being. To be sure, they enjoyed access to an overabundance of the raw materials that were needed for producing more of the vital goods; but, since many of those materials would have to be worked upon at length before they could offer sustenance, a dearth of numerous basic goods could last for quite a long span. We accordingly have to ask how the law of nature and its communitarian imperatives dealt with shortages, or with threatened shortages, that stemmed from misfortune.

Yet, second, we must observe that shortages could ensue not only from freakish accidents but likewise from causes that were much less forgivable. Dogged labor could go awry because of negligence or foolishness, just as easily as because of innocent mishaps. Similarly objectionable was outright slothfulness, another potential cause of scarcity. Although a person could shield himself from productivity-foiling mishaps by never bothering to engage in productive efforts at all, he plainly would not be helping to avert woeful shortages. Even more flagrantly than assiduous but reckless people, loafers violated the natural law that adjured them to advance the prosperity of humankind. When idleness-encouraging mores gained the favor of people generally, the resultant meagerness of overall comforts set in place a world of "needy and wretched inhabitants" (TTG, II, §37). In sum, though a nearly perfect correspondence indeed existed between the striving and the output of wastrels, their scanty output would aggravate shortages as much as would reckless blunders and sheer mischances.

How, then, would the foremost imperative in the law of nature address the problem or the potential problem of acute scarcity? Given that the cardinal precept of natural law imposed an obligation on everybody to maximize the comforts and the conveniences of the human race, what prescriptions would it engender for the possible circumstances of widespread destitution? Would those prescriptions vary in light of variations among the causes of indigence? Because sluggardness and carelessness breached the law of nature palpably, would not sluggards and careless people deserve to be subjected to discipline?

When responding to these questions, we ought to keep in mind that we are not yet taking into account each person's privilege and duty to favor his own most pressing needs above the most pressing needs of everyone else. On the basis of our assumptions hitherto, a person *F* could not snatch away the goods of another person merely because *F* had to have those goods for survival. Rather, *F* was entitled to seize possession of someone else's things if and only if the nonconsensual transfer(s) would directly or indirectly serve the weal of the human race. The same general principle would apply, of course, to items that did not yet belong clearly to anyone; the procuring of such items by human agents would have to go ahead in the ways best promotive of humanity's weal.

After the downfall of the labor theory of ownership, we perceive that the exclusive principle which would undergird every aspect of distributive justice in a Lockean state of nature was the principle of human well-being. Whether that principle operated directly to establish each concrete holding and assignment, or whether it operated by means of criteria which established each specific assignment and which themselves were ordained directly by the principle of human well-being, the drive for such well-being would govern all appropriate answers to all the questions of distributive justice. Therefore, any germane answers to the questions broached in the penultimate paragraph above must unfold by reference to the needs and concerns of humankind. Though highly detailed responses to those queries must depend on the specificities of multitudinous circumstances, we can here entertain some overarching reflections.

We first may note that, in conditions of pronounced shortages, obligations of charity to any person with a crippling illness and to any person with other serious handicaps would partly or wholly disappear. Everyone qua consumer would doubtless be entitled to strictly equal consideration and hence would have a claim-to-crucial-but-exiguous-goods that matched the force of anyone else's claim; but strictly equal consideration would not be due to everyone qua provider of sustenance. Skillful and hardy people were more adept at producing goods and services than were other people, while some people indeed could not produce goods and services at all. In periods of grimness when a severe dearth of basic items excluded the possibility of keeping everybody alive throughout the interval needed for the furnishing of new items, unproductive people had to give way. Whenever necessary to spare a vigorous person, each disabled person would have to undergo the self-sacrifice to which Adam very nearly resorted in Shakespeare's *As You Like It*.[4]

Of course, familial obligations might demand special efforts by any person *Q* to save her handicapped child or spouse or parent; but, if such efforts would divert finished goods from healthy people whose lives depended on their consumption of those goods, the efforts could not proceed. In such circumstances, everybody would have an obligation to forbear from devoting precious resources to the nourishing of a crippled relative. Likewise, each crippled person had a duty to starve.

Whenever acute shortages meant that the continuation of any people's lives would involve the neglect of others' lives, able-bodied people took precedence because of their greater capacity to contribute thenceforward to the fulfilling of everyone's basic needs. (They of course also had a greater capacity to foster everyone's comfort, by producing wealth far beyond the minimum that was necessary for bare subsistence.) If anybody with a sound constitution gained survival at the expense of

[4] I am obviously assuming that badly handicapped people would be unproductive. Though such an assumption is not implausible in regard to the state of nature, it is not necessarily true; for example, a badly handicapped person with a vigorously inventive mind could probably contribute more to human flourishing (even in the state of nature) than most able-bodied people could. My numerous references to the handicapped should therefore be construed as referring only to handicapped people who were largely or wholly unproductive.

anyone infirm, the healthy survivor could proceed to fashion the useful items that would tend to bring about the well-being of himself or other people thereafter. If, by contrast, an irrecoverably enfeebled person survived at the expense of anyone hale, then the survivor would quickly perish or would only retain his grasp on life by getting his future sustenance from provisions made by one or more of his fellows. Those provisions would hence be drained away from meeting the urgent needs of someone robust, who otherwise could have labored to bring forth new provisions. Therefore, until enough provisions for everybody became available through replenishment, the conferring of sustenance on a chronic invalid in preference to any able-bodied person was a breach of the cardinal mandate of God's law. In a situation amounting to a deadly zero-sum game, any substantial catering to the needs of the unproductive would slight the needs of productive people – unless the shortages were sufficiently mild to allow the feeding of all productive persons and *some* disabled persons.

Thus, when scarcities in the state of nature were so acute that a balance had to be struck between the vital interests of healthy people and the vital interests of broken people, the balance always had to favor the healthy. Only such a set of priorities would ensure the preservation and flourishing of humankind to the greatest extent feasible. Ergo, only such a set of priorities would give due heed to God's natural law.

Perhaps these comments on the plight of the sickly in a shortage-torn state of nature will seem unduly bleak and callous. Yet, in fact, the picture just drawn is pretty close *mutatis mutandis* to the picture that we can find in the *Two Treatises*. By presuming that original rights of ownership would all develop through labor, Locke presumed that robust people would generally own more possessions than would the infirm (whose holdings were passively attained through inheritance or gifts or alms, instead of being attained actively through work). In addition, while proclaiming that the owners of assets were duty-bound to relieve the want of the poor, Locke underlined their duties with reference solely to assets that were more than enough to keep alive the people who owned them. In statements which we have previously examined, Locke applied the obligation of charity to the "Surplusage" or the "Plenty" of each owner, but not to items that met the pressing wants of an owner (TTG, I, §42).

Indeed – as was argued earlier – given Locke's well-known view that everyone had a privilege and a duty to preserve himself or herself, the obligation of charity could not have applied to goods that formed the vital sustenance of an owner. Every owner had a prerogative and a duty to retain the things that allowed his or her survival. Hence, because able-bodied people were much more likely to own enough for themselves in times of shortages than were debilitated people, and because the owners of any assets were neither privileged nor duty-bound to divest themselves of the things they had to keep in order to stay alive, a famine would typically involve an unresponsiveness by the healthy to the woes of the sickly. A hale person who did not own anything more than what he needed for his survival would not bear charitable duties to invalids in a time of general want and distress. If no one held any surplus goods, and if no one could amass or produce any extra goods straightaway, no one would be free or obligated to succor an incapacitated person who had run out of goods completely. And because each grossly handicapped person was like everyone else in having to avoid interference with rights of property gained by others, each such person had to resign himself to going the way of all flesh when no one around him could afford to come up with aid. In sum, the state of nature as Locke perceived it was not much less forbidding in times of brutal adversity than the Lockean state of nature redescribed here. In either version of the natural state, the repellent harshness would derive from the harshness of the posited circumstances more than from any ways of dealing with those ghastly circumstances.

If the supreme imperative of natural law demanded the favoring of vigorous people over badly handicapped people during severe shortages of food and other essential goods, it equally weighed in favor of the more vigorous people over the less vigorous people.[5] If human being *Q* was generally more productive than human being *R*, he deserved to be sustained in preference to *R* whenever grievous shortages posed an outright trade-off between the life of *Q* and the life of *R*. The reason for this preference, of course, was very much the same as the reason for the bias in favor of the hearty over the sickly. Just as the preserving of able-bodied people at the expense of bedfast people (when necessary) was the lone way to maximize the prosperousness of the human species at any given juncture, the ranking of each person on the basis of her productive skills was the only standard for preferential treatment that would secure the maximal well-being of humankind. Such a ranking allowed the human species to husband optimal means for the effectuation of the paramount end that was required of the species by its Fashioner.

How would the assigning of preferential positions to adroit workers be affected by anybody's culpableness in aggravating or initiating the severe hardships that brought about the need for the assigning of preferential positions? If someone contributed through carelessness or through slothfulness to a dearth of essential goods, was his or her entitlement to some

[5] People with disabilities that were varyingly severe would doubtless occupy many different positions on the spectrum of productivity.

goods impaired thereby? We may assume that outright misfortunes due to uncontrollable circumstances would not result in the attaining or losing of a preferential posture by anyone on a basis other than his or her productive capacity. Laziness and easily avoidable blunders, however, could not so smoothly be overlooked; they indeed had a bearing on the favored or disfavored positions of people during acute shortages. But their impact on people's statures most certainly did not override the supreme directive in the law of nature, which called for the promotion of humanity's weal. On the contrary, the changing of people's statures came about in fulfillment of that supreme directive.

Because lethargy and careless blunders were violations of natural law, the human beings who had adopted such patterns of behavior would deserve to be brought to book. Moreover, because those violations were serious indeed in a time of imminent or actual famine, everyone then responsible for such violations would deserve to be punished seriously – perhaps even so far as to be denied his very entitlement to adequate sustenance. After all, if no one ever underwent penalties for torpor or sloppiness, the flouting of natural law's prime mandate would surely be encouraged. Of course, even in periods of grave hardship and scarcity, minor instances of sloth or recklessness might occasion fairly lenient chastisements such as scoldings and thrashings. More serious violations of the natural-law ban on indolence and incautiousness, however, would provoke serious penalties. Among such penalties, there might well figure the loss of one's entitlement to enjoy the goods that would allow one to survive during a famine. That entitlement then would go to someone less precipitate or less sluggish. (Note that a situation of dire shortages, in which some people would starve while everybody else would retain a grasp on life with just enough goods, was quite inflexible in regard to the imposing of sanctions through the cutting off of someone's entitlement to have the basic necessities. Withdrawing only a certain portion of a minimally sufficient batch of items would make no sense, because the possessor of the unwithdrawn items would starve while no one else would receive an opportunity to benefit from those items. Thus, in the context of calamitous shortages, the punishment of a lazy or reckless person by the withholding of essential goods was an all-or-nothing affair.)

One of the salient means, then, by which a habit of slothfulness or foolhardiness would have an impact on the entitlements of people in circumstances of dreadful scarcity was the institution of punishment. Disciplinary measures served the cardinal precept of natural law by deterring violations of it. But an even more direct means by which a pattern of sluggardness or foolhardiness could bear on the positions of human agents in times of harrowing shortages was the tendency of each agent's past conduct to bespeak the likely course of his future conduct.

Suppose that person *Q* was a healthy person with good dexterity and strength. From this supposition we can tentatively infer that *Q* enjoyed a pretty high ranking on the scale of people who would deserve to stay alive at the expense of their weaker fellows' lives during periods of harsh shortages. Yet now suppose that *Q* generally did not take proper advantage of her abilities, owing to laziness or to frequent blunders. Not merely did she render herself liable to appropriate chastening; she also substantially impaired her position as an effective worker whose basic needs should be filled in preference to others' needs.

Endowed with a rash or lazy disposition, *Q* was apt to fall short of her productive potential in the months or years leading up to famines and was likewise apt to fall short of that potential in the subsequent months and years. In times of desperate scarcities, therefore, she had a duty to sacrifice herself for the good of more deliberate and more persistent workers. Even as her infringements of natural law that contributed to a state of hardship would subject her to punishments, the likelihood of her future incautiousness or lassitude would deprive her of a cogent claim to be spared (ahead of most other people) from the grievous want that she had helped to intensify. Any framework of distribution saving her from that fate, while neglecting to do at least as much for people who were more conscientious, would have transgressed the law of nature by assigning a preferential perch to somebody unproductive. Favored treatment in desperate circumstances for someone torpid or reckless was quite as indefensible in its flouting of God's mandates as was favored treatment for someone psychologically or physically incapacitated. Only if the idle and the careless were left to starve (in the event of a terrible famine) for the sake of getting sufficient goods to people who labored earnestly, would the overall promotion of humanity's wealth continue apace.

In short, then, distributive guidelines that pursued the well-being of humanity would have to bestow a rank on each human subject in accordance with his productive prowess, diligence, and prudent alertness. Under such guidelines, people who were totally or almost totally incapacitated would have to die before anybody else when a severe shortage of basic goods excluded the possibility that *everyone* could survive. Other human beings, who were capable of producing goods and services, would stand in a general order of precedence decided by their abilities and conscientiousness and verve. Counting in a person's favor were qualities such as strength, dexterousness, caution, and perseverance; counting against a person were qualities such as weakness, clumsiness, rashness, and languor. Such qualities would combine in mixtures that varied from one person to the next. The more a person's valuable qualities outweighed her negative qualities, the more productive the person was, and hence the higher she ranked among her fellows in their respective entitlements to have access to any crucial goods during periods of grave affliction. Conversely, the more a human being's undesirable traits surpassed her laudable traits, the less productive the person was, and so the greater the chance that she would bear a duty to sacrifice herself through starvation in particular contexts.

During intense shortages that required a deadly trade-off between the life of a more productive person and the life of a less productive person, the latter person was obligated to renounce his consumption of the things that he otherwise would have consumed as basic means for survival. In any case, whether we are focused on the duties of unproductive people to abnegate their lives in order to spare their more productive contemporaries, or whether we are focused on the entitlements of productive people to stay alive when their doing so would force unproductive human beings to perish, we have found that any just ways of dealing with famines in the Lockean state of nature had to abide unswervingly by the principal directive of natural law. Like all other eventualities and problems within the state of nature, the circumstances of desperate want would be governed by the overriding imperative that oriented all projects toward the flourishing of the human race.

Communitarianism drawn ever more tightly by individualism

We now introduce the factor that has gone unexplored in this discussion of the communitarianism which underlay every pattern of entitlements in the Lockean state of nature. On the one hand, the central mandate or prime objective of natural law was the enrichment of human welfare. The preservation and comfort of humankind were the paramount ends decreed by the law of nature. Frameworks of entitlements rose or fell on the basis of their suitability or unsuitability for realizing those chief ends. On the other hand, readers might now urge that the whole relationship between the paramount aims of natural law and the concrete webbings of entitlements was disrupted by the prerogative (and furthermore the duty) of each individual to strive for the satisfaction of his own basic needs ahead of anyone else's. Although Locke persistently expressed the foremost concern of natural law as the "*Preservation of all Mankind*" (TTG, II, §7, emphasis in original), he declared that every human being was bound and privileged to get sustenance for herself before trying to sustain other people. Let us look once again at the clearest formulation of this belief: "Every one as he is *bound to preserve himself*, and not to quit his Station wilfully; so by the like reason when his own Preservation comes not in competition, ought he, as much as he can, *to preserve the rest of Mankind*" (TTG, II, §6, emphasis in original). Here we have apparently found that every individual's obligation to promote the good of humanity was tempered by his privilege and obligation to meet his own essential needs first.[6] One's duty to the whole of one's species, when defined from one's own perspective, would clearly not compel or even allow a full-fledged sacrifice of oneself. Unless the succoring of one's fellows was consistent with the succoring of oneself, one's duty to one's fellows carried no weight.

Notice here that the approval which Locke bestowed on the favoring of oneself would extend to the fulfillment of one's pressing needs only. Everyone might have a privilege and a duty to conserve his own *life* at the expense of other people if necessary, but no one in pursuit of various inessential comforts would have a privilege to sacrifice the fundamental well-being of anybody else for those comforts. Once a person's continued hold on life had been appositely achieved, the person was not entitled to favor his own interests above the interests of any other person. Insofar as human beings had to engage in competition for raw survival, everyone could perhaps seek her own good in preference to the good of all the people around her; yet this self-favoritism would not have any purchase insofar as the competition among people centered merely on their striving for luxuries.

The significance of the point made in the last paragraph will soon become evident. Broadly explained, the point is that the limited license for special self-concern by people in the Lockean state of nature would have no role except in circumstances of appalling shortages where trade-offs indeed were necessary between the lives of some and the lives of

[6] There are two easy routes that will allow an escape from Locke's apparent countenancing of self-devoted behavior. First, we might blandly note that his approval of such behavior is detectable solely in the words "when [one's] own Preservation comes not in competition." We can scarcely be faulted for attaching very little importance to a fleeting proviso. Second, we might trade on the manipulability of silence. The phrase just quoted would yield an obvious message when a person was not in competition with anybody else for survival; much less clear, however, would be its message when competition indeed loomed. Should we expound Locke's phrase as "when [one's] own Preservation comes not in competition and even when it does come in competition," or should we alternatively expound the phrase as "when [one's] own Preservation comes not in competition and *only* when it comes not in competition"? Neither construal is resistless or preordained, and therefore neither of them can be dismissed. We hence can warrantedly adopt the first construal – which means that we can warrantedly approach Locke's text in a way that dissipates his endorsement of self-preferring behavior.

Nonetheless, I have here forgone these easy routes of escape. Instead, this chapter proceeds along two paths that are far more complicated and more significant. We first shall see that nothing in Locke's theories compelled or justified the granting of any license to self-favoritism. We then shall find that, if strict self-favoritism were condoned and thus practiced, it would bear implications that would force it to be eschewed on Lockean grounds. Rather than dismiss Locke's proviso through interpretive dodges, I shall counter it by revealing its unacceptableness in any truly Lockean world.

others. Only when human beings had to contend against one another for bare survival, would their leeway for special self-devotion be triggered; and only when there were acute shortages of finished goods in the state of nature, would human beings have to compete against one another for bare survival.[7] Thus, my finally giving attention to the place for self-solicitude in the Lockean state of nature will leave intact the bulk of my extensive analysis concerning the implications of my general critique. Indeed, the only main section of that analysis which will have to be modified is the section on acute scarcities. We shall have to re-examine the topic of that section in order to take account of the individualistic prerogative of self-favoritism. As will presently be explored, the heightened individualism in the Lockean state of nature could not but reinforce the thoroughgoing communitarianism of that state.

However, before we probe the consequences of allowable self-concern in the natural era of humankind, we ought to reflect briefly on the inexplicableness of the endorsement that Locke gave to self-concern. His commending of self-favoritism was decidedly not entailed by any of his chief postulates. And, in fact, only a pretty dubious assumption could square his attitude on this topic with his overriding insistence on the obligation of everyone to promote the flourishing of the human race.

Looking after one's own vital needs first: in search of justifications When Locke stressed that every person was obligated and privileged to look after her own essential needs before looking after the essential needs of anyone else, this contention did not follow from the mere axiom of every person's self-ownership. Such an axiom held that everyone was fully entitled to employ his own strength and skills and abilities as he chose, *within the restraining guidelines of natural law.* Albeit one's prerogative to dispose of oneself in the state of nature was fettered solely by the restrictions of natural law, it indeed was fettered by those restrictions; and hence a natural-law ban on self-favoritism would have defined self-ownership as a mode of dominion which did not permit conduct that placed an agent's own needs and interests above those of fellow agents. Under such a regime of natural law, everyone could dispose of his capacities as he wished, so long as he gave no preference to his own pursuits above the pursuits of anybody else. Though such a framework of natural law would by and large have reduced the ownership of oneself to the moral state of having one's needs and

[7] Of course, any defense of oneself against aggression (not necessarily in circumstances of famine) can perfectly well be classified as an instance of self-favoritism. But since a warranted exercise of the prerogative of self-defense was also justifiable directly by reference to the foremost imperative of natural law, it will not receive attention here.

likings counted on a par with the needs and likings of every other member of humankind – a state or condition that would have very often incorporated as well a reasonable amount of leeway for electing one's specific avenues of compliance with the precepts of natural law – this framework excluding any self-preferential treatment would quite as clearly have been a possible scheme of mandates, applying to every person, as was the framework that allowed self-preferential treatment. For Locke, self-ownership meant precisely that no one could require anyone else to perform an action which was not otherwise obligatory under the law of nature (and that no one could require anyone else to shrink from doing an action which the law of nature condoned). Thus, rights that shielded one from one's fellows in a world governed by natural law which proscribed self-favoritism were indeed the stuff of self-ownership.

If the limited license for the favoring of oneself did not emerge ineluctably from the axiom of human self-proprietorship, it just as plainly did not derive perforce from the tenet that God made human beings "to last during [H]is, not one anothers Pleasure" (TTG, II, §6). Nor did it flow automatically from the tenet that the Deity "made Man . . . that Man should live and abide for some time upon the Face of the Earth, and not that so curious and wonderful a piece of Workmanship by its own Negligence, or want of Necessaries, should perish again, presently after a few moments continuance" (TTG, I, §86). From the notion of God's entitlement to control the destinies of the beings in the human race, and from the notion of God's solicitude for those beings, we cannot infer that everybody was privileged and obligated to pursue her own vital needs ahead of the vital needs of all the people around her.

Attempts to justify self-favoritism by appealing to the premise of God's dominion over His creatures would run afoul of the problem that we studied in chapter 3 of this book with help from Shakespeare's *The Winter's Tale*. In a world fashioned and perpetually sustained by an all-encompassing Deity with blanket omnipotence, anyone's subordination of her own vital needs to the vital needs of anyone else would always come about as an instance of God's workings. Unlike human proprietors, God enjoyed actual control over every facet of the things which He was entitled to control; that is, He enjoyed control over every feature of everything. Hence, a person's sacrifice of himself by starving would proceed via God's design and would therefore warrant the inference that the person had "last[ed] during [God's] . . . Pleasure." As a result, the prohibition of such a sacrifice was unnecessary as a means for effectuating God's entitlement to decide the fates of all creatures.

Similarly, a premise recounting God's concern for the lives of human beings would not per se demand or support the verdict that everyone had a privilege and a duty to seek the conservation of her own life ahead of others' lives. On the one hand, to be sure, Locke's countenancing of people's self-devotion was not unequivocally at odds with the premise of divine concern. Recall that self-favoritism in a Lockean universe was legitimate only when it dealt with choices and undertakings that were essential for a person's capacity to survive. Each human being *P* always had to favor herself when assets crucial for the continuation of someone else's existence were unforgoable also for the continuation of *P*'s existence. But no one was ever privileged or obligated to jeopardize the basic interests of others when her own survival was not at stake. Thus, a ban on self-favoritism would not automatically have spared more lives than it would have doomed. While such a tack would have forced and allowed each human being to save a worthier human being's life by undergoing starvation when necessary, the salvaging of the meritorious person's life would have cost the life of the salvager. On the other hand, as my last few sentences have revealed, the outlawing of self-favoritism would at worst have constrained *n* people to die in lieu of *n* other people during grave hardships; it would not have increased the total number of deaths occasioned by the circumstances of hardship. At worst, then, any ban on self-favoritism would have equaled the strengths of any policy of self-favoritism, when judged by its upholding of God's solicitude for the lives of His human creatures.[8]

[8] These remarks presume that the quantity of sustenance needed by any one person would roughly match the quantity needed by any other person. Plainly, however, some disparities would occur. Small children could survive on rations considerably more meager than the rations that most adults would have to get for survival. In the same way, very short adults generally could preserve their lives with less food than very tall adults would need. These divergences left some room for counterexamples to the proposition that a ban on self-absorption would not enlarge the overall number of fatalities in a period of dire want.

Suppose that children *K* and *L* together could stay alive on the same amount of sustenance that would keep adult *M* alive. Suppose further that *M* was more productive than *K* and *L* in combination would ever be, perhaps because *K* and *L* were badly deformed. In light of these particular circumstances, a scheme of natural law which proscribed self-favoritism and which sought to expand aggregate production would indeed resolve a conflict between *M*'s life and the children's lives by giving the nod to *M* for survival. Because *K* and *L* had to hand over their vital goods to *M*, a single life would trump two lives. Nonetheless, we readily can defuse this example. We initially should observe that background facts like those specified, while clearly possible, would almost certainly be rare. More important, we can specify any number of background facts that would invert the upshot of our example. Suppose, for instance, that *M* was handicapped severely and that both *K* and *L* were fully competent to engage in productive toil. Because *K* and *L* would not then have to hand over their vital goods to *M*, the trade-off between his needs and their needs would result in the sparing of two lives at the cost of one. Given our ability to construct examples that point in opposite directions, we know that Locke could not appropriately derive his stance on people's self-favoritism from his premise that God attached the utmost value to human lives.

In fact, much more can be said for the disallowal of special self-devotion than what has just been said about the worst consequences that the disallowal might engender. God's concern for the lives of human creatures went along with His even more expansive concern for human flourishing – a concern underlying His gift of the world to human beings for "the greatest Conveniencies of Life they were capable to draw from it" (TTG, II, §34). We thus have to gauge the virtues of a ban on self-favoritism by inquiring whether the impact of such a ban would foster human welfare. And we have to ask whether Locke could duly have justified his unleashing of self-devotion if he had argued that normal conduct which emerged from the self-devotion indeed would help to advance human thriving maximally.

As was mentioned briefly above, an effort to justify Locke's position here must trade on a highly doubtful assumption. Locke had to insist that, on the whole, a policy of self-favoritism would augment the welfare of humankind because people generally were much better situated to address their own basic wants than to satisfy the basic wants of their fellows; and thus a natural state in which people were allowed and obligated to put their own needs first would tend to yield better outcomes than a natural state in which everyone was obligated to place his own vital needs on a par with those of everyone else. People looking mainly after

Still more important, the examples presented here have focused exclusively on the *short-term* effects that could have somehow developed from a ban on self-favoritism. As will be argued momentarily, the use of productiveness as the standard for appraising the worth of individuals' lives was aimed at guaranteeing that any short-term retrenchment in the size of the human species during famines would wreak the slightest possible harm on the long-run flourishing and proliferation of humankind. Even in circumstances where the total of unproductive people who had to starve was higher than the total of more productive people who thence were spared, the sparing of the productive people tended to bring about the conditions for the largest possible growth of the human race in the future.

Finally, perhaps the most important fact about the examples above is that the trade-offs in which the vital interests of *M* competed with the vital interests of *K* and *L* were conflicts that would have to be settled on the basis of norms and factors other than people's self-absorption. As the closing arguments of this chapter will explain in depth, the legitimizing of everybody's self-favoritism rendered powerfully clear the utter indispensableness of natural law's perspective-surmounting rules for determining who should live and who should die in times of desperation. A regime of natural law that countenanced self-devotion in the quest for survival had to furnish the overarching prescripts that could resolve the disaccordancies among vantage points, to which self-devotion led. Thus, regardless of whether people were obligated to favor themselves in satisfying their urgent needs, the conflicts or the potential conflicts stirred by their endeavors to fill those needs would have to be governed by criteria that overmastered the conflicts. One's entitlement to pursue one's own basic interests ahead of the basic interests of one's fellows would be beside the point. That entitlement became active only when one's pressing needs were athwart the pressing needs of somebody else; and any such clash of vital interests would call for a resolution based immediately or mediately upon the overriding imperatives in the law of nature.

their own requirements would have greater incentives and more definite knowledge in their striving for the accomplishment of their aims than would people who were bound to look after everyone else's interests as tenaciously as their own. And so the efforts of people looking mainly after themselves would very probably bear more fruit. Such, at least, was the vein of argument that offered itself to Locke (who did not put such an argument forth explicitly, however).

Now, while appraising the argument or assumption which the preceding paragraph has suggested, we shall temporarily disregard the chief snag that afflicts Locke's approval of self-absorption. That is, we shall temporarily overlook the fact that the authorizing of self-absorption would pit the basic interests of some against the basic interests of others during the terrible periods that would activate the prerogative of self-absorption; and we thus can temporarily disregard the fact that the legitimateness of self-absorption within a Lockean world would induce a strikingly manifest reliance on the communitarian prescripts of natural law for the assigning to people of their rightful claims-to-goods. Instead, we shall look exclusively at the thesis that human knowledge and impulses were key factors which supported Locke's stand on self-preferring behavior.

Notice initially that the line of thought which we now are studying is thoroughly consequentialist. Instead of positing the entitlement-to-favor-one's-own-essential-needs as a brute part of the moral universe, the appeals to knowledge and incentives have plumped for such an entitlement by insisting on its efficacy. Were the privilege of personal self-devotion a fundament of morality, the prospects for its fruitfulness would have no bearing upon its force; it would obtain without regard to the likelihood that anyone would succeed in exerting it.

When we ask about the objective which the privilege of individual self-devotion would reputedly help to further, we can know that the lengthening of the life of every self-devoted human creature was not an ultimate goal. After all, if a maximally long life for each person *considered individually* had been the truly ultimate aim toward which the identification and vesting of entitlements always had to be oriented for each person *considered individually*, the prerogative of self-favoritism would have clearly amounted to a part of the moral universe's bedrock. An entitlement to self-favoritism would thus have always obtained, notwithstanding the presence or absence of the conditions which improved its efficacy. Besides, if the whole justification for the prerogative of personal self-solicitude had focused on nothing more than the life of every human agent considered separately, then any surface comparison between that justificatory project and the project of justifying a ban on self-solicitude would have gone amiss. Through such a comparison, we at best could learn that the authorizing of self-absorption would putatively accomplish goal *Y* more efficaciously than a ban on self-absorption would accomplish goal *Z*. But such a comparison on its own would fail to determine whether the pretty fruitful accomplishment of goal *Y* was more desirable than the somewhat less effective accomplishment of goal *Z*. Even when we are sure that one particular set of guidelines would produce apples in greater numbers than the oranges produced by a different array of guidelines, we still must seek a basis for judging whether apples were more desirable than were oranges. And, in the scheme of natural law depicted by the *Two Treatises*, the only fundamental criterion that could ground a choice between goal *Y* and goal *Z* (or between apples and oranges) was goal *Z* itself: the goal of enabling humankind as a whole to flourish.

Hence, if the argument which we now are challenging has made a pertinent point at all, it has sought to reach the conclusion that a limited license for the self-favoritism of everyone would improve humankind's well-being throughout the natural era of human existence (and beyond). Specifically, the argument has reached its conclusion by highlighting the superior knowledge and the stronger incentives that were enjoyed by each human agent who pursued his own fundamental interests as his leading priority, in contrast with the remoter knowledge and the weaker incentives that were characteristic of any human agents who were bound to pursue with equal diligence their own vital needs and the vital needs of their fellows. Thus, we now must ask whether Locke could safely have relied upon the two factors just singled out: the factor of human knowledge and the factor of human motivation.

Clearly, the argument for Locke's position has gone astray by focusing on incentives. Here the sole relevant concern is to ascertain the complex web of entitlements and duties that best fulfilled the needs of humankind in the state of nature. If people felt a suitable urge to heed their God-imposed obligations, they would thereby tend to follow the natural dictates which were most conducive to the flourishing of humanity; if they lacked any strong inclination to comply with God's will, they would tend to flout those natural laws. Nevertheless, in either case the structure of rights and duties and privileges decreed by God was a structure of entitlements aimed at the promotion of human welfare. Anyone's disobedience or observance of natural mandates had not even a tenuous effect on the salutariness and advisability of those mandates. When human agents were so depraved and so stupid as to scorn what was good for their entire species – and good for every individual in the species, when we take account of the otherworldly beatitude and punishments that awaited people in a Lockean universe – the scorned patterns of conduct were abidingly good for the species, all the same. As everyone who has read the Book of Judges or almost any other book of the Hebrew Scriptures will know, a gap could always exist between the modes of behavior that ensured collective well-being and the modes of behavior that enticed people. To admit that each human agent felt a strong drive to seek her own vital interests ahead of everyone else's interests is not automatically to say that her preferential pursuit of her interests was desirable. Though maybe we can surmise that her preferential pursuit of her basic interests would be very likely to achieve some or all of its intended effects (because of the assiduity with which it would be carried on), we hardly can take as given that those effects would promote the weal of humanity.

And so the argument in favor of Locke's position has reduced to the notion that persons striving for the fulfillment of their own basic needs would enhance the good of their species to the utmost because of the particular strengths of their knowledge. Everyone knew much more about his own essential requirements and his own possibilities than did anyone else; thus, a framework of natural law which permitted and compelled everybody to concentrate his exertions on his own essential requirements was a framework that would yield the best outcomes for the large majority of persons who were quite capable of producing sustenance for themselves. To be sure, a framework along those lines would do very little or indeed nothing to attend to the urgent requirements of the badly handicapped in a period of bleak shortages. But such neglect of severely handicapped people's needs accorded well with the prime imperative in the law of nature, which (when necessary) demanded a flow of assets to productive people at the expense of the unproductive.

Furthermore, the defenders of Locke's position can argue, the unleashing of individual self-concern would tend to bestow advantages on the more productive people over the less productive people within the state of nature during arduous times. Although the ability to live through a famine did not seamlessly correspond to the higher levels of persistence and skill in laboring, it did correspond thereto in many respects. As a result of that significant correspondence, a matrix of natural law which gave its blessing to people's self-favoritism in the direst times of hardship would thereby generally be giving its countenance to the sparing of people who were more productive than those who were not spared. Once again, that is, a regime of natural law which sanctioned the favoring of oneself by oneself would help to realize the paramount objective in God's design for the world: the thriving of humanity. Or so the more adept spokesmen for the Lockean viewpoint might seek to have us believe.

The foremost problem with this imagined reassertion of Locke's perspective is that it proposes too little while conceding too much. For the sake of argument we should allow that the favoring of oneself by oneself would oft proceed in exact conformity with the overriding communitarian dictate of natural law. In other words, for the sake of argument we ought to allow two points. First, given that any human being would usually possess an intimate knowledge of her own needs and circumstances, she was generally best positioned to choose the course of behavior that she had to adopt for her survival during periods of acute shortages. Second, the ability of each human agent to turn her knowledge into some life-redeeming action was substantially correlated with her prowess and resolution in productive endeavors. From these two points we can (arguendo) infer that the according of a free rein to people's self-devotion in circumstances of dreadful scarcity would tend to enable any highly productive individuals to take advantage of opportunities for survival more capably than could their maladroit and lazy contemporaries. Such a state of affairs would thus tend to maximize productivity and so would tend to comply with the cardinal precept of natural law as strictly as possible. Yet, unfortunately for Locke's defenders, these conceded points are not enough to sustain the case for self-favoritism. As this paragraph began by remarking, an attempt to uphold Locke's view through an invocation of the foregoing points will assert too little while conceding too much.

An argument like the one synopsized in the last few paragraphs does not assert enough, because it has merely shown that the legitimation of people's self-concern during times of want would commend itself frequently as a product or function of the chief imperative in the law of nature. That is, at the very most the argument can establish that people's self-solicitude in the face of oppressive hardships would deserve to be authorized on an ancillary plane, where the self-solicitude figured as an epiphenomenon of the basic level which it had to serve fully; the argument has not shown in any way that the self-solicitude of each person was on the same level as that occupied by the basic end of humanity's well-being. Presuming to vindicate in consequentialist terms the self-absorption of human agents as the means for securing the collective good of the human species, the posited defense of Locke has made clear that the self-absorption was justified derivatively through its attachment to a primary ground. In other words, the posited defense reveals that the self-absorption of anyone was justified only insofar as it helped to realize the aim for which it had to act as an instrument. Placed in this instrumental and subordinate posture, self-devotion was not an irreducible pivot that could override the objective of humanity's flourishing when it clashed therewith.

Having demonstrated too little, even when explored with the utmost lenience – having demonstrated at best that individuals' self-absorption was valuable *derivatively* in service to the weal of the human race – the attempt to reaffirm Locke's position has also had to concede too much. In fact, that attempt's insufficiency has gained our attention here largely because of the damaging concessions that have rightly been offered along the way. Specifically, the argument in support of Locke has avowed that the favoring of oneself by oneself during famines in the state of nature would sometimes jar with the goal of shoring up the prosperity of humankind. Perhaps a general license for self-preferring routes of behavior in conditions of ghastly hardship would indeed *tend* to carry out the goal of human thriving, which it sought to advance; but this tendency, after all, was at most a tendency and not a certainty. Even if we grant that a policy of self-favoritism for desperate periods would often work to the benefit of productive people and so would work toward the maximizing of productivity, we hardly ought to accept that this desirable pattern came about at every relevant juncture.

Yet, if the principle of self-favoritism would sometimes run athwart the cardinal imperative in the law of nature, why would it ever reign absolutely or universally? Why would any such principle not lapse on the occasions when it would foil the very purpose it was meant to achieve? As was argued here a moment ago, the policy of self-favoritism did not enjoy the fundamental inexpugnableness that strictly characterized the end for which the policy was established. Holding sway merely as an instrument in the service of the most profound imperatives, the license for self-devotion could scarcely trump those basic imperatives. Must we not conclude, then, that the policy of self-favoritism had to go by the wayside when it lessened the flourishing of humanity?

The sole apparent rejoinder for Lockeans to these largely rhetorical questions is a quite familiar thesis about moral rules. Writers in sympathy with Locke's position can declare that the overwhelming advantages to be gained through a smoothly functioning set of moral guidelines would surpass the advantages that could realistically be won through the carving out of many exceptions to the chief guidelines. Although the natural laws condoning self-favoritism would in some circumstances not yield the optimal results that they were supposed to yield, the guaranteeing of optimal results by way of varied exceptions to the laws would breed a host of misfortunes – such as disputes and insecurity and resentment – that would outweigh any advantages. To underpin this theme, Locke's defenders can best point out the dearth of most people's knowledge. That is, they can submit that people generally did not have enough information to distinguish between legitimate and illegitimate self-concern. Not equipped with adequate knowledge, people would become muddled if they had to take account of departures from the norm of self-favoritism in times of hardship; thus, those departures would at best prove futile and would perhaps eventuate in disorder. Hence, because such departures had to be justified on the basis of their serving the cardinal end of natural law (if they were to be justified at all), they were plainly not tenable.

The major problem with the argument just summarized is that the linchpin of its reasoning is quite likely untrue. What causes the argument to stand or fall is the premise that people lacked the information which they would need for judging whether exceptions to the rule of self-concern were applicable to any particular arrays of facts. Such a premise, to say the least, is far from patently correct; its doubtfulness excludes it from performing effectively as the keystone of a sound argument.

If human agents indeed knew enough to understand when the principle of self-devotion was rendered active by painful scarcities throughout a broad region, they could know enough also to perceive the divergences among themselves in their productive abilities. Although, of course, one's knowledge of the widespread affliction hardly *entailed* one's knowledge of the disparities in productiveness, both sorts of knowledge relied upon a general awareness of the constraints and possibilities that marked the conditions of other people's lives. In any event, most human beings could form approximate estimations of other people's talents and verve; hence, they could form reasonable estimations of how they and their contemporaries should be ranked in their claims for adequate sustenance. Perhaps small gradations among the ranks would escape the ken of most human beings, but sharp divergences would be apparent to nearly everyone. Divergences somewhat less pronounced could likewise attract the notice of many people.

Even some fairly crude estimations of the priorities among human beings were sufficient to render useful and workable a number of exceptions to the standard of self-concern for dealing with frightful shortages of essential goods. Insofar as eventualities that required any deviations from the usual authorizing of self-concern would involve some gaps among people (and attendant rankings among people) that were quite conspicuous, natural law did well to provide for the deviations. Though the limits on human knowledge probably undercut the feasibleness of certain departures from the rule of self-favoritism, those general limits were relaxed enough to enable quite a large number of departures.

A supporter of Locke may advance two closely connected replies. He or she can first respond that the vast majority of people within the state of nature would discern none of the substantial differences among their respective talents for producing goods. According to this reply, the sharp distinctions as well as the more subtle distinctions among the levels of workers' prowess lay beyond the grasp of the human mind in the natural state of the species. A kindred riposte goes even further, by declaring that people would in fact notice many differences among their respective skills and strengths but would very frequently err in their evaluations; not only did countless people fail to observe the true discrepancies among the postures of individuals, but they saw discrepancies that did not obtain.

Neither of the retorts just outlined can be altogether dismissed. Each of them describes a state of affairs that could have somehow emerged. Nonetheless, while the hypothesized situations were not utterly inconceivable, they were scarcely probable. Any response affirming the actuality of those situations must ascribe to the members of the human species a shuddersome degree of obtuseness. Such an ascription will be highly doubtful at best, and it will certainly be a shaky pedestal upon which to build an argument for the unalloyed favoring of oneself by oneself in difficult times.

The solidifying and reasserting of communitarianism by way of individualism Having challenged the view that every person always bore an entitlement to favor himself in times of grueling adversity, and having perceived that Locke could not rightly draw such a view from one or more of his basic axioms, we now shall temporarily take that view as a given. At present, we shall abstain from casting doubt on the notion of an unremitting entitlement to the favoring-of-oneself-by-oneself under circumstances of grievous hardship. But the conclusion reached through this temporary acceptance of Locke's premise is not that the ideal of individualism amounted to a bedrock value in the *Two Treatises of Government*; instead, the pertinent conclusion is that Locke's individualism reinforced the sway of communitarianism as the fundament of his thought. Far from rivaling or imperiling the communitarianism of a Lockean world, the individualism of such a world was an outgrowth of the communitarianism.

Before we proceed to study how the individualism of Locke extended or sharpened his communitarianism, we should very briefly review the status of his individualism as a product or function of communitarianism. Three types of individualism merit attention here, in passing. First is the individualism of self-devotion, for people who were confronted with disastrous shortages of essential goods. As has been argued here, this first mode of individualism had to be justified by reference to the chief communitarian prescript in the law of nature. (Yet, as has also been emphatically argued here, the attempts to furnish a constant ground for this sort of individualism by reference to the chief communitarian prescript must rely on some very doubtful assumptions.) Ergo, this mode of individualism was entirely subordinate to communitarianism and was thoroughly in its service; the privilege of self-concern for the people who were threatened with starvation in a Lockean world would serve as the extension and reinforcement of communitarianism.

Next is the individualism of every person's self-ownership. Here we can correctly describe Locke's individualism as a function or product of his communitarianism. Although the precept of universal ownership of oneself was a basic Lockean precept on a par with the fundamental communitarian directive of natural law, it gained the whole of its concrete substance through the terms laid down by the fundamental directive. As has more than once been remarked herein, the diverse prerogatives of self-ownership were strictly prerogatives within the confinements posed by the duties that were established in the law of nature. And, as has lengthily been contended, those duties would encompass all aspects of those prerogatives and thereby would contain the prerogatives as nothing more than various chances for discretion in fixing on the surest paths to compliance with the array of duties. (The view put forward in the preceding sentence will have gone unretracted as we continue to take account of the self-absorption that ostensibly came to be permissible and indeed obligatory when famines struck.) In other words, the cardinal mandate of natural law reduced everybody's self-proprietorship to a mere vehicle by which the mandate could suitably be effected; any human being's self-ownership always had to adjust its course as a function of the paramount principle in the law of nature, which defined the ends of self-ownership and also the range of means by which those ends could be furthered.

Another type of individualism, in a Lockean world, arose through the apportionment of desirable things. Though the structures of entitlements that allotted any number of goods and services would frequently differ in their general outlines (and always would differ in their sundry details) from one broad span of time to the next and from one broad area to the next, those structures could often take individualistic forms. That is, they often could endow people with rights and privileges that enabled each human being to display a frosty lack of concern for the desires and happiness of his fellows. Of course, except during the agony of a famine, people in the Lockean state of nature were bound to provide relief to any well-behaved person(s) among them who would otherwise starve. But, within the curbs imposed by the general obligations of charity, regimes of entitlements could evolve in which everyone was free to show stark indifference toward the welfare of his contemporaries.

We need to explore two points in connection with this third mode of individualism. First, having underscored the potential for individualistic schemes of entitlements by which goods and services were allotted, we can and should still declare that any suitable structure of entitlements emerged as it did because everyone was naturally obligated to ascribe no less importance to everybody else's concerns and interests than to his own concerns and interests. And, second, any justly selfishness-countenancing scheme of entitlements for allotting goods and services would arise as a function of the communitarian sway of natural law.

To understand the first of these points, we have to make a distinction between the plane on which entitlements to goods were set and the plane on which entitlements to goods were enjoyed. Recall that no one in the Lockean state of nature had an originary right to any specific good or any specific batch of goods. In the beginning, the earth and all its fruits were in common. Therefore, the retention of a right to any specific part of the earth or any specific share of the earth's fruits was inevitably and wholly derivative, in the sense that it arose through the operation of factors – such as human toil, or the death of someone who bequeathed things to someone else – which produced all their moral/legal results at a stage posterior to the opening stage of nonownership. For humankind as a whole, and for every portion of humankind, there thus developed two general phases. The fundamental or anterior stage, in which the norms for the gaining of entitlements had yet to be fixed, was analytically and temporally prior to every stage in which such norms became active. Shifts from the antecedent phase to any later phase would confront the questions whether rights of property were advisable and how such rights were to be bestowed (if indeed they were advisable).

Now, a crucial fact which must be highlighted here is that the cleft between origins and subsequent times recurred at each moment of the human condition. At every juncture, choices had to be reached (explicitly or implicitly) between preserving and transforming the regnant modes of entitlements. Every stretch of time would hence serve as an origin, an originary groundwork, for every succeeding stretch of time; at every moment, the norms that would prevail in each future period had yet to be fixed.

With attention trained on the continuously recurring divide between origins and successive periods, we are well positioned to grasp the first of the two key points that were adumbrated above. To emphasize the possibility and the probability of individualistic schemes of entitlements in a state of nature with correctly apportioned assets is to leave abundant room for declaring further that everyone was obligated to place his own interests on a par with those of everyone else. When we indeed refer to a ban on everybody's self-favoritism – when we indeed avouch that everyone was obligated to give no preference to his own aims and ambitions over anyone else's aims and ambitions – we are looking at the originary aspect of every moment or period in the state of nature. This originary aspect related to the justifying of rules for the apportionment of all goods and services. It consisted, then, in the basic level at which prerogatives were grounded, rather than in the level at which prerogatives were won and retained. By contrast, when we affirm that individualistic arrays of entitlements could be perfectly suitable within the Lockean state of nature, we have turned our attention to the secondary or derivative aspect of every moment. This aspect concerned the gaining and enjoyment of goods and services. It consisted in the level at which entitlements were assigned and held and exerted, rather than in the level at which the rules for entitlements were broadly ordained. And so we hardly have perpetrated a clumsy contradiction when we suggest that everyone under normal circumstances was debarred from the favoring of herself and that everyone was often entitled to indulge her selfish proclivities with great zest. An outlook obligatory at the tier of foundation was an outlook discardable at the tier of implementation.

Why would special solicitude for oneself by oneself be improper in the originary aspect of every moment? At the stage of determining the proper guidelines for the distribution of assets, every person was bound immediately by natural law and its prime imperative (the imperative to advance the well-being of humankind). Given the downfall of the labor theory of ownership, matters of distribution in the Lockean state of nature were fully governed by the objective of expanding the total prosperousness of humankind; and, although that objective could determine specific outcomes through intermediate norms, the choice between mediated and direct applications was itself governed squarely by the prime lodestar which the applications had to subserve. That is, the originary phase or aspect of every moment was ruled directly by the law of nature and its principal end. Moreover, because that end was aggregational – because it reduced the comfort of every person to an element or ingredient in the comfort of humankind – it offered no reason for supporting anyone's interests over anyone else's interests on a basis other than the sheer contribution of particular interests to the goal of humankind's flourishing. (*Perhaps* a rare and partial exception to the aggregational drive of the foremost edict in natural law was the right of involuntarily unproductive human beings to be provided with sustenance in every period of plenty. We soon shall warily ponder this disputable and murky exception.)

Thus, since each human being in the originary aspect of every moment was bound immediately by natural law's chief directive, and since that directive would place the interests of anyone on a par with those of anybody else and would always weigh the competing interests by reference solely to the standard of productivity, each human being within the fundamental or foundational aspect of every moment was required to appraise his own and anyone else's interests with a uniform yardstick. At the level of fundaments, given that the cardinal behest of natural law obligated every human being to use the same touchstone of the collective weal for gauging his own ambitions and those of everybody else, no person enjoyed the slightest latitude to regard his own projects and concerns as anything other than vehicles for humanity-wide projects and concerns. No one enjoyed such latitude when making choices in the originary phase of each moment.

In the *posterior* phase of every moment, by contrast, the approved guidelines for the bestowing of entitlements could authorize many avenues of piggish behavior. And thus we come to the second of the two main points that were stated several paragraphs ago. Regardless of how much selfishness the law of nature prescribed in the derivative phase of any moment, the selfishness was indeed derivative and was wholly in the service of natural law's communitarianism. There abided a harmony between the communal wealth and the individual's obligation or freedom. To do what was legitimate from the perspective of any individual would amount to doing what was good from the overall perspective of the community or the species.

We can deal with this second point more quickly than with the first because it merely renews an observation that has already been expounded. Armed with the knowledge that the labor theory of ownership has proved to be indefensible, we have learned accordingly that the sundry distributions of assets in the Lockean state of nature had to develop by reference to the overriding demand of natural law (its demand for the encouragement of human prosperity). That overriding demand itself could yield specific patterns of holdings, or could form such patterns through intermediate rules which were themselves justified strictly by the overriding demand for human prosperousness. At certain junctures, perhaps at many junctures, the norms which interposed between natural law's prime mandate and its specific consequences could vest human beings with selfishness-promotive entitlements. Though the brutal versions of individualism such as an extreme Social Darwinism would almost certainly fail to bring about the maximal thriving of the human race, the quite relaxed and sensible variants of individualism would doubtless often contribute more to such thriving than any communistic schemes of entitlements ever would. Among the milder versions of individualism, of course, was the array of entitlements that Locke described in his labor theory of property – a web of entitlements that we also can construe as a mild version of collectivist fellowship.

At any rate, in just about every context there was surely a possibility that a selfishness-promotive regime of entitlements would best carry out the demands set forth by the law of nature. And whenever such a regime in fact emerged as the most appropriate regime for a given period, it attained its role precisely because of its effectiveness in meeting the natural-law demands. Far from subverting or belying the sway of the communitarian precepts of natural law, a duly individualistic scheme of entitlements in the state of nature would reinforce the natural-law precepts by adhering to them with the utmost fidelity. Any such individualistic scheme of prerogatives and duties would come to pass in the state of nature – i.e. in the state of nature characterized by Lockean justice – if and only if its coming about would help to foster the thoroughly communitarian end of human thriving (on a species-wide scale) to the greatest extent feasible. Any selfishness-breeding latticework of entitlements that unfolded in the Lockean state of nature was fundamentally communitarian.

No disaster, no change

You yourselves know that [my own] hands ministered to my necessities, and to those who were with me. In all things I have shown you that by so toiling one must help the weak, remembering the words of the Lord Jesus, how he said, 'It is more blessed to give than to receive.' (Acts 20:34–35)

Except when the state of nature plunged into famines that stretched broadly or narrowly, it included no problems or conditions that unleashed the self-favoritism of anyone who was helping to establish the guidelines for the bestowal of entitlements concerning key goods and services. When free of dreadful scarcities, then, the natural state did not present any contexts that lay beyond the scope of this chapter's earlier discussions of individualism as an epiphenomenon. My earlier analyses of both the productive side and the distributive side of human beings' control over the earth and all its fruits can remain unamended here, as now we ponder the prerogative and the duty of everyone to place her own vital needs ahead of anyone else's vital needs when supplies of crucial goods dwindled to a life-threatening modicum. After all, my previous discussions were relevant to every possible course of circumstances within the natural era of humankind, excluding only those circumstances where people were entitled to indulge in self-favoritism when tacitly or expressly opting for the criteria that governed the distribution of wealth. And because the only circumstances that ever triggered the entitlement to self-favoritism were circumstances of desperate want,[9] the lone embellish-

[9] Recall that my discussion of self-favoritism is not giving attention to measures of self-defense (against violent attacks) that might occur in ordinary situations unmarked by famine.

ment or refinement that should here be appended to my former discussions is an analysis of what ensued when people favored themselves while on the verge of starving.

An important and rather doubtful assumption lies behind the remarks just made. This assumption, which draws a certain degree of support from quite a few passages in Locke's texts, is that everyone in the state of nature had an entitlement to adequate sustenance when the availability of finished goods warded off any threat of a famine. When life-preserving consumables were abundant enough to go around, each person who behaved well not merely could invoke an entitlement to *quest* for consumables but would also have an entitlement to *get* them. Everyone able-bodied would likewise have a duty to toil for sustenance, of course, but even disabled persons who could never comply with such a duty would be entitled to receive shares of sustenance. So long as some human beings worked hard enough to produce basic goods in ample quantities, no one could be denied such goods altogether by dint of being wholly unable to perform work.

Before examining the soundness or shakiness of the tenet just described, we ought to consider its importance for the present discussion. In the eyes of anyone who eschews that tenet, the gap between the current discussion and the former discussions in this chapter is more pronounced than has hitherto been implied. If we disclaim the view that anyone badly handicapped was entitled to get a decent share of crucial provisions, and if instead we think that productive people were both free and obligated to withhold their aid from badly handicapped people, we must draw an inference which partly clashes with the notion that everybody had an entitlement to care for herself ahead of others when her survival was threatened grievously. From the perspective of humankind as a group and from the perspective of the able-bodied members of humankind, a fully disabled human being would have neither a privilege nor a duty to consume food that could have been devoted to other purposes. Such a human being was obligated to starve. From the perspective of the utterly feeble person, by contrast, her prerogative of self-devotion for circumstances of mortal danger would consist in her privilege to obtain crucial goods at anybody else's expense if necessary. To say the least, a handicapped person from her own viewpoint would hold a privilege to consume food that could have been devoted to other ends. Very likely, any such person could not act efficaciously upon her privilege, but, from her own viewpoint, her retention of the privilege was not in doubt.

Thus, a renunciation of the assumption sketched two paragraphs ago will have led us to posit a gaping discontinuity between the entitlements of the badly handicapped as understood by the healthy and the entitlements of the badly handicapped as understood by the handicapped themselves. Now, our discovering of this tension or conflict should hardly drive us to infer automatically that we must renew our credence in the assumption noted above; as will soon become plain, a host of roughly similar clashes between perspectives would arise in Locke's state of nature during times of severe shortages, and the clashes would obtain among healthy people just as much as between the healthy and the infirm. Instead of presupposing the correctness of a norm that would avert the discontinuity between the standpoints of the able-bodied and the debilitated, we should assess such a norm rigorously. Although this discussion will concede that Locke did avail himself of such a conflict-removing norm explicitly and implicitly, my verdict will rest on portions of the *Two Treatises* that are much more elusive than has generally been realized.

This discussion will proceed as follows. Initially we explore how the general line of argument and the general set of priorities in the *Two Treatises* tend to substantiate the view that the able-bodied were required not to furnish any assistance to their handicapped fellows. Such a view gains support as well from a number of specific passages in the *Two Treatises*, including some passages that are often seen as cutting in a very different direction. Having scrutinized the relevant passages, and having thereby added specific textual support to the argumentative support for heartless indifference toward the plight of the feeble in a Lockean world, we then shall make some concessions by admitting the superior weightiness of pronouncements that tell more clearly (though not indisputably) *against* such cold disregard. At least arguendo, this discussion avows that Locke in fact stressed a right to life which was a right to life and which therefore was not simply a right to be secure from lethal attacks. And the discussion hence avows that the entitlement of each disabled person to acquire food and other items in periods of prosperousness was an exception, though a rare and equivocal exception, to the forcefully aggregating sweep of the prime command in the law of nature.

No one should have great problems in discerning how the overall drift of the *Two Treatises* could militate against the supplying of crucial goods and services to the grimly handicapped. Severely incapacitated people would probably contribute no goods and services to humankind's output, yet of course their very existence would depend on their consuming of goods and services. By the standards of the chief imperative in the law of nature, then, the nourishing of an invalid was an unacceptable drain on resources. It wasted time and effort that could have gone toward expanding the production of useful items and toward enabling an increase in the number of healthy people. Someone's life was saved in the process, to be sure, but the assets spent on the saving of that life could more fruitfully have been dedicated to other uses. Competent workers on whom resources were expended would not merely consume essential goods but would also add to the total output of goods, and would often add far more than their own sustainment required. Unlike the badly handicapped people, the healthy people would serve as means of production – and accordingly as means of promoting the long-term wealth of the human race – and would therefore not serve just as ends of consumption.

In other words, to apportion assets optimally, and thus to bolster the long-term flourishing of humankind, healthy people had to withhold assistance from every person who would make no genuine contributions to satisfying her own material needs or the material needs of anybody around her. Hale people would never kill handicapped people by resorting to acts of slaughter, but would kill them through sheer neglect. Hard-won assets would hence be freed for productive uses, instead of being squandered on the unproductive.[10]

To be sure, this rule for disregarding the fundamental needs of unsound people would very likely contain qualifications in regard to the needs of formerly productive people who had become debilitated in their senescence. Although such people would no longer contribute to the output of services and goods, a policy of supplying them with crucial provisions would encourage a healthy sense of security in human agents who were still productive but who knew that they would grow elderly in turn. If people were confident that their steadfast labors in their vigorous years would earn them the reward of being sustained in their advanced years by their stronger and younger fellows, they thus would have an incentive to engage earnestly in productive toil. And so the offering of support to elderly people who had once been dutiful laborers would very likely further the productivity of the human race.[11]

[10] Some of the points discussed in my present line of analysis will doubtless strike readers (along with me) as repellent and even Hitlerian. I should therefore emphasize that I am exploring the implications of a certain principle, rather than endorsing it.

[11] Of course, a similar argument might be advanced in favor of giving sustenance to *every* handicapped person, on the ground that productive people would all then feel assured of receiving some appropriate alms in the event of becoming handicapped themselves through serious illnesses or serious misadventures. Such an elaboration of the argument, however, runs afoul of two weaknesses. First, the new argument will have reached too broadly by eliminating the tie between present or future sustenance and past work. At most, the new argument can justify the provision of support to handicapped people who had labored sedulously before they were deprived of their health. People totally incapacitated from birth, and other people who had performed no endeavors or virtually no endeavors before total incapacitation, would not be entitled to any support. A thoroughgoing neglect of the vital needs of such people would create no disincentives for anybody hard-working, and in fact would create the proper incentives by ensuring that no emoluments would be available to people who had not displayed industriousness.

Another weakness in the extended version of the above argument is nearly as telling.

Having reviewed the analytical or argumentative reasons for insisting that everyone wholly unproductive in the Lockean state of nature (aside from each elderly person who had formerly been a hard worker) was not entitled to be kept alive by productive contemporaries, we inquire now whether this analytical posture is effectively buttressed by the pertinent views set forward in the *Two Treatises*. Many scholars who study Locke's political principles have taken for granted that everyone in the state of nature was endowed with a right to life, a right that was hence much more than a right to be free from the violence of knaves. Though the entitlements of grimly handicapped people in the state of nature have barely been examined at all in the immense secondary literature on Locke, the putative right-to-life attaching to everyone in the Lockean scheme of things would entail or virtually entail the right of badly handicapped people to get their sustenance from healthy people, except in times of grave scarcity. Is an implicit credence in this entitlement-to-support warranted on the basis of the relevant passages from Locke's text?

Let us begin this survey of the most germane passages by reflecting once again on Locke's famous announcement of a natural right to support. That announcement, in the *First Treatise*, may seem to tell quite strongly in favor of our concluding that everybody during the natural state of the world indeed had a right to be succored whenever he or she was incapable of earning his or her livelihood through toil:

God the Lord and Father of all, has given no one of his Children such a Property, in his peculiar Portion of the things of this World, but that he has given his needy Brother a Right to the Surplusage of his Goods; so that it cannot justly be denyed him, when his pressing Wants call for it. And therefore no Man could ever have a

Not only does the argument fail to show that healthy people were obligated to be solicitous of badly handicapped people who had never done any work, but likewise it fails to show with much cogency that serious handicaps which stemmed from anything other than the thousand natural shocks of senescence would afflict enough people to emerge as important factors in the decisions of the able-bodied. Whereas just about every person who lived to an advanced age would be debilitated, most people would probably not become debilitated unless indeed they had lived to an advanced age. Hence, so long as infirmities relating to sheer elderliness did not entail starvation for the elderly human beings who had once been diligent workers, any younger people with various other kinds of infirmities could rightly be ignored by hale people; given the outlined situation, this cold neglect would probably not result in any marked loss of the security and incentives that encouraged the able-bodied to exert themselves duly. We here have to ask a question along the following lines. Even if a slight augmentation of security and incentives would result from the providing of aid to *every* handicapped person who had constantly toiled when healthy, would the greater secureness and incentives outweigh the loss of valuable finished goods which the rendering of assistance to unproductive people involved? Now, the answer to this question undoubtedly was affirmative at any number of moments in the state of nature. But it likewise was almost certainly negative at other points in that state. Ergo, if confronted with a general argument which has presupposed that the answer to this question was always "yes," we must respond with a charge of oversimplification.

just Power over the Life of another, by Right of property in Land or Possessions; since 'twould always be a Sin in any Man of Estate, to let his Brother perish for want of affording him Relief out of his Plenty . . . *Charity* gives every Man a Title to so much out of another's Plenty, as will keep him from extream want, where he has no means to subsist otherwise. (TTG, I, §42, emphasis in original)

This passage is surely one of the mainstays for interpretations of the *Two Treatises* that presume to find therein a worthy concession to the needs of the handicapped. Eventually we can allow, at least arguendo, that the entitlement described in this passage did indeed bear upon the circumstances of any human agent who lacked a sound body or mind. But at the moment my task lies in showing that such an interpretation is not as obviously correct as many readers may think.

The principal argument against viewing the above extract as well-disposed to the interests of the feeble is that Locke there addressed the needs of only the able-bodied members of humankind. Although his silence on the needs of the handicapped will scarcely have debarred an extension of his theses, it removes any aura of ineluctableness from that extension. Within the quoted passage itself, the general tenor of Locke's pronouncements may appear to embrace all human beings; but the somewhat narrower reach of his concerns is clear in the statement which directly follows the quoted passage. "[A]nd a Man can no more justly make use of another's necessity, to force him to become his Vassal, by with-holding that Relief, God requires him to afford to the wants of his Brother, than he that has more strength can seize upon a weaker, master him to his Obedience, and with a Dagger at his Throat offer him Death or Slavery" (TTG, I, §42). Locke focused not so much on the probability of starvation as on the probability that the fear of starvation would result in the loss of person *J*'s control over her productive activities to person *K*. Locke's chief worry was not that *J* would starve, but that *K* would subjugate *J* and "tye [her] to hard Service" (TTG, I, §41). Bondage, not hunger, stood as the central target of Locke's complaints. Those complaints, then, had reference only to human beings who were capable of doing productive service as bondsmen. Those complaints would bear not at all, or would bear very tenuously, on human beings who were incapable of doing any productive work.

Notice that Locke delivered his complaints about servitude in the context of his discussion whether a single man could own the whole earth. Locke contended that such exhaustive ownership would invest one man with complete authority over the conditions of everybody's access to raw materials for productive endeavors. Anyone wielding that authority could "deny all the rest of Mankind Food, and so at his pleasure starve them, if they w[ould] not acknowledge his Soveraignty, and Obey his Will"

(TTG, I, §41). Locke vehemently objected to this scenario, through a curt riposte that made clear his fundamental preoccupation with the interests and troubles of the healthy:

> [I]t is more reasonable to think, that God who bid Mankind increase and multiply, should rather himself give them all a Right, to make use of the Food and Rayment, and other Conveniencies of Life, the Materials whereof he had so plentifully provided for them; than to make them depend upon the Will of a Man for their Subsistence, who should have Power to destroy them all when he pleased, and who being no better than other Men, was in Succession likelier by want and the dependance of a scanty Fortune, to tye them to hard Service, than by liberal Allowance of the Conveniencies of Life, to promote the great Design of God, *Increase* and *Multiply*. (TTG, I, §41, emphasis in original)

Here we find that Locke was primarily upset about the exclusion of able-bodied people from raw materials that could have been worked upon to yield "Food and Rayment, and other Conveniencies of Life." In a world possessed by a single owner, the healthy would be barred from free and efficient uses of assets and instead would have to submit to the laborious demands of "hard Service." Thus, both when Locke referred to what people could have done in the absence of an all-controlling proprietor, and when he referred to the loathsome peonage that would stifle the human beings who lived under the reign of any such proprietor, he revealed that he was thinking only of able-bodied members of humankind. Though Locke of course did not explicitly write that his remarks had no bearing on the welfare of incapacitated people, his remarks neglected such people all the same.

We therefore can pretty firmly construe Locke's references to down-and-out people – his references to people who had "no means to subsist otherwise [than on charity]" (TTG, I, §42) – as references to people whose inability to attain their own livelihood in the midst of the natural world's abundant raw furnishings was remediable and thus was temporary. Locke envisioned the kinds of setbacks that were wholly surmountable if the human agents who had incurred the setbacks were tided over long enough to regain their footing as independent producers. Throughout the *First Treatise*'s remarks on charity, Locke never had in mind any situations of chronic unproductiveness engendered by disabilities that were irremovable. Of course, as has here been mentioned, we cannot correctly seize on Locke's disregard of the incapacitated and advert to that disregard as *proof* that the incapacitated had no rights to get succor in a Lockean world. Silence can denote many things, and does not perforce bespeak a hostility toward what has been left unstated or unglimpsed. Yet, withal, silence does not perforce bespeak a receptive attitude, either. We cannot safely presume that Locke's discussion of charity within the *First Treatise* was per se an acknowledgment of handicapped people's needs or was so elastic that it could serve implicitly to acknowledge those basic needs.

Another passage that we ought briefly to confront is the overview of the state of nature presented near the beginning of the *Second Treatise* – an overview that we have explored from a different angle in my third chapter:

The *State of Nature* has a Law of Nature to govern it, which obliges every one: And Reason, which is that Law, teaches all Mankind, who will but consult it, that being all equal and independent, no one ought to harm another in his Life, Health, Liberty, or Possessions. For Men being all the Workmanship of one Omnipotent, and infinitely wise Maker; All the Servants of one Sovereign Master, sent into the World by his order and about his business, they are his Property, whose Workmanship they are, made to last during his, not one anothers Pleasure. And being furnished with like Faculties, sharing all in one Community of Nature, there cannot be supposed any such *Subordination* among us, that may Authorize us to destroy one another, as if we were made for one anothers uses, as the inferior ranks of Creatures are for ours. Every one as he is *bound to preserve himself*, and not to quit his Station wilfully; so by the like reason when his own Preservation comes not in competition, ought he, as much as he can, *to preserve the rest of Mankind*, and may not unless it be to do Justice on an Offender, take away, or impair the life, or what tends to the Preservation of the Life, the Liberty, Health, Limb or Goods of another. (TTG, II, §6)

Three features of this passage prevent it from amounting to a clear-cut statement in support of handicapped people's rights. First, and least important, the principle commended in the passage relies to some extent on the notion that human creatures had all been "furnished with like Faculties" – a notion from which the passage draws the conclusion that "there cannot be supposed any such *Subordination* among us, that may Authorize us to destroy one another, as if we were made for one anothers uses." Now, even when we take notice of the disparities among healthy people in strength and intelligence and productive skills, we plausibly can maintain that gravely handicapped human beings were so much lower than normal human beings in physical or intellectual prowess that those two broad classes of human beings were not equipped with "like Faculties." Brawny people and skinny people when judged in accordance with a Lockean yardstick would surely have "like Faculties," and very much the same would be true of people with brilliant minds and people with unexceptional minds; but the task of comparison would cease to unearth a general uniformness as soon as it extended to any human creature with a grimly disabled body or a woefully imbecilic mind. Such, at any rate, is a view which we easily can assign to Locke as we venture to interpret the phrase "like Faculties." On the basis of Locke's vague wording, that imputed view is at least as credible as any opposing stance.

(With regard to people mentally incapacitated, the view just outlined will have gained in force if we turn to some discussions of idiots in the *Essay concerning Human Understanding* [EHU, II, xi, §§12–13; III, vi, §26]. Locke there described idiots as beings who were much closer to brutes than to full-fledged human agents. His remarks on physical deformation were broadly comparable, although they were somewhat disapproving accounts of other people's opinions rather than of his own assessments [EHU, III, vi, §§26–27, 29]. In the *Two Treatises of Government*, Locke again adverted to the capacities of idiots in a pungent manner. However, his comments there were more subtle and extensive and were far more problematic; we shall need to scrutinize them later.)

A second notable feature of the passage above, a feature more significant than the one just mentioned, is the passage's highlighting of destruction rather than of neglect. What the passage condemns is not the overlooking of individuals' urgent needs, but the active harming or slaying of the individuals. No upright person within the state of nature would unprovokedly ever "harm" or "destroy" or "take away" or "impair" the life and weal of anyone else. That is, no one could ever truly be justified in taking aggressive action against the vital interests of one or more of his fellows. But, solely from the information that all aggressive conduct was outlawed, we cannot deduce validly that cold indifference was also outlawed. People barred from forcibly interfering with the projects of one another would scarcely ipso facto be barred from showing only the meagerest solicitude for the welfare of one another. (As will presently be explained, this current point is unweakened by Locke's insistence on the duty of everyone to "preserve the rest of Mankind.") A prohibition on callous unhelpfulness would never stem merely from a prohibition on outright plunder and assaults, but would have to stem from a principle of charity or else from a more far-reaching principle of communitarianism. And thus the excerpt under consideration here will have sent us back to the inconclusive excerpt on charity that we plumbed a moment ago. To determine whether handicapped people were entitled to receive sustenance from healthy people in the Lockean state of nature, we clearly must know more than the fact that the healthy were not allowed to murder the handicapped.

To be sure, the decisive words in the above extract – the words "harm," "destroy," "take away," and "impair" – can easily be construed as applying to omissions quite as much as to actions. An exegete of Locke has plenty of room to argue that a failure to provide any sustenance for wholly disabled human beings would of course harm and destroy and take away and impair the lives of such human beings. A lack of positive help could kill as certainly as a fatal deed of aggression. Locke himself, moreover, declared that any person's inactivity was at one with any person's activity in always or nearly always deriving from the human will. If generous acts of assistance (and violent acts of aggression) were the products of choices, so were any refusals to supply needed assistance:

[I]t being unavoidable that the Action depending on [a man's] *Will*, should exist, or not exist; and its existence, or not existence, following perfectly the determination, and preference of his Will, he cannot avoid willing the existence, or not existence, of that Action; it is absolutely necessary that he *will* the one, or the other, *i.e.* *prefer* the one to the other: since one of them must necessarily follow; and that which does follow, follows by the choice and determination of his Mind, that is, by his *willing* it: for if he did not *will* it, it would not be. So that in respect of the act of *willing*, a Man in such a case is not free: Liberty consisting in a power to act, or not to act, which, in regard of Volition, a Man, upon such a proposal, has not. For it is unavoidably necessary to prefer the doing, or forbearance, of an Action in a Man's power, which is once so proposed to his thoughts; a Man must necessarily *will* the one, or the other of them, upon which preference, or volition, the action, or its forbearance, certainly follows, and is truly voluntary. (EHU, II, xxi, §23, emphasis in original)

Now, if deeds and omissions were alike in having been chosen, why should we interpret Locke in the *Second Treatise of Government* as presuming to discriminate between them at all? Why would lethal *neglect* conform with the law of nature while lethal *actions* would violate that law?

In reply to such worries we can hardly construct an indisputable answer that will fix a single reproachless way of interpreting the *Second Treatise*'s comments. All the same, we suitably can deflect those worries. Let us remember that we here are only interpreting some comments by Locke; we are not considering any independent line of reasoning that might properly take account of the parallels between doing and withholding. For Locke, the act/omission dichotomy retained considerable importance in the assignment of one's duties. Whereas people had to *abstain* in all circumstances from wrongful actions such as murder and plunder, they had duties to *perform* helpful actions only when some opportunities arose. No one was obligated to perform helpful actions without respite. As Locke explained:

There are things of which the outward performance is commanded, for example the outward worship of the Deity, the consoling of a distressed neighbour, the relief of one in trouble, the feeding of the hungry: in these matters we are not under obligation continuously, but only at a particular time and in a particular manner. For we are not obliged to provide with shelter and to refresh with food any and every man, or at any time whatever, but only when a poor man's misfortune calls for our alms and our property supplies means for charity. (ELN, 195)

Locke's basic distinction between charity and justice went along the same lines. Whereas the principle of justice required human beings to abstain from *all* conduct that would interfere unacceptably with the rightful holdings of one another, the principle of charity required nurturant conduct only when appropriate, and thus allowed inactivity on other occasions. Once again we see how important for the structuring of entitlements and duties was the act/omission dichotomy – important enough here to mark and undergird the divide between the two great mainsprings of all entitlements to wealth.

We should hence conclude that the long excerpt from section 6 of the *Second Treatise* does indeed pertain to acts only, rather than to acts and omissions. The key terms within that extract are more suggestive of deeds than of failures to perform any deeds, and the tenor of the extract bespeaks the imposition of categorical duties rather than conditional duties (save, of course, in regard to the general caveat that the wreaking of damage on the life of someone else was allowable when a person's "own Preservation c[ame] . . . in competition" with the preserving of someone else). Given the excerpt's language, and given that Locke normally perceived the act/forbearance divide as pregnant, we should infer that his denunciation of harm was aimed at harmful deeds as opposed to harmful neglect. A contrary interpretation is not at all inconceivable, but it has to overcome a heavy burden of proof.

A third significant feature of the quotation from section 6 of the *Second Treatise* is its announcement that everyone in the state of nature had a duty to "preserve the rest of Mankind." Our noticing of this feature enables us to recall that our whole examination of this extract has been focused on situations in which the good of some particular individuals collided with the good of humanity. That is, one needs to emphasize here the gap – or potential gap – between the flourishing of specific human agents and the flourishing of the human species. (For support in underlining that gap, one can adduce some passages from the *Second Treatise* wherein Locke prioritized the collective weal over any individual's welfare [TTG, II, §§16, 134, 159, 171]. Such passages already have received our attention.) A framework of natural law denying grossly handicapped people any entitlements to obtain essential alms would impose such restrictions not because of sheer callousness, but because the larger good of the human race would thereby be served. Though healthy people's neglect of badly handicapped people's needs would of course endanger the survival of the handicapped people gravely, it also would promote the survival and the flourishing of the human species. It would thus accord with everyone's duty to "preserve the rest of Mankind."

Benefits would accrue to the species from the disregard of helplessly unproductive people's wants because such a policy of disregard would avert a draining of resources that otherwise would take place. Keeping the incapacitated alive would always mean a diversion of crucial goods to people who could not contribute to the shaping of any goods; valuable finished items would go toward the sustainment of people who would do virtually nothing to enhance the stock of items or even to replenish the stock. Items used for satisfying the needs of the disabled would not be used for offering healthy people some productivity-enhancing incentives in the form of more comforts and more security, and would thus not be used for facilitating a long-term expansion in the pool of productive human beings. Consequently, such a diversion of important assets would hinder the long-term preservation and growth and thriving of humankind. Only if the incapacitated were left to fend for themselves and so were left to die, would assets flow to optimal uses in cycles of both consumption *and* production that were essential for the very existence of a flourishing human race.

And hence the law of nature, with its requirements for the broadest possible enlargement and thriving of the human species, demanded that healthy people ignore the basic needs of the unproductive – in the interest of devoting all fruits of toil to building up the aggregate productivity, and thus the expansibility, of the human race. Although healthy people could never rightly slay an enfeebled person through aggressive assaults, they could appropriately kill her by neglecting her vital needs. Such, at any rate, is one plausible interpretation of the insistence by Locke on everybody's duty to "preserve the rest of Mankind."

This reading of Locke is far from incontestable or resistless. While its divide between the good of the collectivity and the good of certain individuals does gain key support from quite a number of passages where Locke ascribed priority to the collective good over the good of specific persons, a disputant nonetheless can credibly argue that the passage under consideration here does not advert to such a duality. A rejoinder along those lines will itself be far from incontestable and definitive, of course; but it enjoys a fair degree of plausibleness, and it cannot be ruled out. Ergo, the reading offered here should profess simply to be one credible approach among others. All the same, the credibility of this reading permits us to observe that the passage under consideration is hardly a clear-cut manifesto for the rights of the prostrate. Unequivocal though the passage might seem to anybody hastily glimpsing at its language about the duty to "preserve the rest of Mankind," it shows itself to be highly equivocal when subjected to a wee bit of probing.

One of the major sources of ambiguity in the excerpt from the *Second Treatise* just studied – the act/omission divide – is also salient in a passage from the *First Treatise*. When Locke described there the role of government, he stated his view in terms with a comprehensive scope that may appear very friendly to the needs of the handicapped:

Government being for the Preservation of every Mans Right and Property, by preserving him from the Violence or Injury of others, is for the good of the Governed. For the Magistrates Sword [is] for a *Terror to Evil Doers*, and by that Terror to inforce Men to observe the positive Laws of the Society, made conformable to the Laws of Nature, for the public good, i.e. the good of every particular Member of that Society, as far as by common Rules, it can be provided for. (TTG, I, §92, emphasis in original)

With the reference in this passage to "every Mans Right," and still more boldly with the fancied equation between the public good and the "good of every particular Member of that Society," Locke used language that can seem unstinting in its support for handicapped people's wants and rights. This semblance of univocalness dissolves, however, almost immediately.

Let us note, in passing, the words "as far as by common Rules, it [i.e. every individual's good] can be provided for" – words that tarnish the ostensible clarity of this latest excerpt. More important is the fact that the excerpt concentrates on the punishing and preventing of baleful *deeds*, as opposed to instances of baleful *neglect*. Locke concerned himself with the "Evil Doers" who would try to inflict "Violence or Injury" on their fellows. He perceived the basic function of government as the thwarting of the evildoers' misconduct, and he felt that any legitimate institutions of government would have to shield everybody within their purviews against violent acts. When Locke here wrote about the "good of every particular Member of that Society," he was thinking of the secureness gained through the wielding of the public sword to deter aggression, fraud, and theft. He was not explicitly thinking of the results of mandatory benevolence (though neither, of course, was he asserting that duties of benevolence would always be absent). In this passage on government, the aim of public officials was to block undesirable interventions by any person into the life of anybody else; the passage does not per se advert to the objective of fostering desirable interventions.

Like the other quotations from the *Two Treatises* on which we have focused in the present analysis, the brief description of government on which we are focused here can lend itself to a number of persuasive construals. Doubtless, interpreters will forbear from arguing that neglect alone would amount to "Violence," but they plausibly can maintain that the neglect would amount to "Injury." They can likewise maintain that the neglect was incompatible with the "Preservation of every Mans Right," and that it therefore had to be banned by any government which fulfilled the central purpose of governance. According to these interpreters, the instillment of terror through the public sword was not only aimed at squelching all evil acts, but was further aimed at squelching any disregard of one's obligations of charity. Thus, the "good of every particular Member of that Society" would include each member's secureness from devastating neglect as well as her secureness from attacks and marauding.

Such an interpretation, with its view that the quoted passage about government does not rest at all upon an act/omission divide, can fairly commend itself as reasonable and colorable. Yet, while colorable, it is far from overwhelmingly cogent. At the very best, it is certainly not conclusive in a way that puts to rout the interpretation submitted here. Of course, the interpretation submitted here is itself not conclusive. Nonetheless, its plausibility is sufficient to rebut the contention that Locke's summary of the public magistrate's general task was an undividedly lucid statement which presupposed that every handicapped person would enjoy a right to be sustained by her healthy fellows. A careless glance at Locke's summary might prompt a complacent interpretation along those lines, but a reading that is more vigilant can hardly fail to disclose substantial ambiguity and unsettledness. Once again a pleasingly solid base for the fundamental rights of the severely disabled in a Lockean world has melted down to a composition far more fluid and hence manipulable.

Any careful exegete should deliver much the same verdict with regard to another portion of the *Two Treatises* that can strike a more hurried analyst as tilting unambiguously in favor of rights-to-sustenance for the incapacitated. In the course of some insightful remarks on executive discretion in civil governance, Locke referred to the "Fundamental Law of Nature and Government, *viz.* That as much as may be, *all* the Members of the Society are to be *preserved*" (TTG, II, §159, emphasis in original). He contended that, if the laws of a society obstructed the realization of this primary Law, "'tis fit that the [l]aws themselves should in some Cases give way" (TTG, II, §159). Now, in light of the emphasis on "all" in "*all* the Members of the Society," a hasty reader of these short excerpts will probably be inclined to view them as plainly supportive of demands by bedridden people to receive succor from able-bodied contemporaries. Yet, once again, the *Second Treatise*'s comments lose their clarity when examined with greater diligence.

Even if we ignore the minor tergiversation of "as much as may be" in the remarks just quoted, we easily can deny that those remarks cover the circumstances of invalids. Let us look at the sprawling statement which expands on Locke's cardinal norm:

> For since many accidents may happen, wherein a strict and rigid observation of the Laws may do harm; (as not to pull down an innocent Man's House to stop the Fire, when the next to it is burning) and a Man may come sometimes within the reach of the Law, which makes no distinction of Persons, by an action, that may deserve reward and pardon; 'tis fit, the Ruler should have a Power, in many Cases,

to mitigate the severity of the Law, and pardon some Offenders: For the *end of Government* being the *preservation of all*, as much as may be, even the guilty are to be spared, where it can prove no prejudice to the innocent. (TTG, II, §159, emphasis in original)

This sentence reveals that Locke was still applying an aggregational standard, such as that of utilitarianism, when he wrote about the need to preserve "*all* the Members of the Society."

Should we tag any number of the disabled as "innocent," we know that they could nevertheless be called upon to suffer privation if a disregard of their elementary wants would further the aggregate well-being of humankind. Just as any innocent man could lose his home when necessary to guard the public weal, an innocent human being with a terrible handicap was required to lose her life for the good of the human race. To be sure, the parallel between forcing someone to lose his home and forcing someone to lose his life is inexact on more than one count; but the divergences between the two situations do not all point the same way. On the one hand, the loss of a person's house was not as shuddersome as the loss of his life, and the person could be fully or partly compensated for the loss of his home. On the other hand, the loss of the domicile ensued from the direct intervention of officials or private actors, whereas the loss of life occurred in a manner not as grievously overbearing. At least when gauged in accordance with Locke's values, a refusal to intervene was less obnoxious than a harmful intervention. We therefore have a good basis for esteeming the mandatory loss of a person's home to be weightier than the mandatory loss of a person's life, and we also have a good basis for a contrary judgment.

But, even if we now have determined that a neglect-induced loss of life was weightier than a loss of residence, we still can ask whether the justifiability of the latter could extend to the former. Recall that the tribulations of neglect-induced starving would proceed for the sake of maximizing the ability of the human species to thrive and hence its ability to surround human beings with the arrangements wherein they best could preserve themselves. Given this underlying focus of the lethal neglect, the remarks by Locke that are under consideration here cannot themselves decide the legitimacy or illegitimacy of the neglect. If we construe the language about "*all* the Members of the Society" as a means of holding that *every* individual at any time was "to be preserved," and likewise if we assume that the "preserving" of every individual encompassed the dispensation of vital alms as well as a full abstention from the active causing of injuries, then a disregard of handicapped people's wants was unacceptable. If on the other hand we construe the phrase "*all* the Members of the Society" as an aggregational reference to the largest possible group of human beings at any time and at any times thereafter, or likewise if we assume that the "preserving" of a society's members did not encompass the handing out of alms to the destitute, then a failure to respond to the needs of the incapacitated was certainly permissible and even obligatory.

Thus, when we opt to think of fully disabled people as "innocent," the latest extract scrutinized here does not afford very sharply defined guidance on the potential claims of the disabled to receive succor. When we characterize the fully disabled people as "guilty," the extract will acquire more definiteness – though not perfect conclusiveness – and will militate in favor of overlooking the urgent needs of such people. After all, Locke confined the sparing of the guilty to circumstances "where it can prove no prejudice to the innocent." Yet claims by disabled people for charity would not count as such circumstances, because any fulfillment of those claims would siphon off basic goods from manifold uses that were more productive. As has been explained, the distribution of goods and services to severely handicapped people would impede the growth of prosperity in the state of nature, because such people were only ends of consumption and were not also means of production. Wealth doled out to those people would generate no returns in productivity and would ergo fail to accomplish what it could have accomplished if it had gone toward reinforcing the strengths and numbers and skills and incentives of healthy people. Reduced to languishing as an arid soil that would suck up items which could have been employed fruitfully, disabled people were always bound to be sacrificed through starvation in order to avert any "prejudice to the innocent." Had the "guilt" of human agents with dreadful handicaps been rectifiable and surmountable, it would not alone have condemned them to the horrors of brusque indifference and starving; but those human agents indeed would be required to undergo such a fate because the very continuing of their lives would curb humanity's total output.

In short, another passage that initially seems to furnish quite an impressive grounding for the rights of the cruelly handicapped is not so clear when probed more attentively. Although the latest excerpt above hardly adopts an unequivocal stance against such rights, it is far less solidly supportive of them than careless readers will have presumed. Before turning to a passage that weighs more strongly in favor of entitlements for utterly unproductive people, we should glance at a warm recollection of Locke's personal attitudes toward almsgiving. An account by one of Locke's closest friends can shed a ray of illumination on topics that have figured importantly throughout our present excursus:

> He [Locke] was naturally compassionate and exceedingly charitable to those in want. But his charity was always directed to encourage working, laborious, industrious people, and not to relieve idle beggars, to whom he never gave anything, or would suffer his friends to do so before him, saying such people as these

were 'robbers of the poor': and asking those that went for to relieve them whether they knew none that they were sure were in want and deserved help? If so, how could they satisfy themselves to give anything they could spare to such as they knew not to be in need, but who probably deserved to be so? . . . People who had been industrious, but were through age or infirmity passed labour, he was very bountiful to, and he used to blame that sparingness with which such were ordinarily relieved, as if it sufficed only that they should be kept from starving or extreme misery whereas they had, he said, a right to live comfortably in the world.[12]

To be sure, we have to approach these comments with some reservations in mind. First, of course, we shall never know if the comments are a reliably unsweetened and accurate portrayal of Locke. Second, even if the remarks are accurate, we ought to be wary of seizing on the characteristics of Locke's personal temperament in order to draw bold inferences about his theoretical postulates. Third, as will soon be argued, the quoted comments do not shed any light on the deepest question facing us here. Despite these reservations, however, we can draw at least one firm inference from the quoted remarks. If the remarks are accurate, then Locke was inclined to favor destitute people who had been conscientious workers – as opposed to the slothful. In everyday life he made the exact distinction that was entailed by general precepts of his political thought. To him the basic line of analysis pursued here would not seem strange. Indeed, given the fire that Locke apparently showed in his withholding of any alms from indolent "robbers of the poor," he would conceivably not have blenched at the proposition that such wastrels ordinarily should be left to starve.

But, even if we have traced some connections between Locke's personal behavior and his philosophical theses, his remarks above fail to answer the central query that we now must address. Those remarks deal only with people who were healthy yet torpid, and with hard-working people who had become infirm. No mention is made of incapacitated people who had not formerly been industrious. As we think about the prescribed fate of such people, let us overlook the standing of anyone who had had opportunities to labor – and who had disdained those opportunities – before becoming wholly decrepit. Let us concentrate on people who were severely handicapped from birth or from infancy. Did these people have entitlements to be kept alive through the provision of food and other basic necessities within the Lockean state of nature? Or did their total incapacity to participate in the production of goods and services deprive them of any claim to receive goods and services?

If we look for guidance from the chief precept of natural law, we must

[12] Maurice Cranston, *John Locke: A Biography* (Oxford: Oxford University Press, 1985), 426 (comments of Lady Damaris Masham).

conclude that human beings utterly disabled at birth would have no entitlements to get succor from their fellows. That chief precept, after all, required the insistent maximizing of human productivity as the groundwork for the largest feasible expansion of human thriving and comfort. A policy of conferring basic necessities on the crippled, however, would impair the overall output of goods and services by directing valuable items to particular uses that would never pay off through the creation of further items. Such a policy, with respect to anyone who was incapacitated from birth, could not be justified on the ground that it strengthened the incentives for healthy people's diligent toil (by making such steady toil a precondition for the obtaining of adequate support from others when needed). In contrast with rules for the supplying of ample goods and services to the once-productive elderly, the handing out of some alms to every innately feeble person would yield no extra incentives for able-bodied human beings to carry out hard work. Incentives would attach to no one, except to evolving fetuses who might acquire congenital ailments and to unconceived fetuses who might arise with genetic ailments. Yet even the diehard anti-abortion activists of the present day can scarcely suppose that fetuses and unconceived fetuses are productive workers who respond to incentives. Maybe those activists cannot endorse Job's assertion that a stillborn fetus has "never see[n] the light" (Job 3:16), but they surely must grasp that fetuses do not perform any toil whatsoever and do not take account of any principles relating to charity.

In short, the creating of incentives for persistent exertions was irrelevant here. And so the parceling out of necessary provisions to human beings with inborn handicaps was not authorized or demanded by the cardinal imperative in the law of nature. Nor have we hitherto discovered any pronouncement from the *Two Treatises* that very clearly upholds the rights of people born incapacitated. Although some of Locke's positions have undoubtedly been suggestive, each has proved to be more equivocal and more knotty than it first may appear. Still, many readers are apt to think that Locke could hardly have been so callous about the plight of grossly handicapped babies as to urge the disregard of their elementary wants on sternly utilitarian grounds. Lending substantial credence to this intuition, we must now contemplate a passage that tells quite vividly in support of those babies' rights.

For such an extract we shall turn to a chapter of the *Second Treatise* where Locke described maturity as the means by which young adults were delivered from the stewardship of their parents. According to Locke, the guidance and authority exercised by parents over their youthful children would stem from the incompetence of the children to deliberate independently and to understand the duties laid upon them by natural law (and also by civil law, when the state of nature had been transcended). Until a person honed his capacity for reasoning, to the point of knowing the laws that trammeled his discretion and conduct, he was bound to be guided by the judgment of authoritative protectors such as parents. "All which seems no more than that Duty, which God and Nature has laid on Man as well as other Creatures, to preserve their Off-spring, till they can be able to shift for themselves" (TTG, II, §60).

Yet, as Locke noticed, there furthermore would be adult members of the human race who were incapacitated from doing any reasoning on their own. Certain people were so deficient mentally that they had to be guided and protected throughout their lives. As Locke explained:

> But if through defects that may happen out of the ordinary course of Nature, any one comes not to such a degree of Reason, wherein he might be supposed capable of knowing the Law, and so living within the Rules of it, he is *never capable of being a Free Man*, he is never let loose to the disposure of his own Will (because he knows no bounds to it, has not Understanding, its proper Guide) but is continued under the Tuition and Government of others, all the time his own Understanding is uncapable of that Charge. And so *Lunaticks* and *Ideots* are never set free from the Government of their Parents. (TTG, II, §60, emphasis in original)

Locke manifestly presumed that the imbeciles and lunatics were indeed allowed to survive and were in fact maintained through the "Tuition and Government of others." He offered nary the slightest hint that mentally incapacitated people would deserve no assistance and would therefore deserve to perish of starvation soon after being born (whenever their handicaps became obvious).

To be sure, not all lunatics and idiots were hopelessly unproductive people. Steered by constant direction from their parents or guardians, some of them could perhaps work fruitfully. But others among them, doubtless, were so severely unattuned to reality that they never could perform any useful work. Very likely, complete unproductiveness would characterize a large proportion of the mentally crippled. Even so, Locke refrained from drawing any distinctions here that would vest some idiots with entitlements-to-survive while shutting out many others from those entitlements. Rather, he presupposed the conferral of such entitlements on all idiots and lunatics, and he took upon himself to explain how those entitlements could be wielded. His silence on the productive/unproductive distinction was an eloquent silence that bespoke few qualms about the correctness of sustaining *every* lunatic's life.

To be sure, as well, in the above passage Locke referred only to incompetent minds and not to languishing bodies. His remarks elsewhere on the physically incapacitated were not as forthright as his remarks here on the mentally incapacitated. However, if unproductive idiots were entitled to receive help and tutelage, then unproductive people with severe bodily handicaps could scarcely be refused assistance. By disclosing that the plight of involuntary unproductiveness would not in itself debar a *mentally* unsound person from getting aid, Locke ipso facto disclosed that such a plight would not in itself debar a *physically* unsound person from getting aid. After all, Locke's religiously grounded stance on human equality forbade the one-sided use of a criterion – i.e. any use that would scotch the rights of only some of the human beings who shared the characteristic(s) singled out by that very criterion.

Let us not be dogmatic. Though the latest extract above is firmer than the previous extracts in its tendency to uphold the rights of grimly disabled people, it of course can always be reinterpreted along very different lines. Readers justifiably can declare that Locke adduced the sad situation of idiots and lunatics merely as a piquant analogy that could help to reinforce his main point about the guidance and safekeeping of children. According to this possible reinterpretation, we ought to shrink from focusing on a passage that was chiefly designed to illustrate an idea which has no bearing on the prime topic of our current discussion. The vivid analogies employed to accentuate that idea were drawn from the social world as it was, rather than from the social world as it should have been; had the social world been what it should have been, unproductive lunatics would not have enjoyed any entitlements to get alms. Or perhaps the analogies indeed were drawn from the social world as it should have been, and Locke simply never bothered to state flatly that unproductive lunatics would not be entitled to receive any alms like those available to productive lunatics. We have noted already that silence can convey any number of meanings. Some analysts might hold that Locke's silence about the gap between unproductive idiots and productive idiots can best be construed as flowing from his belief that such a gap was too obvious to require attention. Far from perceiving Locke's silence as support for the notion that the productive/unproductive dichotomy was inapposite with regard to lunatics, this hypothetical reinterpretation can perceive the silence as a mark of the deep and persistent sway of that dichotomy.

Now, although the reinterpretation above is surely possible, it is not profoundly convincing. It certainly does succeed in showing the equivocalness of some remarks that may have been unduly presented here as limpid, and it fittingly warns against bestowing too great an import on analogies that were not themselves at the focus of Locke's concern. Yet it submits a reading of Locke's comments on lunatics that is pretty strained and also somewhat ungenerous. Not only does that reading provide a rather far-fetched analysis by opting heavily for the canny manipulation of silence, but it encumbers Locke with a wincingly harsh attitude toward involuntary unproductiveness. Therefore, while the appropriate understanding of the latest extract from the *Two Treatises* is plainly not a matter beyond dispute, we can probably best infer that Locke took as given the entitlements of all lunatics and all innately handicapped people to receive succor. Having explored the many ambiguities in the relevant sections of the *Two Treatises*, and hence having found that any conclusions on this topic should be flexible and modest, we now can accept the kindly verdict that has revealed itself to be far from unmistakably preordained; in other words, we now can accept the view that people incapacitated from birth or from infancy would all be entitled to some life-maintaining assistance at the hands of their productive contemporaries in a Lockean world.

This concession implies a limit on the drawing of consequences within this chapter. We can express the limit in a positive way as the entitlement of every human being to get essential goods and services from his fellows when he himself was partly or totally unable to meet his own fundamental needs through his best efforts. That entitlement would conflict very rarely with the foremost imperative in the law of nature – which required the maximal flourishing of the human species – but it indeed would clash therewith now and then; and on the few occasions when a conflict arose, the entitlement would generally outweigh the foremost imperative (which on those occasions, obviously, was not the foremost imperative). Thus, since my current chapter tries to show that all elements of Locke's theory of property were governed through and through by the natural law's prime directive with a focus on the aggregate weal of the human race, we clearly must acknowledge a limit to the applicability of this chapter's thesis.

Nevertheless, we surely also ought to beware of overestimating and oversimplifying the restrictions imposed by my conceding that every person involuntarily unproductive in the Lockean state of nature had a right to be kept alive under most circumstances. This concession has only slightly impaired the force of this chapter's arguments. Most unproductive people would be altogether excluded from the terms of the concession or else would be embraced by those terms in a manner fully consistent with the chief dictate of natural law.

Anyone who was healthy but slothful would enjoy no claims to the goods of others via the right that has just been described. After all, that right would relate only to each person who was unproductive *against his or her will*. Sheer laziness deserved no protection or reward, at least when evaluated by anybody impartial. Similarly, the human agents who had loafed throughout the years before the undoing of their productive capacities would have no entitlements thereafter to obtain assistance from anybody else. Earlier, we perceived one reason for such a lack of entitlements; we observed that the bestowing of the entitlements upon wastrels would infringe the supreme directive of natural law, which called for maximal productivity and which thus called for arrays of entitlements that would not severely dampen industriousness by rewarding the faithful toiler and the shiftless beggar alike. We now can descry a second reason for the withholding of certain rights and privileges from the slouchy. An indolent person who became disabled would not be unproductive against his will. Although he in fact did lose his productive abilities, he had almost never shown a serious inclination to employ those abilities in any event. His aloofness from productive exertions in the aftermath of his own enfeeblement was thus not involuntary. And so the newly handicapped sluggard, who was forced to lead a life of inaction that he would fecklessly have pursued at any rate, did not qualify for alms on the basis of the concession granted to human beings who vainly wished to work.

If torpid people would continue to be excluded from the getting of alms within a framework of natural law that provided for the needs of involuntarily unproductive people, their assiduous counterparts would fare much better – just as they would be faring even if the prime mandate of natural law with its aggregational thrust had not been modified for the good of people handicapped from birth or from infancy. Hard-working people who were unproductive as a result of largely inevasible mishaps would promptly be entitled to ask for aid until their fortunes improved. They held their entitlements-to-support on the basis of the cardinal prescript in natural law and furthermore on the basis of the lone exception to that chief prescript (the exception for the rights of anyone who was unproductive against his or her will).

In a like manner, a person who had conscientiously labored till he somehow became permanently deprived of his health at a fairly early age would always have an entitlement to be nourished by his contemporaries. As this chapter earlier argued, the entitlements of any such man or woman under the supreme imperative in the law of nature were fuzzy to a certain extent. On the one hand, the conferral of entitlements-to-relief on disabled men and women who formerly had been earnest toilers would help to build incentives for earnest toiling; on the other hand, the incapacitation of young and middle-aged people was probably so uncommon that the furnishing of relief to everyone not yet old might tend to make hardly any impact upon the structuring of people's incentives. And since the furnishing of relief would drain away assets from productive uses, its weakly salutary effect on motivations might be too costly. Here, however, our new awareness of the only exception to the supreme requirement in natural law can dispel any lingering doubts. Under the terms of that sole exception, anyone not yet elderly along with anyone elderly would have an entitlement to get succor in the wake of becoming crippled after having labored with perseverance thitherto. We hence should resolve the slight uncertainty in the treatment of this point by the natural law's principal demand, and should now conclude that the promotion of incentives for steady toiling was worth the cost of supplying aid to people who had once toiled diligently but who had later suffered enfeeblement while still young. Such a resolution of the uncertainty has always seemed most plausible, in any event.

Thus, people incapacitated from birth or from early childhood were the exclusive group of handicapped people who would hold entitlements-to-relief on the basis of the one exception to the natural law's chief principle and *not* on the basis of that chief principle itself. In other words, although the exception to the foremost dictate of natural law indeed operated as an exception, its departures from the norm were extremely limited. Only in relation to the small group of people just specified, would anyone's actual entitlement to the fulfillment of basic needs be in competition with the cardinal mandate of natural law instead of being squarely derived from it.

Of course, with a little ingenuity we can go some distance toward blurring the "exceptional" status of the exception to the prime command in the law of nature. That is, we can try to bring the workings of the exception under the reach of the precise mandate to which those workings stood as exceptions. Perhaps the easiest way of pursuing this reconception is to adduce the possible link between deprivation and diligence, a link on which we focused earlier briefly. If healthy people had to allot some goods for the preservation of people who were handicapped from birth or from childhood, then the finished items left over to be used by the healthy would be fewer than they otherwise would have been – unless the healthy people produced enough to feed the disabled *and* to push their own levels of consumption and investment as high as those levels would have gone in circumstances where nothing was earmarked for innately handicapped people. Insofar as we can submit that healthy people would value their consumption and their material security more than they would value their leisure, we can well maintain that the imposing of duties on the healthy for the sustenance of the handicapped would eventuate in a more prolific output of goods and services on the whole. To draw this inference about those duties, in other words, we have to assume here that the able-bodied would enlarge their overall output to provide for the feeble and to satisfy their own basic wants (and indeed their own secondary wants) as richly as ever. Given such a hypothesis about the balance that would be struck between the comforts of material wealth and the opportunities for relaxing, a scheme of fundamental prescriptions which conferred rights-to-be-kept-alive upon the innately handicapped would promote the sheer industriousness of the human species. The establishment of rights-to-succor would hence fulfill the chief natural-law imperative requiring the dogged maximization of human flourishing.

Though the vein of argument that has just been limned is not guilty of outright blunders, it smacks unduly of special pleading. Highly conjectural and rather contrived, it lays down axioms about human preferences and priorities as if those essential axioms can be blithely treated as givens. Indeed, only if those axioms are treated as axioms by being taken for granted, can the posited line of argument succeed. Yet the theses advanced in those axioms are far too contestable and contested to warrant an uncritical endorsement. Maybe my last paragraph above is correct in stating that everybody or almost everybody during the natural phase of the human species would opt for the diminishing of relaxation in preference to the diminishing of consumption and investment. Maybe, however, that paragraph is not correct. How are we to know? Here the crucial point is that that paragraph has traded glibly in speculation and has not offered any theorizing which is suitably rigorous. Albeit its surmisals indeed can foil dogmatic pronouncements from the other direction, those surmisals can never serve to establish any solid verdicts of their own about the likely effects of mandatory help for the incapacitated. Had we only to show that the provision of succor for innately handicapped human beings was *not perforce contrary* to the prime directive of natural law, the broaching of possibilities in the last paragraph would suffice to clinch our case. Instead, however, the argument in that paragraph has needed to confirm that the provision of sustenance was *always compatible* with God's prime directive. As such a proof, the argument does indeed fall short.

Avowing that the rights of innately handicapped people to be kept alive were departures from the normal requirement for the maximization of productiveness, and recalling how seldom those departures would emerge, we should ask about the most appropriate way in which to classify those departures. That is, should we seek to characterize those rare exceptions as individualistic encroachments on the communitarian sway of natural law's cardinal prescript, or should we aim to classify those exceptions as the very products of communitarianism? Plainly, either classification recommends itself in certain respects and not in others, just as either classification can apply to the rules of private ownership. By adopting the perspective of the innately handicapped, we can view their rights-to-succor as individualistic claims that put the well-being of specific persons above the general well-being of the human race as a whole. By adopting the perspective of healthy human beings obligated to aid the handicapped, we can view the handicapped people's rights-to-succor as communitarian burdens that constrained a number of individuals to make sacrifices for the good of their fellows. Yet neither of those perspectives can gain an utterly overwhelming advantage in relation to the other; each to some degree is legitimate, and neither is conclusive.

Let us, however, grant that a right-to-sustenance for disabled people was individualistic by and large. We thus have granted that the cardinal imperative in the law of nature was qualified by an individualistic exception to its reign. How does such an acknowledgment impinge on this chapter's principal line of reasoning, which contends that the inability of self-ownership and labor to operate as the grounds for the distribution of wealth would mean that all apportionments of assets were comprehended and fully shaped by the natural law's chief command?

Of course, in quite an obvious way, the making of a concession here does reveal that the operative reach of the natural law's foremost mandate was not all-encompassing. Nonetheless, the restriction of that mandate's reach along these lines should occasion no bewilderment or dismay. After all, this chapter's drawing of consequences has stemmed from the demise of the labor theory of property. Thus, we should scarcely be bemused or taken aback when our drawing of consequences does not extend to people on whom the labor theory of ownership hardly bore at all (because of the complete incapacity-for-work from which those people had always suffered). What has been demonstrated is that all the decisions seemingly governed by the norms expressed in the labor theory were instead governed totally by the paramount directive of natural law – the directive binding all human agents to maximize the flourishing of their species. Other decisions, such as those concerning human creatures who could not perform any toil, were never putatively based on the norms expounded within the labor theory of ownership; the point of reference for those decisions would accordingly not change as a result of the toppling of the labor theory.

If we assume that the specific norms upheld in the labor theory were presented as decisive for *all* allotments of goods and services in the state of nature, we must assume that people handicapped from birth were supposed to get their shares of the goods and services by way of those particular norms. Were we to give our credence to the latter assumption, we would commit ourselves to thinking that all innately handicapped people were supposed to acquire no goods and services whatsoever (since those people could not manage to carry out any entitlement-generating work). Yet these concluding paragraphs of this long discussion have proceeded from a recognition that innately handicapped human beings did hold entitlements to receive succor in a Lockean world; we hence must know that the standards of the labor theory were not presumed to govern *every* apportionment of valuable things in such a world, and specifically we know that those standards were not presumed to govern the apportionment of essential items for human beings who were always or nearly always incompetent to engage in productive tasks. Thus, we hardly should be surprised to learn that the distribution of some essential items to those unfortunate human creatures could go ahead regardless of how unsound or sound the justification for the labor theory's standards might prove to be. A fundamental critique of the labor theory will have challenged and overturned any view of that theory's norms as the bedrock principles for dividing up goods in the state of nature, but it will tend to fall short of throwing other Lockean precepts into question. To the precise extent that the implications ensuing from this book's overall encounter with Locke are hemmed about slightly, they reflect the limits of the target in the encounter.

A conclusion for hard times: individualism undone by individualism

All the considerations that have just been reviewed here in support of entitlements-to-be-kept-alive for innately handicapped people – insofar as we have paid no attention to the differences among people's standpoints – have primarily borne on contexts in which the finished goods were so abundant that everyone could get enough to survive. Difficulties emerge as soon as we look at contexts in which grave scarcities of key goods prevailed. Such contexts, remember, were the only contexts in which the duty and prerogative of self-favoritism loomed large; self-absorption in the choosing of entitlement-assigning norms was not permissible except when one's very life was threatened, and hence was not permissible unless dire scarcities of essential goods compelled trade-offs among the lives of people who had to use the goods for their sustenance.

In conditions of plenty, when the natural laws relating to alms were fully heeded, the privilege and duty of self-devotion were never activated. In such conditions, then, the variations among the standpoints of people would result in no systematic discrepancies among appropriate views concerning the imputation of rights and privileges; since no one was exercising self-favoritism, no one would ever credit himself with any really vital prerogatives that would not be imputed to him likewise by all the people around him. (Though the formulation in the preceding sentence allows for some interpretive flexibility with regard to the concretizing of natural-law demands, its singling out of the *appropriate* views on rights and privileges has brushed aside the potential for major errors or dishonesty. The possibility of egregious blunders or disingenuousness would certainly be important for some investigations, but not for our investigation of how entitlements were to be assigned in principle.)

Yet, when severe shortages of crucial items arose, the consentaneity of perspectives broke apart on the reef of self-favoritism. Each of the human agents vying with one another for existence was entitled to place her own essential wants above those of everybody else. While each was justified from her own perspective in laying claim to urgently needed goods, her claims were unjustified from anybody else's perspective. Moreover, not simply were the justifiable claims of person *S* at odds with the justifiable claims of person *T*, but either person's warranted claims could prove to be at odds with the claims of humankind as a whole. Here we see the most pronounced form of Lockean individualism – and here we ipso facto shall see the undermining of Lockean individualism.

Near the outset of the discussion on the rights of handicapped people, we observed that the triggering of self-absorption in times of desperate hardship would foster an inconsistency between the entitlements of every handicapped person as construed by that person and the entitlements of every handicapped person as construed from other perspectives. From the vantage point of the overall human species, anybody unfit for labor would have to die before anybody hale whenever some full-blown sacrifices had to be made because of serious shortages. From the vantage point of anybody unfit for laboring, on the other hand, the rescuing of herself was the top priority and indeed was a strict matter of obligation. Nor did the conflicts only lie between the perspective of the whole human race and the perspective of each disabled human being; conflicts also prevailed between individuals. From the viewpoint of any person *J*, a handicapped person *K* would always deserve to die whenever *K*'s continued existence would preclude or sorely imperil *J*'s continued existence. After all, the self-favoritism of *J* – rendered operative by the plight of famine – would clearly entitle *J* to sustain herself at the expense of every one of her fellows, whether handicapped or robust. (Notice that *J* could be a disabled person, and that everything here remarked about *J vis-à-vis K* can thus likewise be maintained about *K vis-à-vis J*.) Hence, the self-devoted perspective of each disabled person *K* in a time of want would collide often with the overarching perspective of humanity as a whole, and furthermore would clash with the individual perspective of every member of humankind whose own basic welfare was at odds with the basic welfare of *K*.

In a situation of grievous hardship, of course, the independent right-to-be-kept-alive that was held by each innately handicapped person would run up against its own restrictions and could therefore prove totally unavailing. In any such situation, with too few ready comestibles to keep everyone alive, a person or group of people would have to starve for the sake of others. The only pertinent question was *who* would have to starve.

Appropriate answers to that question would hinge on the sundry viewpoints from which the answers stemmed. From the viewpoint of an innately handicapped person *K*, her own entitlement to receive some food and thus to avoid starvation was unimpeachable. From the viewpoint of any person other than *K*, however, *K*'s wants could properly be disregarded when such neglect was essential for allowing the other person to live. And from the perspective of humanity as a whole, the basic needs of *K* were all bound to go unmet if the sacrificing of *K* would help a productive human agent to survive during the desperate shortages. The right of *K* to receive assistance, in other words, did not bind every one of *K*'s fellows except when *K*'s reliance upon that right did not involve the neglect of anybody else's key wants. If the supply of food was too skimpy for everyone to survive through a particular period, the entitlement of *K* to get succor would vanish from the sight of everybody or nearly everybody apart from *K* herself. Accordingly, except in the eyes of *K* herself, the right of *K* to due sustenance would have no bearing on answers to the question concerning who was obligated to starve.

For a somewhat different way of elaborating this general point, we ought to remember that the entitlement-to-be-kept-alive was vested in *every*one who generally behaved decently and who was not willfully unproductive. Each person handicapped from birth and each person handicapped after years of diligent toil would hold an entitlement-to-be-kept-alive, of course, but so would each human being in normal health who encountered setbacks and hardships through no real fault of his own. Hence, the entitlement-to-be-kept-alive could scarcely determine who would eat and who would go hungry in the midst of grave shortages which prevented the universal fulfilling of that entitlement. Since ex hypothesi a harsh famine would entail trade-offs among the lives of people who each enjoyed the right to adequate sustenance, that common right in itself could never serve to ground the distinctions that were needed for making any such trade-offs. Natural law could hardly distinguish people from one another on the basis of an endowment which they shared. Some alternative touchstone, drawn of course from the law of nature, would have to underlie the distinctions.

Now, as should be quite apparent already, the considerations adduced here with regard to the feeble must apply in almost every respect to human agents who were perfectly hearty. Just as each incapacitated person would rank below every healthy person in the species-wide order of priorities, each hale person ranked *below* every person who was more productive and ranked *ahead* of each person who was less productive. From the overarching perspective of the human race, healthy people occupied niches on a scale that drew an inverse relation between productiveness and expendability. Though grotesquely handicapped people would be less favored than anyone hearty, just about everybody hearty would be less favored than some other person or set of people (some other person or set of people who respectively could produce even higher levels of normal output).

Albeit the preservation of anyone with a sound body and mind would not so likely clash with the general weal of the species as would the preservation of anyone infirm, the horrors of widespread destitution could result in the sacrifice of myriad healthy people along with every disabled person. And, of the greatest importance here, the standpoints of healthy victims would jar profoundly with the standpoint of humankind – in quite the same way as would the standpoints of crippled victims. Healthy people, like sickly people, had duties and entitlements to favor themselves in periods of harrowing shortages. Each human being at any level of fitness was entitled and obligated to place his own crucial needs ahead of everyone else's needs and ahead of species-wide needs, when famines scotched the possibility that everyone's crucial needs could be satisfied. Thus, no healthy person could accept being called upon to forsake his own survival for the good of the human species. When the good of the species demanded the sacrifice of a healthy person *Q* so that some or all of the more productive contemporaries of *Q* could be spared, a gap would consequently arise between the self-devoted viewpoint of *Q* and the broadly transindividual viewpoint of the species. On this particular count, as much as on several closely related counts, what was true of each feeble person was also true of each robust person. Whether someone was able-bodied or grimly handicapped, his rightful devotion to himself was bound to conflict with the demands of the human species when those demands required him to starve.

Similarly, the contradictions between the rightful claims of any disabled person and the rightful claims of any contemporary (anyone disabled or not) were paralleled by the contradictions between the claims of any hale person and the claims of any other hale person. If the group of healthy people was akin to the group of sickly people inasmuch as the members of both such groups would justly adopt individual perspectives that were apt to be discordant with the perspective of the whole human race during severe scarcities of essential goods, then the groups were furthermore alike in that the members of both such groups would justly adopt individual perspectives which were apt to be discordant with one another during such scarcities. Given the occurrence of lethal shortages, and given the obligation of every person to seek his own survival ahead of anybody else's survival when a trade-off was necessary, a robust person's standpoint could well conflict with the standpoints of other people who were robust. Sometimes a famine would result in the deaths of incapacitated people exclusively, but at other times a famine would also cause the deaths of quite a few hearty people. On occasions when the grisly toll of a famine did extend to the ranks of healthy people, each healthy person's obligation to acquire sustenance was starkly and legitimately unyielding from his own perspective but was wholly and legitimately unrecognized by some or all of his healthy fellows. Though doubtless the able-bodied people were not as prone to starve during famines as were bedridden people, and though the able-bodied were therefore not as prone to become enlocked in clashes of individual perspectives *among themselves* as they would be in relation to the perspectives of their feeble counterparts, they could never be immune from such clashes among themselves.

Sickly people *and* rugged people who were authorized to favor themselves, then, could rightly hold to individual viewpoints that jarred with one another and also jarred with the main requirements of the species to which the rugged and the sickly belonged. Note, moreover, that slothfulness on the part of anyone would not affect the predicament just described. Once we take account of self-favoritism in the Lockean scheme of things, we know that anyone slouchy would from his own perspective be bound and privileged to keep himself alive during famines by obtaining any requisite goods. Earlier in this chapter, before we looked at the role of self-favoritism, we observed that someone who had often been shiftless – and who was thus inclined to continue being shiftless – would incur a duty to starve when necessary to spare the life of an industrious person in a harrowing time of want. We now can see that a shiftless person, from his own viewpoint, was not constrained to be a sunken-cheeked martyr for the cause of industriousness. However clearly the prime imperative of natural law would ordain such a fate for loafers, each loafer from his own self-favoring standpoint was obligated and allowed to quest for his survival even at the expense of the assiduously productive human agents around him. Perhaps each wastrel had forfeited his right to be kept alive by others, but he retained always his entitlement and his duty to concern himself with his own most pressing needs above the various needs of every one of his fellows. (And he thus retained the prerogative and the duty to ignore anyone else's right to be kept alive, whenever his disregarding of such a right was crucial for his own ability to avoid starvation.) Hence, a lazy person was as prone as anyone else to be involved in conflicts between the just priorities of his own perspective and the transindividual focus of the chief command in the law of nature; likewise, such a person was always prone to become ensnarled in clashes between his own viewpoint and the individual viewpoints of any number of his contemporaries. Because past idleness would not disallow current self-absorption throughout periods of bleakness and hardship, any idle person would join his diligent fellows in the tangle of inconsistent stands to which self-absorption led.

In fact, these remarks about the slothful might beckon us to reconsider and slightly modify this chapter's previous assertion that Locke's endorsement of self-preferring behavior would pertain solely to famine-torn periods of humankind's natural state (and also to defenses against aggression, of course). To be sure, the authorizing of self-devotion indeed related exclusively to people whose lives were in competition with other people's lives or well-being. But exactly such a state of dire competition could afflict lazy people despite an absence of widespread misery. Recall here that a pattern of indolence would strip a person of any right to be kept alive by aid from her fellows, a right that would normally become operational when a person lacked enough finished goods to meet her own vital needs. Thus, even in conditions of general plenty, a wastrel might have neither an adequate amount of essential goods nor the dimmest hope of gaining relief through alms from anybody hard-working. If the wastrel did not have any entitlement to put her own urgent needs ahead of other people's needs and apparent rights, she clearly would be duty-bound to starve amid the general prosperity of those other people. Fortunately for her, however, she was privileged and obligated to pursue her own basic weal in preference to that of anybody else. From her own vantage point, indeed, she was authorized to take possession of any finished goods that she would require for her sustainment. In this respect, her viewpoint of course would jar with the chief principle in the law of nature and would jar as well with the viewpoints of the individual human beings whose sundry assets she might attempt to rob. Her perspective clashed also with the perspectives of other loafers, who competed with her for assets. Yet, notwithstanding these overt tensions, she behaved in accordance with the law of nature when she attached a higher priority to her own existence than to any other person's existence or well-being.

Surely, however, we have gone amiss somewhere. Would the self-preferring behavior of a sluggish person indeed accord with the vision of natural law in the *Second Treatise*? Are we not bordering on absurdity if we think that Locke intended to give his blessing to plunder carried out by shiftless people against industrious people? And are we not also verging upon the ludicrous if we declare that Locke intended to give his blessing to a host of wildly discordant stances – equally legitimate stances – on the proper interpretation of natural law's demands?

To be sure, specifically in relation to the problem of idlers, we can dodge the third of these queries by devising apposite responses to both the first query and the second. We can hold that any frequently torpid person lost not merely her entitlement to be kept alive through suitable alms, but also her entitlement to favor her own prospects for survival above the prospects of other people. (To be sure, even a torpid person would of course retain her prerogative of self-defense against aggression.) In light of this additional forfeiture, there would not be any legitimate clash of perspectives that involved wastrels; nor would major legitimate inconsistencies among *any* standpoints occur except through the occurrence of severe shortages.

But, although we can circumvent the last of the above queries when we train our focus on idlers, we shall have to address that query in the course of taking a broader view. As phrased above, that third query – along with each of the other queries – has unwisely asked about Locke's intentions; however, we can revitalize the third query by perceiving that it is principally concerned with some of the general lines of argumentation in the *Two Treatises*. Appropriately reframed, our question asks whether the accounts of natural law and natural entitlements within the *Two Treatises* should incline us to think that famine-ravaged periods in the Lockean state of nature were akin to the turbulence in the Hobbesian state of nature.

My discussion of the conflicts among the viewpoints in the Lockean state of nature – i.e. in the Lockean state of nature temporarily riven by acute shortages – does bear indeed a striking resemblance to Hobbes's picture of a brutish presocietal state (although the clashes in the *Leviathan*'s state of nature arose from linguistic and psychological and even epistemological grounds as well as from moral/legal grounds). When the survival of person *A* excluded the survival of person *B* in a desperate period of the Lockean natural state, the rights-to-sustenance held by each of these people would be rights from his or her own perspective exclusively. From the vantage point of the other person, those rights at best were construable as privileges; much more often they would not be construable as prerogatives of any sort, but instead would be construable only as some obligations of noninterference. In effect, that is, the Lockean state of nature during the throes of famines became the Hobbesian state of nature. Everyone's rights would function merely as privileges, and would jostle with the putative rights of everybody else whenever those so-called rights were invoked. And, for all practical purposes, the transindividual duties flowing from the prime command in the law of nature were inoperative. Here, apparently, the individualism of the Lockean state of nature would reach its summit.

Given the dominant conception of natural law within the *Two Treatises*, should we now conclude that this picture of extreme individualism has correctly portrayed the chief entitlements and the role of self-devotion in a state of nature where the supplies of goods available for immediate consumption were direly scant? Or should we conclude, rather, that the extreme individualism was itself the first casualty of the dreadful hardships that might have served to bring it about? On the one hand, there were always abundant opportunities in the state of nature for disagreements about the specificities of the outcomes that were to be derived from the general mandates of natural law. Conflicts among the well-made judgments of individuals would emerge almost unavoidably in relation to quite a number of particular problems. Moreover, the onset of a famine was so terrible in itself that any means of coming to grips with it would generate some cruel and ghastly effects; thus, the dreadfulness of a plunge into Hobbesian conditions was mainly a consequence or an aspect of the dreadfulness of excruciating scarcity. Though a Hobbesian way of dealing with the perils of famines was rebarbative, *any* way of dealing with the perils of famines was bound to have rebarbative consequences.

On the other hand, the considerations telling against a scheme of Hobbesian atomism were far stronger. Albeit the law of nature left some room for interpretive discretion and hence some room for varied interpretations of its concrete demands, the fact of this interpretive leeway would hardly warrant the tumult of a Hobbesian free-for-all in which interpretations clashed wildly as they received expression from self-devoted people whose interests wildly clashed. For Locke, interpretive latitude pertained to different conceptions of a shared project – not to wholly discordant projects. As was mentioned above, the overarching duties of natural law would effectively cease to function insofar as the Lockean state of nature became a Hobbesian state of nature during times of want and distress; thus, the scope for differences of interpretation in fleshing out those natural-law duties would be largely or entirely irrelevant as a grounding and a backdrop for the Hobbesian scheme of things.

Furthermore, although any response to famines was indeed bound to be unpleasant because the famines themselves were so lamentable, the problem to be confronted was how to make the best of an evil plight. Such a question derived not only from common sense but also from the paramount principle in the law of nature. Yet a Hobbesian answer to that question would doubtless fare very poorly. A framework of entitlements along Hobbesian lines would scarcely keep the toll of disasters to a minimum.

Besides, such a framework in its effects would constitute an arrant departure from the general relationship between human strife and natural law as presented by the *Two Treatises*. Never in the course of all other circumstances – all circumstances other than grinding scarcities – would the fundamental directives in a Lockean world authorize a lethal state of disorder; on the contrary, the threat of deadly brawls and disorder came from the tendency of human beings to slight their natural-law duties. Even the individualized duty of enforcement and punishment, which could certainly ignite tussles on the part of resistant malefactors, was triggered only by the occurrence of wrongful deeds and was not productive of any violence except when malefactors compounded their original crimes by stubbornly refusing to make amends. Throughout the *Two Treatises*, a constant fidelity to natural law would result in the harmonious coexistence of people. And thus we should refrain from ascribing any conflict-promotive message to Locke's endorsement of the self-favoritism of human beings. Our ascription of such a message, after all, must entail the verdict that people in any famine-torn periods of the state of nature had to fulfill their natural-law duties by contending ferociously against one another when their key interests collided. Any such verdict upends the usual slant of natural law. Everywhere else within the *Two Treatises*, the law of nature encouraged peace and aimed to advance prosperity. In regard to famines, apparently, the law of nature would significantly reduce the orderliness of interaction among people and would largely forsake the goal of maximizing the prosperousness of humankind. Confronted with this disturbing picture of radically shifted priorities, we ought to withhold assent. The allowance of self-devotion would have produced unbearable consequences that would have made imperative a rescinding of the allowance.[13]

[13] Here a subtle caveat is important. As was argued earlier, the cardinal directive in the law of nature could possibly though improbably yield at certain junctures a regime of entitlements that inspired an atomistic unruliness. Nothing in my current line of argument conflicts with that previous point, because my two sets of arguments have worked at quite different levels. The atomistic unruliness here decried would ensue directly from wholesale conflicts over the implications of natural law, whereas the unruliness described before was a product of entitlements which in turn arose as epiphenomena of natural-law commands that were not themselves the direct sources or objects of controversy.

More important, the clashes here envisaged were life-and-death scuffles that would cruelly override all the normal checks on the committing of harm within the Lockean state of nature. A justifiably self-devoted person in the midst of terrible shortages of essential goods could justifiably trample on the basic rights of others as much as necessary to secure his own life. By contrast, the disharmonious interaction that was mentioned earlier as a possibility would never rightly encompass brawling and certainly would never rightly encompass *lethal* brawling. In any Lockean state of nature where the access to finished items was duly governed by a scheme of privileges without concrete rights of ownership, discord among people could well ensue if goods were frequently snatched away from their holders through the widespread exertion of the privilege-to-snatch; nonetheless, the altercations that might develop were strictly bounded in times of plenty by people's basic rights. Everybody could seize belongings in such a world, but no one could gravely jeopardize the survival or the decent well-being and secureness of others. Unlike the mortal combat in a famine-plagued state of nature where everyone was required to put his own vital needs ahead of everyone else's, the routine skirmishes in happier periods would never come close to being fights-to-the-death. Such skirmishes

Oppressive shortages were bitter indeed, and they surely stretched the natural law to its limits. All the same, we have no reason to think that such shortages would reverse the basic tenor of natural law. Instead of sparking divisions and enmities, the law of nature would demand the avoidance of those evils. Dissension and antagonisms could well arise with frequency, but they always would occur in spite of God's law and not in fulfillment of it. Rather than occasion a multitude of explosive conflicts among individual standpoints without an overall prioritizing of standpoints, the law of nature would uphold an exacting scale of priorities – determined, of course, by the paramount objective of human thriving and comfort. Such a ranking of individuals would try to stanch the development of clashes and bloodshed by requiring various human agents to subordinate their needs and their very lives to the needs and lives of their more productive contemporaries. The less that anyone could contribute to the attaining of human welfare, the more substantial the likelihood that she would be called upon to starve in order to leave precious sustenance for the use of her fellows. (Notice that a duty to starve was squarable with the duty to abstain from all acts of suicide. One's observance of the duty-to-starve proceeded not through any active self-slaughter, but through passive noninterference with the gaining of nourishment by one's fellows – a passive noninterference that admittedly sealed one's own demise, in conditions of acute shortages.)

Now, although the preceding paragraph has described a way of coming to grips with hellish scarcities that was most attuned to the general purport of natural law and most suitable for making the best of an extremely unpleasant situation, the verdict of that paragraph has

would leave everyone with his or her fundamental rights intact, though some people would fare much better from the skirmishes than would others.

However small were the chances that a network of privileges with no rights of ownership would fulfill the supreme behest in the law of nature by maximizing the comforts and the conveniences of the human race, such a network could on occasions prove indeed an optimal structure for the distribution of assets. If people were inclined generally to care more about retaining some levels of their comforts and conveniences than about relaxing, the potentially greater vulnerableness of holdings in a regime of privileges-without-concrete-rights could strengthen aggregate productivity by strengthening people's incentives to be productive. Very different were the life-and-death struggles fueled by the authorizing of self-devotion in a period of shuddersome want; people who lost those struggles did not emerge therefrom with opportunities to toil even harder. During a time when finished goods were acutely limited in supply, a human agent who was unsuccessful when jousting fiercely with others for those goods would not live to compensate for his misadventures. His losses, so to speak, were dead losses. Hence, given that mortal strife within a famine-plagued state of nature would yield no profitable effects on the incentives of losers, all advantages to be won through the strife could more appropriately be won through a matrix of entitlements which barred self-devotion and which strictly ranked people for the fulfilling of a duty-to-starve.

expunged the role of self-centeredness within Locke's account. A ranking of people in connection with the duty-to-starve would scotch the privilege of self-devotion for everyone whose duty to starve was activated and for every other person as well. Now, the privilege of self-devotion was available only under circumstances of ghastly hardship; hence, given that that privilege was wholly excluded under just such circumstances, it was excluded altogether.[14] In other words, if the thesis of my last paragraph is true, self-devotion would never be allowed in the only settings where it was ever warranted. That paragraph has reconciled Locke's insistence on the cardinal mandate of natural law and his putative authorizing of self-favoritism for desperate people, but has achieved this maneuver by eliminating the role of self-favoritism completely. To defend the integrity and the scope of the communitarian impulse in the supreme directive of natural law, we have had to brush Locke's comment on self-devotion out of existence. Should we harbor any compunctions?

In grappling with this latest question, we initially should observe that Locke never seemed to notice the vexing problems which surrounded his thesis of legitimate self-absorption. He apparently failed to grasp that the privilege of self-favoritism would apply only in the torturous circumstances posed by a crushing scarcity of essential goods, and so he never explored such circumstances in his reflections on the state of nature. Perhaps the latter omission stemmed as well from Locke's having run together two quite distinct varieties of superabundance – a superabundance of the raw materials furnished by the Deity, and a superabundance of the items which were made from those raw materials by human exertions and which thereafter were ready to be employed for nutriment or for comfort. Within the Lockean state of nature, there was indeed a superabundance of the earth's resources; but, because of factors that have already been explained, a superabundance or even a sufficiency of the products created from the earth's natural resources by human beings could occasionally dissolve for weeks or months at a time. In any case, whether or not Locke did confuse these types of superabundance when he neglected to discuss famines, he surely did neglect to discuss famines. Our verdict here must accordingly proceed as a sympathetic extrapolation, not as a direct analysis of specifically pertinent remarks.

By insisting that the general priorities of natural law would reach to the woes of famine in the state of nature as much as to any normal developments in that state, we seem to have excluded the notion that a course of self-preferring behavior and self-preferring choices would ever be legiti-

[14] Once again, I am not here taking account of anyone's legitimate measures of self-defense against aggressive attacks (which would not occur only during periods of grievous shortages). I am considering solely the varieties of self-favoritism that would not be in harmony with the prime imperative of natural law.

mate. Must our loyalties to the principles of Locke be sharply divided? Doubtless, the most suitable answer here is to show that the division of loyalties is far less gaping than has just been implied. Although a faithful exposition of Locke cannot wholeheartedly accept his stray words about the favoring of oneself during grievous trials, we can reconstrue *as self-preferring behavior* the instances of people's conformity with the overriding directive of natural law. To achieve this new understanding of their conformity, we must redirect our focus from sheer survival and concentrate instead on some matters even more urgent.

When Locke referred to legitimate self-devotion, he clearly framed his comment as a remark about survival. Everyone in the state of nature had to contribute to the well-being of humanity "when his own Preservation c[ame] not in competition" (TTG, II, §6). Because of the disagreeable consequences to which this policy of self-favoritism would have led, a careful exposition of Locke cannot include his specific version of such a policy; his version was too resoundingly at odds with his basic precepts. However, we can extract the general principle of self-favoritism from his concrete formulation of that principle. Having borrowed from Locke that general principle, then, we can expand upon it in two chief ways to harmonize it with his communitarian view of natural law (and natural law's prime command). Each of these ways will mark a shift of orientation, from the objective of survival to a deeper objective.

First, we can follow Jesus in holding that it "is the spirit that gives life, the flesh is of no avail" (John 6:63). In other words, we can focus on a consideration which Locke highlighted in his *Essay concerning Human Understanding*: the surpassing excellence of eternal glory in relation to any comforts or any fruitful projects within this vale of tears. A Lockean universe was governed by a Creator, before whom "each of us shall give account of himself" (Romans 14:12). Therefore, in the background of all the conduct chosen by anybody during her years on earth were the punishments and rewards that structured the afterlife. A person whose deeds complied with the law of nature could expect heavenly bliss. And given that that unceasing bliss would far outweigh all earthly desiderata, every sensible human being would comply with the natural law regardless of any worldly ills occasioned by such compliance. Only by submitting oneself to undergo some earthly hardships when necessary for due obedience to the law of nature, could one avoid infernal woes and obtain celestial rewards.

Thus, as soon as we have moved our attention from the worldly domain to the otherworldly domain, we find precisely how someone's heeding of a duty-to-starve would count as self-preferring behavior. For Locke, the importance of enjoying felicity in the age to come would overshadow entirely the importance of keeping oneself alive in the here and now. Since the attaining of ultimate felicity depended on one's adherence to one's natural-law duties, a regime of natural law which encumbered anyone with a duty-to-starve in desperate times would make his or her adherence to that duty a self-devoted course of behavior. Ergo, we have harmonized the communitarianism of the natural law's foremost imperative with the general principle of self-favoritism for circumstances of acute hardship. With eyes trained firmly on the hereafter, someone who complied with an obligation to starve was thereby favoring his own weal.

To discern yet another way of reconciling Locke's focus on the good of humanity with his license for individual self-absorption in periods of dreadful want, we shall have to turn our attention from the posture of human beings in their presocietal stages to their posture in the presence of government. In the state of nature, the earthly weal of a person would rarely be advanced through his or her heeding of a duty to starve. Unless the people interacting with person *Q* could threaten him believably with some brutal tortures that would be triggered by his snatching away the vital goods of anyone more productive, he would lack any self-preferring reasons for withholding his hand from plundering in times of miserable destitution. At worst, he would meet with failure when pillaging and would lose his life straightaway; but, of course, he would quickly lose his life in any event if he fulfilled his obligation to starve. A self-devoted (and unreligious) person would have no more than the meagerest of incentives to exercise the restraint demanded by such an obligation.

Quite a different state of affairs would come about when a full-fledged apparatus of governance had emerged. While all disciplinary workings would improve by becoming lodged in central mechanisms, perhaps the most notable improvement would lie in the capacity of a government to inflict appalling torture on anybody who scouted natural law by refusing to accept an obligation to starve-when-necessary. Though an array of punishments involving the imposition of prolonged agony might sometimes be feasible in the state of nature, they could be accomplished far more deftly when a government was in charge of punitive tasks. And so, with the introduction of government, there could arise a strong incentive for people to abide by their obligations to starve-when-necessary. As Locke acknowledged when he wrote that a slave could find "the hardship of his Slavery out-weigh the value of his Life" (TTG, II, §23), the suffering of exquisite torment could very frequently be a fate worse than death. Anyone self-devoted would therefore tend to acquiesce in his own starvation when called upon for that purpose by a hard-line government, in a setting of acute scarcities. A death through starvation would amount to the lesser of two evils, when compared with a more excruciating death through torture wrought by disciplinary agents. In other words, once again we see that the principle of self-favoritism could be squared with the establishment of strict priorities among people for entitlements to remain alive and for duties to starve. If a government emerged to enforce with brutal rigorousness the set of priorities established by the cardinal directive in the law of nature, a self-devoted person who was required to starve because of some grueling shortages would indeed elect to starve in order to promote his own interests under the deplorable circumstances.

Let us conclude by taking note of the ties between this discussion and the rest of this book. When we focused on Locke's specific version of the principle of self-favoritism, we discovered that a famine-racked state of nature would witness many life-and-death conflicts where the contenders all were justified in their various warring standpoints by the natural law's putative endorsement of self-preferring decisions. To avoid such an undesirable situation – a situation grotesquely undesirable when judged by Lockean standards – we have looked at two other conceptions or applications of the principle of warranted self-concern. Those alternative conceptions allow the harmonizing of Lockean individualism and Lockean communitarianism, by reducing the former to a vehicle for the latter.

With those two alternative understandings of self-devotion, we have found that a truly Lockean endorsement of the favoring of oneself would lead not to countless warring perspectives on the implications of natural law, but to potent means of removing any clashes among the countless perspectives. The eliding of clashes would proceed through constant referrals or displacements from the level of competing needs to a level of greater harmony. Conflicts arising from incompatible needs could get referred to the will of God, whose intentions for humanity would overpower the conflicts by prioritizing the needs. God as Judge of the World attached never-ending punishments to the flouting of His priorities, and He thereby made one's adherence to His priorities a matter of keen self-interest. Conflicts arising from incompatible needs could also get referred to the penal organs of government, with officials who truly acted as "ministers of God" (Romans 13:6). Such ministers would enforce God's intentions and priorities with a harshness that would make one's observance of those priorities a matter of keen self-interest.

In short, whether the backing up of the paramount prescript in the law of nature would come from God directly or would come from Him indirectly through officials of government, the backing would operate as the means by which that starkly transindividual prescript could be rendered congruent with the self-devotion of individuals. Without the determination of priorities and enforcement of priorities by external commands, the individuals who were bound to favor themselves in desperate times would unavoidably clash with one another during such times. Only through the felt presence of an authoritative arbiter and disciplinarian, would the otherwise ineludible conflicts among self-favoring people have no legitimate purchase. And since God was *always* present, there indeed would never be any purchase – never a legitimate purchase – for those life-and-death conflicts. Disasters, as the occasions for the extreme development of Lockean individualism, were therefore settings which would reveal most poignantly the systematic constraints that always kept the normative fundaments of Locke's individualism in service to the normative fundaments of his wholesale communitarianism. Because of those systematic constraints, a license for self-preferring behavior would ensconce everybody all the more roundly in a matrix of communitarianism, as the license received its tenor and its scope from that very matrix. A license for self-preferring activity was a license to pursue communitarian ends.

That is, in all respects which here are germane, a situation of grievous scarcities would closely resemble other situations in any Lockean world – situations on which Locke's theory of property was supposed to bear. During a time of grievous scarcities, self-devoted people had to refer beyond themselves to know what their interests were and hence to know what their self-absorption would incline them to do. They had to refer beyond themselves to the overriding directive in the law of nature (and to the Deity who had issued that prime directive). In a like manner, the exploitation of the earth and its fruits by human beings in times of plenty could not determine how the resulting products would be assigned. People owned themselves, and of course they would also own their other proprietary possessions; but they had to refer beyond themselves to ascertain what the ownership of oneself involved and to know which things were included in their batches of other proprietary possessions. They had to refer beyond themselves to the overriding directive in the law of nature.

Just as a flat endorsement of self-preferring conduct was thoroughly insufficient to establish which modes of conduct were allowed and required, the norm of self-ownership was thoroughly insufficient to establish which other things a person would own – or even to establish what was entailed by the quality of ownership. And just as the natural law's endorsement of self-preferring behavior would utterly depend on the cardinal mandate of natural law for specific substance, the norm of self-ownership would utterly depend on that cardinal mandate for the determination of distributive outcomes and the specification of entitlements. In periods of bleak destitution and in periods of high flourishing, the chief command in the law of nature would set the range of proper decisions. It prescribed all apposite choices and embraced individualistic choices as functions of its communitarian sway. Locke's service as an apostle of individualism was merely part of his service as an apostle of collectivism.

Citational appendix

This appendix's wide-ranging list of books and dissertations and essays dealing with the labor theory of property has been distilled – at the pleasant but firm insistence of my publisher – from a much longer list of all the relevant secondary works that I have read. The first of the three main sections of this appendix contains my citations to writings that have criticized the labor theory of property on philosophical or analytical grounds (and sometimes also on political grounds, but not only on political grounds). The second and longest section contains my citations to works that have not sought to impugn the philosophical merits of the labor theory; some of those works, despite being predominantly uncritical or defensive in regard to the labor theory's argumentational soundness, have denounced the theory's political bearings. Finally, the third chief section contains my citations to writings that deal with topics very closely related to the labor theory.

ANALYTICAL CRITICISMS OF THE LABOR THEORY

Richard Aaron, *John Locke* (Oxford: Clarendon Press, 1971), 276–8.

Lincoln Allison, *Right Principles* (Oxford: Basil Blackwell, 1984), 100–1, 109.

Richard Arneson, "Lockean self-ownership: towards a demolition," 39 *Political Studies* 36 (1991).

R. F. Atkinson, "Locke on government," in Indira Mahalingam and Brian Carr (eds.), *Logical Foundations* (Basingstoke: Macmillan, 1991), 175, 179, 182–3.

Michael Ayers, *Locke* (London: Routledge, 1991), vol. II, 267–8.

Lawrence Becker, "The labor theory of property acquisition," 73 *Journal of Philosophy* 653 (1976).

Property Rights: Philosophic Foundations (London: Routledge and Kegan Paul, 1977), 32–74.

Christopher Berry, "Property and possession: two replies to Locke: Hume and Hegel," in J. Roland Pennock and John Chapman (eds.), *Nomos XXII: Property* (New York: New York University Press, 1980), 89–90, 93–4.

James Bonar, *Philosophy and Political Economy* (London: Swan Sonnenschein, 1893), 99–102, 117.

J. Budziszewski, *The Nearest Coast of Darkness* (Ithaca: Cornell University Press, 1988), 51–4.

Alan Carter, *The Philosophical Foundations of Property Rights* (Hemel Hempstead: Harvester Wheatsheaf, 1989), passim.
Melvin Cherno, "Locke on property: a reappraisal," 68 *Ethics* 51 (1957).
G. A. Cohen, "Marx and Locke on land and labour," 71 *Proceedings of the British Academy* 357 (1985).
Morris Cohen, "Property and sovereignty," 13 *Cornell Law Quarterly* (1927), 8, 16–18.
Frank Coleman, *Hobbes and America: Exploring the Constitutional Foundations* (Toronto: University of Toronto Press, 1977), 82–4, 102–5, 107.
Rosemary Coombe, "Author/izing the celebrity: publicity rights, postmodern politics, and unauthorized genders," 10 *Cardozo Arts and Entertainment Law Journal* (1992), 365, 369, 373.
"The properties of culture and the politics of possessing identity: native claims in the cultural appropriation controversy," 6 *Canadian Journal of Law and Jurisprudence* (1993), 249, 259, 263.
Joseph Cropsey, *Political Philosophy and the Issues of Politics* (Chicago: University of Chicago Press, 1977), 40–2, 102, 164, 209–10.
Casimir Czajkowski, *The Theory of Private Property in John Locke's Political Philosophy* (Notre Dame: University of Notre Dame doctoral dissertation, Committee on Graduate Study, June 1941), 68–102 et passim.
J. P. Day, "Locke on property," 16 *Philosophical Quarterly* 207 (1966).
John Dunn, *Interpreting Political Responsibility* (Oxford: Polity Press, 1990), 12, 16–18.
Ronald Duty, *The Theory of Property in British Political Thought: Locke, Hume, Burke and Bentham* (Minneapolis: University of Minnesota doctoral dissertation, Graduate School, August 1979), 13–132, 389–91.
David Ellerman, "On the labor theory of property," 16 *Philosophical Forum* 293 (1985).
Richard Ely, *Property and Contract in their Relations to the Distribution of Wealth* (New York: Macmillan, 1914), vol. II, 541–43.
Richard Epstein, "Possession as the root of title," 13 *Georgia Law Review* 1221 (1979).
Takings (Cambridge: Harvard University Press, 1985), 10–12, 334–44.
"Taxation in a Lockean world," in Jules Coleman and Ellen Frankel Paul (eds.), *Philosophy and Law* (Oxford: Basil Blackwell, 1987), 49, 51.
"The utilitarian foundations of natural law," 12 *Harvard Journal of Law and Public Policy* (1989), 713, 730–7.
William Fisher III, "Reconstructing the fair use doctrine," 101 *Harvard Law Review* (1988), 1659, 1688–9, 1691–2, 1756–7.
Milton Fisk, *The State and Justice* (Cambridge: Cambridge University Press, 1989), 80–4.
David Friedman, "Comment on Brody," 1 (1) *Social Philosophy and Policy* 88 (1983).
Norman Geras, "'The fruits of labour': private property and moral equality," in Michael Moran and Maurice Wright (eds.), *The Market and the State* (New York: St. Martin's Press, 1991), 59–80.
Allan Gibbard, "Natural property rights," 10 *Noûs* (1976), 77, 82–5.
Robert Goldwin, *Locke on Property* (Chicago: University of Chicago doctoral dissertation, Department of Political Science, December 1963), 55–123.

J. W. Gough, *The Social Contract* (Oxford: Clarendon Press, 1957), 140–2.
Carol Gould, "Economic justice, self-management, and the principle of reciprocity," in Kenneth Kipnis and Diana Meyers (eds.), *Economic Justice: Private Rights and Public Responsibilities* (Totowa: Rowman and Allanheld, 1985), 202, 205–7, 211–13.
Ruth Grant, *John Locke's Liberalism* (Chicago: University of Chicago Press, 1987), 111–14.
James Grunebaum, *Private Ownership* (London: Routledge and Kegan Paul, 1987), 15–18, 52–69, *et* passim.
Amy Gutmann, *Liberal Equality* (Cambridge: Cambridge University Press, 1980), 19, 30–3, 157–9, 237 n.45.
Eugene Hargrove, "Anglo-American land use attitudes," 2 *Environmental Ethics* (1980), 121, 138–48.
Jonathan Harrison, *Hume's Theory of Justice* (Oxford: Clarendon Press, 1981), 81–2, 109–11.
Virginia Held, *Rights and Goods: Justifying Social Action* (New York: Free Press, 1984), 132, 172–3.
Agnes Heller, *Beyond Justice* (Oxford: Basil Blackwell, 1987), 29, 155, 180.
Roderick Hills, Jr., "The reconciliation of law and liberty in James Wilson," 12 *Harvard Journal of Law and Public Policy* (1989), 891, 927–9.
A. M. Honoré, "Ownership," in A. G. Guest (ed.), *Oxford Essays in Jurisprudence* (Oxford: Oxford University Press, 1961), 107, 135–6.
"Property, title and redistribution," in Carl Wellman (ed.), *Equality and Freedom* (Wiesbaden: Franz Steiner Verlag, 1977), 107–15.
Kenneth Hoover, *A Politics of Identity* (Urbana: University of Illinois Press, 1975), 10 n.5, 18–22, 47–51.
David Hume, *A Treatise of Human Nature* (Oxford: Clarendon Press, 1978) (L. Selby-Bigge and P. Nidditch eds.), 505–6 n.1 (book III, part II, §III).
E. J. Hundert, "The making of *Homo Faber*: John Locke between ideology and history," in Richard Ashcraft (ed.), *John Locke: Critical Assessments* (London: Routledge, 1991), 438–56.
Dudley Knowles, "Hegel on property and personality," 33 *Philosophical Quarterly* (1983), 45, 46–8.
Emile de Laveleye, *Primitive Property* (London: Macmillan, 1878) (G. Marriott trans.), 341–3, 346–53.
Herman Lebovics, "The uses of America in Locke's *Second Treatise of Government*," in Richard Ashcraft (ed.), *John Locke: Critical Assessments* (London: Routledge, 1991), 252–66.
Richard Lichtman, "The façade of equality in liberal democratic theory," 12 *Inquiry* (1969), 170, 179–85.
George Lodge, *The New American Ideology* (New York: Alfred Knopf, 1976), 10, 100–6, 109.
Loren Lomasky, *Persons, Rights, and the Moral Community* (New York: Oxford University Press, 1987), 114–19.
William Lucy and François Barker, "Justifying property and justifying access," 6 *Canadian Journal of Law and Jurisprudence* (1993), 287, 296–304.
David Lyons, "The new Indian claims and original rights to land," in Jeffrey Paul (ed.), *Reading Nozick* (Totowa: Rowman and Littlefield, 1981), 355, 361–2.
J. D. Mabbott, *John Locke* (London: Macmillan, 1973), 147–9.

Alasdair MacIntyre, *After Virtue* (Notre Dame: University of Notre Dame Press, 1981), 230–4.

John Mackie, *Ethics: Inventing Right and Wrong* (Harmondsworth: Penguin, 1977), 174–7.

Kingsley Martin, *French Liberal Thought in the Eighteenth Century* (London: Phoenix House, 1962, 2nd edn.), 120, 221–4, 238–9.

Thomas Mautner, "Locke on original appropriation," 19 *American Philosophical Quarterly* 259 (1982).

John McCall, "Welfare reform: cost reductions or increased work incentives," in Kenneth Kipnis and Diana Meyers (eds.), *Economic Justice: Private Rights and Public Responsibilities* (Totowa: Rowman and Allanheld, 1985), 190, 191–4.

A. I. Melden, *Rights and Persons* (Berkeley: University of California Press, 1977), 179, 182–3, 229–31, 242–3.

David Miller, "Justice and property," 22 *Ratio* 1 (1980).

Kenneth Minogue, "The concept of property and its contemporary significance," in J. Roland Pennock and John Chapman (eds.), *Nomos XXII: Property* (New York: New York University Press, 1980), 3, 9–10, 17–21.

T. I. Mulcahy, "Locke's theory of property," 59 *Irish Monthly* 319 (1931).

Stephen Munzer, "Book review of Lawrence Becker, *Property Rights*," 63 *Minnesota Law Review* (1979), 531, 532–6.

A Theory of Property (Cambridge: Cambridge University Press, 1990), 56–8, 66, 67, 75, 256–7 n.1.

Thomas Nagel, *Equality and Partiality* (New York: Oxford University Press, 1991), 120–1, 140.

Kai Nielsen, "Capitalism, socialism and justice," in Tom Regan and Donald VanDeVeer (eds.), *And Justice for All* (Totowa: Rowman and Littlefield, 1982), 264, 270–3.

Equality and Liberty (Totowa: Rowman and Allanheld, 1985), 198, 254–7.

Robert Nozick, *Anarchy, State, and Utopia* (New York: Basic Books, 1974), 174–82.

D. J. O'Connor, *John Locke* (New York: Dover Publications, 1967), 209–10.

Onora O'Neill, "Nozick's entitlements," 19 *Inquiry* (1976), 468, 473–9.

William Paley, *Moral Philosophy* (London: John W. Parker and Son, 1859), 107–10 (bookk III, part I, ch. 4).

Thomas Pangle, *The Spirit of Modern Republicanism* (Chicago: University of Chicago Press, 1988), 158–71.

Geraint Parry, *John Locke* (London: George Allen and Unwin, 1978), 49–57.

John Plamenatz, *Man and Society* (London: Longmans, 1963), vol. I, 219–20, 241–8.

Frederick Pollock, "Locke's theory of the state," in Richard Ashcraft (ed.), *John Locke: Critical Assessments* (London: Routledge, 1991), 1, 6.

Ross Poole, "Locke and the bourgeois state," 28 *Political Studies* 222 (1980).

Hastings Rashdall, "The philosophical theory of property," in *Property: Its Duties and Rights* (London: Macmillan, 1915, 2nd edn.), 33, 40–7.

Leo Rauch, *The Political Animal* (Amherst: University of Massachusetts Press, 1981), 63–6, 74, 79–81.

Andrew Reeve, *Property* (Atlantic Highlands: Humanities Press International, 1986), passim.

"The theory of property: beyond private versus common property," in David Held (ed.), *Political Theory Today* (Stanford: Stanford University Press, 1991), 91–114.

John Richetti, *Philosophical Writing: Locke Berkeley, Hume* (Cambridge: Harvard University Press, 1983), 68–9, 72–3.

David Ritchie, *Darwin and Hegel* (London: Swan Sonnenschein, 1893), 178–95.

Natural Rights (London: George Allen and Unwin, 1894), 266–71.

Gerald Runkle, *A History of Western Political Theory* (New York: Ronald Press, 1968), 293–4.

Alan Ryan, "Property, liberty, and *On Liberty*," in A. Phillips Griffiths (ed.), *Of Liberty* (Cambridge: Cambridge University Press, 1983), 217, 226–7.

Property and Political Theory (Oxford: Basil Blackwell, 1984), 14–38.

"Locke and the dictatorship of the bourgeoisie," in Richard Ashcraft (ed.), *John Locke: Critical Assessments* (London: Routledge, 1991), 419–37.

Husain Sarkar, "The Lockean proviso," 12 *Canadian Journal of Philosophy* 47 (1982).

Richard Schlatter, *Private Property: The History of an Idea* (New York: Russell and Russell, 1973), 151–61.

A. Allan Schmid, *Property, Power, and Public Choice* (New York: Praeger, 1978), 24–5, 28.

Ian Shapiro, "Resources, capacities, and ownership: the workmanship ideal and distributive justice," 19 *Political Theory* 47 (1991).

James Smith, "The scope of property rights," in Samuel Blumenfeld, *Property in a Humane Economy* (LaSalle: Open Court, 1974), 225–43.

Hillel Steiner, "The natural right to the means of production," 27 *Philosophical Quarterly* (1977), 41, 44–5.

"Justice and entitlement," in Jeffrey Paul (ed.), *Reading Nozick* (Totowa: Rowman and Littlefield, 1981), 380–2.

"Book review of Jeremy Waldron, *The Right to Private Property*," 101 *Ethics* 201 (1990).

An Essay on Rights (Oxford: Blackwell, 1994), 105, 229–48, et passim.

Peter Stillman, "Property, freedom, and individuality in Hegel's and Marx's political thought," in J. Roland Pennock and John Chapman (eds.), *Nomos XXII: Property* (New York: New York University Press, 1980), 130, 140–1.

"Hegel's analysis of property in the *Philosophy of Right*," 10 *Cardozo Law Review* (1989), 1031, 1040–1.

C. E. Vaughan, *Studies in the History of Political Philosophy before and after Rousseau* (New York: Russell and Russell, 1960), vol. I, 174–85.

Thorstein Veblen, "The beginnings of ownership," 4 *American Journal of Sociology* 352 (1898).

Jacob Viner, "'Possessive individualism' as original sin," 29 *Canadian Journal of Economics and Political Science* (1963), 548, 557–8.

Jeremy Waldron, "Two worries about mixing one's labour," 33 *Philosophical Quarterly* 37 (1983).

The Right to Private Property (Oxford: Clarendon Press, 1988), 137–252 et passim.

"Property, justification and need," 6 *Canadian Journal of Law and Jurisprudence* (1993), 185, 198–202, 209–10.

Patrick Gordon Walker, *Restatement of Liberty* (London: Hutchinson, 1951), 19–20, 75–80, 101–2.
Lloyd Weinreb, *Natural Law and Justice* (Cambridge: Harvard University Press, 1987), 79–80.
Walter Weisskopf, *Alienation and Economics* (New York: E. P. Dutton, 1971), 57–63.
Frederick Whelan, "Property as artifice: Hume and Blackstone," in J. Roland Pennock and John Chapman (eds.), *Nomos XXII: Property* (New York: New York University Press, 1980), 101, 103–4, 110.

WORKS ANALYTICALLY UNCRITICAL OF THE LABOR THEORY

Bengt Abrahamsson and Anders Broström, *The Rights of Labor* (Beverly Hills: Sage Publications, 1980), 84–7, 140–4.
Willi Paul Adams, *The First American Constitutions* (Chapel Hill: University of North Carolina Press, 1980) (Rita and Robert Kimber trans.), 190–1.
Robert Albritton, "The politics of Locke's philosophy," 24 *Political Studies* (1976), 253, 265.
S. Alexander, *Locke* (London: Archibald Constable and Co., 1908), 76–7.
C. Fred Alford, *The Self in Social Theory* (New Haven: Yale University Press, 1991), 112–39.
Edward Andrew, "Inalienable right, alienable property and freedom of choice: Locke, Nozick and Marx on the alienability of labour," 18 *Canadian Journal of Political Science* 529 (1985).
Shylock's Rights: A Grammar of Lockian Claims (Toronto: University of Toronto Press, 1988), 58–63, 93–7, 132–3, 167.
John Anglim, "On Locke's state of nature," 26 *Political Studies* (1978), 78, 81–6.
Anthony Arblaster, *The Rise and Decline of Western Liberalism* (Oxford: Basil Blackwell, 1984), 27–8, 106, 163–6, 241.
Hannah Arendt, *The Human Condition* (Chicago: University of Chicago Press, 1958), 70, 99–104, 110–16, 134–6.
Barbara Arneil, "Trade, plantations, and property: John Locke and the economic defense of colonialism," 55 *Journal of the History of Ideas* 591 (1994).
Richard Ashcraft, "The *Two Treatises* and the exclusion crisis: the problem of Lockean political theory as bourgeois ideology," in J. G. A. Pocock and Richard Ashcraft, *John Locke* (Los Angeles: William Andrews Clark Memorial Library, 1980), 25–114.
Revolutionary Politics and Locke's Two Treatises of Government (Princeton: Princeton University Press, 1986), 257–82.
Locke's Two Treatises of Government (London: Allen and Unwin, 1987), 123–50.
"Introduction," in Richard Ashcraft (ed.), *John Locke: Critical Assessments* (London: Routledge, 1991), vii, x–xiii.
"The politics of Locke's *Two Treatises of Government*," in Edward Harpham (ed.), *John Locke's Two Treatises of Government: New Interpretations* (Lawrence: University Press of Kansas, 1992), 14, 30–2, 35–40, 45.
"Locke's political philosophy," in Vere Chappell (ed.), *The Cambridge Companion to Locke* (Cambridge: Cambridge University Press, 1994), 226, 238–51.

R. W. Baldwin, *Social Justice* (Oxford: Pergamon Press, 1966), 26–7, 88–93.

Benjamin Barber, "Against economics: or, capitalism, socialism, but whatever happened to democracy?" in Fred Baumann (ed.), *Democratic Capitalism?* (Charlottesville: University Press of Virginia, 1986), 22, 28–9, 46 n.8.

Ernest Barker, *Traditions of Civility* (Cambridge: Cambridge University Press, 1948), 236 n.1, 238.

Charles Bastide, *John Locke. Ses théories politiques et leur influence en Angleterre* (Paris: Ernest Leroux, 1907), 231–2.

Lawrence Becker, "Rights: an introduction," in Lawrence Becker and Kenneth Kipnis (eds.), *Property: Cases, Concepts, Critiques* (Englewood Cliffs: Prentice-Hall, 1984), 70, 73.

"Property rights and social welfare," in Kenneth Kipnis and Diana Meyers (eds.), *Economic Justice: Private Rights and Public Responsibilities* (Totowa: Rowman and Allanheld, 1985), 71, 74–84.

Max Beer, *Early British Economics* (London: George Allen and Unwin, 1938), 56–7, 173–6.

A History of British Socialism (London: George Allen and Unwin, 1953), vol. I, passim.

A. J. Beitzinger, *A History of American Political Thought* (Charlottesville: Ibis Publishing, 1986), 9, 10–11.

Stanley Benn, "Property," in *The Encyclopedia of Philosophy* (New York: Macmillan and The Free Press, 1967), 491–2.

S. I. Benn and R. S. Peters, *The Principles of Political Thought* (New York: Free Press, 1965), 184, 185–6.

Isaiah Berlin, "Hobbes, Locke and Professor Macpherson," 35 *Political Quarterly* (1964), 444, 460–8.

Joseph Bien, "Freedom and the concept of property in John Locke's *Second Treatise of Government*," in Carl Wellman (ed.), *Equality and Freedom* (Wiesbaden: Franz Steiner Verlag, 1977), 189–94.

William Blackstone, *Commentaries on the Laws of England* (New York: Evert Duyckinck, George Long, Collins and Co., 1822), 5–9.

Mark Blaug, *Ricardian Economics* (New Haven: Yale University Press, 1958), 34–5, 140–9.

William Bluhm, *Theories of the Political System* (Englewood Cliffs: Prentice-Hall, 1965), 314–15, 321.

H. R. Fox Bourne, *The Life of John Locke* (London: Henry S. King and Co., 1876), vol. II, 171–3.

William James Booth, *Households: On the Moral Architecture of the Economy* (Ithaca: Cornell University Press, 1993), 116, 126–35, 138, 160–75.

John Bowle, *Western Political Thought* (London: Jonathan Cape, 1947), 365–6.

Teresa Brennan and Carole Pateman, "'Mere auxiliaries to the commonwealth': women and the origins of liberalism," 27 *Political Studies* (1979), 183, 192–3.

John Brigham, *Property and the Politics of Entitlement* (Philadelphia: Temple University Press, 1990), 19, 39, 112.

Baruch Brody, "Redistribution without egalitarianism," 1 (1) *Social Philosophy and Policy* 71 (1983).

J. Bronowski and Bruce Mazlish, *The Western Intellectual Tradition* (New York: Harper and Row, 1960), 213–14.

Norman O. Brown, *Love's Body* (New York: Vintage, 1966), 6–7, 139, 145–6.

Stephen Buckle, *Natural Law and the Theory of Property* (Oxford: Clarendon Press, 1991), 149–90.

James MacGregor Burns and Stewart Burns, *A People's Charter* (New York: Alfred Knopf, 1991), 20, 81–2.

Melissa Butler, "Early liberal roots of feminism: John Locke and the attack on patriarchy," in Richard Ashcraft (ed.), *John Locke: Critical Assessments* (London: Routledge, 1991), 639, 655, 659–60.

E. F. Carritt, *Morals and Politics* (Oxford: Clarendon Press, 1935), 74–5, 77.

Alfred Chalk, "Natural law and the rise of economic individualism in England," 59 *Journal of Political Economy* (1951), 332, 344–7.

James Chandler, "A reconsideration of the concept of property," in Carl Wellman (ed.), *Equality and Freedom* (Wiesbaden: Franz Steiner Verlag, 1977), 147–51.

Jean-Jacques Chevallier, *Histoire de la pensée politique* (Paris: Payot, 1979), vol. II, 36.

John Christman, "Can ownership be justified by natural rights?" 15 *Philosophy and Public Affairs* 156 (1986).

James Clapp, "Locke, John," in Paul Edwards (ed.), *The Encyclopedia of Philosophy* (New York: Macmillan, 1967), vol. IV, 487, 499.

Lorenne Clark, "Women and John Locke; or, who owns the apples in the Garden of Eden?" 7 *Canadian Journal of Philosophy* (1977), 699, 717–24.

G. A. Cohen, "Self-ownership, world-ownership, and equality," in Frank Lucash (ed.), *Justice and Equality Here and Now* (Ithaca: Cornell University Press, 1986), 108, 122–5.

"Self-ownership, world-ownership, and equality: part II," in Ellen Frankel Paul, Jeffrey Paul, Fred Miller, Jr., and John Ahrens (eds.), *Marxism and Liberalism* (Oxford: Basil Blackwell, 1986), 77–96.

E. Paul Colella, "The commodity form and socialization in Locke's state of nature," 16 (3) *International Studies in Philosophy* 1 (1984).

Janet Coleman, "Medieval discussions of property: *Ratio* and *Dominium* according to John of Paris and Marsilius of Padua," 4 *History of Political Thought* (1983), 209, 210, 219–21.

"*Dominium* in thirteenth and fourteenth-century political thought and its seventeenth-century heirs: John of Paris and Locke," 33 *Political Studies* (1985), 73, 81–4, 95–100.

John Colman, *John Locke's Moral Philosophy* (Edinburgh: Edinburgh University Press, 1983), 187–92, 196–8.

John Commons, *Institutional Economics* (Madison: University of Wisconsin Press, 1959), vol. I, 31–40.

Paul Conkin, *Self-Evident Truths* (Bloomington: Indiana University Press, 1974), 95–9.

Prophets of Prosperity (Bloomington: Indiana University Press, 1980), 227–8, 256.

Thomas Cook, *History of Political Philosophy from Plato to Burke* (New York: Prentice-Hall, 1936), 522–3, 531.

Edward Corwin, *The "Higher Law" Background of American Constitutional Law* (Ithaca: Cornell University Press, 1955), 69–70.

Richard Cox, *Locke on War and Peace* (Oxford: Clarendon Press, 1960), 87–94, 181–2, 187–8.
"Justice as the basis of political order in Locke," in Carl Friedrich and John Chapman (eds.), *Nomos VI: Justice* (New York: Atherton Press, 1963), 243, 254–61.
Maurice Cranston, *John Locke: A Biography* (Oxford: Oxford University Press, 1985), 210.
Robert Denoon Cumming, *Human Nature and History* (Chicago: University of Chicago Press, 1969), vol. II, 4–5, 123–37, 144–6, 173, 182–3.
Robert Cunningham, "Introduction," in Samuel Blumenfeld, *Property in a Humane Economy* (LaSalle: Open Court, 1974), ix, xv–xvi.
Peter Cvek, "Locke's theory of property: a re-examination," 11 *Auslegung* 390 (1984).
James Daly, *Sir Robert Filmer and English Political Thought* (Toronto: University of Toronto Press, 1979), 158–9.
J. P. Day, "Self-ownership," 20 *Locke Newsletter* 77 (1989).
Frank Derringh, *Personal Autonomy and Locke's Theory of Property, With Special Attention to Modern Commentators* (New York: Columbia University doctoral dissertation, Faculty of Philosophy, 1980), 1–96 *et* passim.
H. T. Dickinson, *Liberty and Property* (New York: Holmes and Meier, 1977), 68, 87.
Gottfried Dietze, *In Defense of Property* (Chicago: Henry Regnery Company, 1963), 26–7.
John Patrick Diggins, *The Lost Soul of American Politics* (New York: Basic Books, 1984), 5, 61, 147–9.
Maurice Dobb, *Theories of Value and Distribution since Adam Smith* (Cambridge: Cambridge University Press, 1973), 137–40, 146.
C. H. Driver, "John Locke," in F. J. C. Hearnshaw, *The Social and Political Ideas of Some English Thinkers of the Augustan Age* (New York: Barnes and Noble, 1967), 90–2.
S. B. Drury, "Robert Nozick and the right to property," in Anthony Parel and Thomas Flanagan (eds.), *Theories of Property: Aristotle to the Present* (Waterloo: Wilfrid Laurier University Press, 1979), 360–79.
"Locke and Nozick on property," 30 *Political Studies* 28 (1982).
Louis Dumont, *From Mandeville to Marx* (Chicago: University of Chicago Press, 1977), 48–54, 189–91.
Essays on Individualism: Modern Ideology in Anthropological Perspective (Chicago: University of Chicago Press, 1986), 41, 80–1.
John Dunn, *The Political Thought of John Locke* (Cambridge: Cambridge University Press, 1969), 66–7, 166 n.4, 211.
Locke (Oxford: Oxford University Press, 1984), 36–44.
Steven Dworetz, *The Unvarnished Doctrine: Locke, Liberalism, and the American Revolution* (Durham: Duke University Press, 1990), passim.
William Ebenstein, *Great Political Thinkers* (New York: Holt, Rinehart and Winston, 1960) (3rd ed.), 389–91.
Eldon Eisenach, *Two Worlds of Liberalism* (Chicago: University of Chicago Press, 1981), 95–100.
David Ellerman, "Property and production: an introduction to the labor theory of

property," in Lawrence Becker and Kenneth Kipnis (eds.), *Property: Cases, Concepts, Critiques* (Englewood Cliffs: Prentice-Hall, 1984), 220–35.

Richard Epstein, "Takings: of Maginot lines and constitutional compromises," in Ellen Frankel Paul and Howard Dickman (eds.), *Liberty, Property, and the Future of Constitutional Development* (Albany: State University of New York Press, 1990), 173, 188–91.

Edward Erler, "The great fence to liberty: the right to property in the American founding," in Ellen Frankel Paul and Howard Dickman (eds.), *Liberty, Property, and the Foundations of the American Constitution* (Albany: State University of New York Press, 1989), 43, 52–6.

James Farr, "'So vile and miserable an estate': the problem of slavery in Locke's political thought," in Richard Ashcraft (ed.), *John Locke: Critical Assessments* (London: Routledge, 1991), 666, 676–7, 683.

Leslie Francis and John Francis, "Nozick's theory of rights: a critical assessment," 29 *Western Political Quarterly* (1976), 634, 639–40, 641–2.

Alexander Fraser, *Locke* (Edinburgh: William Blackwood and Sons, 1907), 101–2.

Michael Freeden, *Rights* (Milton Keynes: Open University Press, 1991), 15–16.

Anthony Fressola, "Liberty and property: reflections on the right of appropriation in the state of nature," 18 *American Philosophical Quarterly* 315 (1981).

George Gale, "John Locke on territoriality: an unnoticed aspect of the *Second Treatise*," in Richard Ashcraft (ed.), *John Locke: Critical Assessments* (London: Routledge, 1991), 511, 518–20.

William Galston, *Justice and the Human Good* (Chicago: University of Chicago Press, 1980), 228–32.

Dante Germino, *Modern Western Political Thought: Machiavelli to Marx* (Chicago: Rand McNally, 1972), 130–3.

Otto Gierke, *Natural Law and the Theory of Society* (Boston: Beacon Press, 1957) (E. Barker trans.), 103, 294 n.39.

Harry Girvetz, *From Wealth to Welfare* (Stanford: Stanford University Press, 1950), 28–32, 89–90.

Mark Glat, "John Locke's historical sense," in Richard Ashcraft (ed.), *John Locke: Critical Assessments* (London: Routledge, 1991), 622, 631–2.

Daniela Gobetti, *Private and Public: Individuals, Households, and Body Politic in Locke and Hutcheson* (London: Routledge, 1992), 99–100.

Mark Goldie, "Introduction," in John Locke, *Two Treatises of Government* (London: J. M. Dent, 1993) (M. Goldie ed.), xv, xxxvii–xliii.

M. M. Goldsmith, "The entitlement theory of justice considered," 27 *Political Studies* (1979), 578, 580–2.

Robert Goldwin, "John Locke," in Leo Strauss and Joseph Cropsey (eds.), *History of Political Philosophy* (Chicago: University of Chicago Press, 1987) (3rd ed.), 476, 486–95.

Barbara Goodwin, "The political philosophy of money," 7 *History of Political Thought* (1986), 537, 541–2, 553–4.

J. W. Gough, *John Locke's Political Philosophy* (Oxford: Clarendon Press, 1973), 80–103.

Frank Grace, *The Concept of Property in Modern Christian Thought* (Urbana: University of Illinois Press, 1953), 35–6.

Robert Grady II, "Property and 'natural political virtue': the implications of Locke as a 'liberal,'" 10 *Polity* 86 (1977).

John Gray, "John Stuart Mill on the theory of property," in Anthony Parel and Thomas Flanagan (eds.), *Theories of Property: Aristotle to the Present* (Waterloo: Wilfrid Laurier University Press, 1979), 257, 271–6.

W. H. Greenleaf, *The British Political Tradition: The Ideological Heritage* (London: Methuen, 1983), vol. II, 35–6.

Knud Haakonssen, *The Science of a Legislator* (Cambridge: Cambridge University Press, 1981), 106–7, 142.

Andrew Hacker, *Political Theory: Philosophy, Ideology, Science* (New York: Macmillan, 1961), 253–61.

Elie Halévy, *The Growth of Philosophic Radicalism* (London: Faber and Faber, 1952) (M. Morris trans.), 43–4, 211.

Henry Hallam, *Introduction to the Literature of Europe in the Fifteenth, Sixteenth, and Seventeenth Centuries* (London: John Murray, 1855) (5th ed.), vol. IV, 203–4.

John Hallowell, *Main Currents in Modern Political Thought* (New York: Holt, Rinehart and Winston, 1950), 107–10.

Walton Hamilton, "Property according to Locke," 41 *Yale Law Journal* 864 (1932).

Iain Hampsher-Monk, *A History of Modern Political Thought* (Oxford: Blackwell, 1992), 88–95.

Richard Handler, "Who owns the past? History, cultural property, and the logic of possessive individualism," in Brett Williams (ed.), *The Politics of Culture* (Washington: Smithsonian Institution Press, 1991), 63, 64–5.

Ian Harris, *The Mind of John Locke* (Cambridge: Cambridge University Press, 1994), 213–30.

F. A. Harper, "Property and its primary form," in Samuel Blumenfeld, *Property in a Humane Economy* (LaSalle: Open Court, 1974), 1, 14–21.

Govert den Hartogh, "Tully's Locke," 18 *Political Theory* 656 (1990).

Virginia Held, "John Locke on Robert Nozick," 43 *Social Research* 169 (1976).

Don Herzog, *Without Foundations: Justification in Political Theory* (Ithaca: Cornell University Press, 1985), 70–2.

Christopher Hill, *A Nation of Change and Novelty* (London: Routledge, 1990), 126–7.

The English Bible and the Seventeenth-Century Revolution (London: Penguin, 1993), 131, 166.

L. T. Hobhouse, "The historical evolution of property, in fact and in idea," in *Property: Its Duties and Rights* (London: Macmillan, 1915, 2nd edn.), 1, 26–7.

Thomas Hodgskin, *Labor Defended against the Claims of Capital* (New York: Augustus M. Kelley, 1963), 82–92.

Popular Political Economy (New York: Augustus M. Kelley, 1966), 19–23, 27–31, 45–52, 236–7.

The Natural and Artificial Right of Property Contrasted (Clifton: Augustus M. Kelley, 1973), 24–43, et passim.

Michael Hoffheimer, "Locke, Spinoza, and the idea of political equality," 7 *History of Political Thought* (1986), 341, 356, 357–9.

Henry Scott Holland, "Property and personality," in *Property: Its Duties and Rights* (London: Macmillan, 1915, 2nd edn.), 169, 177.

Istvan Hont and Michael Ignatieff, "Needs and justice in the *Wealth of Nations*: an introductory essay," in Istvan Hont and Michael Ignatieff (eds.), *Wealth and Virtue* (Cambridge: Cambridge University Press, 1983), 1, 35–8.

Hans-Hermann Hoppe, *The Economics and Ethics of Private Property* (Boston: Kluwer Academic Publishers, 1993), 48, 184–6, 195, 246, et passim.

Thomas Horne, "Book review of James Tully, *A Discourse on Property*," 9 *Political Theory* 451 (1981).

Property Rights and Poverty (Chapel Hill: University of North Carolina Press, 1990), 48–65, 69–71, et passim.

John Hospers, "Property (comments on Professor Mavrodes' address)," 53 *The Personalist* 263 (1972).

Alan Craig Houston, *Algernon Sidney and the Republican Heritage in England and America* (Princeton: Princeton University Press, 1991), 111–14.

Justin Hughes, "The philosophy of intellectual property," 77 *Georgetown Law Journal* (1988), 287, 296–330.

Peter Hulme, "The spontaneous hand of nature: savagery, colonialism, and the enlightenment," in Peter Hulme and Ludmilla Jordanova (eds.), *The Enlightenment and its Shadows* (London: Routledge, 1990), 16, 25–34.

E. J. Hundert, "Market society and meaning in Locke's political philosophy," in Richard Ashcraft (ed.), *John Locke: Critical Assessments* (London: Routledge, 1991), 457–71.

M. W. Jackson, *Matters of Justice* (London: Croom Helm, 1986), 62, 64.

Herbert Johnston, "Some remarks about Locke's teaching on property," 24 *The New Scholasticism* 146 (1950).

W. T. Jones, *Masters of Political Thought: Machiavelli to Bentham* (Boston: Houghton Mifflin, 1947), vol. II, 177–81.

Philip Kain, *Marx and Modern Political Theory* (Lanham: Rowman and Littlefield, 1993), 37–64.

David Kelley, "Life, liberty, and property," 1 (2) *Social Philosophy and Policy* 108 (1984).

Patrick Kelly, "Book review of James Tully, *A Discourse on Property*," 21 *Journal of the History of Philosophy* 240 (1983).

"'All things richly to enjoy': economics and politics in Locke's *Two Treatises of Government*," 36 *Political Studies* 273 (1988).

Willmoore Kendall, *John Locke and the Doctrine of Majority-Rule* (Urbana: University of Illinois Press, 1959), 69–72.

"John Locke revisited," 2 *Intercollegiate Review* (1966), 217, 222–6, 232.

Nannerl Keohane, "Rousseau on life, liberty and property: a comment on MacAdam," in Anthony Parel and Thomas Flanagan (eds.), *Theories of Property: Aristotle to the Present* (Waterloo: Wilfrid Laurier University Press, 1979), 203, 204–6, 208, 210–11.

John Boyd Kinnear, *Principles of Property* (London: Smith, Elder and Co., 1914), 2–20.

Israel Kirzner, "Producer, entrepreneur, and the right to Property," in Samuel Blumenfeld, *Property in a Humane Economy* (LaSalle: Open Court, 1974), 245–62.

"Entrepreneurship, entitlement, and economic justice," in Jeffrey Paul

(ed.), *Reading Nozick* (Totowa: Rowman and Littlefield, 1981), 383, 402, 404–5.
John Kleinig, *Valuing Life* (Princeton: Princeton University Press, 1991), 66–7, 91–2, 124–5, 237 n.53.
Kirk Koerner, *Liberalism and Its Critics* (London: Croom Helm, 1985), 57–76, 232–7.
Erazim Kohák, "Possessing, owning, belonging," 21 *Dissent* 344 (1972).
Serge-Christophe Kolm, *Le Contrat Social Libéral* (Paris: Presses Universitaires de France, 1985), 127–68 passim.
Linda Lacey, "Of bread and roses and copyrights," 1989 *Duke Law Journal* (1989), 1532, 1539–40, 1564–5.
Sanford Lakoff, *Equality in Political Philosophy* (Cambridge: Harvard University Press, 1964), 92–3, 100–1, 127, 149–50.
Robert Boyden Lamb, *Property Markets and the State in Adam Smith's System* (New York: Garland Publishing, 1987), 60–93.
Sterling Lamprecht, *The Moral and Political Philosophy of John Locke* (New York: Columbia University Press, 1918), 123–4.
Paschal Larkin, *Property in the Eighteenth Century with Special Reference to England and Locke* (New York: Howard Fertig, 1969), 54–81.
Harold Laski, *The Rise of Liberalism* (New York: Harper and Brothers, 1936), 126–9.
Political Thought in England: Locke to Bentham (London: Oxford University Press, 1949), 31.
Peter Laslett, "Market society and political theory," 7 *The Historical Journal* (1964), 150, 152–4.
"Introduction," in John Locke, *Two Treatises of Government* (Cambridge: Cambridge University Press, 1967, 2nd edn.) (P. Laslett ed.), 3, 100–6.
Ramon Lemos, *Hobbes and Locke: Power and Consent* (Athens: University of Georgia Press, 1978), 139–59.
"Locke's theory of property," in Richard Ashcraft (ed.), *John Locke: Critical Assessments* (London: Routledge, 1991), vol. III, 343–61.
Thomas Lewis, "An environmental case against equality of right," 8 *Canadian Journal of Political Science* 254 (1975).
"Adam Smith: the labor market as the basis of natural right," 11 *Journal of Economic Issues* (1977), 21, 46–7.
"Acquisition and anxiety: Aristotle's case against the market," 11 *Canadian Journal of Economics* (1978), 69, 71–2 n5.
Wolfgang von Leyden, "John Locke and natural law," 31 *Philosophy* (1956), 23, 25–6.
Hobbes and Locke: The Politics of Freedom and Obligation (London: Macmillan, 1982), 101–9.
George Lichtheim, *The Origins of Socialism* (New York: Frederick Praeger, 1969), 91, 108, 124–5.
D. G. Long, "Bentham on property," in Anthony Parel and Thomas Flanagan (eds.), *Theories of Property: Aristotle to the Present* (Waterloo: Wilfrid Laurier University Press, 1979), 221, 226, 235–6.
R. Jeffrey Lustig, "Freedom, corporations, and the new Whiggery," in Fred

Baumann (ed.), *Democratic Capitalism?* (Charlottesville: University Press of Virginia, 1986), 127, 130–1, 137.
D. C. MacDonald, "Preface," in William Ogilvie, *Birthright in Land: An Essay on the Right of Property in Land* (New York: Augustus M. Kelley, 1970), ix–xvii.
Alasdair MacIntyre, *A Short History of Ethics* (New York: Macmillan, 1966), 157–8.
Eric Mack, "Individualism, rights, and the open society," in Tibor Machan (ed.), *The Libertarian Reader* (Totowa: Rowman and Littlefield, 1982), 3, 12–13.
John Mackie, "Book review of James Tully, *A Discourse on Property*," 32 *Philosophical Quarterly* 91 (1982).
"Rights, utility, and universalization," in R. G. Frey (ed.), *Utility and Rights* (Minneapolis: University of Minnesota Press, 1984), 86, 88–90.
K. A. B. Mackinnon, "Giving it all away? Thomas Reid's retreat from a natural rights justification of private property," 6 *Canadian Journal of Law and Jurisprudence* (1993), 367, 369, 372, 375, 381–2.
James Mackinnon, *A History of Modern Liberty* (London: Longmans, Green, 1941), vol. IV, 499–500.
C. B. Macpherson, "Locke on capitalist appropriation," 4 *Western Political Quarterly* 550 (1951).
"The social bearing of Locke's political theory," 7 *Western Political Quarterly* 1 (1954).
The Political Theory of Possessive Individualism (Oxford: Oxford University Press, 1962), 194–262, 269–70.
Democratic Theory (Oxford: Clarendon Press, 1973), 231–4.
"Capitalism and the changing concept of property," in Eugene Kamenka and R. S. Neale (eds.), *Feudalism, Capitalism and Beyond* (London: Edward Arnold, 1975), 104, 112–14, 115–16, 118–20.
Pierre Manent, *Histoire intellectuelle du libéralisme* (Paris: Calmann-Lévy, 1987), 93–106.
Harvey Mansfield, Jr., "On the political character of property in Locke," in Alkis Kontos (ed.), *Powers Possessions and Freedom* (Toronto: University of Toronto Press, 1979), 23–38.
John Marshall, *John Locke: Resistance, Religion and Responsibility* (Cambridge: Cambridge University Press, 1994), 265–71, 280–82.
Paul Marshall, "John Locke: between god and Mammon," 12 *Canadian Journal of Political Science* 73 (1979).
Karl Marx, *Theories of Surplus Value, Part I* (London: Lawrence and Wishart, 1969) (E. Burns trans.), 365–7.
Chester Maxey, *Political Philosophies* (New York: Macmillan, 1949), 258–9.
Charles McCoy, *The Structure of Political Thought* (New York: McGraw-Hill, 1963), 209–11.
Forrest McDonald, *Novus Ordo Seclorum: The Intellectual Origins of the Constitution* (Lawrence: University Press of Kansas, 1985), 61–6.
Richard McKeon, "The development of the concept of property in political philosophy: a study of the background of the constitution," 48 *International Journal of Ethics* (1938), 297, 344–6, 360–2.

David McNally, "Locke, levellers and liberty: property and democracy in the thought of the first Whigs," 10 *History of Political Thought* 17 (1989).
Vicente Medina, *Social Contract Theories* (Savage: Rowman and Littlefield, 1990), 32–7.
Ronald Meek, *Studies in the Labour Theory of Value* (London: Lawrence and Wishart, 1956), 20–2, 125–6.
Social Science and the Ignoble Savage (Cambridge: Cambridge University Press, 1976), 20–3.
Uday Singh Mehta, *The Anxiety of Freedom: Imagination and Individuality in Locke's Political Thought* (Ithaca: Cornell University Press, 1992), 148–9.
Anton Menger, *The Right to the Whole Produce of Labour* (New York: Augustus M. Kelley, 1962) (M. Tanner trans.), 42 n.3, 75 n.2, et passim.
Carolyn Merchant, *The Death of Nature* (San Francisco: Harper and Row, 1980), 78.
Ecological Revolutions (Chapel Hill: University of North Carolina Press, 1989), 163.
Daniel Merino, *Natural Justice and Private Property* (Washington: Catholic University of America doctoral dissertation, Faculty of Philosophy, 1922), 13–60.
Max Milam, "The epistemological basis of Locke's idea of property," in Richard Ashcraft (ed.), *John Locke: Critical Assessments* (London: Routledge, 1991), 402–18.
David Miller, *Social Justice* (Oxford: Clarendon Press, 1976), 78–9, 158–9.
Philosophy and Ideology in Hume's Political Thought (Oxford: Clarendon Press, 1981), 69–70, 189.
Fred Miller, Jr., "The natural right to private property," in Tibor Machan (ed.), *The Libertarian Reader* (Totowa: Rowman and Littlefield, 1982), 275–87.
Geoffrey Miller, "Economic efficiency and the Lockean proviso," 10 *Harvard Journal of Law and Public Policy* 401 (1987).
Neil Mitchell, "John Locke and the rise of capitalism," 18 *History of Political Economy* 291 (1986).
Charles Monson, Jr., "Locke and his interpreters," in Richard Ashcraft (ed.), *John Locke: Critical Assessments* (London: Routledge, 1991), 13–26.
James Moore and Michael Silverthorne, "Gershom Carmichael and the natural jurisprudence tradition in eighteenth-century Scotland," in Istvan Hont and Michael Ignatieff (eds.), *Wealth and Virtue* (Cambridge: Cambridge University Press, 1983), 73, 81–3.
Gaetano Mosca, *A Short History of Political Philosophy* (New York: Thomas Crowell Company, 1972) (S. Koff trans.), 149–50.
Henry Moulds, "Private property in John Locke's state of nature," 23 *American Journal of Economics and Sociology* 179 (1964).
"John Locke and rugged individualism," 24 *American Journal of Economics and Sociology* 97 (1965).
Jerry Muller, *Adam Smith in His Time and Ours* (New York: Free Press, 1993), 60, 65.
Gunnar Myrdal, *The Political Element in the Development of Economic Theory* (Cambridge: Harvard University Press, 1965) (P. Streeten trans.), 70–4.

Émilienne Naert, *Locke ou la raisonnabilité* (Paris: Éditions Seghers, 1973), 77–9.

Roderick Nash, *The Rights of Nature* (Madison: University of Wisconsin Press, 1989), 14–15.

Stephen Newman, *Liberalism at Wits' End* (Ithaca: Cornell University Press, 1984), 54–8.

"Locke's *Two Treatises* and contemporary thought: freedom, community, and the liberal tradition," in Edward Harpham (ed.), *John Locke's Two Treatises of Government: New Interpretations* (Lawrence: University Press of Kansas, 1992), 173, 182–6.

C. Reinold Noyes, "Property and sovereignty," 1 (3–4) *Journal of Legal and Political Sociology* (1943), 72, 79–80.

Karl Olivecrona, "Appropriation in the state of nature: Locke on the origin of property," 35 *Journal of the History of Ideas* 211 (1974).

"Locke's theory of appropriation," 24 *Philosophical Quarterly* 220 (1974).

"An insertion in para. 25 of the *Second Treatise of Government*?" 6 *Locke Newsletter* 63 (1975).

"The term 'property' in Locke's *Two Treatises of Government*," 61 *Archiv für Rechts- und Sozialphilosophie* 109 (1975).

"A note on Locke and Filmer," 7 *Locke Newsletter* (1976), 83, 87, 92–3.

Vernon Parrington, *The Colonial Mind* (New York: Harcourt, Brace and Company, 1927), vol. I, 270–1, 316, 338, 344.

Geraint Parry, "Book review of James Tully, *A Discourse on Property*," 12 *Locke Newsletter* 108 (1981).

J. E. Parsons, Jr., "Locke's doctrine of property," 36 *Social Research* 389 (1969).

Carole Pateman, "Sublimation and reification: Locke, Wolin and the liberal democratic conception of the political," in Richard Ashcraft (ed.), *John Locke: Critical Assessments* (London: Routledge, 1991), 690, 696.

Edwin Patterson, "A pragmatist looks at natural law and natural rights," in Arthur Harding (ed.), *Natural Law and Natural Rights* (Dallas: Southern Methodist University Press, 1955), 48, 61–2, 63–4.

Ellen Frankel Paul, *Moral Revolution and Economic Science* (Westport: Greenwood Press, 1979), 20–1, 87, 175–9.

"The just takings issue: can it be resolved by contemporary theories of justice?" in Tibor Machan (ed.), *The Libertarian Reader* (Totowa: Rowman and Littlefield, 1982), 184, 188–9.

Roy Harvey Pearce, *The Savages of America* (Baltimore: Johns Hopkins University Press, 1965, rev. edn.), 67–8.

Harold Perkin, *The Origins of Modern English Society: 1780–1880* (London: Routledge and Kegan Paul, 1969), 51–5, 225–6, 232–4.

J. G. A. Pocock, "A discourse of sovereignty: observations on the work in progress," in Nicholas Phillipson and Quentin Skinner (eds.), *Political Discourse in Early Modern Britain* (Cambridge: Cambridge University Press, 1993), 377, 418–20.

Raymond Polin, *La Politique Morale de John Locke* (Paris: Presses Universitaires de France, 1960), 255–73.

"Justice in Locke's philosophy," in Carl Friedrich and John Chapman (eds.), *Nomos VI: Justice* (New York: Atherton Press, 1963), 262–83.

"The rights of man in Hobbes and Locke," in D. D. Raphael (ed.), *Political Theory and the Rights of Man* (Bloomington: Indiana University Press, 1967), 16, 22–4.

Margaret Jane Radin, "Property and personhood," 34 *Stanford Law Review* (1982), 957, 958 n.3, 961 n.7, 965, 973–4, 979.

Ayn Rand, *Capitalism: The Unknown Ideal* (New York: New American Library, 1967), 18, 122–5, 129, 321–5.

Andrzej Rapaczynski, "Locke's conception of property and the principle of sufficient reason," 42 *Journal of the History of Ideas* 305 (1981).

Nature and Politics (Ithaca: Cornell University Press, 1987), 171–217.

D. D. Raphael, *Problems of Political Philosophy* (Atlantic Highlands: Humanities Press International, 1990, 2nd edn.), 150.

Piercy Ravenstone, *A Few Doubts as to the Correctness of Some Opinions Generally Entertained on the Subjects of Population and Political Economy* (New York: Augustus M. Kelley, 1966), 197–206.

Samuel Read, *Political Economy: An Inquiry into the Natural Grounds of Right to Vendible Property or Wealth* (Fairfield: Augustus M. Kelley, 1976), 94–100, 105–8.

David Resnick, "Rationality and the *Two Treatises*," in Edward Harpham (ed.), *John Locke's Two Treatises of Government: New Interpretations* (Lawrence: University Press of Kansas, 1992), 82, 100–1, 104.

David Richards, *Foundations of American Constitutionalism* (New York: Oxford University Press, 1989), 61—2, 83, 147 n.64.

Judith Richards, Lotte Mulligan, and John Graham, "'Property' and 'people': political usages of Locke and some contemporaries," in Richard Ashcraft (ed.), *John Locke: Critical Assessments* (London: Routledge, 1991), 472, 478–80.

Patrick Riley, *Will and Political Legitimacy* (Cambridge: Harvard University Press, 1982), 72, 84, 91–2, 96–7.

"On finding an equilibrium between consent and natural law in Locke's political philosophy," in Richard Ashcraft (ed.), *John Locke: Critical Assessments* (London: Routledge, 1991), 557, 566, 568, 575–6, 579–80.

Caroline Robbins, *The Eighteenth-Century Commonwealthman* (Cambridge: Harvard University Press, 1959), 64, 66.

H. Mark Roelofs, *Ideology and Myth in American Politics* (Boston: Little, Brown and Company, 1976), 62–9, 87.

The Poverty of American Politics (Philadelphia: Temple University Press, 1992), 30–2, 37–9.

Michael Paul Rogin, *Fathers and Children: Andrew Jackson and the Subjugation of the American Indian* (New York: Alfred A. Knopf, 1975), 78–80, 88–9.

Johannes Rohbeck, "Property and labour in the social philosophy of John Locke," 5 *History of European Ideas* 65 (1984).

Eric Roll, *A History of Economic Thought* (Englewood Cliffs: Prentice-Hall, 1956) (3rd ed.), 113–14.

Mark Rose, "The author as proprietor: *Donaldson v. Becket* and the genealogy of modern authorship," 23 *Representations* (1988), 51, 54–9, 69–73.

Authors and Owners: The Invention of Copyright (Cambridge: Harvard University Press, 1993), 5–7.

Murray Rothbard, *Man, Economy, and State* (Princeton: D. Van Nostrand Company, 1962), vol. I, 78–80, 147–152.

"Justice and property rights," in Samuel Blumenfeld, *Property in a Humane Economy* (LaSalle: Open Court, 1974), 101, 106–22.

The Ethics of Liberty (Atlantic Highlands: Humanities Press, 1982), 21–2, 33, 46–9.

For a New Liberty (New York: Libertarian Review Foundation, 1985) (rev. ed.), 31–7.

Alan Ryan, "Utility and ownership," in R. G. Frey (ed.), *Utility and Rights* (Minneapolis: University of Minnesota Press, 1984), 175, 179–80, 186–7.

Property (Minneapolis: University of Minnesota Press, 1987), 63, 68–9.

"Locke on freedom: some second thoughts," in Knud Haakonssen (ed.), *Traditions of Liberalism* (St. Leonards: Centre for Independent Studies, 1988), 33, 36–47.

"Property," in Terence Ball, James Farr, and Russell Hanson, *Political Innovation and Conceptual Change* (Cambridge: Cambridge University Press, 1989), 309, 311, 322–4.

Cheyney Ryan, "Yours, mine, and ours: property rights and individual liberty," in Jeffrey Paul (ed.), *Reading Nozick* (Totowa: Rowman and Littlefield, 1981), 323–4, 338.

George Sabine, *A History of Political Theory* (New York: Holt, Rinehart, and Winston, 1961, 3rd edn.), 527–8, 689.

John Sanders, "Justice and the initial acquisition of property," 10 *Harvard Journal of Law and Public Policy* 367 (1987).

Rolf Sartorius, "Persons and property," in R. G. Frey (ed.), *Utility and Rights* (Minneapolis: University of Minnesota Press, 1984), 196–214.

Thomas Scanlon, "Nozick on rights, liberty, and property," 6 *Philosophy and Public Affairs* (1976), 3, 23–4.

George Scherger, *The Evolution of Modern Liberty* (New York: Longmans, Green, 1904), 60–1.

Herbert Schneider, "Pragmatism and property," 1 (3–4) *Journal of Legal and Political Sociology* 5 (1943).

Gordon Schochet, "Radical politics and Ashcraft's treatise on Locke," 50 *Journal of the History of Ideas* (1989), 491, 501–2, 506.

David Schultz, *Property, Power, and American Democracy* (New Brunswick: Transaction Publishers, 1992), 14–16, 19–21, 129–37, 174–5.

Sibyl Schwarzenbach, "Locke's two conceptions of property," 14 *Social Theory and Practice* 141 (1988).

Thomas Scott-Craig, "John Locke and natural right," in Arthur Harding (ed.), *Natural Law and Natural Rights* (Dallas: Southern Methodist University Press, 1955), 29, 35–6, 41–3.

Martin Seliger, *The Liberal Politics of John Locke* (New York: Frederick Praeger Publishers, 1969), 141–208.

W. G. Serra, *Property: Its Substance and Value* (London: Figurehead, 1935) (T. Holmes trans.), 9–12.

Ian Shapiro, *The Evolution of Rights in Liberal Theory* (Cambridge: Cambridge University Press, 1986), 89–96, 294.

Political Criticism (Berkeley: University of California Press, 1990), 190–3.

Kiyoshi Shimokawa, "A critique of Laslett's treatment of the *Two Treatises*," 16 *Locke Newsletter* (1985), 35, 48–9.

Kristin Shrader-Frechette, "Locke and limits on land ownership," 54 *Journal of the History of Ideas* 201 (1993).

Mulford Sibley, *Political Ideas and Ideologies* (New York: Harper and Row, 1970), 377–8, 385, 590.

Henry Sidgwick, *The Principles of Political Economy* (London: Macmillan, 1887, 2nd edn.), 502–3.

Paul Sigmund, *Natural Law in Political Thought* (Cambridge: Winthrop Publishers, 1971), 86–7.

A. John Simmons, "Inalienable rights and Locke's *Treatises*," in Richard Ashcraft (ed.), *John Locke: Critical Assessments* (London: Routledge, 1991), 185, 193, 198.

The Lockean Theory of Rights (Princeton: Princeton University Press, 1992), 222–352 et passim.

On the Edge of Anarchy: Locke, Consent, and the Limits of Society (Princeton: Princeton University Press, 1993), 67, 106–7 n.20, 111–13, 117–18.

Wilhelm Sjöstrand, *Freedom and Equality* (Uppsala: Almqvist and Wiksell, 1973), 19, 21, 43.

Rogers Smith, *Liberalism and American Constitutional Law* (Cambridge: Harvard University Press, 1985), 22–4, 45–9, 56–7, 140–3.

David Snyder, "Locke on natural law and property rights," 16 *Canadian Journal of Philosophy* 723 (1986).

A. W. Sparkes, "Trust and teleology: Locke's politics and his doctrine of creation," 3 *Canadian Journal of Philosophy* (1973), 263–7.

Henry Spiegel, *The Growth of Economic Thought* (Durham: Duke University Press, 1983) (rev. ed.), 164, 166.

Kathleen Squadrito, "Locke's view of dominion," 1 *Environmental Ethics* 255 (1979).

John Locke (Boston: Twayne Publishers, 1979), 108–12.

William Stafford, *Socialism, Radicalism, and Nostalgia* (Cambridge: Cambridge University Press, 1987), 56–7, 107–10, et passim.

Werner Stark, *The Ideal Foundations of Economic Thought* (Fairfield: Augustus M. Kelley, 1976), 9–26.

Hillel Steiner, "Capitalism, justice and equal starts," in Ellen Frankel Paul, Fred Miller, Jr., Jeffrey Paul, and John Ahrens (eds.), *Equal Opportunity* (Oxford: Basil Blackwell, 1987), 49–71.

J. L. Stocks, "Locke's contribution to political theory," in J. L. Stocks and Gilbert Ryle, *John Locke: Tercentenary Addresses* (London: Oxford University Press, 1933), 3, 6–7.

Leo Strauss, *Natural Right and History* (Chicago: University of Chicago Press, 1953), 202–51.

What is Political Philosophy? (Glencoe: Free Press, 1959), 49, 217–19, 270, 305.

An Introduction to Political Philosophy (Detroit: Wayne State University Press, 1989), 50–1.

"On Locke's doctrine of natural right," in Richard Ashcraft (ed.), *John Locke: Critical Assessments* (London: Routledge, 1991), 161–84.

Nathan Tarcov, "A 'non-Lockean' Locke and the character of liberalism," in

Douglas MacLean and Claudia Mills (eds.), *Liberalism Reconsidered* (Totowa: Rowman and Allanheld, 1983), 130–3, 137–8.

Nathan Tarcov, *Locke's Education for Liberty* (Chicago: University of Chicago Press, 1984), 142–8, 177–80, 205–6.

R. H. Tawney, *The Acquisitive Society* (New York: Harcourt, Brace and World, 1920), 13–14, 52–83.

Judith Jarvis Thomson, "Property acquisition," 73 *Journal of Philosophy* 664 (1976).

Adriano Tilgher, *Homo Faber: Work through the Ages* (Chicago: Henry Regnery Company, 1958), 85, 87–8.

Keith Tribe, *Land, Labour and Economic Discourse* (London: Routledge and Kegan Paul, 1978), 46–51.

Richard Tuck, *Natural Rights Theories* (Cambridge: Cambridge University Press, 1979), 169–72.

James Tully, "The framework of natural rights in Locke's analysis of property: a contextual reconstruction," in Anthony Parel and Thomas Flanagan (eds.), *Theories of Property: Aristotle to the Present* (Waterloo: Wilfrid Laurier University Press, 1979), 114–38.

A Discourse on Property (Cambridge: Cambridge University Press, 1980).

"Locke," in *The Cambridge History of Political Thought* (Cambridge: Cambridge University Press, 1991) (J. Burns and M. Goldie eds.), 616, 627–9.

"Placing the *Two Treatises*," in Nicholas Phillipson and Quentin Skinner (eds.), *Political Discourse in Early Modern Britain* (Cambridge: Cambridge University Press, 1993), 253, 255–7, 263–80.

An Approach to Political Philosophy: Locke in Contexts (Cambridge: Cambridge University Press, 1993), chapters 2–5.

Catherine Valcke, "Locke on property: a deontological interpretation," 12 *Harvard Journal of Law and Public Policy* 941 (1989).

Karen Vaughn, "John Locke and the labor theory of value," 2 *Journal of Libertarian Studies* 311 (1978).

John Locke: Economist and Social Scientist (Chicago: University of Chicago Press, 1980), 77–107.

"Book review of James Tully, *A Discourse on Property*," 14 *History of Political Economy* 441 (1982).

"The economic background to Locke's *Two Treatises of Government*," in Edward Harpham (ed.), *John Locke's Two Treatises of Government: New Interpretations* (Lawrence: University Press of Kansas, 1992), 118, 129–33, 138–9.

Michel Villey, "Notes sur le concept de propriété," in Carl Wellman (ed.), *Equality and Freedom* (Wiesbaden: Franz Steiner Verlag, 1977), 69, 70–1, 76–7.

Ursula Vogel, "When the earth belonged to all: the land question in eighteenth-century justifications of private property," 36 *Political Studies* (1988), 102–3, 106, 108–9.

Jeremy Waldron, "Enough and as good left for others," 29 *Philosophical Quarterly* 319 (1979).

"Locke, Tully, and the regulation of property," 32 *Political Studies* 98 (1984).

Michael Walzer, *Spheres of Justice* (New York: Basic Books, 1983), 104–5.

Joel Weinsheimer, *Eighteenth-Century Hermeneutics* (New Haven: Yale University Press, 1993), 28–31.
Walter Weisskopf, *The Psychology of Economics* (London: Routledge and Kegan Paul, 1955), 23–7, 145–6.
Patricia Werhane, *Adam Smith and His Legacy for Modern Capitalism* (New York: Oxford University Press, 1991), 61–8, 134–5.
John Weymark, "Money and Locke's theory of property," 12 *History of Political Economy* 282 (1980).
Morton White, *The Philosophy of the American Revolution* (New York: Oxford University Press, 1978), 214–17.
Edmund Whittaker, *A History of Economic Ideas* (New York: Longmans, Green and Co., 1940), 195–8.
Schools and Streams of Economic Thought (Chicago: Rand McNally, 1960), 67–8, 194, 227–8, 375.
Andrew Williams, "Cohen on Locke, land, and labour," 40 *Political Studies* 51 (1992).
Donald Winch, *Adam Smith's Politics* (Cambridge: Cambridge University Press, 1978), 18–22, 49, 58–9, 89–90.
John Winfrey, "Charity versus justice in Locke's theory of property," in Richard Ashcraft (ed.), *John Locke: Critical Assessments* (London: Routledge, 1991), 385–401.
Jonathan Wolff, *An Introduction to Political Philosophy* (Oxford: Oxford University Press, 1996), 23, 25–6, 152–8.
Robert Paul Wolff, *The Poverty of Liberalism* (Boston: Beacon Press, 1968), 57.
Sheldon Wolin, *Politics and Vision* (Boston: Little, Brown and Company, 1960), 309–10, 341–2.
Neal Wood, *The Politics of Locke's Philosophy* (Berkeley: University of California Press, 1983), 34–40, 141–2, 159–60.
John Locke and Agrarian Capitalism (Berkeley: University of California Press, 1984), 49–71.
John Yolton, *Locke and the Compass of Human Understanding* (Cambridge: Cambridge University Press, 1970), 187–95.
Locke: An Introduction (Oxford: Basil Blackwell, 1985), 68–72.
Michael Zuckert, "An introduction to Locke's *First Treatise*," in Richard Ashcraft (ed.), *John Locke: Critical Assessments* (London: Routledge, 1991), 121, 135–7.
Natural Rights and the New Republicanism (Princeton: Princeton University Press, 1994), 216–88.

RELATED TOPICS

Bruce Ackerman, *We the People* (Cambridge: Harvard University Press, 1991) [Locke's possessive individualism], vol. I, 25–31.
Larry Alexander and William Wang, "Natural advantages and contractual justice," 3 *Law and Philosophy* (1984) [libertarian conception of self-ownership], 281, 292–7.
Joyce Appleby, "Ideology and theory: the tension between political and economic

liberalism in seventeenth-century England," 81 *American Historical Review* (1976) [tension between Lockean doctrine of self-ownership and early capitalism's need for a disciplined work force], 499, 512–15.

Capitalism and a New Social Order (New York: New York University Press, 1984) [Locke's individualism and his emphasis on the productiveness of labor], 35–7.

John Arthur, "Resource acquisition and harm," 17 *Canadian Journal of Philosophy* 337 (1987) [untenability of Nozick's neo-Lockean approach to original acquisition].

Richard Ashcraft, "Locke's state of nature: historical fact or moral fiction?" in Richard Ashcraft (ed.), *John Locke: Critical Assessments* (London: Routledge, 1991) [role of government as preserver of natural rights of property], 212, 226–9.

Patrick Atiyah, "The liberal theory of contract," in *Essays on Contract* (Oxford: Oxford University Press, 1986) [insufficiency of Lockean labor theory as a ground for the details of contract law], 121, 131, 133–4.

Robin Attfield, *The Ethics of Environmental Concern* (Athens: University of Georgia Press, 1991, 2nd edn.) [Locke's "enough and as good" proviso, applied intergenerationally], 44, 97, 107–10, 185, 187.

Leland Baldwin, *The American Quest for the City of God* (Macon: Mercer University Press, 1981) [Locke as proponent of bourgeois individualism], 27–8, 87, 90, 109, 289–90.

Thomas Baldwin, "Tully, Locke, and land," 13 *Locke Newsletter* 21 (1982) [status of natural property after transition to political society in Lockean world].

William Batz, "The historical anthropology of John Locke," 35 *Journal of the History of Ideas* (1974) [Locke's emphasis on proprietary rights as natural and presocietal], 663, 668.

A. L. Beier, "'Utter strangers to industry, morality and religion': John Locke on the poor," 12 (3) *Eighteenth-Century Life* 28 (1988) [Locke's moderately enlightened attitude toward the poor].

J. H. Bogart, "Lockean provisos and state of nature theories," 95 *Ethics* 828 (1985) [problematic status of the "enough and as good" proviso within Nozick's neo-Lockeanism].

David Braybrooke, *Meeting Needs* (Princeton: Princeton University Press, 1987) [Lockean "spoilage" and "sufficiency" limitations on ownership], 286–9.

J. Budziszewski, *The Resurrection of Nature: Political Theory and the Human Character* (Ithaca: Cornell University Press, 1986) [Locke's theory of property as a doctrine of human excellence], 137.

George Bull, "What did Locke borrow from Hooker?" 7 *Thought* (1932) [Locke's bourgeois individualism], 122, 126–8.

Martin Carnoy, *The State and Political Theory* (Princeton: Princeton University Press, 1984) [Locke's unstinting emphasis on private property; and the role of civil society in preserving natural property], 17–20, 24.

John Christman, "Self-ownership, equality, and the structure of property rights," 19 *Political Theory* 28 (1991) [complexities of self-ownership, and its compatibility with egalitarianism].

Joshua Cohen, "Structure, choice, and legitimacy: Locke's theory of the state," 15

Philosophy and Public Affairs 301 (1986) [Locke's theory of the "property owner's state"].

Conal Condren, *The Status and Appraisal of Classic Texts* (Princeton: Princeton University Press, 1985) [Locke's calculated ambiguity in his use of the term "property"], 245–8.

Charles Covell, *The Defence of Natural Law* (New York: St. Martin's Press, 1992) [Lockean proprietary rights as natural and presocietal], 9, 114–19.

Martin Diamond, "Democracy and *The Federalist*: a reconsideration of the Framers' intents," in Jack Greene (ed.), *The Reinterpretation of the American Revolution* (New York: Harper and Row, 1968) [Locke's emphasis on comfortable self-preservation as opposed to bare self-preservation], 504, 517–18.

Frank Donovan, *Mr. Jefferson's Declaration* (New York: Dodd, Mead and Company, 1968) [relationship between Locke's and Jefferson's views of property], 138–41.

Graeme Duncan, "Comments on some radical critiques of liberal-democratic theory," in Pierre Birnbaum, Jack Lively, and Geraint Parry (eds.), *Democracy, Consensus and Social Contract* (London: Sage Publications, 1978) [the possessive individualism of Lockean liberalism], 59, 62–3.

John Dunn, *The Political Thought of John Locke* (Cambridge: Cambridge University Press, 1969) [Locke's work ethic, based on the notion of one's "calling"], 214–67.

Western Political Theory in the Face of the Future (Cambridge: Cambridge University Press, 1979) [religious roots of Locke's individualism, and defense of Locke against charges of uncritical bourgeois lackeyism], 37–40.

"Justice and the interpretation of Locke's political theory," in Richard Ashcraft (ed.), *John Locke: Critical Assessments* (London: Routledge, 1991) [tension between Lockean justice and Lockean charity], 43–63.

"Consent in the political theory of John Locke," in Richard Ashcraft (ed.), *John Locke: Critical Assessments* (London: Routledge, 1991) [status of natural property in the transition to civil society], 524, 530–2, 535.

Carl Friedrich and Robert McCloskey, "The roots of American constitutionalism," in *From the Declaration of Independence to the Constitution* (New York: Liberal Arts Press, 1954) [connection between Lockean property rights and Lockean right to self-preservation], vii, x–xi, xii–xiii.

Alan Goldman, "The justification of equal opportunity," in Ellen Frankel Paul, Fred Miller, Jr., Jeffrey Paul, and John Ahrens (eds.), *Equal Opportunity* (Oxford: Basil Blackwell, 1987) [desert and self-realization as grounds for keeping the fruits of one's labor], 88, 92, 98–100

Robert Goldwin, "Locke's state of nature in political society," 29 *Western Political Quarterly* 126 (1976) [Locke's emphasis on the right and duty of self-preservation].

Ruth Grant, "Locke's political anthropology and Lockean individualism," in Richard Ashcraft (ed.), *John Locke: Critical Assessments* (London: Routledge, 1991) [Lockean individualism], 64–84.

W. H. Greenleaf, *The British Political Tradition: The Rise of Collectivism* (London:

Methuen, 1983) [Locke's emphasis on the presocietal right of property as the safeguard and expression of individuality], vol. I, 16–17.

Knud Haakonssen, "Hugo Grotius and the history of political thought," 13 *Political Theory* (1985) [similarities and differences between the Lockean theory and the Grotian theory of property], 239, 243–4, 256.

Thomas Haggard, "Work, government, and the constitution: determining the proper allocation of rights and powers," in Ellen Frankel Paul and Howard Dickman (eds.), *Liberty, Property, and the Future of Constitutional Development* (Albany: State University of New York Press, 1990) [Lockean ideas concerning self-ownership and property, in the nineteenth-century United States], 241, 246, 250–2.

Ronald Hamowy, "*Cato's Letters*, John Locke, and the republican paradigm," in Edward Harpham (ed.), *John Locke's Two Treatises of Government: New Interpretations* (Lawrence: University Press of Kansas, 1992) [labor theory of property in the Lockean *Cato's Letters*], 148, 157–8.

Iain Hampsher-Monk, "Resistance and economy in Dr. Anglim's Locke," 26 *Political Studies* (1978) [crucial role of human productiveness in Locke's state of nature], 91, 95–7.

Christopher Hill, *Society and Puritanism in Pre-Revolutionary England* (New York: Schocken, 1967, 2nd edn.) [the work ethic in seventeenth-century England], 124–44, 507–10.

Thomas Horne, "Bourgeois virtue: property and moral philosophy in America, 1750–1800," 4 *History of Political Thought* 317 (1983) [moderate importance of Locke's theory of property in eighteenth-century American political thought].

Martin Hughes, "Locke on taxation and suffrage," 11 *History of Political Thought* (1990) [Locke's view of the productivity-enhancing effects of private ownership], 423, 428–30.

Lucien Jansse, *La propriété* (Paris: Les Editions Ouvrières, 1953) [Lockean property rights as natural and presocietal], 144–5.

Anthony Kronman, "Contract law and distributive justice," 89 *Yale Law Journal* (1980) [critique of libertarian doctrines that tie together self-possession and self-ownership], 472, 493–4.

Catherine Larrère, *L'invention de l'economie au XVIIIe siècle* (Paris: Presses Universitaires de France, 1992) [relations between Locke's labor theory of property and the physiocratic theory of property], 199–200, 202, 272–3.

Steven Lukes, *Individualism* (Oxford: Basil Blackwell, 1973) [Locke as *laissez-faire* individualist], 84, 138–9.

J. D. Mabbott, *The State and the Citizen* (London: Hutchinson's University Library, 1947) [Locke as individualist who viewed society as a mere means for preserving natural property], 23–4.

Tibor Machan, *Capitalism and Individualism* (New York: Harvester Wheatsheaf, 1990) [Lockean view of property as safeguard of autonomy], 9, 76–81.

Eric Mack, "Locke's arguments for natural rights," 11 *Southwestern Journal of Philosophy* (1980) [duty of each person to preserve others], 51, 58–9.

"Distributive justice and the tensions of Lockeanism," 1 (1) *Social Philosophy and Policy* 132 (1983) [tension between Lockean individualism and Lockean communitarianism in the theories of property developed by Robert Nozick and Hillel Steiner].

C. B. Macpherson, "Scholars and spectres: a rejoinder to Viner," 29 *Canadian Journal of Economics and Political Science* 559 (1963) [Locke's broad and narrow uses of the word "property"].

Thomas Mautner, "Locke's own," 22 *Locke Newsletter* 73 (1991) [Lockean self-ownership].

Ronald Meek, *Smith, Marx, and After* (London: Chapman and Hall, 1977) [relations or nonrelations between Locke's theory of property and certain doctrines propounded by Adam Smith and David Ricardo], 30, 159.

Diana Meyers, "A sketch of a rights taxonomy," in Kenneth Kipnis and Diana Meyers (eds.), *Economic Justice: Private Rights and Public Responsibilities* (Totowa: Rowman and Allanheld, 1985) [difficulties in Locke's view of property as fundamental], 87, 92–3.

Jeffrie Murphy and Jules Coleman, *Philosophy of Law* (Boulder: Westview Press, 1990) [libertarian conception of one's entitlement to the fruits of one's labors], 172.

R. S. Neale, "'The bourgeoisie, historically, has played a most revolutionary part,'" in Eugene Kamenka and R. S. Neale (eds.), *Feudalism, Capitalism and Beyond* (London: Edward Arnold, 1975) [Locke as proponent of absolute rights of private property], 84, 95, 98.

Philip Newman, *The Development of Economic Thought* (Englewood Cliffs: Prentice-Hall, 1952) [Locke as defender of sanctity of property with a theory inapplicable to modern conditions], 349, 356.

Michael Novak, *The Spirit of Democratic Capitalism* (New York: Simon and Schuster, 1982) [Locke's emphasis on the productivity of labor as the means of complying with God's demand for the promotion of human flourishing], 39–40, 366 n.8.

William Ogilvie, *Birthright in Land: An Essay on the Right of Property in Land* (New York: Augustus M. Kelley, 1970) [the partially conflicting relations between the natural right to the fruits of one's labor and the natural right to an equal share of land], 7–17.

Onora O'Neill, "Rights to compensation," in Ellen Frankel Paul, Fred Miller, Jr., Jeffrey Paul, and John Ahrens (eds.), *Equal Opportunity* (Oxford: Basil Blackwell, 1987) [dubiousness of Nozick's "Lockean proviso" dealing with the need to compensate people after no more unowned resources are available for appropriation], 72, 78–9 n.6.

Constructions of Reason (Cambridge: Cambridge University Press, 1989) [Locke's emphasis on charity as well as on justice], 219–23.

Geraint Parry, "Individuality, politics and the critique of paternalism in John Locke," 12 *Political Studies* 163 (1964) [Locke's individualism].

Carole Pateman, *The Sexual Contract* (Stanford: Stanford University Press, 1988) [Lockean self-ownership], 13, 55–6, 71, 214.

Jeffrey Paul and Ellen Frankel Paul, "Locke's usufructuary theory of self-ownership," 61 *Pacific Philosophical Quarterly* 384 (1980) [Lockean self-ownership].

J. G. A. Pocock, "The mobility of property and the rise of eighteenth-century sociology," in Anthony Parel and Thomas Flanagan (eds.), *Theories of Property: Aristotle to the Present* (Waterloo: Wilfrid Laurier University Press, 1979) [unimportance of Locke's theory of property in the eighteenth century], 141, 146–50.

"The myth of John Locke and the obsession with liberalism," in J. G. A. Pocock and Richard Ashcraft, *John Locke* (Los Angeles: William Andrews Clark Memorial Library, 1980) [unimportance of Locke's "bourgeois" theory in the eighteenth century], 1–4.

"Negative and positive aspects of Locke's place in eighteenth-century discourse," in Martyn Thompson (ed.), *John Locke und/and Immanuel Kant* (Berlin: Duncker and Humblot, 1991) [unimportance of Locke's theory of property in the eighteenth century], 45, 49, 60–1.

Pierre-Joseph Proudhon, *What is Property?* (New York: Howard Fertig, 1966) (B. Tucker trans.) [the invalidity of countless defenses of property, including some versions of the labor theory], passim.

Jeffrey Reiman, "The fallacy of libertarian capitalism," 92 *Ethics* 85 (1981) [dubiousness of Nozick's neo-Lockean theory of property].

Ron Replogle, *Recovering the Social Contract* (Totowa: Rowman and Littlefield, 1989) [interplay between one's Lockean proprietary acquisitions and the status of other people], 53–5, 201–6.

John Roemer, "A challenge to neo-Lockeanism," 18 *Canadian Journal of Philosophy* 697 (1988) [dubiousness of Nozick's neo-Lockean justification of material inequality].

Alexander Rosenberg, "The political philosophy of biological endowments: some considerations," in Ellen Frankel Paul, Fred Miller, Jr., Jeffrey Paul, and John Ahrens (eds.), *Equal Opportunity* (Oxford: Basil Blackwell, 1987) [the complexities of self-ownership as the ownership of one's own capacities], 1–31.

Michael Sandel, *Liberalism and the Limits of Justice* (Cambridge: Cambridge University Press, 1982) [self-ownership and desert, as understood in modern liberalism], 66–103.

Hannah Sewall, *The Theory of Value before Adam Smith* (New York: Augustus M. Kelley Publishers, 1968) [Locke's emphasis on the value-creating role of labor], 73–6.

Jeremy Shearmur, "The right to subsistence in a 'Lockean' state of nature," 27 *Southern Journal of Philosophy* 561 (1989) [satisfiability of the rights of the indigent to basic subsistence in the Lockean state of nature without any governmental coordination or intervention].

George Sher, *Desert* (Princeton: Princeton University Press, 1987) [the complexities of desert], 99–108, et passim.

Frank Snare, "The concept of property," 9 *American Philosophical Quarterly* 200 (1972) [general concept of property, with references to Locke].

Lawrence Stone, "The results of the English revolutions of the seventeenth century," in J. G. A. Pocock (ed.), *Three British Revolutions: 1641, 1688, 1776* (Princeton: Princeton University Press, 1980) [Locke as individualistic defender of private rights of property], 23, 35, 36–7, 44.

R. H. Tawney, *Religion and the Rise of Capitalism* (Gloucester: Peter Smith, 1962) [Locke's view of proprietary rights as natural and presocietal], 189, 258.

James Tully, "A reply to Waldron and Baldwin," 13 *Locke Newsletter* 35 (1982) [Locke's nonacceptance of the alienability of labor power in the state of nature; and the status of natural property after the transition to political society in a Lockean world].

Jacob Viner, "The perils of reviewing: a counter-rejoinder," 29 *Canadian Journal of Economics and Political Science* 562 (1963) [Locke's broad and narrow uses of the word "property"].

Jeremy Waldron, "'The turfs my servant has cut,'" 13 *Locke Newsletter* 9 (1982) [Locke's acceptance of the alienability of labor power in the state of nature].

Ernest Weinrib, "Right and advantage in private law," 10 *Cardozo Law Review* (1989) [differences between Nozick's Lockean theory of proprietary acquisition and Hegel's theory], 1283, 1293–7.

Samuel Wheeler III, "Natural property rights as body rights," in Tibor Machan (ed.), *The Main Debate: Communism versus Capitalism* (New York: Random House, 1987) [attempted derivation of proprietary rights-in-things from personal self-ownership], 272–89.

John Yolton, "Locke on the law of nature," 67 *Philosophical Review* (1958) [Lockean individualism], 477, 496–8.

Naomi Zack, "Locke's identity meaning of ownership," 23 *Locke Newsletter* 105 (1992) [Lockean self-ownership].

Index

Printed in the United States
38819LVS00006B/46-48

9 780521 548908